Why the
CHURCH
Needs
BIOETHICS

Why the
CHURCH
Needs
BIOETHICS

A GUIDE TO WISE ENGAGEMENT WITH
LIFE'S CHALLENGES

John F. Kilner, *Editor*

 **ZONDERVAN**®

ZONDERVAN.com/
AUTHORTRACKER
follow your favorite authors

We want to hear from you. Please send your comments about this book to us in care of zreview@zondervan.com. Thank you.

ZONDERVAN

Why the Church Needs Bioethics
Copyright © 2011 by John F. Kilner

This title is also available as a Zondervan ebook.
Visit www.zondervan.com/ebooks.

Requests for information should be addressed to:

Zondervan, *Grand Rapids, Michigan 49530*

Library of Congress Cataloging-in-Publication Data

Why the church needs bioethics : a guide to wise engagement with life's challenges / John F. Kilner, general editor.
      p. cm.
   ISBN 978-0-310-32852-0 (softcover)
   1. Medical ethics—Religious aspects—Christianity. 2. Bioethics—Religious aspects—Christianity. 3. Christian ethics. I. Kilner, John Frederic. II. Title: Guide to wise engagement with life's challenges.
   R725.55.W55 2011
   174.2—dc22   2010052141

Cover design: Rob Monacelli
Interior design: Matthew Van Zomeren

Printed in the United States of America

11 12 13 14 15 16 /DCI/ 23 22 21 20 19 18 17 16 15 14 13 12 11 10 9 8 7 6 5 4 3 2 1

CONTENTS

Part Three
BETTER DEATH

Part Four
BETTER LEARNING

TEAM OF AUTHORS AND CRITIQUERS

AUTHORS

BIBLICAL/THEOLOGICAL STUDIES FIELDS

New Testament

D. A. Carson, PhD, Research Professor of New Testament at Trinity Evangelical Divinity School, author of more than fifty books, President of the Gospel Coalition.

Old Testament

Richard E. Averbeck, PhD, Professor of Old Testament and Semitic Languages and Director of the PhD Program (Theological Studies) at Trinity Evangelical Divinity School, widely published author.

Theology

Kevin J. Vanhoozer, PhD, Blanchard Professor of Theology at Wheaton College Graduate School, author of numerous award-winning books, including a *Christianity Today* Book of the Year.

MINISTRY FIELDS

Pastoral Care

Steven C. Roy, PhD, Associate Professor of Pastoral Theology at Trinity Evangelical Divinity School, many years of experience as a pastor in multiple church settings.

Counseling

Stephen P. Greggo, PsyD, Professor of Counseling at Trinity Evangelical Divinity School, many years of counseling and speaking in settings all around the world, author of *Trekking toward Wholeness*.

Miriam Stark Parent, PhD, Chair of the Counseling Department at Trinity Evangelical Divinity School, licensed clinical psychologist, extensive experience in professional and ministry counseling.

Intercultural Ministry

Harold A. Netland, PhD, Professor of Intercultural Studies and Philosophy of Religion at Trinity Evangelical Divinity School, a decade of work in Asia, author of several leading books on pluralism.

Bruce L. Fields, PhD, Associate Professor of Theology (especially black and liberation theology) at Trinity Evangelical Divinity School, many years of cross-cultural ministry experience (especially with African and Native Americans).

Elizabeth Y. Sung, PhD, Assistant Professor of Biblical and Systematic Theology (especially theology and social theory: race, ethnicity, culture) at Trinity Evangelical Divinity School, extensive experience in campus ministry.

OTHER PROFESSIONAL (CASE-ORIENTED) FIELDS
Business

Scott B. Rae, PhD, Professor of Ethics (Business Ethics and Bioethics) at Biola University's Talbot School of Theology, ethics consultant, author of numerous books on business ethics and bioethics.

Helen Eckmann, EdD (Leadership), Associate Professor of Business Management at National University, consultant with Fortune 500 companies, minister.

Law

Paige Comstock Cunningham, JD, Executive Director of The Center for Bioethics and Human Dignity, author of US Supreme Court briefs, past President of Americans United for Life.

Health Care

Robert D. Orr, MD, CM, Director of Clinical Ethics at Loma Linda University, American Medical Association Award for Medical Ethics, author of *Medical Ethics and the Faith Factor*.

Susan Salladay, RN, PhD, Professor of Nursing at Cedarville University, extensive nursing experience and administrative experience in medical and bioethics centers.

COMMUNICATION FIELDS
Preaching/Worship

Greg R. Scharf, DMin, Professor of Pastoral Theology at Trinity Evangelical Divinity School, past President of the Evangelical Homiletics Society, Board Chair of John Stott Ministries of Langham Partnership International.

Teaching/Education

Miriam L. Charter, PhD, Director of the PhD Program (Educational Studies) at Trinity Evangelical Divinity School, extensive teaching experience in Central/Eastern Europe, specialist in Problem-Based Learning.

BIOETHICS

William P. Cheshire, MD, MA (Bioethics), Professor of Neurology in the College of Medicine at Mayo Clinic, Senior Research Fellow in Neuroethics at The Center for Bioethics and Human Dignity, more than one hundred publications.

John T. Dunlop, MD, MA (Bioethics), internist and geriatrician, trained at Johns Hopkins University and practicing medicine at Zion Clinic, author of *Finishing Well to the Glory of God*.

John F. Kilner, PhD, MDiv, Director of Bioethics Programs and Forman Chair of Ethics at Trinity International University, author/editor of twenty bioethics books, leader of numerous research and writing projects.

CRITIQUERS

BIBLICAL/THEOLOGICAL STUDIES FIELDS

New Testament

Robert Yarbrough (Covenant Theological Seminary, Missouri)

Old Testament

Andrew Schmutzer (Moody Bible Institute, Illinois)

Theology

Oliver O'Donovan (Edinburgh University, Scotland)

MINISTRY FIELDS

Pastoral Care

Richard Shenk (Village Church, Minnesota)

Counseling

Philip Monroe (Biblical Seminary, Pennsylvania)

Intercultural Ministry

Scott Moreau (Wheaton College Graduate School, Illinois)

OTHER PROFESSIONAL (CASE-ORIENTED) FIELDS
Business

Kenman Wong (Seattle Pacific University, Washington)

Law

Morse Tan (Florida Coastal School of Law, Florida)

Health Care

Alvin Moss (West Virginia University, West Virginia)

COMMUNICATIONS FIELDS
Preaching/Worship

Greg Strand (Evangelical Free Church of America Headquarters, Minnesota)

Teaching/Education

Ted Ward (Michigan State University, Michigan, and Trinity Evangelical Divinity School, Illinois)

BIOETHICS

Dennis Hollinger (Gordon-Conwell Theological Seminary, Massachusetts)

INTRODUCTION

WISDOM FOR LIFE'S CHALLENGES

JOHN F. KILNER

To say that the church needs bioethics is simply to insist that the church needs to help people handle bioethical challenges well. Bioethical challenges have to do with life and health ("bio"), and what one does about them should flow from wise discernment about what is good and right ("ethics"). For instance, which of the dozens of ways to make a baby are ethically acceptable for infertile couples seeking to be faithful Christians? Is it ever godly to "pull the plug" when a person appears to be dying? As pills and other means to expand our capacities beyond the normal human range increasingly become available, can it be virtuous to use them?

"That person needs ethics!" is a frequent exclamation today. It typically indicates two things: (1) there are some challenges in that person's life or work that need serious attention; and (2) the resources necessary to engage those challenges well are available. To maintain that the church needs bioethics is to make similar claims regarding some of the greatest challenges today facing individuals, families, communities, societies, and the world. The church needs to give these challenges serious attention, and the church has the necessary resources to engage such challenges well.

The problem is that most people in the church, including pastors and other church leaders, do not realize what these resources are. Such resources do not depend upon congregations having special bioethics expertise. Rather, they involve the biblical, theological, ministerial, and other sources of wisdom to which congregations have ready access. Wisdom is at the heart of understanding and engaging the world in a God-honoring way. It is desperately needed everywhere, but perhaps nowhere more than in the face of challenges to life and health that make up the arena of bioethics. Those who learn to find wisdom for bioethical challenges can find wisdom for all of life's predicaments.

Consider some of the most common bioethical challenges.

Infertility, for instance, afflicts millions of people in the United States alone, and the global statistics are staggering. Various treatments and technologies pledge to produce a "good birth." Not only can a couple likely have the baby they have longed for, but the baby can be healthy and even have certain other desired characteristics. But at what moral cost? If this couple is to flourish, they and all who advise and support them will need wisdom.

Death, needless to say, eventually afflicts more people than any other malady. Various interventions and decisions not to intervene claim to provide "a good death." A dying man can end life support or life itself in his own time, on his own terms. But at what moral cost? If this man during his dying and all who advise and support him are to flourish, they will need wisdom.

Between birth and death, people constantly receive offers promising "the good life." This pill will cure that ill; this machine will compensate for that weakness. Increasingly, people will be hearing, "This technology will make you better than well—even more than human; it will enable you to transcend the limits that constrain most people." But even the tiny print in the footnotes will not spell out the moral cost. If people are truly to flourish, they will need wisdom.

Wisdom is not so much a single destination or even a particular journey as it is a way of traveling. Wisdom is what enables the sifting, organizing, and interpreting of information that leads to understanding and engagement. No wonder the wise man Solomon exclaims that wisdom "is more profitable than silver and yields better returns than gold. She is more precious than rubies; nothing you desire can compare with her" (Prov. 3:14–15).

It is easy to assume that Solomon had such wisdom because he was born with a unique capacity for it. By implication, most other people would have little hope of being nearly as wise. Yet this same Solomon insists that wisdom is something that people can "get": "The beginning of wisdom is this: Get wisdom" (Prov. 4:7).

But where are they to get it? They are to begin by looking in deepest reverence to God, not to a prestigious university or the internet or the latest self-help guru. ("The fear of the LORD is the beginning of wisdom"; Prov. 9:10.) Solomon himself received wisdom by committing himself to God and asking God for it (1 Kings 3:7–12). New Testament authors echo Solomon's counsel and example with such reminders as "if any of you lacks wisdom, you should ask God, who gives generously.... But when you ask, you must believe" (James 1:5–6). Believe what? And what does that have to do with wisdom?

The apostle Paul was constantly bringing wisdom to bear on life's predicaments, nowhere more so than in his letters and visits to Corinth. Yet he summarized his ministry there by saying, "I resolved to know nothing while I was with you except Jesus Christ and him crucified" (1 Cor. 2:2). The belief necessary for wisdom is not best described simply as belief in God or in Jesus Christ—though both are accurate; rather it is best described as belief in Jesus Christ and him crucified. It is wisdom that is accessible because of the cross and the accompanying resurrection.

The cross demonstrates how offensive sin is to a holy God and the magnitude of God's love even for people in whom sin rules. Understanding these two truths provides a foundation for a wise response to bioethical challenges. Without the cross, people would be unable to recognize and do all that is wise, because sinful self-centeredness would dominate. Without the resurrection, people would not have the new life and power they need in the face of life's predicaments.

Christ " 'himself bore our sins' in his body on the cross, so that we might die to sins and live for righteousness" (1 Peter 2:24). Christ's crucifixion makes possible a related crucifixion in people: "Those who belong to Christ Jesus have crucified the sinful nature with its passions and desires" (Gal. 5:24). Similarly, Christ's resurrection makes possible a related resurrection in people: "If we have been united with him in a death like his, we will certainly also be united with him in a resurrection like his.... Offer yourselves to God as those who have been brought from death to life; and offer every part of your-self to him as an instrument of righteousness" (Rom. 6:5, 13). In Christ, the power of the Holy Spirit becomes available to do what cannot be done in human strength and wisdom alone.

Being wise requires not only life-giving freedom from within but also a freedom from without. Ironically, another great obstacle to being wise is "wisdom" itself—the wisdom that is common in the "world" (*kosmos*). The world, in this biblical sense, commonly operates by a set of values and principles that have no necessary reference to God, rooted in an understanding of the world in which God has no necessary place. This frame of reference can easily shape people's understanding and actions unless they consciously reorient their lives around Christ. The result is not a way of life constantly at odds with the world, because God has written his ethical standards on everyone's hearts (Rom. 2:15) and people intuitively will sometimes act accordingly. But a biblical-Christian outlook will also at other times be at odds with the world's outlook, since the "wisdom of the world" looks elsewhere for counsel than to "Christ ... the wisdom of God" (1 Cor. 1:20–24).

The goal of this book, then, is not just any wisdom but the wisdom of Christ. God makes it available to those willing to set aside personal preoccupation and worldly recognition in order to follow Christ and glorify him with their lives. It has always been the case that "the LORD gives wisdom" to "his faithful ones" (Prov. 2:6–8). Implicit in these and other biblical discussions of wisdom is the understanding that the pursuit of wisdom involves revering and believing God, learning about God and his ways, and living in accordance with those ways.

Learning about God and his ways is an endeavor that necessarily involves far more than one field of study. Biblical studies, theology, pastoral care, and bioethics are but a few of the many fields in which such learning takes place. The idea that simply by participating in a bioethics class or two, people can gain sufficient wisdom for understanding and engaging bioethical challenges is badly mistaken. Yet that narrow approach is how most people, including Christians, generally seek bioethical wisdom.

A different approach is necessary today, one that brings to bear on bioethical challenges all of the subjects that people formally study in a theological curriculum or less formally learn through the church. As understanding those subjects helps people to develop a genuinely Christian view of the world and everything in it, people's capacity to receive from God wisdom for bioethical challenges will grow. Bioethics needs the insights and perspectives of many other areas of study if there is to be sufficient wisdom to address its challenges. And, just as important, all of these other areas of study need bioethics if their content is to be evidently relevant to the toughest challenges of contemporary life.

Accordingly, this book is for far more people than those already involved in bioethics per se. It also has much to offer to every Christian, and to unbelievers interested in learning what difference Christian faith makes for living. However, the authors have written with certain people particularly in mind: leaders in churches and Christian ministries, and students preparing for such leadership roles. These are the people in their communities who have the greatest say in how preparation for life's challenges takes place. They also have the greatest access to the range of fields that provide the best sources of wisdom and serve as the primary resources for this book. Old Testament, New Testament, theology, counseling, pastoral care, intercultural ministry, preaching, and education are prominent among them. Rather than simply pulling from the New Testament a passage here and there, or from theology a quotation here and there, the approach here is to let all of these fields speak in their own voices, in a way that allows the richness of their outlook and insights to address situations directly. Of particular interest is the contribution each makes to equipping people with an understanding of and commitment to the gospel in all of its biblical richness.

Such an approach has implications for the authorship and focus of this book. All parts of it cannot be written by the same author or two, because the integrity of each voice requires a speaker who has extensive experience in that particular field. And the authors must focus on concrete situations — case studies — to ensure that discussions do not remain too general and removed from life. This case-oriented approach suggests that other case-oriented fields such as medicine, law, and business have much to contribute as well. Although they are not as much a part of many people's weekly experiences in church or seminary, they encompass information and insight that Christians need access to in order to bring other more familiar fields to bear on life's predicaments.

For the purposes of this book, three rich cases provide the necessary focus. One spotlights the quest for a better birth, one the quest for a better life, and one the quest for a better death. The team of authors has rooted each case in real life by crafting it from actual bioethical challenges which huge numbers of people are facing today. The first case includes such matters as reproductive technologies, genetic diagnosis, and stem cell research. The second considers human enhancement and the use of drugs to function well in academic and other settings. The third examines individual, family, and societal well-being in the midst of decisions to end medical treatment or life itself.

While it would in some ways be illuminating to allow every field to demonstrate what it can contribute to a wise approach to each case, the repetition would be quite cumbersome. So for each case, the planning team has selected three particularly appropriate fields to address the case: one biblical-theological field (Old Testament, theology, or New Testament), one ministry field (counseling, intercultural ministry, or pastoral care), and one other profession (business, law, or health care). A fourth chapter on each case then makes sure that various contributions of the field of bioethics itself are a part of the mix; it also underscores some of the important insights which the three preceding chapters on the case have contributed and notes some of the important contributions of the six other fields.

Following the first three parts of the book, each with four chapters focusing on one case, part 4 considers how in the course of everyday living people can gain the wisdom they need to prepare for and engage such cases in real life. Although the people in the case studies exemplify the many people in churches who have not learned to handle bioethical challenges well, better learning is indeed possible. In the two chapters of this final section, leaders in the fields of preaching and education draw on the three case studies and the previous twelve chapters to consider what such learning can look like.

As noted earlier, wisdom is a way of traveling through life, committed to God and his ways, and seeking to understand and live faithfully with the help of a wide range of available resources. To that end, each chapter of this volume features numerous resources in its footnotes which readers may want to consider for further insight. The authors have also produced four bibliographies which include explanations of the contents of each resource listed. There is one bibliography on each of the three clusters of issues addressed by the cases in this book, and one encompassing the entire broader range of bioethical challenges today. These lists of resources, along with other helpful materials, are located on an internet website (*everydaybioethics.org*) rather than printed here, to facilitate periodic updating there. Meanwhile, the book's conclusion offers suggestions for ways that readers can put the insights of this book to work in their lives and spheres of influence. Wisdom is not mere head knowledge; it is insight lived out in the situations of life.

This book is the fruit of many people working over many years. The entire author team is grateful to family, friends, colleagues, and others who have provided invaluable support and encouragement. The initiative began with a grant that the Wabash Center for Teaching and Learning (Indiana) awarded in 2006 for an exploratory project on teaching bioethics in the context of theological education. The setting for this project was Trinity Evangelical Divinity School in Deerfield, Illinois, USA, because of the leadership role that this school (and Trinity International University, of which it is a part) has provided in pioneering courses and degree programs in bioethics. The Dean of TEDS, Tite Tienou, graciously supported the project and helped lead one of the project sessions. Lydia Leggett faithfully administered the funds and related correspondence. The Center for Bioethics and Human Dignity and the Carl F. H. Henry Center for

Theological Understanding kindly provided numerous educational materials during the Wabash project and the subsequent book project. And special thanks goes also to Ben Mitchell and John Dunlop for leading the entire series of Wabash sessions with me and participating in the initial brainstorming for this book project.

Some of the faculty from the Wabash project — energized by the challenges of exploring how their fields contribute to understanding and engaging bioethical challenges — continued to work on this subsequent book project. Others joined the author team to increase its gender balance, ethnic participation (African-American, Asian-American, etc.), and representation from other schools (Talbot School of Theology, Wheaton College Graduate School, Loma Linda University, Cedarville University, etc.).

The involvement of leaders from other academic institutions and churches also increased considerably as a result of the decision to include an official critiquer for each chapter, thanks to the generous financial support of an anonymous funder (to whom all involved in this project owe much thanks for making the entire project possible). The author team is immensely grateful to the chapter critiquers, absolves them of all shortcomings of this book, and credits them with a much more insightful book than would have been possible without them. A complete list of the book's authors and critiquers, with their affiliations, appears at the front of the book.

I want to add a special word of thanks to the two physician-bioethicists, William Cheshire from Mayo Clinic and John Dunlop from Zion Clinic, who served with me on the planning team for this project. Each of them helped conceive and carry out the whole, while playing a special role in one part of the book. That special role included meeting with authors and reviewing early drafts to help authors develop their ideas, and writing the final chapter of the part in coordination with the others on the planning team. John Dunlop repeatedly went above and beyond the call of duty, offering ideas for many different chapters and other sections of the book. It has been an immense privilege for me to work with these two godly and talented people, and with such a gifted team of nineteen authors and twelve critiquers. I have gained renewed appreciation for the importance of the body of Christ, which can do so much more together than its members can do alone, and in which each member plays an important part. This book would be significantly impaired were any one of its contributors missing.

Many other churches, organizations, and individuals too numerous to list have had a formative influence on the development of this book, for which all involved in this project are grateful. For instance, several of us had the privilege of refining the case studies and strategies for engaging them through interacting with large groups of people at such churches as Willow Creek (Illinois), Harvest Bible (Illinois), Menlo Park Presbyterian (California), Sanibel Community (Florida), the Orchard (Illinois), and Winnetka Bible (Illinois). Concepts central to designing this book gained clarity from interactions following plenary addresses I presented at Harvard University (Cambridge, Massachusetts), Johns Hopkins University (Baltimore, Maryland), Evangelical Theological Society (in

New Orleans, Louisiana), Wheaton College (Wheaton, Illinois), ACR Homes (Minneapolis, Minnesota), the Center for Bioethics and Human Dignity (in Phoenix, Arizona), Evangelical Free Church of America (in East Troy, Wisconsin), and Talbot School of Theology (La Mirada, California); and through courses I taught at Trinity International University (in Deerfield, Illinois, and Miami, Florida), Asbury Theological Seminary (in Wilmore, Kentucky), Bethel College (in Mishawaka, Indiana), and Gordon-Conwell Theological Seminary (in South Hamilton, Massachusetts). I am very grateful for their welcome and interest.

The thirty-one Christian leaders producing this book have invested substantial time and energy in this project out of a shared vision for the importance of learning how to gain wisdom for engaging tough bioethical challenges. For them, human intuition is insufficient. So are biblical prooftexting and simplistic assumptions about what the right position on something "obviously" is. It is time to do the challenging work necessary, drawing on the many resources God has provided, to learn more about what being wise actually looks like in the face of life's predicaments. No better arena for this investigation exists than today's great bioethical challenges.

Part One

BETTER BIRTH

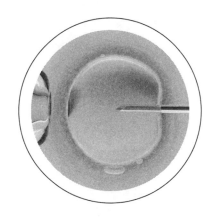

HAVING A BABY THE
NEW-FASHIONED WAY

Betty (43) and Tom (45) have been married for ten years. As a couple, Tom and Betty are requesting an in vitro fertilization (IVF) team at a nearby infertility clinic to assist them in achieving a pregnancy using Betty's sister's eggs and Tom's sperm. In this process, Betty's sister, Laura, will undergo a superovulation process to increase the number of eggs she can contribute. Just before ovulation, her eggs will be removed from her body and fertilized in the laboratory. Some of the resultant embryos will be transferred into Betty's uterus two days after fertilization. The medical risks are small but real.

As a couple, these college-educated professionals are financially secure. Betty is a buyer for a major retail chain. Tom does accounting in a county office. Building a fine house while advancing in their careers had pushed childbearing interests into the background. Betty began to raise the idea of having children about five to six years into the marriage. As she approached forty, Betty noticed that she had the house she always wanted but no children. Following intense discussion, Tom and Betty decided to have children. After being off birth control for a year with no pregnancy, Betty became concerned. She became meticulous about tracking her cycle and having sex. What surprised them both was a heightened interest in spirituality. They began to attend an active Christian church with a contemporary-style service. Later they accepted a cordial invitation to join a small home fellowship group, and they participated whenever it was convenient.

As cycle after cycle passed without her becoming pregnant, Betty could no longer let the matter rest. The couple began to seek out medical advice. In the meantime, Betty was finding it difficult socially to be around children and couples who had children. She was progressively feeling more isolated and "on the outside." This increasingly affected the couple's social life, which added tension to their relationship with each other as well.

Tom and Betty have since received extensive unsuccessful treatment for infertility. Betty has responded poorly in her IVF cycles, and despite six attempts has never reached the stage of egg retrieval. Her age is thought to be a significant factor in her inability to produce mature eggs. Prior to their marriage, Betty became pregnant by

Tom; however, the couple chose to terminate the pregnancy because they felt they were neither emotionally nor financially ready for parenthood. Adoption is not an option for them. Their desire is for either a genetically related child or none at all. Tom seems to be more ambivalent than Betty about parenthood at this season in his life, but "wants to make his wife happy." The relationship and marriage have been stormy at times but are currently stable. Tom is concerned that Betty is putting all of her energy into becoming pregnant. Consequently, being together is far more stressful and less enjoyable.

Betty has asked her sister, Laura, age thirty-eight, to donate her eggs so that Betty and Tom can have a child. Laura is on the other side of a contentious and costly divorce. Her marriage was troubled from the start by out-of-control spending and a husband who had trouble remaining faithful. His business bankruptcy left her in desperate straits financially. She finds comfort in raising her two children, ages three and five. She states that she has finished her family and desires no more children. She expresses delight in being able to help her sister. She lives 150 miles away, however, and will have to accept the inconvenience of staying with Betty and Tom for several weeks while preparing for the procedure. Her children will come to stay also.

There are several areas of potential conflict:

1. *Disagreement over the issue of secrecy.* Laura believes the entire family should know about the procedure and that the child should be told, in Laura's words, "about my contribution to its genetic heritage." Betty is adamant that the donation be a closely held secret with no one else knowing. On this matter, Tom and Betty speak with one voice.

2. *The use of preimplantation genetic diagnosis (PGD) and amniocentesis.* Laura wants to be sure that any child she is partly responsible for bringing into the world is healthy, whereas Betty does not think she wants to know about problems. She is certain she could not go through an abortion if genetic abnormalities were discovered by using amniocentesis to test the genetic health of the developing fetus. Tom agrees with Laura's commitment to doing whatever it takes to ensure that only a healthy child is born. But he suggests that abortion could likely be avoided by genetically screening the embryos using PGD before any are implanted, so that only healthy embryos are implanted.

3. *Plans for unwanted healthy embryos.* Tom, Betty, and Laura learn that the embryos not transferred to Betty's uterus will be frozen for future use, but may never be needed by Betty and Tom if all goes well the first time. So Betty suggests that any extra embryos be made available to other couples who, like her and Tom, cannot conceive and do not have a sister such as Laura to provide the eggs. Tom and Laura indicate they would prefer to sell the embryos for stem cell research, since they have heard about dozens of ways that sick people are already being helped by stem cell treatments.

4. *Superovulation versus surrogacy.* There is a level of uncertainty about whether

Betty can successfully become pregnant and carry a child through to birth, even if healthy embryos are produced. So Betty and Tom have also asked Laura if she would be willing to serve as a surrogate mother and handle the pregnancy stage for her sister. They have pointed out to her that she could simply be inseminated with Tom's sperm and not have to risk the dangers of drug-induced superovulation. Laura replied that pregnancy would require a much greater effort on her part, and that Betty and Tom would need to pay her for that. In fact, she has added, all this talk of the risks of superovulation has made her think that she should also be paid something even if she provides only her eggs and not her uterus.

5. *The complex relationship among them.* Betty denies any concerns about her relationship with Laura. She and Tom stood by her sister during her tumultuous marriage. She feels that her sister owes her this help. As Betty puts it, "Laura got all the good eggs." Laura and Tom have always gotten along well. Laura says she has the best brother-in-law in the world and would love to help him have a child. So Betty encourages Tom to try to negotiate favorable terms with Laura.

CHAPTER 1

WISDOM FROM THE OLD TESTAMENT

Richard E. Averbeck

The situation of Betty and Tom, on which this chapter is based, is reminiscent of millions of similar situations today and throughout human history. It is part of our human groaning: "We know that the whole creation has been groaning as in the pains of childbirth right up to the present time. Not only so, but we ourselves, who have the firstfruits of the Spirit, groan inwardly as we wait eagerly for our adoption as sons, the redemption of our bodies" (Rom. 8:22–23).[1]

For a woman, the anguish of not being able to have a child can far exceed "the pains of childbirth." We live as fallen people in the midst of a fallen world, all of which are in "bondage to decay" (v. 21). For some couples, this particular kind of groaning becomes an all-consuming part of their lives, at least for a time, if not permanently. It spoils everything, so to speak. Once they encounter this obstacle, no part of their marriage relationship or any family or other social relationship escapes its dark shadow. They will do almost anything to overcome it, no matter what tactics may be involved. Some handle it better than others, but the pain involved in not being able to have a baby is very real and can be overwhelming.

After long-term disappointing failure at trying to have a child naturally, Betty and Tom try in vitro fertilization (IVF) with Betty's eggs, but without success. As a result, they now intend to use eggs provided by Betty's sister, Laura, or perhaps even have her serve as a surrogate mother for them by being artificially inseminated with Tom's sperm. Meanwhile, a considerable amount of marital and social distance and conflict have arisen between them and with others. So they are trying to manage the complications of both the infertility itself and the ways they have been handling it. It is not a happy situation and, realistically, there is a great deal of potential for serious ongoing problems

---

1. Unless otherwise noted, all biblical quotations in this chapter are from *The Holy Bible, New International Version* (Grand Rapids, Mich.: Zondervan, 1985).

even if they should manage to find a way to have a baby "in the new-fashioned way." As noted above, this is not a new story. Each instance of it, however, has different people involved and, therefore, its own peculiarities.

The goal of this chapter is to look at the issues Betty and Tom face from the perspective of Old Testament Scripture. First, we will consider passages that deal directly with barrenness (i.e., infertility). According to the Bible, this was just as serious and difficult a problem in ancient Israel as it is today — perhaps even worse. Some of the ways and means available to deal with it were different, but not all of them were. Moreover, the harsh personal, marital, relational, and social repercussions were much the same as today. It is not difficult to find biblical correspondences with this case study. Second, after working through the infertility accounts, we will focus our attention on Genesis 1–4 and its implications for dealing with infertility from a biblically based bioethical point of view. Our purpose will be to discover what biblical framework of thinking and acting is available to guide Tom, Betty, and Laura through such a troubling dilemma in a way that is pleasing to God.

We cannot escape groaning in life, even if we are among the redeemed (Rom. 8:23). It comes with the condition and circumstances of being fallen people in a fallen world. Yes, God can and sometimes does step in supernaturally to change people's situations. Praise him! As harsh and painful as it may be to face, however, God is generally more interested in changing people than he is in changing their circumstances. This is a reality that all need to grasp no matter what their circumstances may be. The Lord wants people to walk faithfully and prayerfully with him in the midst of their life situations, whatever they may be. This is the only route to "the peace of God, which transcends all understanding" (Phil. 4:7).

INFERTILITY AND BARRENNESS IN THE OLD TESTAMENT

It is a good and natural God-given desire for a man and woman, committed to one another in a loving marriage, to want to have a baby together. That God's original and perfect design welcomes reproduction needs to be affirmed with gentle care amid the difficulties faced by a couple struggling with infertility. Psalm 127:3–5 makes the point from a man's point of view: "Sons are a heritage from the LORD, children a reward from him. Like arrows in the hands of a warrior are sons born in one's youth. Blessed is the man whose quiver is full of them. They will not be put to shame when they contend with their enemies in the gate." From the woman's point of view, Psalm 113:9 praises the Lord for his grace when "he settles the barren woman in her home as a happy mother of children."

One of God's covenant promises to the ancient Israelites as a nation was that if they remained faithful to their covenant with him, he would bless them with fertility (Exod. 23:26; Deut. 7:14). Fertility was a sign of God's favor toward them as part of his plan to prosper his covenant people, who were the especially blessed nation in the midst of all the other nations. Conversely, there are instances in which infertility is portrayed as a judgment from God, whether within Israel (e.g., 2 Sam. 6:23, regarding the barrenness of David's wife Michal) or among other peoples (e.g., Gen. 20:17–18, regarding Abimelech's entire household).

In the case of Betty and Tom, all that has gone wrong flows ultimately from the corruption of God's original design physically, relationally, and spiritually as seen in Genesis 3–4 and the rest of the Bible. We will come back to all this later, but it is important to note here that, on the one hand, some elements of the case are not necessarily a direct result of the people's personal corruption. The physical reality of infertility, for example, is a medical problem that can occur beyond people's control. On the other hand, the case study suggests that they may have contributed to the problem by waiting so long. Betty's "clock" has been "ticking" for a long time. The previous pregnancy and abortion shows that she was fertile earlier in life. It also shows, however, that something has gone terribly wrong in their thinking about having a baby in the first place. The disregard for the life of the earlier baby and the self-centered pragmatic reasons for the abortion are not the focus of this chapter, but they are emblematic of the underlying corruption that is in full view in the case study.[2]

BARRENNESS AND INHERITANCE IN THE OLD TESTAMENT WORLD

There are a number of cases of barrenness in the Old Testament, beginning with Israel's three main ancestral women: (1) Sarai, Abram's wife (Gen. 11:30; they were later renamed Sarah and Abraham, respectively, Gen. 17:5, 15–16), (2) Rebekah, Isaac's wife (Gen. 25:21), and (3) Rachel, Jacob's wife (Gen. 29:31; Jacob was given a second name, Israel, in Gen. 32:28).[3] In some ways, infertility was even worse in the Old Testament world than today because of the legalities associated with inheritance rights in the patricentric tribal clan culture of that day.

Consider, for example, the case of the daughters of Zelophehad (Num. 27:1–11; cf. also 26:33 and chap. 36). Their father had no male heirs, which meant that his line of descent would vanish from his tribal clan in the next generation. These women asked for and were granted their father's inheritance alongside their father's brothers in order to avoid the consequences of no male heir for their family's line of descent (Num. 27:4, 7).[4]

---

2. For some helpful discussions of the issues involved, see James K. Hoffmeier, ed., *Abortion: A Christian Understanding and Response* (Grand Rapids, Mich.: Baker, 1987).

3. Some of the most useful secondary sources for the discussion of barrenness in the Old Testament are Hemchand Gossai, *Barrenness and Blessing: Abraham, Sarah, and the Journey of Faith* (Eugene, Ore.: Cascade Books, 2008), and Warren McWilliams, *Where Is the God of Justice? Biblical*

Perspectives on Suffering (Peabody, Mass.: Hendrickson, 2005), 53–64.

4. In fact, the standard inheritance practices in Israel were adjusted for just such circumstances in the future (Num. 27:8–11). See the extended explanation in Timothy R. Ashley, *The Book of Numbers* (Grand Rapids, Mich.: Eerdmans, 1993), 541–45, 658–59.

For some men even today, having a male heir is of some considerable concern. This does not appear to be the case with Tom. But in the ancient Israelite world, one can imagine the pressure not only to have children but especially to have a male heir.

Abraham, the eventual "father of the Jews" and the nation of Israel, felt heart-wrenching pain over the matter of an heir in his own life (Gen. 15:1–3). Because of his previous faithfulness to the Lord in the battle against the four kings and his subsequent interchange with Melchizedek (Gen. 14:1–2, 13–24), the Lord promised Abraham "your reward shall be very great" (15:1 NRSV). Abraham's response was anything but enthusiastic. From his point of view, what difference would a reward make anyway, since he was still "childless" and, therefore, without someone from his own body to pass the reward down to, along with everything else that he owned? Yes, he could leave it all to his household steward, Eliezer of Damascus (v. 2), but that was not a very satisfying solution to the dilemma.[5]

Similarly, after Sarah bore Isaac, her concerns also turned to the problem of inheritance when she reacted strongly in a rage against Hagar and Ishmael: "Get rid of that slave woman and her son, for that slave woman's son will never share in the inheritance with my son Isaac" (Gen. 21:10). Admittedly, Sarah's reaction here arose out of jealousies that had developed over the years, not just the economics of inheritance, as will be noted below.

ABRAHAM, SARAH, AND HAGAR: GOOD INTENTIONS GONE WRONG

The Abraham narratives (Gen. 11:27–25:11) raise the problem of Sarah's infertility to the level of a major driving force in their story. Right from the beginning, we are told that "Sarai was barren; she had no children" (Gen. 11:30). This emphatic dual statement of Sarah's infertility comes as early as possible in the text, as an element attached to the genealogical introduction to the Abraham narratives. Just a few verses later, Genesis 12:1–3 records God's call and commission of Abraham, beginning with "Leave your country, your people and your father's household and go to the land I will show you" (v. 1).

The next verse is especially important for our purposes here: "I will make you into a great nation and I will bless you" (v. 2). One of the promises God gives Abraham is that leaving everything behind and going to this other land will result in his growing into a great nation. In other words, he will have a great multitude of descendants even though Sarah is infertile. Multiple divine reaffirmations of this promise state that he will have as many descendants as the particles of dust on the earth (Gen. 13:16) and the stars in the sky (Gen. 15:5), so to speak.

5. See the explanation and literature cited in Gordon J. Wenham, *Genesis 1–15* (Waco, Tex.: Word, 1987), 327–29, 334.

Sarah's infertility persists, however, for twenty-five years (compare Gen. 12:4 with 17:1, 24; 21:5). In the meantime, both Sarah and Abraham struggle with the problem. Genesis 15:1–5 reveals how much this troubles Abraham. (See certain elements of this passage treated above.) He has come to a point where God's other blessings in his life mean little to him. But the Lord makes the same promise of an abundant seed again, and, by faith, Abraham once again accepts the promise by faith: "Abram believed the Lord, and he credited it to him as righteousness" (v. 6). Sarah's infertility is no small matter to Abraham. It occupies his heart continually. Nevertheless, he is willing to reaffirm his trust in the Lord's promise in spite of all appearances. This becomes one of the most important statements of faith in the Bible for all who are children of Abraham by faith, whether Jew or Gentile. (See the apostle Paul's reference to it, e.g., in Rom. 4:3, 11–12, 16, 18–22 and Gal. 3:6–9, 26–29.)

After living ten years in Canaan (Gen. 16:3), Sarah is the one who initiates Abraham's marriage to Hagar as a secondary wife: "Sarai his wife took her Egyptian maidservant Hagar and gave her to her husband to be his wife." The previous verse (v. 2) reveals that Sarah intends this as a form of surrogacy: "Go, sleep with my maidservant; perhaps I can build a family through her" (lit. "perhaps I will be built up from her"). This arrangement is for the benefit of Sarah, not Hagar, and not just for Abraham's posterity either. Sarah's plan is to solve the problem of her own infertility through the body of Hagar.[6] This tactic arises out of Sarah's own pain and frustration over not being able to have a child (Gen. 16:1–2). As she puts it, "The Lord has kept me from having children" (v. 2).

Although Sarah knows that the whole matter is really under the Lord's control, she takes it into her own hands anyway. At the same time, there is good reason to believe that what Sarah proposes here was not out of the ordinary in that culture. According to documents from the late third millennium BC down through the first millennium BC, surrogate marriages were common in cases of infertility.[7] Hagar oversteps her position: "When she knew she was pregnant, she began to despise her mistress" (cf. v. 4; i.e., she treated Sarah disrespectfully). When Sarah turns to blame Abraham for this (v. 5), he simply responds, "Your servant is in your hands…. Do with her whatever you think best" (v. 6). Among other things, this verse shows that becoming this kind of wife to Abraham does not remove Hagar's status as a maidservant as far as Abraham is concerned.

ISAAC AND REBEKAH, JACOB AND RACHEL: AM I IN THE PLACE OF GOD?

The story of Rebekah's infertility is relatively simple. She has been barren. Apparently Isaac and Rebekah struggled with that at first, but we are not told a great deal

---

6. Jacob's wife Rachel uses her handmaid Bilhah in the same way (Gen. 30:3, lit. "and I will be built up, even I, from her"), and so does Leah (Gen. 30:9, 12).

7. E.g., see M. J. Selman, "Comparative Customs and the Patriarchal Age," in *Essays on the Patriarchal Narratives*, ed. A. R. Millard and D. J. Wiseman (Winona Lake, Ind.: Eisenbrauns, 1983), 119, 123–28, 136–37.

about it. Instead, her husband, Isaac, prays for her, and the Lord answers his prayer so that Rebekah becomes pregnant with twins (Gen. 25:21–23). The term for prayer here is relatively unusual in the Hebrew Bible ʿātar, "to plead, make supplication"). Sometimes it seems to emphasize the intensity or persistence of the prayer, often on behalf of others (cf., e.g., Exod. 8:30; 10:18; Judges 13:8). The twins, however, struggle with each other even in the womb, and that leads to struggles with and between the parents throughout their lives. This ongoing struggle motivates most of the story of Isaac and Rebekah, Jacob and Esau (Genesis 25–35).

Embedded within this framework of struggle between Jacob and Esau, however, is the pain-filled story of the struggle between Jacob's two wives, Leah and Rachel, with particular attention to Rachel's infertility: "When the LORD saw that Leah was not loved, he opened her womb, but Rachel was barren" (Gen. 29:31). This leads to Rachel's demand, "Give me children, or I'll die!" (30:1), and Jacob's response, "Am I in the place of God, who has kept you from having children?" (30:2). Even though Rachel is loved and is the favored wife, she is tormented by having no children, and she, in turn, torments Jacob. One can feel the wild emotions oozing out of the passage: frustration, rage, a sense of unfairness in life, trying to blame, demand for action to fix the problem.

So Rachel's next step is to take up the standard practice of surrogacy (Gen. 30:3): "Here is Bilhah, my maidservant. Sleep with her so that she can bear children for me [lit. "on my knees"] and that through her I too can build a family" (lit. "I myself can be built up from her"; the same expression as Sarah's in 16:2, cited above). The plan works, so Rachel responds, "God has vindicated me; he has listened to my plea and given me a son" (30:6). Similarly, Leah has borne four sons to Jacob before she stops bearing (29:32–35), at which point she gives her own handmaid Zilpah to Jacob, and through her obtains two more sons (30:9–13).

These women see this form of surrogacy as an act of faithfulness. After bearing a fifth son, Leah proclaims, "God has rewarded me for giving my maidservant to my husband" (Gen. 30:18). The fierce battle between Rachel and Leah, therefore, continues (30:14–24).[8] For Leah it is primarily a struggle for the affections of her husband in the face of his special devotion to Rachel (29:30–31; 30:14–20). Jacob prefers Rachel's bed over Leah's (30:14–16). However, after the birth of her sixth son, Leah hopes that this will change: "God has presented me with a precious gift. This time my husband will treat me with honor, because I have borne him six sons" (v. 20). There is no evidence, though, that it makes any difference.

The point of reviewing all these machinations is to show that, even though there are many cultural and situational differences between these patriarchal narratives

---

8. For a helpful treatment of the battle between these two women, see Gordon J. Wenham, *Genesis 16–50* (Dallas: Word, 1994), 246–48.

and the Tom and Betty case study, there are also substantial similarities. Tom is ambivalent about having children at this relatively late stage in life but wants to make Betty happy. In the biblical story, Jacob has already obtained heirs through Leah, but he loves Rachel and wants to make her happy. In this regard, however, it is in God's hands, and he knows it (Gen. 30:1 – 3). It is important to note that Tom and Betty experience increased interest in spiritual things as they grow older and encounter this struggle with infertility.

The case study indicates neither the degree to which they submit their struggle to the Lord, nor the kind of faith they have in the Lord in the first place. For their faith to make any real difference in the face of such a severely troubling difficulty, they would need to go deep and stay long in a personal relationship with the Lord, both individually and as a couple. Being "religious" will simply not do, although engaging in sympathetic human relationships through their fellowship group could at least help them not feel alone in their struggle. The case study reveals, however, that they are becoming increasingly isolated as Betty becomes uncomfortable being around children and couples who have children. Tom and Betty represent a large number of couples whose marital relationship is threatened by tension, conflict, and social isolation.[9] They are enjoying life together less and less.

One can see similar tensions and relational dynamics in the kinds of marital and relational disappointments, jealousies, and competitions that are evident in the stories of the patriarchal wives referenced above. There are, of course, many elements of the Tom and Betty case study that have no direct correspondence to Old Testament times simply because they involve "new-fashioned" science. Moreover, it is significant that Laura is not a slave woman and that Tom would not engage in sexual relations with Laura but would have his semen collected for artificial insemination.

Nevertheless, certain core similarities remain in this updated version of the patriarchal narratives, in which "who deserves what" is a preoccupation. Laura demands payment for surrogacy services, because carrying the child full term as a surrogate would require much more from her than just providing eggs. Meanwhile, Betty feels that her sister owes her this, and she is trying to use Laura's good relationship with Tom to manipulate the situation. She is a desperate woman acting in desperate ways to get what she so badly wants and is determined to get by whatever means she can.[10]

ELKANAH AND HANNAH

Consider also the experience of Elkanah and Hannah. Elkanah was a Levite who lived in the tribal territory of Ephraim (1 Sam. 1:1; note the genealogy in 1 Chron.

---

9. I personally know an infertile woman who has insisted that she and her husband stay away from church and family gatherings altogether because she wants to avoid being around children and couples who have them.

10. There are other biblical stories of infertility outside of the patriarchal narratives—e.g., the mother of Samson (Judges 13:2), possibly Ruth (suggested to some by Ruth 4:13, "the LORD enabled her to conceive"), Elisha's benefactor, the Shunamite woman (2 Kings 4:8 – 17), and Elizabeth (Luke 1:7).

6:22–28, 33–34). The story of his wife Hannah and the birth of their son, Samuel, is an extraordinarily powerful account of faithfulness to the Lord amid an agonizing struggle with infertility.[11] Elkanah has two wives, Hannah and Peninnah; "Peninnah had children, but Hannah had none" (1 Sam. 1:2). Hannah is referred to as the "first" wife and Peninnah the "second," which suggests that Elkanah has taken Peninnah as a second wife because of Hannah's infertility (v. 2; recall the discussion of this ancient Near Eastern practice above).[12] Every year, Elkanah has brought his whole family to Shiloh to worship the Lord there because that is where the tabernacle sanctuary was located at the time, with the ark of the covenant (1 Sam. 4:3–4).

On these occasions, and assuredly on many others, her adversary (i.e., rival wife) Peninnah torments Hannah because it is a family celebration and Hannah has no children to celebrate with. All she has is Elkanah, and that is simply not enough, even though he loves Hannah more than Peninnah (recall Jacob with Rachel and Leah). Yes, Hannah is the object of his special affections, but the agony of having no children regularly ruins the occasion for Hannah, and for Elkanah too because the one he loves so deeply is so unhappy and is weeping in distress (1 Sam. 1:4–8). As he puts it, "Don't I mean more to you than ten sons?" (v. 8).

The parallels to the plight of Tom and Betty are many. Betty's pain over not having a child is wreaking havoc on their family and social life. Betty "was progressively feeling more isolated and 'on the outside.' This increasingly affected the couple's social life, which added tension to their relationship with each other as well." As Elkanah complains that having children is more important to Hannah than their love for each other, "Tom is concerned that Betty is putting all of her energy into becoming pregnant. Consequently, being together is far more stressful and less enjoyable." The main difference in the situations is that, in the case of Hannah, the other woman has already borne children for Elkanah and is using them to torment her, whereas problems are arising with Betty's potential "surrogate" before surrogacy has even been attempted. Nothing is working. But Betty is determined to make it work anyway.

Who knows what Hannah might have tried if there were any number of biological options available to pursue in her day. In any case, at a particular point Hannah takes the situation to the Lord (1 Sam. 1:9–18). It is likely that she has done this in previous years as well, but on this occasion she makes a special vow to the Lord, and Eli the priest intercedes for her. Making vows was a common practice in Israel and in the surrounding territories.[13] When people were in some kind of special distress, they would sometimes promise something to the Lord if he would deliver them from that distress (see, e.g.,

---

11. See the helpful discussion of this story in light of reproductive bioethical issues today in Gilbert Meilaender, "A Child of One's Own: At What Price?" in *The Reproductive Revolution: A Christian Appraisal of Sexuality, Reproductive Technologies, and the Family*, ed. John F. Kilner et al. (Grand Rapids, Mich.: Eerdmans, 2000), 40–42.

12. David Toshio Tsumura, *The First Book of Samuel*, NICOT (Grand Rapids, Mich.: Eerdmans, 2007), 108.

13. See ibid., 117–18n77 and the literature cited there.

Lev. 7:16; 2 Sam. 15:7–8; Pss. 50:14–15; 66:13–15). As part of her desperate prayer, Hannah vows that if the Lord gives her a son, "then I will give him to the LORD for all the days of his life, and no razor will ever be used on his head" (1 Sam. 1:11; cf. the perpetual Nazirite vow of Samson from his birth in Judges 13:5, and the Nazirite vow regulations in Numbers 6).

The depth of Hannah's understanding of the Lord and commitment to him is what carries her through her agony over the years. Her faith comes to its fullest expression in her prayer of dedication when she presents Samuel to Eli (1 Sam. 2:1–10). There she celebrates God's care for and exaltation of the poor and needy. From Hannah's perspective, barrenness is a severe neediness.

The main point for us to consider here is that the robust pursuit of God by Hannah (and Elkanah too) shines through in the narrative, and that is what makes all the difference in the world when it comes to dealing with Hannah's agonizing infertility. Tom and Betty can also be greatly blessed by pursuing God and God's ways. So it will be helpful in the remainder of this chapter to consider what direction God's Word—particularly the Old Testament—provides for dealing with the challenges that this couple faces. However, offering this biblical guidance could well make no difference to such a couple unless they are deeply committed to the will and work of the Lord in the first place. A superficial spiritual life will tend to lead toward a merely superficial concern for the Lord's guidance in such important matters. In the end, there is no substitute for a close relationship with God as the starting point of ethical living.

In light of the biblical examples that we have considered above, it is not surprising that people devote so much time, money, and other resources today to seeking biotechnological options for having a baby. Many wonderful therapeutic procedures and products can now help people with ailments from head to toe. There is much to be thankful for and make use of, particularly in trying to overcome infertility. However, the desperate determination to have a baby can tempt even Christians to set aside biblical guidance and overstep ethical boundaries in spite of their faith—that is, if they even consider the ethical questions in the first place. The combined influence of personal desires, biotechnical possibilities, and moral relativism contributes to this temptation.

A BIBLICAL BASIS FOR HAVING A BABY

As noted above, good bioethical decisions for Betty and Tom will flow out of a way of thinking, living, and relating that derives from a robust pursuit of God individually and together as a couple. The early chapters of Genesis can help them to understand what that means and looks like. These chapters are the foundation for everything else in the Bible. They tell us where we came from, how we fit into the world, and what our purpose is according to God's design.

The so-called generations formula provides the structural frame for Genesis.[14] It appears eleven times throughout the book, beginning with Genesis 2:4: "these are the generations of the heavens and the earth when they were created" (NRSV). The New Testament opens with the same genealogical emphasis, this time from Abraham to Jesus. In fact, all human history up to this very day is dependent on the birth of babies. We are all part of the same story even today, whether we know it or not, and whether we like it or not.

Through the genealogies and the stories of barrenness strewn throughout the Bible, we can see how central marriage and the bearing of children are in God's plan, and yet how troublesome the whole matter can become. Being denied what seems so natural and central to one's place and purpose in the world is no small matter. Betty's reaction to her infertility and her desperation to overcome it arise from something that is good and natural in her, even if some of the ways she is handling it are making life difficult for her and others around her. Yes, there were cultural patterns in the ancient biblical world that contributed to the struggle with this problem in ways peculiar to that day. But many of the basic issues were the same then as they are today.

Genesis 1–4 can help us build a biblical base for dealing with "having a baby the new-fashioned way," and for many other bioethical challenges as well. First, and probably most important, is our place and purpose as human beings in God's creation as those whom he created in his image (Genesis 1). This is where we need to start, because everything else flows out of this basic principle of human design and dignity. Second, we need to consider the essential nature of the one man and one woman marital bond as God designed it (Genesis 2). Third, the corruption of God's design has had disastrous effects on our situation in the world and how we handle it (Genesis 3). Even though the original design is still in place, everything we do is also deeply affected by our corruption. Fourth, the only good way to handle life is to allow whatever we face along the way to drive us toward the Lord, calling on his name in the midst of it all (Genesis 4). Each of these elements provides meaningful direction for Tom, Betty, and all of the many others who have a stake in the situation before us.

GENESIS 1: HUMANITY CREATED IN THE IMAGE AND LIKENESS OF GOD

Although "image and likeness" language is not present often in the Bible, its appearance at strategic locations in the text elevates it to a high level of importance. The first occurrence is in Genesis 1:26–28, at the point of the original creation. In fact, it is the main topic of the first clause that God speaks when he creates humanity: "Then God said, 'Let us make humankind in our image as our likeness, that they may rule'" (my trans.).

14. I have discussed this in some detail in Richard E. Averbeck, "Factors in Reading the Patriarchal Narratives: Literary, Historical, and Theological Dimensions," in *Giving the Sense: Understanding and Using Old Testament Historical Texts*, ed. David M. Howard Jr. and Michael A. Grisanti (Grand Rapids, Mich.: Kregel, 2003), 115–37, esp. 117–20, 127–30, and 136.

What does it mean that humanity is created in God's "image and likeness"?[15] There is virtually no end to the debate over this basic question.[16] However, four broad observations are sufficient for our purposes.

First, being created in God's image is primarily a physical matter, not in terms of looking like God in some physical way but rather in terms of being physical people who stand within the physical creation as God's "statue," so to speak.[17] Second, as his statue, humanity's purpose is to stand for him, his authority, and his divine purposes amid the whole creation. Genesis 1:26 explains that people are called to "rule" as managers of his creation. They represent him in this world. It is their responsibility to do this, and to do it well—that is, according to God's character and creative design. Third, fulfilling this function requires appropriate relationships with both God and one another. On the human level, the basic bond is that between a man and a woman. Genesis 2 develops this point further and will be treated below.[18]

Finally, God designed people, even with all of their limitations,[19] to function as his image and even to have children in their own image (Genesis 5), but not to replace him or become his equal.[20] In fact, people are dependent even on the creation around

---

15. In Gen. 5:2, the term *likeness* is used alone for the image and likeness of God, whereas Gen. 1:27 uses *image* the same way. We should not try to distinguish between image and likeness, as if they refer to different aspects of our correspondence to God.

16. The secondary scholarly literature on the so-called *imago Dei* (the Latin term for "the image of God" in humanity) is voluminous. A particularly discerning, thorough, and current summary of the exegetical and theological discussion, the history of interpretation, and its application to current issues is J. Richard Middleton, *The Liberating Image: The Imago Dei in Genesis 1* (Grand Rapids, Mich.: Baker, 2005). An extensive exegetical and theological discussion is also provided in Andrew J. Schmutzer, *Be Fruitful and Multiply: A Crux of Thematic Repetition in Genesis 1–11* (Eugene, Ore.: Wipf and Stock, 2009), 89–203.

17. In addition to the five times the image and likeness terminology refers to human beings in the image of God (Gen. 1:26–27 twice; 5:1; 9:6), the term *image* occurs only eleven more times in the Hebrew Old Testament and seventeen times in the Aramaic part of Daniel (all in Dan. 2:31–35 for the great dream image of Nebuchadnezzar, and Dan. 3:1–19 for the giant image of gold that Nebuchadnezzar set up). Most often *image* refers to statues or other three-dimensional replicas, primarily statues of gods or men (e.g., Num. 33:52; 2 Kings 11:18; 2 Chron. 23:17; Ezek. 7:20; 16:17; Amos 5:26). A further clue to the meaning of the terms, as they were used in the broader culture, resides in the bilingual (Aramaic and Akkadian) ninth-century-BC Tell

Fekheriye inscription from northern Mesopotamia/Upper Syria. See Andreas Schüle, "Made in the 'Image of God': The Concepts of Divine Images in Gen 1–3," *Zeitschrift für die alttestamentliche Wissenschaft* 117 (2005): 1–20.

18. As pictured in Genesis 1 (esp. vv. 26–28), people were created as relational beings by a relational God. As the *imago Dei*, humanity's function is primarily representational and necessarily relational. See the extensive discussion in Claus Westermann, *Genesis 1–11: A Commentary*, trans. John J. Scullion, SJ (Minneapolis: Augsburg, 1984), 147–61, esp. his conclusion on pp. 155–58.

19. In Gen. 9:6 God declares people once again to be those made by him in his own image: "Whoever sheds the blood of man, by man shall his blood be shed; for in the image of God has God made man." Thus, humanity remains God's statue in the world even though ravaged by sin and corruption. To disrespect the image is to disrespect the one whom the image represents.

20. Gen. 5:3 goes on to say that "Adam lived one hundred thirty years and generated [lit. 'caused to be born'] a son in his likeness as his image, and named him Seth" (Gen. 5:3, my trans.). Adam "generated" Seth; he did not "create" him. The verb *bārāʾ*, "to create," is used of God's creative work in Gen. 1:27; 5:1–2, and elsewhere, but never of human reproduction. The verb *generated* is another form of the verb "to give birth," which is the same verb that underlies the term *generations* discussed earlier in this chapter. Human beings are not creators but "reproducers." This is an important distinction.

them for sustenance (see, e.g., Gen. 1:29). Humanity has made numerous attempts over the millennia to take the place of God, beginning in the original garden itself (see the remarks on Genesis 3 below), and it has always come to no good. It comes to no good when people try to do this in their personal and relational lives as well.

Humanity has been created with human dignity by God as his own image, with responsibility for all of creation. This is who people are. In the case study, although they may not put it this way, Tom and especially Betty find themselves in a place of struggle that feels like an assault on their God-given purpose and potential. It is heart-wrenching. What would it look like for them to handle themselves well amid their circumstances? The answer to this question begins with understanding and accepting the implications of being created in the image of God, but *not* being God. Sometimes it is tempting to try to play God in this or that situation, but when people do that, they are stepping out of line, much like Rachel did when in desperation she demanded of her husband, Jacob, "Give me children, or I'll die!" Jacob loved her, but how else could he respond other than to say, "Am I in the place of God, who has kept you from having children?" (Gen. 30:1–2).

At the same time, not being able to contribute personally to fulfilling the mandate to "be fruitful and increase in number; fill the earth" (Gen. 1:28) could naturally feel to Betty and Tom like they are left out of the full experience God designed for Betty as a mother and for them as a couple. They are not wrong to try to overcome their infertility problem by legitimate means. So the question is, What are legitimate means and what are not, from a biblical point of view?

Betty became pregnant by Tom before they were married. The given reason for aborting the baby was that "they were neither emotionally nor financially ready for parenthood." Whether or not this past abortion itself has anything to do with why Betty cannot get pregnant at her present stage in life, earlier in life she could and she did. She and Tom just did not want to have a child then, so they chose to abort. Betty's age now is likely at least part of the problem. In fact, she may not be able to bring a child to term even if she were to get pregnant "in the new-fashioned way."

While aborting the earlier child had little if anything to do with eugenics directly, some of the practices Tom, Betty, and Laura are considering are part of a new eugenic agenda.[21] Eugenics has to do with using the principles of heredity to improve the quality of human beings born into the world. Experience with this practice has been controversial. Positively, eugenics can promote reproduction among those who have the qualities that are considered advantageous to the improvement of humankind overall. Negatively, there can be attempts to limit reproduction among less desirable people. During the first half of the twentieth century, some Western nations, including the United States,

---

21. See especially R. Kendall Soulen, "Cruising toward Bethlehem: Human Dignity and the New Eugenics," in *God and Human Dignity*, ed. R. Kendall Soulen and Linda Woodhead (Grand Rapids, Mich.: Eerdmans, 2006), 104–20.

embraced selected eugenic practices. In Nazi Germany, eugenics turned into a program that became coercive to the point of madness and overwhelming brutality. This "old eugenics" has been widely rejected because it is coercive and racist.

The new eugenics has the same basic goal, supposedly without the coercion and racism. However, advances in the biological science of human reproduction (e.g., "custom options" increasingly open to parents today through gene manipulation) involve new forms of lethal discrimination. Parents increasingly have the freedom to choose whether an embryo is good enough to be implanted, and whether a fetus is healthy enough or sufficiently wanted to be given birth.[22]

This eugenics mentality is quite visible in our present case. First, Betty and Tom plan to use preimplantation genetic diagnosis (PGD) of the embryos as part of the in vitro fertilization (IVF) process. Only the best of Laura's fertilized eggs would be implanted into Betty. In addition, there is disagreement about what to do with the leftover embryos, whether to make them available to other couples with infertility problems or sell them for stem cell research. Since it is reasonable to consider embryos to be human beings—created in the image of God like every other human—they need to be treated accordingly.[23]

Another eugenic issue concerns the use of amniocentesis to check for deformities in order to determine whether to allow the fetus to come to term. Betty herself resists this option because she does not want to go through another abortion. Tom and Laura, however, think this approach offers an important way to ensure that only a healthy child is born. Eugenics is involved here in the form of intentionally aborting a baby who does not match the parents' lifestyle, hopes, and expectations. However, this fetal human being is already created and designed according to the image of God. Just as important is the fact that the parents have been created to function in God's image as well. That entails supporting the child, not aborting the child as an act of human defiance of God's plan and purpose. The fetus does not make the decision. The parents do. So it is their moral character—their living according to the image of God—that is at issue here.

GENESIS 2: THE RELATIONSHIP BETWEEN THE MAN AND THE WOMAN

Genesis 2:4–25 adds a more complete narrative description of the nature and importance of the relationship between the man and woman to the account in Genesis 1. The Lord himself notes here that "it is not good for the man to be alone" (v. 18; contrast "very good" in Gen. 1:31), so God determines to make "a helper suitable" for him (lit. "a helper as his opposite"). The man has been designed relationally from the start. He needs a suitable companion. Note that God is already there and is in relationship with

---

22. This account of eugenics comes from Soulen, "Cruising toward Bethlehem," 108–10.

23. The problem of the status of human embryos is taken up by Evans, "The Moral Status of Embryos," in *Reproductive Revolution*, ed. Kilner et al, 60–76.

the man, but God himself sees the need for the man to have a companion who will be on his own level, a helper who is his corresponding and complementary opposite.

The attraction that the man has for the woman as his corresponding feminine opposite is clear from his response in Genesis 2:23: "This at last is bone of my bones and flesh of my flesh; this one shall be called Woman, for out of Man this one was taken" (NRSV). Woman and Man are personal names here, and there is a play on words: Woman (Hebrew *ʾiššâ*) is a feminine Man (Hebrew *ʾîš*; the standard feminine ending in Hebrew is *â*). The narrator draws out the implication of this in verse 24: "Therefore a man leaves his father and his mother and clings to his wife, and they become one flesh." Some have mistakenly interpreted "they become one flesh" as a reference to sexual intercourse, or even the children that they conceive and bear, thinking that the man and the woman become literally one flesh in the body of a child. The expression may include sexual relations, but it is not limited to that, and it certainly does not apply to the children born of it.

The issue is the naked, open, and exclusive bondedness of the relationship itself (contrast 2:24 with 3:7), not sexual intercourse or reproduction (see more on Genesis 3 below). The point in Genesis 2:24 is that the man will bond with the woman in permanent personal commitment that will never come apart. They become "one flesh" in the sense that they become one functional unit, dealing with life together in bond with one another (including sexual relations). He will grab hold of her tightly with no intention of letting her go. Nothing and no one will come between them because there is no room.

This one-flesh concept is important to the case at hand because the way Tom and Betty are dealing with their infertility is causing significant problems between them as husband and wife. Their one-flesh bond is being compromised. Their design and dignity in the image and likeness of God as it is described in Genesis 1:26–28 are bound up in their relationship not only to God but also to one another. It took "intense discussion" for Betty to convince Tom that they should have children in the first place, and the tension between them is building over social issues and the pressure to get pregnant at virtually any cost.

So far Tom and Betty have not violated their one-flesh union by using IVF, because they have been using Betty's eggs and Tom's sperm in the procedure. That approach, however, has been unsuccessful. So now they are considering using Laura's eggs, which compromises the exclusivity of their bond. Even worse, they are considering whether to go farther and have Laura serve as a surrogate for Betty by bearing the child.[24] This would compound the breach of the union between Tom and Betty.

The patriarchs and their wives sometimes sought to deal with their infertility problems through surrogacy. Because they did not have these other reproductive technolo-

---

24. See the helpful remarks on this in Dennis P. Hollinger, "Sexual Ethics and Reproductive Technologies," in *The Reproduction Revolution: A Christian Appraisal of* *Sexuality, Reproductive Technologies, and the Family*, ed. John F. Kilner et al. (Grand Rapids, Mich.: Eerdmans, 2000), 88–89.

gies available to them in their day, this was basically their last human resort. It was something they did, but that does not mean that it was pleasing to God, any more than various other behaviors described in the Old Testament that fall short of God's good intentions for humanity. Surrogacy is not a part of God's original design (Genesis 1), which includes the one-flesh marital unit of one man with one woman (Genesis 2). It is a weakening of the one-flesh bond by its very nature. God resisted blessing it, for example, in the lives of Abraham and Sarah: Hagar's son Ishmael was not allowed to be the son of promise even though Abraham wished it (Gen. 17:18, "If only Ishmael might live under your blessing!").

The Old Testament picture as a whole emphasizes God's design of the one-flesh bond in a way that includes only one man and one woman. God worked then and still works today, sometimes in spite of our violations of his design. His grace can overcome. Nevertheless, we need to take seriously God's design and live in the light of it. Isaac prayed for Rebekah, and Hannah prayed, and God answered both of them, but not without both women going through the struggle of barrenness. Eventually, God delivered Sarah and Rachel from their barrenness too. God can deliver anyone from such painful circumstances, but he does not always do so. The issue becomes how far people will go to circumscribe or overcome those circumstances, and whether they will stay within the boundaries of God's design while doing so.

GENESIS 3: VIOLATION OF GOD'S DESIGN

The third chapter of Genesis brings us to the original violation of God's design. There is much here that sheds light on the case before us.[25] Tom and Betty's decision-making process is driven almost completely by the pragmatic possibilities available through reproductive technologies and the involvement of Betty's sister, Laura. Little concern for basic human or ethical responsibilities is evident. Genesis 3 tells us that in our fallen human condition this is no surprise. Rapidly advancing developments in biotechnology have generated temptations that are beyond humanity's capacity to resist.[26] History has shown this. And the deceptively destructive new eugenics is not as far off from the old eugenics as some might think.

As discussed above, the various kinds of pain that people experience in this fallen world can overwhelm them to the point where they will seek escape in any way they can, even if that way involves knowingly violating God's design. The basic problem here is that people keep on replaying the dynamics of the fall scene in Genesis 3:1–13. This passage presents a narrative theology that is not just about what happened in the begin-

---

25. For a much fuller treatment of the personal and interpersonal dynamics of the corruption of the human person as seen in Gen. 3:1–13, see Richard E. Averbeck, "Creation and Corruption, Redemption and Wisdom: A Biblical Theology Foundation for Counseling Psychology," *Journal of Psychology and Christianity* 25, no. 2 (2006): 111–26.

26. See, e.g., the brief remarks in Soulen, "Cruising toward Bethlehem," 104–5.

ning but is also about what continues to happen. It serves as a prototype for the sinful dynamics that continue to plague everyone today. People are deceived in their thinking (Gen. 3:1, 13). This raises doubts in people's minds about God's goodness and the serious repercussions of rebellion against him (vv. 3, 4–5). The combination of deception and doubt causes people to have illegitimate desires for things that violate God's explicit design (v. 6a), and this, in turn, leads to acts of sinful behavior in disobedience to God and his design (v. 6b). This combination of dynamics in people's minds and lives leads to an overwhelming sense of shame that they find very difficult to live with (v. 7), resulting in fear and scrambling about as they try to deal with the whole mess (vv. 8–13).

We have already discussed some of these elements reflected in the case before us (e.g., the deception involved in not really considering basic ethical issues, the previous abortion, the social distancing, and the self-serving interests of the people involved). One especially relevant insight in Genesis 3 is the observation that the woman, even in her fallen condition and the accompanying pain, will desire to have a man to cherish her and to bear children with (Gen. 3:16). This is such a deeply embedded part of the design that it cannot be erased even by the fall, and it is evident in the case before us as well. Betty cannot suppress the desire to have a baby with Tom in one way or another, even if it does not involve her own eggs. Again, there is nothing wrong with this desire. And to Tom's credit he is willing to fulfill his wife's desire as best he can.

However, the situation has gotten out of hand in so many ways. Betty cannot contribute the eggs and is bringing another woman into the reproductive process; Tom, Betty, and Laura are suffering serious relational problems; and adoption has been ruled out. Perhaps Betty and Tom just would not be able to muster the nurturing love to raise an adopted baby in a way that would be good for both them and the baby. This is unfortunate. Adoption is very close to the heart of God even in terms of the building of his own kingdom.[27] It may be possible that, if they could move close to the heart of God, Tom and Betty might become passionate about this compassionate answer to their infertility.

GENESIS 4: CALLING ON THE NAME OF THE LORD

The ancients did all they were able to do to try to overcome their infertility problems, and we can expect the same from people in the modern world. There is little hope of restraint actually winning the day in the culture, unless perhaps some kind of atrocity brings about its discrediting, as with the "old eugenics." Short of that, however, for people of sincere Christian faith—believers who have entrusted their lives now and for eternity into the hands of God—there is hope that comes from another whole way of approaching life. This is the main point of Genesis 4.

---

27. See especially the article by Sarah Hinlicky Wilson, "Blessed Are the Barren: The Kingdom of God Springs Forth from the Empty Womb," *Christianity Today* 51, no. 12 (December 2007), 21–28. See also the extensive biblical studies of adoption by God in Trevor J. Burke, *Adopted into God's Family: Exploring a Pauline Metaphor*, New Testament Studies in Biblical Theology 22 (Downers Grove, Ill.: InterVarsity, 2006).

The chapter begins with Eve ("the mother of all the living," Gen. 3:20) bearing two sons, Cain and Abel (Gen. 4:1–2). Tragedy follows when Cain kills Abel. The results are catastrophic for Cain too, since his livelihood becomes threatened. He is a tiller of the ground for whom the ground will no longer produce (Gen. 4:2, 11–14). Toward the end of the chapter, Lamech, the last man in the Cain genealogy, boasts to his wives, "Adah and Zillah, listen to me; wives of Lamech, hear my words. I have killed a man for wounding me, a young man for injuring me. If Cain is avenged seven times [cf. v. 15], then Lamech seventy-seven times" (Gen. 4:23–24). Lamech is boasting that he is in charge and that no one had better challenge him.

By way of contrast, the last two verses recount the birth of a third son to Adam and Eve to replace Abel, whose name is Seth, and he in turn has a son named Enosh (vv. 25–26). The last clause of this chapter reports, "At that time people began to call on the name of the Lord" (v. 26). The only real answer ever given to the problem of humanity's fallen condition is found initially here. It is to "call on the name of the Lord."[28] This becomes a powerful theological refrain through the entire canon of Scripture in many places and at pivotal points (see, e.g., Gen. 12:7–8; 26:25; 1 Kings 18:24; Pss. 55:16; 56:9; 80:18; 86:5; 99:6; and esp. 116:4, 13, 17; Joel 2:32, quoted in Acts 2:21 and Rom. 10:13; etc.). It all starts here.

God can change people's circumstances, even though it is not always his will to do so for reasons apparent sometimes only to him. Those who live for the Lord call on the name of the Lord in the midst of their circumstances whatever they are, and they leave the decision in his hands, as hard as that can be. If Tom and Betty can turn in this direction, they may or may not get the answer they are seeking. But if God does not answer their desires the way they wish him to, he may work in them individually and as a couple to shift their desires toward something that would bring meaning to their lives and their relationship that they have never imagined, and would not want to miss. The pain of not having a child from their own bodies will not necessarily go away. However, in the end "having a baby the new-fashioned way" will not really overcome that problem either, since the baby would not actually be "from their own bodies."

INSIGHT AND PERSPECTIVE

The Old Testament, then, provides great insight into the Romans 8 "groaning" that Tom and Betty are dealing with in their infertility. The stories of women and men who

---

28. The expression "call on the name of the Lord" can mean (1) to proclaim the Lord's name and character, as, e.g., in Exod. 34:5–6 and Ps. 116:5, (2) to call upon the Lord (in prayer) to answer in the midst of difficult circumstances, as, e.g., in 1 Kings 18:24, 36–38 and Ps. 116:4, and (3) to invoke the Lord in worship, which may include either or both of the above, as, e.g., in Ps. 116:17, etc. The overall point is that this expression always involves turning to the Lord and pointing oneself and perhaps also others to him as the only one worthy of our worship, devotion, and dependence in the midst of any and all circumstances and situations of life.

suffer with infertility in the pages of Scripture make it clear that this is no small matter and, in fact, is central to the human predicament. Genesis 1–4 is particularly helpful in reminding us that the bearing of children is central to God's design in the first place. Infertility is a serious problem that understandably causes great pain, but the real issue for people in the midst of it is how they handle such groaning.

They can go the way of Lamech in Genesis 4:23–24 and try to take over by their own willful human power without regard to God's design, or they can turn and "call upon the name of the LORD" right in the face of it. They can allow pain to drive them toward God or away from him. Unfortunately, people today, as in ancient times, often fail to take into consideration God's design and its ongoing implications for making bioethical decisions. The Old Testament offers keen insight for appreciating, at least to some degree, the suffering of those who are wrestling with infertility. It also provides invaluable perspective to help people recognize how to move forward in the midst of their suffering. Both are essential to helping people in the midst of the heartbreaking circumstances of infertility.

CHAPTER 2

WISDOM FROM BUSINESS

Scott B. Rae and Helen Eckmann

Tom and Betty are facing the agonizing experience of infertility. The pain involved is difficult for anyone who has not been through it to understand fully. Betty's apparent obsession with becoming pregnant is not unusual for women in the midst of infertility, and the added stress in their relationship is the norm for couples dealing with such difficulty conceiving a child. No more unusual is their social isolation, which has resulted from understandable feelings of tension and envy when around couples with children. Perhaps their church unwittingly contributes to their feeling of being on the outside, if many couples there do have children and the church advertises itself as a "family friendly" church. They may even have stopped going to church on Mother's Day and Father's Day—for them the two most difficult days of the year—especially if the worship service does not include anything to comfort people for whom those two days are so uncomfortable.

This situation raises profound biblical, relational, and other questions which are addressed in other chapters of this book. Our concern in the present chapter is more related to the infertility clinic where Tom and Betty have already spent considerable energy, effort, and money on six attempts at egg retrieval. The egg harvesting process constitutes over half of the expense of the entire IVF (in vitro fertilization) procedure. So Tom and Betty have already spent thousands of dollars pursuing IVF, without getting past the first stage in the process. That is one of various business ethics issues that the clinic ought to face. Such issues will be the focus of this chapter. We will discuss the moral obligations of the clinic to the couple and to the children who may be born through its procedures, including any half sisters or brothers who could be born to Betty's sister.

THE INFERTILITY INDUSTRY

The business side of infertility treatment is a largely unaddressed topic. The infertility industry has long had a reputation for being underregulated and for pushing the boundaries of social acceptance in creating new forms of families. Many of the relevant ethical issues have been left unaddressed by the law, thereby allowing the clinics to focus solely on achieving a successful pregnancy and the resulting revenue. Taking advantage of a long legal tradition of procreative liberty in the United States,[1] the infertility business has flourished financially while providing the dream of a child to countless couples. But the overall success rate of IVF is not high, with only around 25 to 30 percent of couples achieving a live birth.[2] The dream of having a child through IVF is unrealized by more than half of the couples who invest emotionally and financially in the process. They spend many thousands of dollars and come away empty-handed, a situation in which Tom and Betty find themselves.

Interestingly, the industry is more regulated in Europe than in the United States, and some countries, such as Germany, have far more restrictions on biotechnology in general, not just on infertility treatments.[3] Most infertility clinics in the United States are members of the Society for Assisted Reproductive Technology (SART), which publishes the success rates of member clinics and provides voluntary operational guidelines for them. These guidelines do not have the force of law, and the degree of adherence varies from clinic to clinic.

This overall lack of regulation has given the industry somewhat of a maverick reputation in the field of health care, and the law frequently must catch up to the latest technological innovations.[4] It is not difficult to see how ethical issues could arise for an infertility clinic, given the combination of underregulation, desperate infertile couples, expensive procedures that generate substantial profits, and physicians who are often perceived as giving the gift of life. The business ethics of infertility treatment is often neglected, as though the only stakeholder facing ethical decisions is the couple. The couple is the primary, but not sole, party with ethical decisions to make in the present case.

---

1. The following court cases are widely considered to have established this precedent of procreative liberty: *Meyer v. Nebraska*, 262 U.S. 390 (1923); *Skinner v. Oklahoma*, 316 U.S. 535 (1942); *Griswold v. Connecticut*, 381 U.S. 479 (1965); *Eisenstadt v. Baird*, 405 U.S. 438 (1972); *Carey v. Population Services International*, 431 U.S. 678 (1977). For discussion of these cases, see Scott B. Rae, *The Ethics of Commercial Surrogate Motherhood* (New York: Praeger, 1994).

2. This success rate is usually higher when donor eggs are involved, and other procedures, such as GIFT (Gamete Intrafallopian Transfer), have success rates of 40 to 50 percent. But these technologies are dealing with problem cases to begin with, so the expectation of a high rate of success is not realistic.

3. The United States, a nation with a Christian heritage, has been rather slow on the world stage to engage in intelligent discussion which could lead to a framework of law. European hesitation to embrace some biotechnologies as fully as they are welcomed in the US may be a result of the particularly destructive European eugenics movement in the earlier half of the twentieth century.

4. One often-cited example of how the law trails new reproductive arrangements occurred in the mid to late 1990s at the infertility clinic of the University of California, Irvine. The clinic was run by one of the pioneers of assisted reproductive technologies and was financially very successful. It was involved in an egg-swapping program, in which the clinic appropriated eggs from women who produced more than they needed and gave them to women who did not produce enough. The clinic ran into trouble because it did not disclose the transfer of eggs either to the "donor" or to the recipient. While this was obviously an unethical business practice, the clinic did not violate any state or federal laws. The law was changed shortly thereafter to prohibit such activity. The UCI clinic is no longer in operation.

Tom and Betty should not be under any illusions about the profit-driven side of the clinic to which they have entrusted their infertility treatment.[5] It is not a nonprofit medical clinic but a for-profit business. The doctors, nurses, and staff of this organization have worked hard and devoted considerable amounts of hours and dollars to earning degrees. Most of them likely have deferred debt from student loans. Moreover, it is costly day-to-day to run a business. Salaries for staff average more than fifty thousand dollars a year with 30 percent expenses above that amount for benefits, payroll taxes, and training. Thus, each employee of the clinic costs on average a minimum of sixty-five thousand dollars a year and a maximum of several times that amount, depending on their position and training. Additionally, the partners or doctors who own the clinic have deferred earning an income for more than ten years to get their advanced degrees and are probably at a time in their lives when they need to generate enough income to live the lifestyle to which they have long aspired. Many small- to mid-sized businesses, the size of our clinic, are running an overhead of seventy-five thousand dollars a month or more.[6]

A BUSINESS ETHICS FOR HEALTH CARE

When discussing infertility treatment, people commonly assume that two different sets of ethical standards are in fundamental conflict. Traditional medical ethics emphasizes patient well-being and the physician's obligation to the patient. This stands in apparent conflict with the way business ethics is perceived, with its emphasis on profit maximization. For example, Wendy Mariner puts it like this: "The ethical principles that promote free and fair competition are quite different from the ethical principles that preserve the integrity of the physician-patient relationship and specifically those that protect patient welfare, and these principles can lead to quite different outcomes."[7] In other words, the goal of medicine is the health of the patient, while the goal for business is the maximization of profit.

It is a standard maxim in business that the goal of a corporation is to maximize shareholder wealth. The classic statement of this is by Milton Friedman, who held that

---

5. For a helpful descriptive view of the business side of infertility, see Deborah Spar, *The Baby Business: How Money, Science and Politics Drive the Commerce of Conception* (Cambridge, Mass.: Harvard Business School Press, 2006). While not a discussion of the ethical issues involved, the book accurately portrays the industry as a *business* first and foremost. See also Liza Mundy, *Everything Conceivable: How Assisted Reproduction Is Changing Our World* (New York: Random House, 2007).

6. For further information on these cost figures, see *www.payscale.com*.

7. Wendy Mariner, "Business Ethics vs. Medical Ethics: Conflicting Standards for Managed Care," *Journal of Law, Medicine and Ethics* 23 (1995): 236. See also Andrew C. Wicks, "Albert Schweitzer or Ivan Boesky? Why We Should Reject the Dichotomy between Business and Medicine," *Journal of Business Ethics* 14 (1995): 339; and Arnold Relman, "What Market Values Are Doing to Medicine," *Atlantic Monthly* (March 1992), 106. Relman suggests that "medical care is in many ways uniquely unsuited to private enterprise. It cannot meet its responsibilities to society if it is dominated by business interests."

corporations exercise all the social responsibility they need to simply by making a profit. In doing so, they provide the public with a useful product or service and provide jobs for people in the community. Friedman further argued that for corporations to act in socially responsible ways that do not contribute to their profit is actually stealing from shareholders.[8]

By contrast, Friedman's framework has been challenged by what is known as "stakeholder theory," which suggests that there are other stakeholders, such as employees, the community, the environment, and so on, whose interests should be taken into account along with shareholders' in the decisions a company makes.[9] We would argue that most investors would not consider it theft if the firms in which they invest were to be socially responsible, even at the expense of profit. For example, most mission statements balance elements such as the excellence of the service or product, service to the community, and a fair rate of return for investors. In addition, the work of Georgetown professor Pietra Rivoli suggests that investors who consider social and ethical concerns and act on those concerns constitute a significant portion of equity investment in the United States. As she puts it, "wealth maximization is *a constrained objective*, and the constraints are social and ethical values."[10] This constraint is magnified in the way that companies are urged today toward sustainability and environmental responsibility. In fact, sustainability is often considered synonymous with a stakeholder view.[11]

This stakeholder view is arguably consistent with Adam Smith's original vision of capitalism. Smith considered business to be a profession in which service to the community through a product was the mission, and profit was an anticipated by-product of excellence in that service. The service, not the profit, was the end. The "bottom line" was not the bottom line. His legacy for modern capitalism is *not* that which is widely attributed to him — that the sole goal of a corporation is to maximize shareholder wealth. He never suggested that greed is good. Smith's original vision involved restraint of the very self-interest that is necessary for a properly functioning economic system. As Catholic theologian Michael Novak argues, "A firm committed to greed unleashes social forces that will sooner or later destroy it. Spasms of greed will corrupt its executives, anger its patrons, injure the morale of its workers, antagonize its suppliers and purchasers, embolden its competitors and attract public retribution."[12]

8. Milton Friedman, "The Social Responsibility of Business Is to Increase Its Profits," *New York Times Magazine*, September 13, 1970, 33, 122–26.

9. The classic statement of the stakeholder view is found in Kenneth Goodpaster, "Business Ethics and Stakeholder Analysis," *Business Ethics Quarterly* 1, no. 1 (January 1991): 53–73.

10. Pietra Rivoli, "Ethical Aspects of Investor Behavior," *Journal of Business Ethics* 14 (1995): 265–77.

11. See, e.g., how this is articulated in Andrew Savitz

with Karl Weber, *The Triple Bottom Line: How Today's Best-Run Companies Are Achieving Economic, Social and Environmental Success — and How You Can Too* (San Francisco: John Wiley and Sons, 2006).

12. Michael Novak, *The Spirit of Democratic Capitalism* (Lanham, Md.: University Press of America, 1991), 92. By extension, for a detailed discussion of the trust necessary for an efficient economy, see Francis Fukuyama, *Trust: The Social Virtues and the Creation of Prosperity* (New York: Free Press, 1996).

Though it is true that some firms operate on the greed-is-good corporate philosophy, to characterize that as central to business ethics is inaccurate. The stakeholder model provides a distinct alternative to the charge that corporations exist for the sole purpose of profit maximization. Such a model applies well to the case before us; there is much more to the business ethics of the clinic than simply maximizing profit.[13]

BACKGROUND DYNAMICS

Infertility clinics do not presently engage in routine in-depth counseling of the couples that they treat. They are more concerned with a couple's medical history and the medical issues underlying their difficulty in becoming pregnant. However, some background dynamics such as the psychological and relational health of the couple warrant the clinic's attention as well. These dynamics may well not come out during the clinic's interview of many couples. In such cases, the clinic will not be in as good a position as it could be to serve the couple. The clinic does not have any obligation to resolve background problems, but they are pertinent to the well-being of the couple undergoing infertility treatment. To the degree that such considerations are important in treating the couple, the clinic ought to elicit this kind of information.

The clinic arguably has the responsibility to turn down couples who are not fit to be parents, analogous to the way in which adoption clinics screen the parental fitness of adopting couples. Should Tom's ambivalence about being a father become apparent, the clinic could refer him and Betty to counseling in order to obtain genuine consent for IVF, since a successful result would mean fatherhood for Tom. However, this kind of screening is unlikely to occur, given the American legal tradition of procreative liberty and the clinic's desire to maximize revenue.

Several other important background dynamics are evident in the situation as well. One is Laura's desperate financial straits, which may be coloring her ethical decision-making. Another is the disagreement between Betty and Laura over disclosing the upcoming child's origins both to the child and to the extended family. Still another, in stark contrast to Tom's ambivalence, is Betty's increasingly desperate obsession over becoming pregnant and how that affects her marriage, social life, relationship with her sister (and other family members), and prospects for becoming pregnant. This obsession is magnified by the way that the hyperovarian stimulation medications used in IVF create heightened emotional states in the women who receive them. Furthermore, there is the dynamic that Betty feels her sister owes her some of her eggs, given her relative ease in conceiving her own children and Betty's support for her during her difficult divorce.

---

13. For further discussion of the stakeholder model for business ethics, see Scott B. Rae and Kenman L. Wong, *Beyond Integrity: A Judeo-Christian Approach to Business Ethics*, 2nd ed. (Grand Rapids, Mich.: Zondervan, 2004), chap. 4. For more on the application of business ethics to health care, see Kenman L. Wong, *Medicine and the Marketplace* (Notre Dame, Ind.: Univ. of Notre Dame Press, 2000), and Marc Rodwin, *Medicine, Money and Morals* (New York: Oxford Univ. Press, 1992).

Finally, there are the dynamics related to abortion and adoption. It would be helpful for the clinic to know about Betty's abortion, in light of its possible effects on her physically (e.g., difficulty in becoming pregnant again) and on the couple emotionally (e.g., guilt over ending a previous pregnancy). Desperation to erase the guilt of ending an otherwise successful pregnancy may make them vulnerable to consenting too readily to additional infertility treatments. Meanwhile, at least Betty seems to have rejected adoption somewhat irrationally, since the reason given (requiring a genetic relationship) does not even seem to cause her hesitation over using Laura's eggs.

DECIDING WHEN TO MAKE CHANGES

One of the most glaring ethical issues involving the clinic is one that has already arisen. Betty has already undergone six IVF egg retrieval cycles, a costly and emotionally draining process that involves taking medications that enable her to release as many eggs as possible in any given cycle. This is roughly half the cost of the entire IVF procedure. Chances are that Tom and Betty have already invested at least fifty to one hundred thousand dollars in IVF with nothing but stress, anxiety, and disappointment to show for it so far.

Though it is possible that there are sound medical reasons for each attempt, it is unlikely that simply trying the same procedure repeatedly would markedly increase the chance of success, especially at Betty's age of forty-three. It appears somewhat irregular if the clinic did not suggest using an egg donor well before the sixth failed attempt at egg retrieval. Unless there were very unusual medical indications, the repetition sounds a bit like the definition of insanity—trying the same thing repeatedly and expecting a different result.[14] Without exceptional medical justification, the clinic was acting irresponsibly toward the couple if it did not recommend an egg donor, or other alternatives, much earlier in the process. The couple would have spent thousands of dollars unnecessarily and would have been no closer to having a child than when they began. The picture here would be troubling indeed: a clinic taking advantage of a desperate infertile couple, in which the woman is especially vulnerable to trying it "just one more time." The worst-case scenario would be that the clinic is doing something analogous to a stockbroker who is "churning" his or her clients' accounts (repeatedly buying and selling stocks beyond what is in the clients' interests) simply to generate commissions.

The clinic in all likelihood had an obligation to the couple to guide them to an alternative far earlier than the sixth failed attempt. In fact, the clinic would have done well to have a conversation with the couple about whether they should continue with IVF at all, should the couple not be inclined to consider an egg donor. Were an egg donor not an option, the clinic should have helped the couple to consider when it would be in their interest to stop putting their money into an IVF process that looked likely to continue to fail to achieve a pregnancy.

14. This quote is variously attributed to Albert Einstein, Benjamin Franklin, and an unspecified Chinese proverb, but it comes from Ruby Mae Brown in her novel *Sudden Death* (New York: Bantam, 1983), 68.

Of course, protecting the couple's interests in this way could have jeopardized some revenue for the clinic, which suggests why the clinic may not have taken this initiative.

Such financial reflections raise the broader question of whether it is right for the clinic to get paid at all when its procedures fail to achieve a pregnancy. After all, in many other businesses, payment is generally contingent on successful completion of the job or provision of a working product. For example, if a person's electricity does not come on after an electrician completes the recommended work, the electrician generally does not get paid. Likewise, if a plumber completes a repair and the pipes still leak, the plumber is not paid until the leaks are gone. And when products do not work properly, people return them either for products that do or for a full refund. Such is the routine way in which many customers and businesses relate to each other.

However, providers of medical procedures generally are not held to the same standards as providers of many other services and products. For example, if surgery fails to stop the spread of cancer, patients and their insurance carriers are usually still responsible to pay for the costs of surgery, hospitalization, and other related care. On a smaller scale, if one antibiotic fails to stop an infection, the patient (perhaps at least partly through an insurance company) usually pays the full cost of an alternate medication. One difference between medicine and home repair is that a surgeon, for example, does not indicate that surgery will arrest cancer, and part of the informed-consent process is communicating the relevant probabilities to the patient. In other words, the patient consents to surgery knowing that failure is one of the possible outcomes. Such a failure is not considered the physician's fault, unless there is negligence or other error involved. If mistakes are made, then the physician is obligated to make the situation right to the extent possible and not burden the patient with additional costs.

In the case before us, the clinic is not quite analogous to other types of business in which payment for failure is not acceptable. There is nothing fundamentally wrong with the clinic being paid for attempting to treat infertility, as long as the clinic makes full and truthful disclosure about the likelihood of success. Such disclosure would involve, at a minimum, revealing the success rates for the individual clinic and the industry as a whole for the procedures the couple is considering. Clinics that offer "money-back guarantees" may be a step in the right direction.[15] Discounts on successive attempts with the same procedure would also be appropriate.

DISCLOSURE OBLIGATIONS

The ethical questions regarding the use of donor eggs per se are discussed in the previous chapter. The specific egg donor in view in the present case raises another ethical

---

15. Some clinics offer a money-back guarantee if three attempts at IVF — all paid for in one lump sum at the outset — do not result in a live birth. The catch is that if the couple succeeds on the first attempt, they would be overpaying the clinic for that one round of IVF.

issue for the clinic. Betty's sister, Laura, is thirty-eight years old—hardly the ideal age for an egg donor. Were she not related to Betty, she surely would not be considered for egg donation because of her age. This is the first of several disclosure issues facing the clinic.

DISCLOSING RISKS INVOLVED WITH EGG DONATION

The clinic is obligated, first and foremost, according to the law mandating informed consent, to explain to Laura the risks involved with egg donation. The process of donating eggs is highly invasive, and it is not clear whether the clinic has adequately informed her of its short- and long-term health risks before Betty and Tom bring up the subject in connection with the surrogacy alternative. Short-term, there is the risk of ovarian hyperstimulation syndrome (OHSS), which occurs in one-third of IVF cycles, with roughly 8 percent of patients showing moderate to severe reactions.[16] OHSS can cause dangerous blood clots, liver and renal problems, and respiratory distress, and in rare instances even death. Long-term risks include reducing donors' own future fertility (not an issue in Laura's case) and exposing donors to risk of later development of cancers, particularly breast cancer (something Laura would want to know).

The clinic is obligated to inform Laura about such risks, and Betty should not suggest that Laura owes her anything that justifies taking these risks if Laura chooses not to undergo them. If Laura understands the risks and freely chooses nevertheless to proceed, then the clinic has fulfilled its obligation when it comes to informed consent for Laura to donate her eggs. But they must openly explain the risks to her, not downplay them, even at the risk of Laura's deciding to forgo donating her eggs (not an unreasonable decision). Tom, Betty, and Laura must all be aware of the business side of the clinic's operations. The clinic has a competing obligation to make a profit that, in light of the large sums of money involved, acts as an incentive against full disclosure to Laura.

DISCLOSING RISKS INVOLVED WITH AN OLDER EGG DONOR

Closely related to this obligation of disclosure is the clinic's obligation to disclose to Tom and Betty the risks of selecting a thirty-eight-year-old egg donor. As mentioned above, Laura is a long way from the ideal age for an egg donor, which is between the

16. UK Royal College of Obstetricians and Gynecologists, *2006 Guidelines in Ovarian Hyperstimulation*, available at *http://www.rcog.org.uk/womens-health/clinical-guidance/management-ovarian-hyperstimulation-syndrome-green-top–5* (accessed April 29, 2010). See also *Ovarian Hyperstimulation: What You Need to Know*, available at *http://www.rcog.org.uk/womens-health/clinical-guidance/* *ovarian-hyperstimulation-syndrome-what-you-need-know* (accessed April 29, 2010). The journal *Science* has reported that up to 10 percent of egg donors may experience severe OHSS. See David Magnus and Mildred K. Cho, "Issues in Oocyte Donation for Stem Cell Research," *Science* 308 (June 17, 2005): 1747–48.

ages of eighteen and twenty-five. The clinic is obligated to be forthright with Tom and Betty about the prospects of a successful pregnancy with the eggs of someone in her late thirties. They must also explain the risks of various genetic abnormalities that come with using the eggs of someone Laura's age. Were Laura not a relative, it is hard to see how the clinic could encourage Tom and Betty to use an egg donor her age. It is highly likely that they would suggest that Tom and Betty obtain the necessary eggs from someone much younger.

Given the potential conflicts over the issue of secrecy concerning the child's heritage, the clinic should at least suggest to Tom and Betty that they might be better off with an unrelated and younger egg donor. This alternative would lessen the risk and avoid some of the later disclosure challenges related to the child. Yet it might risk alienating Tom, Betty, and Laura, which the clinic is not inclined to do. This is another area in which the clinic's business interests might well conflict with what is best for Tom and Betty. In the disclosure matters just described, the clinic should weight the obligations of disclosure more heavily than its business interests. It should opt for full disclosure even if that means jeopardizing the chance to do further business with Tom and Betty. The law actually reinforces such a weighting by requiring the informed consent of all participants. The clinic has the obligation to ensure that the consent is genuinely informed and uncoerced.

DISCLOSING ALTERNATIVES TO IVF

A further disclosure obligation of the clinic is to present alternatives to IVF. Of course, the clinic staff should have encouraged Betty and Tom to consider other alternatives earlier in the process, and they should put a variety of alternatives on the table at this point. They have already suggested surrogacy, which would trade off some of the risks of egg donation for risks of labor and delivery for Laura (see discussion of surrogacy option below). They could and should also suggest embryo adoption as an alternative, which would rescue embryos whose genetic parents have abandoned them.

The benefits of such a form of adoption are multiple. There is continuity between the woman who gives birth to the child and the mother who raises the child, as opposed to the break in the relationship at birth in traditional adoption. Further, the likelihood of the embryos' genetic parents returning and reclaiming their child after birth is small, since usually the reason embryos are abandoned is that the genetic parents have completed their family and are no longer interested in bearing any additional children.

Although Tom and Betty have stated that they are not interested in adoption, there is no indication that the clinic has presented them with the alternative of embryo adoption. Since embryo adoption allows the experience of pregnancy and birth, perhaps they may see it differently than traditional adoption. Admittedly, embryo adoption would not give them any genetic connection with their child. However, it would prevent Betty from feeling like she has had a "procreative pinch hitter," giving her instead a significant biological role as the child's birth mother.

DISCLOSING THE CHILD'S GENETIC HERITAGE

The most complicated disclosure issue for the couple may be the one involving the child's knowledge of his or her genetic heritage. Some would argue, with Laura, that the child has a right to know his or her biological parents, and Tom and Betty's insistence on secrecy could undermine such a right. However, others would argue that disclosure of this information needs a specific purpose, such as knowledge of medical history should it become medically necessary to know it. Without such a purpose, there would be little gained by revealing that information. Should the child come to the clinic wanting to know who the biological mother is for reasons of medical history, the clinic would be obligated to assist in providing that information if there is reason to think that Tom and Betty would not object to the child's knowing the identity of his or her genetic mother under those conditions.

The counseling challenges involved at this point are discussed in the next chapter. The business ethics issue for the clinic is a somewhat different matter. The staff may have strong feelings about whether the child's genetic heritage should be disclosed, but their obligation to Tom and Betty, as their clients or patients, is to honor their wishes in this matter. The clinic may be able to refer Tom and Betty to other couples who have wrestled with the issue of confidentiality. The clinic should also refer them and Laura for counseling to work this out, since this kind of disagreement at the very beginning has the potential to cause serious harm to all of the relationships involved.

If Laura decides to break the news to the child or to the extended family at some point, no new ethical issue arises for the clinic. They have a fiduciary obligation to their patients, who are Tom and Betty, to follow their wishes and to respect their desire for confidentiality. They cannot prevent Laura from disclosing this information to whomever she chooses. However, the clinic remains legally obligated to protect the confidentiality of the couple, as any physician would be in dealing with any patient.

One way for fertility clinics to avoid this type of potential legal entanglement is to self-govern according to the high standard of virtue ethics. The Hippocratic oath has been a standard for virtue medical ethics since the fourth century. Its clarion call has always been to "above all else, do no harm."[17] If the fertility clinic were to hold itself to the virtue ethics standard, it would need at least to attempt to address the dynamic, complicated, and unpleasant relationships between the various stakeholders. It would be a virtuous undertaking for the clinic to help facilitate agreement in the critical area of disclosing the child's genetic heritage.

The virtuous action for the clinic is to be sure that the beginning for this child is well thought out, not just financially but also spiritually and emotionally. Acting virtuously by doing more than the law mandates, the clinic would need to avoid facilitating this

17. For further reading on the Hippocratic oath, see Steven H. Miles, *The Hippocratic Oath and the Ethics of Medicine* (New York: Oxford Univ. Press, 2004).

child's being born into an emotional whirlwind, should this critical disclosure issue be left unresolved. Allowing Laura to become an egg donor or surrogate if she disagrees with Tom and Betty now about her future relationship with the child is foreseeably asking for trouble.

PAYMENT FOR EGG "DONATION"

Once Laura recognizes the risks involved in making her eggs available to Tom and Betty, she appears less inclined to make an altruistic gift of them. Her growing insistence on being paid emerges in part from her difficult financial situation.

THE DONOR'S VULNERABILITY

Laura's financial instability (not to mention her divorce) increases her vulnerability to doing something that she might not otherwise do if she were not in such financially difficult circumstances. In other words, if money enters the equation, she may be quite vulnerable to Betty and Tom's wishes for a child regardless of what her moral compass is telling her. The clinic has an obligation to discuss this vulnerability with her and to ensure that she is genuinely consenting to the sale of her eggs, not being taken advantage of by Tom and Betty.

Even were Laura not selling her eggs, Tom and Betty would pay for all the expenses she incurs, including the egg harvesting (the hyperovarian stimulation hormones and the minor surgical procedure to extract the matured eggs), child care, and the cost of lost wages. If she receives an additional payment, she would be like most egg "donors," who are paid a substantial sum of money beyond the medical expenses involved, normally somewhere between $2,500 and $10,000. (This payment can be even higher if the recipient couple imposes special conditions, such as specific traits that the donor must have.) Unless Laura offers to forgo payment beyond expenses, her offer to make her eggs available is really egg *selling*, not egg donation.

The clinic can argue that as long as egg selling is legal, there is no reason why Laura ought not be paid for her eggs, at the least to compensate her for taking the risks involved. However, in order to induce women to go forward with a risky procedure, the clinic may understate these risks. Such risks are different than the risks that ill people undergo for their own benefit, or that a potential mother undergoes for the benefit of her yet-unborn child. The woman who sells her eggs is an otherwise healthy woman, not an infertile "patient" who chooses to assume health risks for the benefit of a baby. It is not unusual for women who have sold their eggs to have deeply conflicted feelings about doing so once they are married and have their own children.[18]

---

18. See Erika Blacksher, "On Ova Commerce," *Hastings Center Report* 30, no. 5 (September–October 2000): 29–30.

THE CHILD'S GENETIC HERITAGE

A second concern about paying for eggs is that it further undermines the likelihood that a child will be able to know his or her biological parents. Those who sell eggs tend to be less altruistic than those not requiring payment. They are more likely not to want to be identified. In the few parts of the world where the law requires donor identification, not surprisingly, the number of available donors has diminished quickly. In this case, that preference is actually reversed, as Laura is the one who desires disclosure and Tom and Betty want confidentiality. But assuming that the clinic upholds confidentiality, the child is still being denied the opportunity (some would say right) to associate with a biological parent. The Donor Sibling Registry has thousands of children still looking for their unidentified biological parent. They often connect with many (ten or more) of their half siblings. This phenomenon suggests that the desire to associate with one's biological parents is a very strong desire. It should be denied only with very compelling reasons.

EUGENIC CONCERNS

A third concern with egg selling as a public policy has to do with the eugenic slant that has moved many societies toward "designer children." Some would-be parents require donors to have particular traits—one advertisement for an egg donor offered seventy-five thousand dollars if the donor was five foot ten or above, blond, blue-eyed, athletic, and scored above 1400 on her SAT exams.[19] In a way that is counterproductive for a culture that values diversity, producing designer children runs the risk of reinforcing damaging stereotypes. Though not at issue in this specific case, should Laura withdraw her offer to make her eggs available, Tom and Betty could easily end up paying more for eggs from a woman who meets criteria that they would set.

THE UNDERMINING OF ADOPTION

A final concern about paying egg donors for their eggs is that the availability of this option tends to undermine traditional adoption, and embryo adoption as well. It is not uncommon for a clinic to suggest adoption of embryos to a couple who is contemplating using an egg donor, because embryo adoption still gives the couple the experience of pregnancy and birth, and prevents one parent from feeling genetically left out of the procreative process. If egg donors were not so available because of the financial inducements involved, perhaps Tom and Betty would consider adoption more seriously.

---

19. This advertisement came from the Brown University student newspaper, cited in Teri Yabalonsky Stat, "Premium Human Eggs Unsettling Practitioners," *Chicago Tribune* (August 1, 2006), Q8. See also Aaron D. Levine, "Self-Regulation, Compensation, and the Ethical Recruitment of Oocyte Donors," *Hastings Center Report* 40, no. 2 (March–April 2010): 27–28, 31. Egg donation websites have potential donors list their critical traits and suggest that their compensation can range from fifty to one hundred thousand dollars. E.g., see Elite Donors, *http://www .elitedonors.com/index2.html* (accessed April 29, 2010).

There are so many available adoptable children, particularly at the embryonic stage, who would benefit greatly were this couple and others like them willing to consider adoption more seriously. Though a public policy that allows for and often encourages the sale of women's eggs is undesirable, few clinics will in fact restrict the number of available options for Tom and Betty unless the law prohibits them from doing so, or unless Tom and Betty request that some options be off the table.

PAYMENT FOR SURROGACY

Another option that should be off the table is the option of paid surrogacy. If Laura is understandably hesitant over the risks of harvesting her eggs, surrogacy simply subjects her to a different set of risks and inconveniences. Instead of a one-month process to procure her eggs, she faces nine months of pregnancy with the risks of labor and delivery, a substantial concern in light of her age. The increased involvement has motivated her demand to be paid more money for surrogacy than for selling her eggs.

A surrogacy arrangement rather than simply egg donation would bring many other complications that increase Laura's vulnerability. For example, if Laura becomes a surrogate mother for this child, who will pay for the approximately fifty thousand dollars worth of financial obligations she likely will incur during the pregnancy? She will need child care for her children; food, clothing, and shelter for at least a year; hospital expenses; after-birth care; and perhaps counseling. The amount involved may be increased significantly if Tom and Betty are responsible for payment of lost wages during the period of pregnancy and recovery, which is the norm in surrogacy contracts. Whoever drafts the arrangement, either the clinic or a surrogacy agency, will be responsible for brokering the assignment of responsibility for such costs.

GENETIC SURROGACY

The type of surrogacy involved here would be a *genetic surrogacy*, in which the surrogate (Laura) is genetically related to the child she is carrying. Laura would contribute both the egg and the womb. If all went as intended, she would become pregnant by intrauterine insemination with Tom's sperm. If Betty had been able to produce retrievable eggs, then Laura would be serving as a *gestational surrogate*. In that case, she would provide only the gestational environment for the child. An IVF procedure would bring together Betty's eggs and Tom's sperm, and resulting embryos would be inserted in Laura's uterus for her to carry to term. However, Betty appears unable to produce retrievable eggs, so she and Tom are considering a genetic surrogacy.

The degree to which the clinic would be involved in the surrogacy arrangement is not clear. Some infertility clinics offer surrogacy services, but many do not. Most refer their patients to surrogacy agencies, which locate and screen the surrogate, draft and monitor the agreement, and distribute all payments to the surrogate from an escrow account. If the clinic only refers Tom and Betty to a surrogacy center, then the ethical issues, and in some states legal issues, shift to the surrogacy agency and away from the clinic. If the clinic also offers surrogacy services, which is possible in this case, then the clinic would face these issues directly.[20]

Since a genetic surrogacy is in view here, the issues are somewhat clearer than if this were a gestational surrogacy. In the latter type, there is significant debate over which biological contributor is the mother of the child—the woman who contributes the egg, or the woman who gives birth to the child.[21] Should Tom and Betty hire Laura to be their genetic surrogate, instead of having her sell her eggs, Laura would be the mother of the child both under the law and under most conceptions of motherhood. She is both the genetic and gestational contributor, and Betty's only contribution (other than paying her sister to perform the biological functions for her) is yet to come—that of the rearing mother. Laura would be the undisputed biological mother of the child, and Tom the child's father. As long as Laura is willing to follow through on her original agreement with Tom and Betty to give them the child for them to raise as their own, things may go smoothly, assuming the communication issues are resolved. But if Laura becomes attached to the child she is carrying and wants to keep the child, the scenario becomes very complicated and may involve a court to effect a final resolution.

The clinic would be bound by the law in whichever state it is operating. Most state laws on genetic surrogacy prohibit removing a child from the child's mother simply because a contract calls for that. They rightly recognize a woman's fundamental right to associate with her child, and this would indeed be Laura's child, not Betty's. It also would be Tom's. Should a dispute arise about custody of the child, Tom and Laura would be analogous to a married couple who have had a child together, then divorce and have to decide custody.

Whoever handles the surrogacy arrangement, either the clinic or a separate surrogacy center, is obligated to inform all the parties of these risks, as well as of the applicable laws governing surrogacy in the center's state. Since the surrogate in the present case also is a family member, there is the potential for confusion about Laura's role in the child's life, especially if there is a disagreement about disclosing the child's origins. As the child grows up in Betty and Tom's home, Laura may feel a special affinity with this child and a strong desire to act on those feelings. This would not be uncommon in the case of a genetic surrogacy like this one.

---

20. For a full discussion of the ethics and legality of surrogacy, see Scott B. Rae, *The Ethics of Commercial Surrogate Motherhood: Brave New Families?* (Westport, Conn.: Praeger, 1994). For a shorter treatment of the commercial aspect of surrogacy, see "Surrogate Motherhood," in *The Reproduction Revolution: A Christian Appraisal of Sexuality, Reproductive Technologies and the Family*, ed. John F. Kilner et al. (Grand Rapids, Mich.: Eerdmans, 2000), 113–23.

21. To explore this difficult subject further, see Rae, *Ethics of Commercial Surrogate Motherhood*, chap. 4. Legally, motherhood may be clearer in gestational surrogacy, since in many states, gestational surrogates have no rights to the child they carry.

SURROGACY AS BABY SELLING

The principal reservation concerning genetic surrogacy when done for a fee beyond reasonable expenses (prenatal care, labor and delivery care, etc.) is that it constitutes the purchase and sale of children. In this case, Laura would be paid a substantial fee, normally anywhere from ten to fifty thousand dollars, in exchange for her waiving parental rights to her child. It is, after all, her child, and if she wants to give the child up to Tom and Betty, she does so knowing that the child is hers to give up. She is signing a waiver of parental rights in exchange for a sizable fee. In other words, she is selling her child to Tom and Betty. To be sure, the child is not only hers but partially Tom's too. So to be more precise, she is selling her "interest" in her child, analogous to selling her share in a business partnership or piece of property.

If these three people were involved in adoption proceedings (with Laura as the birth mother and Tom and Betty as the adoptive couple paying her for her child), they all would be in violation of the law. Adoption law in every state prohibits birth mothers from selling their children to adoptive couples, though the couple may pay the expenses involved. Black market adoptions do exist, and the reason they are called "black market" is that the proprietors illegally buy children from birth mothers and sell them to adoptive couples.

OPERATING ACCORDING TO THE COUPLE'S VALUES

Should Tom and Betty proceed with IVF using eggs from Laura or another donor, they may have some of their own hesitations about IVF. For example, Betty already has indicated an aversion to abortion. When the clinic informs her about the risk of multiple pregnancies and the option of "selectively terminating" one or more of the fetuses if too many embryos successfully implant, she likely will insist that under no circumstances is abortion an option. Avoiding the risk of too many fetuses is not difficult. She can simply require the clinic to limit the number of embryos implanted into her uterus to the number she can safely carry, or even to the number of children she and Tom want to raise (though there are no guarantees that all pregnancies will go to term). From the clinic's profit and performance standpoint, though, more embryos implanted increases the likelihood of a live birth. To help arbitrate this difficult ethical conflict between the clinic's interests and the couple's ethical sensibilities, SART has instituted voluntary guidelines limiting the number of embryos implanted to no more than three.[22] To avoid

---

22. It is not clear that all clinics follow this voluntary guideline, as the well-publicized case of "Octomom" illustrates. Nadya Suleiman had six embryos implanted in her final IVF procedure (two of which split, giving her eight pregnancies total). Her physician was widely considered irresponsible, especially given Suleiman's reluctance to consider selective termination. For one of the numerous accounts of the Octomom case, see "Doctor Octo-Mom's Track Record Not So Great," NBC News, February 10, 2009, *http://www.nbcnewyork.com/news/archive/Meet-Doctor-Octo-mom.html* (accesssed April 29, 2010).

the temptation to abort for genetic abnormalities, Tom and Betty propose screening the embryos through PGD, implanting the healthy ones and discarding the rest, though Betty may have a problem with discarding any embryos.

Tom and Betty also have a concern about embryos left over at the end of the IVF process, and they are not of one mind about the disposition of these embryos. Betty's suggestion to donate them to other infertile couples is analogous to putting them up for adoption, whereas selling them for stem cell research would result in destroying the embryos. The clinic cannot ethically dispose of any extra embryos until Tom and Betty reach a resolution. Meanwhile, the leftover embryos will remain in frozen storage.[23] Since egg sales involve giving up any maternal rights to a child, Laura technically would have no say in what happens to the embryos. The clinic's client is Betty and Tom, not Laura.

If Tom and Betty want to limit the number of embryos created to minimize the likelihood of having any left over, they can ask the clinic to take steps to help them achieve that goal. The result may be higher cost or less success, but if they are insistent about not discarding embryos, the clinic may consider it good business to accommodate their desires. Given her obsession with becoming pregnant, Betty may decide that she wants to optimize her chances of a successful pregnancy, even if that comes with discarding embryos or donating them to research. In any case, the clinic's obligations here are quite limited. The clinic must disclose the possibilities of both leftover embryos and selective termination, but it is not obligated to deviate from the standard of practice to accommodate the couple's values. So Tom and Betty would be wise to remember that the clinic is a business and that they are customers who can take their business elsewhere if the clinic disregards their values.

TOM'S AMBIVALENCE TOWARD BECOMING A FATHER

The clinic has probably worked with ambivalent fathers in the past. This ambivalence may relate to becoming a parent or to the costs involved in IVF and other procedures. On the surface, the clinic could say that as long as Tom consents to the procedures, the clinic has fulfilled its legal and moral obligations. However, the clinic arguably has an ethical obligation to consider how committed both parents are to any IVF, surrogate-parenting, or egg-donation procedures under consideration. If Tom is ambivalent about becoming a father, there is good reason to doubt that Tom and Betty are good candi-

---

23. Many couples are terribly ambivalent about how to deal with the remaining embryos because their intuitions tell them that their embryos are qualitatively different from clumps of cells. Thus their reluctance to discard or donate them to research is understandable. But storing them indefinitely amounts to putting off a decision, which is no resolution either.

dates for the clinic. Ambivalent fathers have sent many children into the rest of their lives with unresolved and sometimes irresolvable issues.

The clinic has a responsibility beyond making a profit and improving its pregnancy rate, and the clinic should do its best to confront discernible problems with the prospective parents before facilitating a pregnancy. For example, a counselor could be assigned to find out the level of Tom's ambivalence, as discussed in the next chapter. Should the clinic become aware of significant ambivalence, ensuring genuine consent obligates the staff to facilitate further exploration of Tom's feelings.

CONCLUSION

Tom and Betty have faced a long, agonizing, expensive, and unsuccessful experience with infertility and its treatment. The amount of pain involved is difficult for anyone who has not been through it to comprehend. Betty's apparent obsession with having a child is common for women experiencing infertility, and the added stress in her marriage relationship is not unusual under the circumstances. This chapter has addressed the ethical concerns related to the infertility clinic where Tom and Betty have spent considerable energy, effort, and money on six attempts at egg retrieval.

Fertility clinics have very few standards to follow. However, the Hippocratic oath's mandate to "above all else, do no harm" is a good measuring rod for fertility clinics that desire to be more than merely legal and to gain a reputation for using high ethical standards in decision-making. Ethical behavior often goes beyond the legal requirements. As fertility clinics decide to operate in harmony with the Hippocratic oath, they will risk being less profitable, at least in the short term. It costs money and time to deal with Betty's frustration over six consecutive unsuccessful IVF attempts, Tom's ambivalence about becoming a father, Laura's uncertainty about being an unpaid egg donor or surrogate mother, and the child's need to be born into a sufficiently stable family environment. In the long run, however, as other businesses have learned,[24] the fertility clinic will likely discover that it pays to be known as trustworthy.

---

24. For a general discussion of this important point that trustworthiness contributes to the success of a business, see John A. Byrne, "After Enron: The Ideal Corporation," *Business Week* (August 19/26, 2002), 68. Byrne puts it like this: "Following the abuses of the '90s, executives are learning that trust, integrity and fairness do matter, and are crucial to the bottom line." See also Francis Fukuyama, *Trust: The Social Virtues and the Creation of Prosperity* (New York: Free Press, 1996).

CHAPTER 3

WISDOM FROM COUNSELING

Stephen P. Greggo and Miriam Stark Parent

A man and a woman who anticipate that their oneness will result in a new human life are connected by an emerging bond to a person who does not yet exist. They hold precious in their mind's eye a vision of a child, *their* child. The exuberance of love as two become one spills over to an idealized child who is central to their dream of family and hope for the future. This is a normal experience for creatures created male and female in God's image — *imago Dei* — charged with a divine mandate to "be fruitful and increase in number" (Gen. 1:28). An authentic love for a child may take on a life of its own well before the reality of pregnancy and birth.[1]

In the case before us, Betty and Tom are in the midst of a severe life crisis: the struggle with the painful injustice of infertility.[2] Neither may recognize the depth or intensity of the drama embedded in their crucial decisions.[3] This developmental crossroads will have profound implications for their oneness as a couple as well as their personal identities as gendered human beings and mature adults striving to achieve the status of parenthood. Perhaps most critical, the integrity of their journey with the Alpha

---

1. Ps. 139:13–16 states that the creator God lovingly knits together the intricacies of body and soul when people are yet "secrets" within their mothers' wombs. It is a powerful truth to recognize that human beings are personally cherished, nurtured, and sustained by the Lord himself, well before birth. Human parents can also love a child long before birth.

2. This chapter will refer to those such as Tom and Betty using variations of the phrase "couples who are struggling with infertility." This practice follows the sage advice of researchers who found that this language portrays these couples in an active position with a sense of agency. Conventional terms such as *childless* and *childfree* are fraught with unintended messages. The streamlined label of *infertile* conveys notions of defectiveness and failure. See Ronny Diamond, David Kezur, Mimi Meyers, Constance N. Scharf, and Margot Winshel, *Couple Therapy for Infertility* (New York: Guilford, 1999), 1–4.

3. Infertility may be as perturbing to one's development as any overt loss. Unfortunately, persons experiencing the secret suffering of infertility are not granted the attention or support that typically fosters recovery from a serious trauma. See Jane Goodman, Nancy Schlossberg, and Mary Anderson, *Counseling Adults in Transition: Linking Practice with Theory*, 3rd ed. (New York: Springer, 2006).

and Omega, the source and goal of all creation, is about to be revitalized in ways they could never imagine (James 1:2–12). Regrettably, locating a mental-health clinician with a reasonable level of expertise regarding the biological as well as the psychosocial intricacies associated with infertility—*and* one who is committed to a Christian world-view—is quite difficult in most locations. So an important opportunity to link Christian resources with bioethical challenges is commonly missed.

The term *bioethics* may bring to mind extreme medical dilemmas, intriguing legal controversies, and science-fiction stories. Bioethics is actually nothing more grandiose than the application of ethical insights to problems in biomedicine, many of which are everyday occurrences.[4] The association of bioethics with the exceptional perpetuates a false sense that most medical decisions are not filled with potential ethical controversies. In fact, they are.

Christian bioethics searches for theologically and biblically informed wisdom to guide what one should and should not pursue in matters of life and health.[5] Counseling is focused conversation within a uniquely defined relationship to resolve concerns, realize growth, and promote health. Counseling that is uniquely Christian involves a quest to apply wisdom so that the Lord is honored in both the process and results. Christian counseling with an eye toward the exploration of bioethical decisions appears reasonable and advisable. Unfortunately, the way to overcome the complex obstacles to bringing the disciplines of bioethics and counseling together may prove to be as elusive as the solutions to the medical dilemmas themselves! Such can particularly be the case in the controversial arena of reproductive ethics. The case of Betty and Tom illustrates the barriers, displays the risks, and suggests the potential of Christian counseling as a resource to enable believers to achieve greater bioethical clarity for living well.

Christian bioethicist Gilbert Meilaender captures well the ethical pitfalls that Christians encounter when assessing reproductive technology: "The seemingly innocent desire to have 'a child of one's own,' combined with the high-tech possibilities of modern medicine and the ever-present pursuit of commercial gain, has fashioned a world in which we regularly create moral conundrums that are beyond our ability not only to solve but even to name."[6] The following list of twelve ethical dilemmas at least names some of the moral conundrums represented in the case of Betty and Tom which cry out for counseling help. The list is representative and suggestive, not comprehensive.

1. To date, extensive biological treatment for infertility has proven unsuccessful. Betty and Tom are about to pursue medical options that involve third parties

4. See Nancy S. Kader and Dorothy A. Greenfield, "Ethical Aspects of Infertility Counseling," in *Infertility Counseling: A Comprehensive Handbook for Clinicians*, 2nd ed., ed. Sharon N. Covington and Linda Hammer Burns (New York: Cambridge Univ. Press, 2006), 508–20.

5. John F. Kilner and C. Ben Mitchell, *Does God Need Our Help? Cloning, Assisted Suicide, and Other Challenges in Bioethics* (Wheaton, Ill.: Tyndale, 2003), vii.

6. Gilbert Meilaender, "A Child of One's Own: At What Price?" in *The Reproduction Revolution: A Christian Appraisal of Sexuality, Reproductive Technologies, and the Family*, ed. John F. Kilner et al. (Grand Rapids, Mich.: Eerdmans, 2000), 36–37.

in the reproductive process itself. Has the season arrived for Betty and Tom to accept the losses associated with infertility? How far can a Christian go in making use of available technology? A theologically informed response to these questions involves consideration of the marriage covenant. How will their decision-making process nurture that covenant to promote oneness, or undercut it and rend it asunder?

2. Betty and Tom once elected to terminate a pregnancy. Might the present press to have a biologically related child be connected to a remote underlying effort to undo or redeem the past? Biblical explorations of divine and interpersonal forgiveness would indeed stir painful memories, resentments, and regrets. The potential for acceptance and freedom in the true redemption found in the gospel is beyond description.

3. There are subtle hints in the narrative that Betty and Tom have experienced the bounty of material blessings associated with financial security. Furthermore, Tom and Laura wish to screen for genetic defects. Has the quest for a child taken on dimensions of obtaining the most desirable product as opposed to a humble request for the privilege of parenting a beloved child?

4. One phrase magnetically draws attention: "adoption is not an option for them." In light of the biblical endorsement of adoption, the personal underlying beliefs of Betty and Tom warrant unpacking and further mutual discussion.[7]

5. Marital strain is evident and becoming increasingly severe. How might persistence in this complex course of action to obtain a child of their own place the integrity and quality of their marital bond in jeopardy?

6. The current venture in infertility treatment involves egg procurement from a known versus an anonymous donor. Beyond the personal and medical risks associated with the procedure itself, there are ethical concerns regarding the relational and psychological well-being of Laura, Betty, and Tom.[8] There is indeed a complex relationship between these individuals. With the deep-seated, values-laden differences already evident, is this an alliance in which the parties can be appropriately yoked on all essential levels, including the spiritual?

7. Laura remains in the midst of recovery from a traumatic divorce. What are the psychological risks of egg donation or surrogacy for her, both now and later? Has the plan taken into account the extensive needs of one who may well be

---

7. Discussion of adoption should not be automatic. Adoption itself raises an entire range of serious considerations. It is the rigidity of this couple's position on adoption that warrants exploration.

8. A survey of ethical and psychological questions to explore in counseling related to egg donation is available from the European Society for Human Reproduction and Embryology (ESHRE); see Patricia Baetens, "Oocyte Donation," *ESHRE Monographs* 1 (2002): 35–36.

considered from a biblical standpoint to warrant special care, as someone who is in poverty, widowed, or socially outcast?

8. Tom expresses willingness to participate in infertility treatment. His language regarding commitment to having and raising a child is ambivalent. Is his yes really a yes?

9. There is open disagreement over issues of secrecy regarding the genetic origin of the child. Outside the obvious latent explosive elements within this shaky truce, tenuous conspiracies do not contribute to an optimal interpersonal climate in which to raise a child. Young adults who discover deceit regarding biological heritage can experience psychological trauma.

10. The potential application of preimplantation genetic diagnosis raises the need for all involved to clarify their definition of a human being.[9] Many Christians hold that embryos are fully human and created in the image of God. People with that view tend to resist the idea that a health concern or handicapping condition justifies supporting some embryos and discarding others.

11. The option of extra unneeded embryos for stem cell research raises the question of whether such disposition of offspring is appropriate, who has authority to make such decisions, and how important agreement is within the family on this matter. Those who recognize embryos as human beings made in the image of God and under God's care will be reluctant to reduce them to transferable property.

12. Laura has raised the possibility of surrogacy for a fee. This broaches weighty matters for Christians to consider at length regarding the sanctity of marriage, the value of human life, and the idea of a human being as a commodity.

To discover what Christian counseling can contribute to understanding and handling these issues, it will be necessary to consider some broader questions about the processes and contributions of Christian counseling. Several such questions will help guide the explorations in the rest of this chapter:

- In the contemporary medical climate, what types of services and resources from an informed mental-health professional (MHP) would a couple like Betty and Tom be likely to experience?
- What benefits might be added to the infertility counseling that Betty and Tom need if faith-based approaches from a Christian counselor or pastor were provided?
- Drawing on the empirical evidence that favors merging spiritually integrated therapy into mental-health services, how might distinctively Christian counseling strategically be implemented with couples struggling with infertility?

---

9. Robert W. Evans, "The Moral Status of Embryos," in *The Reproduction Revolution*, ed. Kilner et al., 63–76.

- Within the contemporary-practice frameworks for pastoral and professional counseling, what are latent clashes between bioethics, professional ethics, and kingdom ethics that require careful explanation and attention?

REASSESSING THE MEDICALIZATION OF INFERTILITY

Throughout history and across cultures there is a close association between fertility and divine blessing. Linda Burns and Sharon Covington provide a helpful overview of the psychological dynamics in their comprehensive text on infertility counseling.[10] Their historical review selects examples ranging from ancient Greece to more recent practices observed in Africa and India. Global illustrations continue into the twentieth century. Until recently, the conventional and worldwide tendency of couples seeking a remedy for infertility has been to turn to religious faith as the decisive source for solutions. The birth of a vigorous child appears indelibly linked to our deepest human notions of health, spiritual well-being, and the delight of divine favor. People commonly speak of childbirth as the *miracle* of birth. Conversely, involuntary childlessness evokes personal anguish that undermines identity, stirs sensations of social shame, and instigates acute spiritual fears of divine abandonment.

The three notable domains for infertility intervention are medical, social, and spiritual. Medical remedies utilize the best available and affordable technology. Social options might include the suffering couple reaching out to other relationships and avenues to meet their parenting needs (e.g., foster parenting). Social solutions could also attempt to redefine or end the partnership (e.g., through divorce or extramarital affairs), involve third parties (e.g., a surrogate mother), or tap into community options for adoption. Over the years, the spiritual domain has retired ever farther into the background as cutting-edge medical options have dominated the foreground. Why petition an unseen deity when assisted reproductive technology (ART) offers proven results?

Those with advanced education often view the prominence throughout history of religiously sanctioned fertility symbols, rites, and customs as a mere curiosity. Such things are primitive religious relics, antiquated mythical beliefs, or erotic art. Advanced, precise scientific knowledge has removed the mystery associated with the physiology of reproduction. There is no incentive to resort to spiritual procedures such as purification, worship, or prescribed offerings when biologically based options are readily available, backed by scientific explanations, and validated with empirical evidence. This phenomenon is the so-called medicalization of infertility. Pragmatically speaking within the

---

10. Linda Hammer Burns and Sharon N. Covington, "Psychology of Infertility," in *Infertility Counseling*, ed. Covington and Burns, 1–19.

Western cultural context, the supremacy of the medical infertility treatment is essentially absolute. Burns and Covington review the medicalization trend, but they include this caveat: faith as a means of solution or comfort remains powerfully influential. Why do people persistently associate fertility with spirituality?

Consider the following. Because medical facts, knowledge, and technology related to reproduction have advanced with stunning results, viewing infertility from an objective and dispassionate perspective may appear plausible. Individuals in the midst of infertility, however, wrestle with perhaps the most intense existential, personal, and spiritual crisis of their lives. Accordingly, as ART applications have increased, so has the inclusion of medically oriented infertility counseling, which addresses psychological and relational concerns. At the same time, though, any extensive and satisfying resolution must address at a core level one's religious and worldview convictions. Consider the case of Betty and Tom. It is no surprise that Betty and Tom discover a growing interest in spiritual matters as the awareness of their infertility emerges. Those who would promote the gospel to people open to Christian faith would do well to include in their vision couples like Betty and Tom. Their souls simultaneously yearn for a child of their own in this material world and for peace with a transcendent other. Internally, they assume a connection between the two.

A subspecialty of counseling has arisen to assist couples facing infertility. Concentrated clinical research has produced material useful for those who would dare to dialogue meaningfully with Betty and Tom. Despite this development, the amount of misunderstanding at the popular level is extensive. People commonly assume that *only* undue tension is inhibiting conception. Messages abound implying that if the uptight partners would basically relax, pregnancy would naturally occur. Stress may indeed contribute to difficulty achieving a pregnancy. But this is only one factor within a complex range of interactive variables. How unfortunate is the amount of preventable torment unintentionally inflicted through ignorance. Christian helpers not only need to increase their awareness of the current literature but also need to educate others within their ministry sphere.

The Freudian psychoanalytic tradition has had an enduring impact on prevailing depictions of infertility.[11] In this tradition, the cause of infertility is connected with an individual's unresolved inner conflicts. For men this may involve harboring inner doubts regarding masculinity, parenthood, or a controlling maternal figure. More often, women bear the blame. Neurotic conflicts regarding motherhood, sexual feelings, or persistent emotional immaturity purportedly prevent pregnancy. When medical reasons are unavailable, the popularity of such models is understandable. Psychological hypotheses modernize the shame-based assumptions fostered by outdated, religiously influenced social networks in which infertility is a sign of divine disfavor. While an exclusively psychological theory is no longer tenable or empirically supported, vestiges of these stigmatizing viewpoints persist

---

11. Ibid.

in the common statements to infertile couples mentioned above. Intended for good, these words perpetuate a message of personal accusation.

A different sort of model — one defining the progression through infertility — is more helpful in the way that it captures common emotional and relational struggles.[12] Broadly speaking, there are five phases.[13]

1. The *dawning* phase is when the couple begins to sense a gnawing anxiety that something is wrong. They entertain seriously the thought that they are having trouble conceiving. As the evidence mounts and cycles pass, they seek medical advice. It becomes necessary to speak out loud the inner fear that could become a festering sore.

2. *Mobilization* is when they attempt to take control and apply a first round of remedies. Diagnostic testing begins and disbelief diminishes. Blame emerges despite rational objections.

3. *Immersion* is an intensive and disruptive period. There are frequent medical appointments, interventions commence, and achieving conception becomes life's highest priority. There is no longer a storehouse of patience to wait for nature to take its course. Infertility treatment becomes not only more intrusive but costly, ethically complex, and psychologically demanding. Couples report a severe sense of life disruption with an accompanying lack of control over their privacy, bodies, and future. They unmercifully question their identities, roles, and direction in life.

4. *Resolution* is the phase in which the couple determines either voluntarily or by external constraint to discontinue medical treatment. This phase is all about mourning the loss of the dream for a genetically related child and coming to terms with the alternatives. It is during this phase that the most demanding and difficult courses of action may be attempted (i.e., third-party reproduction, adoption, or childlessness).

5. The *legacy* phase is when a sense of hope returns, despite the sadness that lingers. The couple recognizes that they have survived a life-quake. In spite of everything, there is a future for them, although it will not unfold according to their previous plan. For those couples who are able to cope, suffering may stimulate a compelling bond of companionship.

Addressing these stages in infertility counseling is similar to using stage theories in crisis and bereavement counseling. Discussing common encounters that others have survived affords those afflicted with a unique opportunity to soothe the internal pain of isolation through the profound gift of normalization. Tom and Betty's frantic attempts to find a solu-

---

12. Diamond et al., *Couple Therapy.*

13. This description is only an overview without detail regarding gender variations and emotional cycles within each phase. Education about substages, gender variations, and cycles within phases can enable couples to better understand the physical and emotional experience.

tion leave them swirling and on the verge of discord, typical of the resolution phase. Were a counselor to help them understand their experience in terms of these five phases, it might actually become easier for them to find meaning within their crisis, and a way forward.

Eventually any forward movement will prompt individuals to contemplate the comprehensive narratives that guide their lives. Following a review of the empirical psychotherapy literature, Kenneth Pargament argues that professional counseling is better when it skillfully integrates the role of spirituality.[14] Survey data documents that the majority of clients within today's postmodern, pluralistic, and multicultural climate explicitly desire such integration. If ever there were clients in need of spiritually integrated therapy, it is the individuals and couples such as Betty and Tom in a struggle with infertility. A person's faith identity may cause tension with medical specialists when theological convictions limit options for intervention on moral grounds. On the other hand, that faith may provide a compass through the ethically explosive and emotionally charged wilderness of medical options.

Alice Domar, a psychologist and researcher who specializes in health psychology and women's issues, acknowledges that women who experience infertility suffer considerable distress, as evidenced by the presence of significant psychological symptoms.[15] The key stressor regarding spirituality identified by Domar has potential applications to those with ministry interests. "There are many reasons why infertile women experience such high levels of distress—the process impacts their relationship with their partner, their sex life, their relationships with family and friends, their job, their financial security, and their relationship with God. ... The majority of individuals in this country pray and believe in a higher power. For many, this is the first time that God has not answered their prayers, leading many to question either their own level of goodness or the existence of God."[16]

From a medical viewpoint, dealing with the psychosocial concerns of those facing infertility is required. Management of psychosocial stressors may facilitate treatment in the biological domain. Accordingly, even treatment with a medical orientation should include the assessment of a patient's religious needs.[17] Several additional considerations follow, for those committed to counseling as Christian ministry.

The first consideration relates to the previously noted trend toward an exclusively medical approach to infertility treatment and the serious reevaluation that requires.[18]

---

14. See Kenneth I. Pargament, *Spiritually Integrated Psychotherapy: Addressing and Understanding the Sacred* (New York: Guilford, 2007). This is not a theological work. Spiritual terms are given psychological definitions that may not conform to a traditional Christian understanding.

15. Alice D. Domar, "The Mind/Body Connection," in *The Boston IVF Handbook of Infertility*, ed. Steven R. Bayer, Michael M. Alper, and Alan S. Penzias, 2nd ed. (Abingdon, England: Informa Healthcare, 2007), 178.

16. Ibid.

17. It is interesting to note that the qualifications for

mental-health professionals who offer infertility counseling do not include any particular expertise in bringing a client's faith perspective into the helping process. See Burns and Covington, "Psychology of Infertility," in *Infertility Counseling*, ed. Covington and Burns, 559–60.

18. To consider the shift in psychiatry to incorporate views of spirituality into practice, see Allan M. Josephson and John R. Peteet, eds., *Handbook of Spirituality and Worldview in Clinical Practice* (Arlington, Vir.: American Psychiatric Publishing, 2004).

For the patient's welfare, it would be prudent to incorporate a definitive spiritual-pastoral component into the treatment process. This would be particularly crucial for those who firmly believe in their salvation through the cross and who identify themselves on a journey into eternity with Jesus Christ. Bringing a new life into the world is intricately tied to one's spiritual walk.

Second, assisting individuals through the experience of infertility requires helping them to find new meaning as they come to grips with their losses. A Christian counseling approach seamlessly merges worthy biblical themes and principles into the helping process. For instance, comfort is available from the God of all comfort and mercy.[19] Counselors can connect individuals who are struggling with infertility with others in the Christian community who have experienced the strength the Lord conveys to believers who are distressed and suffer (2 Cor. 1:3–11).

Third, explicitly biblical and Christian traditions have an important place among the mind-body techniques that have empirical support. Prayer, worship, meditation, and the ministry of the Word may be useful as long as they affirm that the struggle of those grappling with infertility is indeed real and may represent a profound crisis of faith. There is no room here for counterfeit or superficial Christianity that denies suffering. No one should subject people who are experiencing the fallenness of the world to unnecessary shame for presumed personal sins of commission or omission, as befell ancient Job (see, e.g., Job 8:1–6; 11:1–20; 42:1–6).

Betty has turned her suffering inward. It is difficult for her to be around others with children. Christ-oriented care would not condemn her for these tendencies but would help her locate and be transparent with those who could fellowship with her in this season of grief. A supportive network of select mature Christian women might not only enable her to manage her symptoms but also contribute to a growth in faith. What freedom might Betty find in the recognition of the unfathomable depth of divine forgiveness and in the richness of grace provided for her by the cross?

Tom is ripe for coaching on what actually is required to be a loving husband. His views on adoption and biological fatherhood may need gentle but realistic challenge. After all, Scripture frequently mentions adoption. Gentile believers are the adopted children of God (e.g., Eph. 1:5; Rom. 8:15).

Most important, the yearning for Christian community that this couple has already experienced should be affirmed and nurtured.[20] There is much that a qualified and Spirit-anointed Christian counselor or pastoral caregiver could offer Tom and Betty. Their struggle must first be known, then embraced. This requires that there be Chris-

---

19. E.g., 2 Cor. 1:3; Ps. 94:19.

20. The case description never states that Tom and Betty have made the firm commitment of faith in Jesus Christ as their Savior and Lord that Scripture calls for (e.g., John 3:16; 1 John 5:10, 12; Rom. 5:1, 8; 2 Cor. 5:19–21). A crisis such as the infertility struggle they now encounter is often a critical crossroads in people's spiritual journeys. Christian counseling services are ideally suited for those who have decided to invest a lifetime in discipleship as a Christ-follower.

tian counselors who are prepared to come alongside those enduring what may become the most monumental challenge of their adult lives.

COUNSELING SERVICES ADDRESSING INFERTILITY

Betty and Tom have already traveled far down the highway of medical-treatment options. Infertility is commonly defined as a medical condition that exists when a year of sexual intercourse does not result in an expected or desired pregnancy.[21] It does not take a mental-health professional to recognize that within their story, both separately and as a couple, there are indisputable signs of psychological and marital strain. For Betty, becoming pregnant and having a child has become a consuming priority. She is experiencing social withdrawal, isolation, pervasive unhappiness, and obsessive rumination. Tom silently harbors ambivalence over the decision to have a child, along with substantial regret over decreasing marital satisfaction.

"Being together is far more stressful and less enjoyable." No prophetic anointing is required to discern with confidence that moderate to severe relational tension now exists. More intensive discord looms on the horizon. Will their covenant vows survive this season of uncertainty regarding sickness and health? After medical intervention, are Betty and Tom more likely to find their marriage better or worse? What potential psychological and relational concerns are tied to Laura's assuming the role of egg donor or surrogate? Will family bonds be strengthened or severely strained?

The field of ART has advanced dramatically in recent decades. Medical options for stimulating ovulation, intrauterine insemination (IUI), and in vitro fertilization (IVF) have increased. The valuable contributions of MHPs to successful treatment have been legitimized and clarified. Although terminology varies, four roles are now common. First, MHPs can perform *mental-health assessments* via brief screening consultations or through comprehensive psychosocial evaluations. These may focus on individual participants or on the couple as a unit. The purpose is to formulate specific recommendations regarding their vulnerabilities as well as their level of readiness to venture farther into the ambiguities of infertility treatment. (Further considerations are involved if options for third-party reproduction are under consideration, as in the present case.)

Second, MHPs may offer *supportive counseling* to soothe emotional turmoil and maintain the quality of interpersonal relationships. Obstacles and disappointments arise during treatment, leading to serious personal and relational distress. For example, the case of Tom and Betty highlights a particular concern that supportive counseling would typically address—namely, the shift from sex for relational intimacy to sex planned for

---

21. William R. Keye Jr., "Medical Aspects of Infertility for the Counselor," in *Infertility Counseling*, ed. Covington and Burns, 20–36.

conception. The phrase "sex on demand" signifies the intrusion of early-phase infertility treatments such as ovulation tracking, scheduling, timing, positions, and postcoital tests. Once private and spontaneous, intimate activities become topics for medically relevant discussion and are painfully scrutinized. Supportive counseling is useful to maintain perspective and marital vitality.

A third type of counseling, *therapeutic counseling*, addresses expectations regarding parenting, gender, and personal identity; grief and loss related to failed pregnancies or miscarriages; and adjustment to diagnosed medical conditions. Betty and Tom likely would find such counseling helpful in light of the past abortion and their decision to delay childbearing.

Finally, *implication counseling* aimed at considering the progressively challenging decisions about treatment could explore with the participants the implications of pursuing various ART applications. Betty and Tom might benefit from conversations that address the emotionally and morally loaded matters before them. A significant portion of counseling activity could identify and address the repercussions of such routes as egg donation, genetic screening of eggs, embryo donation for stem cell research, surrogate motherhood, and embryo and born-child adoption.

While medical personnel are prepared to handle many aspects of these conversations, mental-health clinicians with expertise in infertility are making important contributions today both to treatment teams (consultation) and directly to couples (counseling).[22] Several patient indications trigger a referral to an MHP. The most obvious indication is when symptoms of stress become disruptive to one's daily functioning. A sample list of such disturbances includes persistent sadness, guilt, agitation and anxiety, changes in weight or sleep patterns, and/or increasing marital discord.[23]

Beyond the presence of actual mental-health issues, any documented history of a past mental-health diagnosis likely would prompt a medical team to suggest consultative or counseling services by an MHP. Reports of past marital discord, separations, affairs, or persistent social-emotional dysfunction would be enormously important to address. Furthermore, medical professionals typically recommend or require mental-health services when the medical options include third parties (e.g., sperm or egg donation, surrogacy) or genetic screening (preimplantation genetic diagnosis).

In light of all these considerations, it is remarkable that the description of Betty and Tom's experience contains no mention of involvement by an MHP. Perhaps they did not follow through on a previous referral. Given the intensity of Betty's drive to parent, she may have prematurely terminated counseling if it raised questions about the

---

22. In broad terms, mental-health *consultations* are professional services that provide information useful to other members of medical teams. Such input facilitates making sound treatment decisions. Consultation tends to serve the patient indirectly. *Counseling* refers to preventive or restorative services that clients directly receive.

23. American Society for Reproductive Medicine (ASRM), "Infertility Counseling and Support: When and Where to Find It," *Patient Fact Sheets*, revised January 2004, *ASRM, http://www.asrm.org/uploadedFiles/ASRM_Content/Resources/Patient_Resources/Fact_Sheets_and_Info_Booklets/Counseling-Fact.pdf* (accessed May 5, 2010).

ways she was proceeding. It is also possible that appropriate services were unavailable. The number of clinicians who specialize in infertility may not be sufficient to meet the expanding need.[24] Nonetheless, there are ample indicators within the case history that plainly endorse referral to an MHP.

In fact, the current literature would suggest such referral as standard procedure for reputable medical-infertility programs. One expert, Johannes Bitzer, a gynecologist and psychotherapist, reminds medical personnel that while reproductive medicine has seen stunning progress on the biological front, the psychosocial dimension remains fraught with drama. Intense emotion accompanies the creation of a new life. "Only by including the psychosocial dimension into the infertility consultation will we be able to make biological reproduction *human* reproduction."[25] Counseling can help the participants in the reproductive process to face their limitations, frailties, contradictions, wills, and wishes.

A CALL FOR CHRISTIAN INFERTILITY COUNSELING

A recent search of the leading peer-reviewed journals that inform Christian MHPs and pastoral counselors yielded only a single article to guide a Christian counselor who might be dialoging with Betty and Tom.[26] This dearth of relevant theologically and psychologically informed literature from a Christian perspective requires remediation. The lone contribution does offer a commendable foundation rooted in biblical wisdom and confirmed by personal experience.[27] Kimberly and Philip Monroe compare a Christian couple's struggle with infertility to how people of faith in the Scriptures move through sorrow associated with a disappointed desire. As the writers remind Christian helpers, believers will indeed grieve when encountering the devastating effects of sin in a fallen world. They offer these directives for counselors who seek to relate biblically to folks like Betty and Tom.

First, mourning losses in earnest is a necessary and faithful response to suffering. A broken world produces seasons of suffering. Grieving does encompass crying out to the Lord for relief and to pursue meaning. When the pain of mourning produces anguish and groaning, counselors listen with compassion to the cries of the suffering who seek the Lord's presence. Second, godly anger is as real as are the effects of the fall that ignite

---

24. Guidelines to determine qualifications and training requirements have been published for well over a decade by the Mental Health Professional Group of the American Society for Reproductive Medicine (ASRM). See "Qualification Guidelines for Mental Health Professionals in Reproductive Medicine," in *Infertility Counseling*, ed. Covington and Burns, 559–60. See also Jacky Bolvin and Heribert Kentenich, eds., "Guidelines for Counseling and Infertility," *ESHRE Monographs* 1 (2002).

25. Johannes Bitzer, "Counselling in Infertility Treat-

ment," *ESHRE Monographs* 1 (2002), 14–20. Italics in original.

26. The search included the *Journal of Psychology and Theology* (JPT), *Journal of Psychology and Christianity* (JPC), and *Journal of Biblical Counseling* (JBC). The range included the year 2000 to Spring 2009.

27. Kimberly Monroe and Philip Monroe, "The Bible and the Pain of Infertility," *Journal of Biblical Counseling* 23 (2005): 50–58.

it. Christian helpers aid those in their care to discern injustice and to respond with a form of anger that moves them closer to God. Third, waiting on the Lord is an act of faith. Godly waiting reorients human beings from demanding that God perform, to prayerfully declaring that God's character is holy, good, just, full of mercy, abounding in grace, and the source of all comfort. God's gifts are good, both to desire and receive. The human heart tends to strive stubbornly for its wishes rather than rest in the contentment that flows from acknowledging God's faithful blessings.

If Tom and Betty are earnest about their Christian faith, consideration of biblical passages that extol these themes would be of great benefit. The Christian counselor will discern that working with those who are facing infertility is similar to aiding others who have suffered different losses and breaches of trust. Infertility counseling can appropriate biblical themes and principles without forcing the particulars of this unique challenge into any formulaic remedial plan.

Christian counseling does offer a distinct perspective. Like counseling in general, it addresses mental-health symptoms by helping clients to manage stress, discover meaning, and come to terms with severe disappointment. However, it goes farther by encouraging clients to enrich their faith journeys by walking with ever-increasing transparency and confidence in the Lord. Another important distinctive is apparent when clients face a moral dilemma. Counseling that is thoroughly Christian not only seeks to clarify what the individuals may want but also strives through the Word and sound theology to discern the leading of the Holy Spirit. This point surfaces a source of tension regarding professional ethics and how to fully respect client autonomy and the right to self-determination, and how to avoid the imposition of counselors' values on vulnerable clients. How can a Christian who offers infertility counseling honor the Lord without violating or ignoring one's professional code of ethics?

PROFESSIONAL AND PASTORAL ETHICS IN CHRISTIAN BIOETHICS

Many of the activities, attributes, and outcomes of pastoral counseling and Christian mental-health professional counseling are similar. Nevertheless, there are distinct differences in the ethical responsibilities involved in each form of counseling. These differences become most apparent when values are critical to a case.

Professional groups have developed codes of ethics to provide guidelines for the practitioner and to protect the public served by that practitioner.[28] For the mental-health practitioner, attention to the appropriate ethics code is vital.[29] State law often specifies

---

28. Gerald Corey, Marianne Schneider Corey, and Patrick Callanan, *Ethics and Issues in the Helping Profession*, 8th ed. (Pacific Grove, Calif.: Brooks Cole, 2010).

29. For an example, see the American Counseling Association, *Code of Ethics and Standards of Practice* (Alexandria, Vir.: ACA, 2005).

such codes as the reasonable standard of practice that recognized practitioners must follow. In addition, state and federal laws may define a separate requirement for specific practices (e.g., mandated reporting of child abuse).

Clergy, however, have no code of ethics to guide their people-helping practices, other than godly character and principles set forth in Scripture. Personal, denominational, or local interpretation of God's expectations tends to operate in place of standards of practice and relational guidelines. Small-group leaders and church elders may have even less understanding or awareness of guidelines to determine ethical practice. While clearly defined guidelines for nonlicensed counselors in ministry settings may not exist, such guidelines may well be implied. "To the extent that pastoral counseling activities parallel those of a secular professional counselor, society will hold that pastoral counselor to the same standards regarding ethics and quality of care as established for the professional."[30]

Laws and ethics codes are more often reactive than proactive. More often they respond to situations that have occurred than anticipate situations that have not yet occurred. The field of bioethics is a prime example of this pattern, with laws and ethical guidelines emerging in response to dilemmas that scientific and technological innovation generate. Consequently, Christian caregivers committed to honoring their ethical responsibilities and all legal requirements in situations such as Tom and Betty's do not have an easy task.

If Tom and Betty receive counseling from either their pastor or a designated church leader, certain expectations and obligations may apply that would differ significantly from those involved if they were to see a Christian MHP for such counseling. Three basic areas of difference that might significantly affect the direction and outcome of the counseling are informed consent, confidentiality, and values conflicts.

INFORMED CONSENT

For the mental-health professional, informed consent has taken on new meaning and power in the twenty-first century as laws and ethical codes have become more stringent. There are two central aspects to informed consent in medical- and behavioral-health settings. The first involves *disclosure* of all important information, and the second involves *free consent*.[31] The concept of informed consent assumes respect for people and for their individual right to make autonomous decisions regarding their care. Professionals disclose the possible harms and benefits of—and alternatives to—any anticipated intervention so that the individuals involved can take ownership of the decisions and become willing participants in treatment.[32]

Clergy and pastoral counselors also have a responsibility to establish some level of informed consent before proceeding with counseling, if only because wise practice dic-

30. William B. Berman, "Ten Commandments for Avoiding Clergy Malpractice in Pastoral Counseling," *Journal of Psychology and Christianity* 16 (1997): 268.

31. Elizabeth Reynolds Welfel, *Ethics in Counseling and Psychotherapy: Standards, Research and Emerging Issues*, 2nd ed. (Pacific Grove, Calif.: Brooks Cole, 2002), 105.

32. Corey, Corey, and Callanan, *Ethics and Issues*, 161.

tates that it be done. While arrived at much less formally than in professional settings, expectations, potential outcomes, boundaries, and risks need to be articulated to avoid misunderstandings, gain commitment, display integrity in the process, and facilitate planning for intervention.

A critical question in Tom and Betty's situation is, Who is the client? Who will be the main focus of any counseling intervention? In this case, it could potentially be *Betty*, whose desire for a child is intense; *Tom*, who is ambivalent about parenthood but wants to make the marriage work; the *marital relationship*, which requires a focus on Betty and Tom together; *Laura*, who is looking at a surrogacy pregnancy; the *potential unborn child*, who has few rights but is at the center of all of this adult interaction; *others*, such as Laura's children or Betty and Tom's church community; or *some combination* of these participants. In this situation, differing agendas and the different status of those involved complicate informed consent.

In the best-case scenario, informed consent involves all three primary adults (Laura, Tom, and Betty), along with appropriate attention to the interests of the potential child. In reality, due to the distance at which Laura lives and everyone's family and work schedules, the initial counseling focus likely would be the marital relationship, involving both Tom and Betty, including their desire to have a child. However, attempting to make any decisions in this case without Laura's involvement limits both the scope of the counseling and any potential outcome. Some counselors would insist on having everyone present at all sessions in order to keep the counseling focused and balanced. Others would be willing to work with whoever could arrange to be present. Dialogue is at the heart of good informed consent, whether pastoral or professional.

The relational as well as bioethical issues inherent in the case before us render the issue of informed consent particularly complex here. What does "disclosure of all important information" mean in this situation? Finding the balance between too much information and too little information in such cases is difficult. "To give valid consent, it is necessary for clients to have adequate information about both the procedure and the possible consequences. The information must include the benefits and risks of procedures, possible adverse effects from treatment, the risk of forgoing treatment and available alternative procedures."[33]

For the counselor, it is essential that those involved understand the potential intrapersonal, interpersonal, familial, and organizational issues that may emerge from counseling in this situation. The potential in this case for negative relational dynamics to emerge is high. Open discussion of Laura's relationship with Tom compounded by Betty's resentment of Laura's capacity to have children may lead to healthier interactions, or it may fracture already fragile relationships. While the support of church members in this situation may substantially benefit Betty and Tom, there is also a substantial risk of losing some of that support if counseling does not go well.

---

33. Ibid.

Informed consent should also include a clear understanding of how information given and received in counseling will be handled. Understanding and agreement regarding confidentiality are critical if communication is to be open and productive in the emotionally charged case before us. Those issues warrant special consideration here.

CONFIDENTIALITY

Throughout Scripture, the sins of the tongue are prominent because they are so deadly. "A gossip betrays a confidence; so avoid anyone who talks too much" (Prov. 20:19). "But no one can tame the tongue. It is a restless evil, full of deadly poison" (James 3:8). Pastors and counselors receive the great gift of free access to the "hidden heart" of the person they counsel. They should use the knowledge they gain in counseling carefully and graciously. Breaching this trust is the most common ethical violation in counseling. It results from careless conversation, providing too much identifying information when discussing cases with others, confiding details to a spouse, elder, or accountability partner without consent, or a hundred other ways that the tongue runs ahead of careful thought.[34]

The expectation of trust is so great in helping relationships that the law grants both clergy and counselors in North America protection that limits the information even the government can force them to divulge. While the scope of that protection is narrowing, communications with one's counselee or parishioner are still generally "privileged." People receiving counsel have the "privilege" of determining what information clergy and counselors can release, and to whom. On the other hand, conversations with lay counselors, elders, and church staff, while expected to be confidential, do not have the legal protection of privileged communication.

Confidentiality is an important consideration in the case before us. Inappropriate disclosure of information to the church elders board or congregation as part of the church's efforts to help Tom and Betty could do irreparable damage to the lives and reputations of these young spiritual seekers. While Tom and Betty are probably assuming that any counseling done with their pastor or with a professional counselor is confidential and legally privileged, they need to know that this is not necessarily the case. In many states, communications in the presence of a third party are not subject to privilege, which means the law does not protect them. While confidentiality is still warranted ethically when two or more clients are involved, there may be no legal protection or remedy if someone violates it.[35] For example, if Laura participates in counseling with Tom and Betty, she could later legally reveal statements made in that setting, especially if the disagreement over disclosure of her biological contribution were to escalate at some future date.

---

34. Miriam Stark Parent, "Boundaries and Roles in Ministry Counseling," *American Journal of Pastoral Counseling* 8 (2005): 1–25.

35. Corey, Corey, and Callanan, *Ethics and Issues*, 214.

VALUES CONFLICTS

Various moral values play an important role in Betty and Tom's situation, whether or not they have carefully articulated them. Such values include convictions regarding the beginning of human life, the right to be a parent, and the commodification of human life, among other values. Clarifying everyone's values and role expectations, as well as negotiating conflicting values and expectations among family members, can provide powerful opportunities for growth. However, this process creates challenges for the mental-health counselor, as well as for the pastoral counselor.

Even as Betty, Laura, Tom, and the church community must struggle with defining their positions on the bioethical issues involved, so must the MHP who may be called on to facilitate that work. Both the pastoral and the professional counselor have a responsibility to think carefully about their positions on the relevant bioethical issues. Both may proceed from a specific theological perspective. Both may incorporate that theological perspective into their counsel. Differences in practice will readily emerge. The pastor, while listening and empathizing, should also explain moral beliefs that the counselee ought to consider. Part of the expectation for pastoral counseling is to provide scriptural and spiritual insight as well as perspective to assist the counselee in living within the context of that insight.[36] This role need not even have been an explicit part of the informed consent, as it is assumed to be part of the pastoral counseling role. That the authority vested in the pastoral counseling role would serve to graciously help the counselee to understand a particular biblical perspective is not an abuse of power.

The community role expectation is that the counselor will operate within the client's values system, a premise that every mental-health organization's code of ethics supports, including that of the American Counseling Association. Counseling is not values free.[37] Counselors bring their own worldviews, including moral values, to every counseling situation. Yet to use the power of the counseling relationship to impose the counselor's values on clients is unethical. When assumptions about values and authority have been articulated in initial informed-consent agreements, the counselor's moral values are in the open and can play a role in the counseling process. For Christian MHPs, this disclosure often takes place in advertising literature or in written agreements citing the authoritative use of biblical principles as the basis for counseling.

So for the pastoral counselor seeing Tom and Betty, there is inherent permission to address the spiritual and moral values involved in their bioethical and reproductive choices. For the Christian MHP, however, that permission requires explicit discussion and agreement in writing before the start of any counseling.

Even with such agreements negotiated up front, values conflicts may still become

---

36. Bill Blackburn, "Pastors Who Counsel," in *Christian Counseling Ethics: A Handbook for Therapists, Pastors and Counselors*, ed. Randolph K. Sanders (Downers Grove, Ill.: InterVarsity, 1997), 75–85.

37. Corey, Corey, and Callanan, *Ethics and Issues*, 78.

a critical piece of the counseling process. Part of the necessary work that Tom, Betty, Laura, and the church community need to do is to consider carefully the intertwined theological, relational, and moral issues involved in their surrogacy plan. The idea that all involved will reach exactly the same theological discernment on each issue may well be "a heavenly ideal" reachable only by miraculous intervention. Given the likelihood of differing positions emerging, the MHP needs to prepare for handling such conflicts.

Where the counselor's position differs from the client's, the default is to the client's values. This is not to say that the counselor's values are irrelevant or invisible. There is a thin line between challenging clients' values to enable clients to think through positions well, and imposing one's own values. Helping Tom, Betty, and Laura to clarify their views and to grapple with the implications of those views is essential. However, the object of such critical conversations is to help them reach conclusions that they can take ownership of spiritually, theologically, and morally, rather than to lead them to agreement with the counselor's convictions.

In pastoral counseling, the default is not necessarily to work with the client's values. If those values could cause the exclusion of the client from the faith community, then the counselor who represents the faith community will understandably commend the community's values. Partly because of the lack of education in the church regarding bioethical issues, Tom and Betty may well encounter some opposition regardless of the decisions they make. The more widely known are their decisions, the greater the likelihood that Tom and Betty will experience relational difficulties with others.

Clarifying values is a critical need for all involved in this case. It is demanding and discerning work. For the Christian MHP, such values-laden work offers unique challenges. It is not easy to be faithful to God's calling and to one's own convictions, while steadfastly honoring the autonomy of counselees to make their own decisions. In Scripture, Peter lays out a general principle when he reminds people always to be prepared to speak for Christ, but to do so "with gentleness and respect, keeping a clear conscience" (1 Peter 3:15 – 16).

MHPs do well to anticipate the options their clients may want to consider, in case there are options that the MHPs cannot ethically facilitate. To the degree that they can foresee such conflicts, MHPs should negotiate them initially as part of informed consent. In the present case, if an MHP were not confident that he or she could work with whatever decision Tom and Betty might make regarding surrogacy, egg donation, egg disposal, or other issues, then the MHP should refer them to another counselor before any serious work begins.

CONCLUSION

ART now offers many possible ways to remediate infertility for those who desire to parent. Due to its medical and psychosocial benefits, infertility counseling has become an established practice specialty for mental-health clinicians. Addressing religious and moral issues is routine in these conversations. Therefore, counselors with Christian convictions, theological proficiency, and explicit training in blending spiritual formation with counseling and psychotherapy are sorely needed today. So are pastoral caregivers who can enter this critical area, with understanding, to spiritually nurture and guide saints as well as seekers.

As we have seen above, employing mental-health services to include the psychosocial dimension in infertility consultation is necessary in order to ensure that biological reproduction remains truly human. There is a pressing need to reverse the current trend toward the absolute medicalization of infertility treatment. For Christ-followers, careful consideration of the theological and scriptural implications of each available infertility treatment is essential to maintain human reproduction as the wise fulfillment of the creation mandate to the glory of God.

Those who offer Christian and pastorally oriented dialogue to explore the implications of infertility treatment options must proceed with caution. Professional expectations regarding informed consent, confidentiality, and values conflicts have been established as sound guidelines for important reasons. With strategic foresight, however, counselors can put procedures into place that meet the best ethical-practice expectations of one's professional guild, respect clients, and truly honor the Lord.

For many couples like Betty and Tom, clinic-style counseling is not the sole solution. It takes a community to support folks who are in a season of confronting infertility. The social domain has much to offer in terms of solutions for infertility. Medical infertility clinics will continue to promote psychosocial support because of its documented benefits.[38] Ministries and congregations can offer educational forums and helping networks in which biblical values foster understanding and healing. There is ample room for Christian ministries to offer groups in which people can acknowledge their spiritual struggles and victories. Infertility is a prime area in which both self-help and leader-directed care groups can thrive.[39]

Yes, it is good to love a child who has not yet entered one's life. The Lord God may indeed fulfill and bless this love. "Children are a heritage from the Lord" (Ps. 127:3). Nevertheless, the road to claiming that heritage can be challenging. The twists, turns, disappointments, and joys along the way of human reproduction become the sites where the Spirit reveals the Lord's presence and makes authentic in human experience the Lord's unfailing love for all his children.

---

38. Group interventions for those struggling with infertility are well documented in the literature throughout the world. There is ample evidence that group interventions ease psychological distress, help people to perceive other treatments as more satisfying, and provide a level of support that positively impacts pregnancy rates. For a thorough review of group treatment options, see Sharon N. Covington, "Group Approaches to Infertility Counseling," in *Infertility Counseling*, ed. Covington and Burns, 156–68.

39. The development and leadership of kingdom-oriented care groups is examined from an empirical, biblical, and practical perspective in Stephen P. Greggo, *Trekking toward Wholeness: A Resource for Care Group Leaders* (Downers Grove, Ill.: InterVarsity, 2008).

CHAPTER 4

BIOETHICS AND A BETTER BIRTH

John F. Kilner

Tom and Betty want to have a baby. They already have achieved a pregnancy—more than a decade earlier—but they did not want a child then. So Betty aborted the fetus. Now she cannot even produce mature eggs, so she and Tom are considering having the child they desire "the new-fashioned way." Using her sister's eggs and/or uterus seems to offer a solution. The question is whether it is a good solution. As Paige Cunningham will remind us in chapter 6, just because something is legal does not mean it is ethical.

To unpack the challenge here, we will need to look at the situation from the perspective of those who have the most at stake. But who counts as a stakeholder here? In the first act of this drama, the primary characters are Betty, Tom, and the aborted fetus. But does a fetus have the full moral status that other human stakeholders have? In the second act, Betty, Tom, Laura, and the embryos are central. But what about the embryos' moral status?

Certainly others are involved, such as the church engaged in biblical teaching through worship services and small groups. Richard Averbeck (chap. 1) alerts us to how much the Bible contributes to an understanding of the challenges Betty and the others face. The infertility clinic has various business interests in this case, as Scott Rae and Helen Eckmann (chap. 2) remind us. Stephen Greggo and Miriam Stark Parent (chap. 3) add an explanation of the roles and responsibilities of various counselors. While these organizations and professionals—and others as well—do have some stake in the predicament at hand, central here is the life-shaping stake of Betty, Tom, Laura, and the progeny they hope to bring into the world. So these will receive particular attention in this chapter, with other stakeholders noted along the way.

However, should we really consider the fetus and embryos to be major stakeholders here? Are they truly people, as the adults are people? There is no way to assess adequately the values and actions of Betty, Tom, Laura, and others without answering that question first. So as eager as we may be to look at the situation from their perspective, we need to do that in two stages.

First, we must carefully consider whether the embryos and fetus are stakeholders to the same degree that the adults are. Are they actually people (or persons—the two terms are synonymous in this chapter)? People not only are biologically human but also have any other characteristics necessary to warrant protecting their lives as adult human lives are normally protected. If the embryos and fetus are people, then we need to consider the situation from the joint perspective of all shareholders together. Only in that context can we look further at the individual needs of Tom, Betty, and Laura and how these three can best pursue the better lives that they seek.

ARE ADULTS THE ONLY MAJOR STAKEHOLDERS IN THIS CASE?

There are good scientific, logical, and biblical reasons to think that embryos are people in the same basic sense that adults are.[1] If that is so during the embryonic period (the first eight weeks following fertilization), then the same is true for fetuses, who are even farther along in development.

CONSIDERATIONS FROM SCIENCE

First, does it make sense scientifically to speak of embryos as human beings? For that category to be appropriate, embryos would need to be both human and beings. To identify something as human, as opposed to plant, animal, or otherwise nonhuman, is scientifically a matter of genetics. The embryos that Tom and Laura would produce would genetically be human. That is scientifically verifiable.

The matter of what constitutes a being (sometimes called an organism, as opposed to merely a group of cells) is also well defined scientifically. The US National Institutes of Health's long-standing definition of the embryo is "the developing organism from the time of fertilization until the end of the eighth week of gestation." Or as various embryology textbooks put it, the life history of a new individual begins at conception.[2]

Accordingly, even the early embryo is not just human life, as blood cells are alive and human. Rather, a human embryo is a human organism—a being that is human—who, unless fatally disabled or injured, can typically develop throughout the human life span if suitable nurture and environment are provided. The same is true for a child or

---

1. These reasons are expanded from considerations originally proposed in John F. Kilner, "An Inclusive Ethics for the Twenty-First Century: Implications for Stem Cell Research," *Journal of Religious Ethics* 37 (December 2009): 683–722.

2. Ronan O'Rahilly originated the international Carnegie Stages of Human Embryological Development for the International Terminologica Embryologica Committee, which determines scientifically correct terms for embryology worldwide. According to his basic embryology textbook (*Human Embryology and Teratology* [Wilmington, Del.: Wiley-Liss, 2001], 8, 33), fertilization "is a critical landmark because, under ordinary circumstances, a new, genetically distinct human organism is formed.... The embryo now exists as a genetic unity."

an adult. While living adult bodies could also be described as "some cells," adults, like embryos, are not "*just* some cells." They are also biologically integrated (self-organizing) beings.

That human embryos are, biologically, human beings is enough to persuade many that they warrant the protections due to all other human beings. Others resist making this equation because they see something added to human beings during or after the embryonic stage that gives them a more protectable status as persons (people). Such a judgment, though, is not a scientific argument per se but more involves a broader appeal to reason and logic.

CONSIDERATIONS FROM LOGIC

Those who think that something must be added to the youngest embryos before they become persons most often have in mind a change in location, formation, individuation, or intention.

Consider first the appeal to *location*. The claim here is that even if embryos implanted in a womb are persons, those in a lab are not, because they cannot develop there into born human beings. However, people are people regardless of where someone puts them. If someone chooses not to put adults where they can obtain what they need in order to live, that does not invalidate their personhood; nor is location relevant to the personhood of embryos.

Avoiding genetic determinism is important here. Genetics and environment, for example, are both important influences on who people become over time. But who people become over time is not the same issue as what their moral status is at a particular moment. At a given moment, genetics helps define whether one is human, whereas environment helps define whether a human is thriving, not whether one is human.

The appeal to *formation* is that only embryos whose neurological "primitive streak" has formed — generally by about fourteen days after fertilization — should be considered persons. The primitive streak provides biological evidence that these organisms will eventually have human brains and related capacities such as self-awareness and reasoning. However, if what matters is the biological evidence that such capacities will eventually develop, such evidence is already present genetically from day one. If it is the capacities themselves that matter, rather than the biological basis for them, then it would be acceptable to kill born children who have not yet developed such capacities as self-awareness or adults who have lost them, an approach relatively few would espouse.

The appeal to *individuation* flows from the observation that early embryos can divide and become more than one embryo, as in the case of identical twins. Because early embryos are not in their final form yet, they allegedly do not qualify as persons. However, embryos change form in all sorts of ways throughout their development. So the question really is what difference division per se makes. Division is not an unusual phenomenon. For instance, a country may divide into two countries. The division does not mean that a country was not present before the division. Division simply suggests that multiple entities (countries or persons) were in some unofficial sense present previously—or at least can be in the future. One (or more) was genuinely present prior to division.

The appeal to *intention* has primarily to do with embryos produced through cloning for the purpose of embryonic stem cell research. The idea is that embryos produced through cloning and intended to be implanted and born may be persons, but they are not persons if they are intended only for research and thus death before they are fourteen days old. However, people are people regardless of what others intend to do to them. Such is the case with people at any stage of their development, whether embryonic or adult.

Throughout their development, human organisms are rightly called human beings, persons, or people. In developmental terms, embryos are *persons with potential* rather than *potential persons*. Sperm and eggs—in fact, all body cells in this age of cloning—have the potential to become persons. So some may understandably refer to them as potential persons. But such language is inappropriate regarding human embryos. They already are beings—organisms—that are human. Their moral significance is rooted in what they are, not merely in what they have the potential to become.

That human embryos have not yet lived out their full potential no more invalidates their personhood than young adults' personhood is invalidated by the fact that they have not yet lived out their full potential. Potential persons rightly do not receive the same protections as actual persons. But embryos are not potential persons; they *are* persons—with potential.

CONSIDERATIONS FROM SCRIPTURE

This view fits well with the writings of the Bible. Because the biblical authors lacked the genetic and biological knowledge of today, they do not speak of embryos and fetuses with the precision that people use now. However, they do make some references to humans in the womb, and to humanity as a category in contrast with nonhuman things. So it is appropriate to ask what view of the human embryo makes the most sense in light of those references. What view of the human embryo is in greatest harmony with what the Bible does say? The Bible's great themes include creation, corruption, and redemption.[3] So that is an appropriate framework in which to consider biblical teaching on a matter related to humanity.

---

3. A more overtly future-oriented (eschatological) theme such as glorification would also be true to the biblical writings, but would be more speculative in light of the paucity of passages connecting life in the womb to this theme. Nevertheless, what if the significance of human life did not depend on the attributes and capacities that some invoke to justify greater protection for born humans than for those not yet born? Rather, what if human significance was tied to the eternal future that lies ahead for all by God's grace? Arguably, the distinction between humans before and after birth would then lose any ultimate significance.

According to the creation account in Genesis 1, God created primarily according to categories rather than descriptive characteristics. For example, God created that which was not living, such as dry ground (vv. 1–10); and living plants, such as trees (vv. 11–13); and living creatures, such as birds (vv. 20–25). That God created all of these things signals that they are all important and that people should treat them with respect.

However, when God creates the category of humanity (vv. 26–27), there are some distinguishing features that mark people not only as different but as warranting special protection. Unlike the case with all previous categories of creation, where God simply states what is to be created (e.g., "God said, 'Let there be light,'" v. 3), humanity's creation begins with God referring to his own participation in the process ("God said, 'Let us make humanity,'" v. 26). This anticipates the upcoming affirmations (in vv. 26 and 27) that there is to be a special connection between God and people; they are to be "in the image of God" (*betselem elohim*). The identical expression appears later in Genesis 9:6 to explain why human beings are so special among all of creation and are not to be killed.[4]

As is the case with nonhumans, humans most fundamentally constitute a category, not a set of varying characteristics. Humans are in the image of God because God says they are, without qualification. The biblical texts that discuss the image of God never indicate that being in the image of God means having certain traits (though certain human capacities and functions do normally flow from being in the image of God).[5]

Who falls within this category of human beings, created in God's image, who are so special that they are not to be killed? All that the text of Genesis 1 indicates is that beings who are human, as opposed to nonhuman creatures, plants, and other things, are included. Human embryos fall into that category, as we have seen from the scientific evidence. So it is more plausible than not to include them among those whom others ought not kill because they are created in the image of God. Some of the characteristics of embryos, such as physical and mental abilities, differ from those of adults, at least temporarily. But that is not what the image of God attaches to, according to the biblical texts.

If there is reason in the context of creation to see human embryos as having the same moral status as adults, there is similar reason in the context of corruption. Just as the creation of humanity (*adam*, Gen. 1:26) in God's image means that all subsequent humans are in God's image, so Adam's rejection of God's way in favor of his own means that all subsequent humans are also in the corruption of sin. As Paul observes, "sin entered the world through one man, and death through sin, and in this way death came to all people" (Rom. 5:12).

---

4. For a more detailed explanation of this biblical passage and others addressing the image of God, see John F. Kilner, "Humanity in God's Image: Is the Image Really Damaged?" *Journal of the Evangelical Theological Society* 53 (September 2010): 601–17.

5. Ibid.

Sin may involve rejecting specific commands of God, as was the case with Adam and has been the case with God's people ever since God gave them the written law through Moses. But sin and thus death are also unavoidably connected with being human even apart from choosing to reject a command of God. So Paul continues in verse 14 to note that "death reigned from the time of Adam to the time of Moses, even over those who did not sin by breaking a command, as did Adam." Sin simply becomes a hallmark of all who are human, from Adam onward, and thus "in Adam all die" (1 Cor. 15:22).

If that is the case, then one's moral status and responsibility before God would not merely reflect a stage of development (e.g., whether one has developed a mental capacity to make choices). Rather, a biblical understanding of humanity would more plausibly support viewing children, fetuses, and embryos as defiled by sin, just as they are all in the image of God. While the prescientific writings of the Bible do not say much about embryos specifically, there are several instances of references to the time when people first begin forming in their mothers' wombs (now called the embryonic stage of development). The biblical view of that period accords well with the biblical understanding of humanity in general described above.

For example, in Psalm 51, David reflects on his life as a morally responsible (sinful) human person after Nathan prompts him to acknowledge his sinful adultery with Bathsheba. He confesses that such sinful acts are, sadly, merely specific manifestations of the sinful person that he has been from the very beginning. As he puts it, "Surely I was sinful at birth, sinful from the time my mother conceived me" (v. 5). The Hebrew parallelism, essentially equating these two different starting points, suggests that there is no biologically precise affirmation here. The point David is making is that he has been sinful (i.e., a morally responsible human being) as long as he has been present in this world. That he considers his time in the womb to be a part of his life in this world, though, is suggested elsewhere, such as Psalm 139, where he refers to his body as "his" (i.e., "my body") and to himself as "I" when he was merely in an unformed state in his mother's womb (vv. 15–16). David, like others in Scripture,[6] refers to himself as the same person — the same "I" — when he is developing in the womb as when he is an adult. He did not become the person David at some later point.

If it makes sense biblically to see embryos as persons created in the image of God and as persons corrupted by sin, it is also important to see what light the redeeming work of God can shed on the personhood of human embryos. The biblical theme of redemption centers around the earthly life, death, and resurrection of Jesus Christ, a series of events that begins with the incarnation. As Paul writes in Philippians 2:6–7, Christ had equality with God, but rather than "grasping" or "promoting" that, he became a human being (*anthropos*) — in fact, a slave (*doulos*). This process could have involved Christ's materializing directly as an adult man, much as he appeared decades later after his resurrection.

---

6. E.g., Job. See Job 31:15. Cf. the analogy with corporate Israel in Isa. 44:2.

But instead the gospel writer Luke describes this becoming a human being as beginning with Jesus as a newly conceived embryo.

According to Luke 1, after the conception of Jesus within Mary by the Spirit of God, she travels with haste (*spoudes*, v. 39) to visit her relative Elizabeth, who is also pregnant, exclaiming to Elizabeth that what God has done (aorist tense = completed action, v. 49) for Mary is great. The Bible knows no intermediate prehuman stage in which Christ is a mere clump of cells without the full moral status of a human being. Rather, the baby jumps in Elizabeth's womb in recognition of the presence of the woman carrying Jesus Christ as an early embryo in her womb, and Elizabeth praises Mary, calling her now "the mother of my Lord" (v. 43). That makes sense: she truly already is a mother, because her son, Jesus, is already present. Christ has not remained God only but has become a human being as well. (In fact, sonship before birth is not unique to Jesus, for God's own messenger, the angel Gabriel, has just told Mary [v. 36] that Elizabeth has "conceived a son" [*suneilephen huion*]. Elizabeth, like many women, conceives not a mere cell but a son — not that which *will be* a son but that which is appropriately called a son already.)[7]

Ironically, the text describing the incarnation in Philippians notes that Christ became not only a human but also a slave. It was not long ago that many people around the world thought that slaves, like embryos, were not persons. In 1857, even the United States Supreme Court ruled that it was "too clear for dispute" that one such slave, Dred Scott, was not a person but was instead mere property that could be owned.[8] Today few would misinterpret Christ's becoming a slave to be suggesting that he became a nonperson, because slaves are persons (though lowly ones in people's eyes, which is the point of the text). Hopefully one day most people will also recognize that Christ's becoming an embryo similarly does not suggest that he became a nonperson. Rather, he took on the lowliest forms of humanity, from a human perspective, to demonstrate that he is the redeemer of all humans.

There are strong biblical reasons, then, to consider embryos and fetuses to be human beings who warrant the basic respect and protections accorded to other persons. However, it is important for Christians and others to remember that this view is not merely a religious idea. Science and logic, as we have seen, support the same outlook. Charles Krauthammer, a *Washington Post* journalist who has served on the US President's Council on Bioethics, offers a pointed reminder to this effect: "Many secularly inclined people such as myself have great trepidation about the inherent dangers of wanton and unrestricted manipulation — to the point of dismemberment — of human embryos.

---

7. Elizabeth's son in the womb is also here called a "child" (*brephos*, vv. 41, 44), the same term used six times elsewhere in the New Testament (e.g., Luke 18:15), always for one who is already born. Being a child is not a function of whether one has been born yet. For more on this and related biblical passages, see John J. Davis, "The Moral Status of the Embryonic Human: Religious Perspectives," *Ethics and Medicine* 22 (Spring 2006): 9–21.

8. US Supreme Court, *Dred Scott v. Sandford* 60 U.S. (19 How.; 1857), 393.

You don't need religion to tremble at the thought of unrestricted embryo research. You simply have to have a healthy respect for the human capacity for doing evil in pursuit of the good."[9]

CONSIDERING ALL STAKEHOLDERS TOGETHER

In the case before us, then, the fetus and embryos are among the people who have the greatest stake in the decisions that Betty, Tom, and Laura make. Accordingly, it is important first to take a look at the case in a way that includes their perspective before considering issues unique to Betty, Tom, and Laura. The goal of this investigation is not primarily to criticize dubious decisions, though some critique will take place along the way. Rather, the goal is to identify constructive ways forward that would have helped each person to flourish. What flourishing entails will need careful consideration as this discussion proceeds.

THE ADULTS AND THE FETUS

Before Betty and Tom's marriage a decade ago and their later joining a church community, Betty became pregnant. What could this couple have learned about marriage and parenthood had they already been part of a church community? The various preaching and education venues that Greg Scharf (chap. 13) and Miriam Charter (chap. 14) discuss in this volume could have communicated much to them. Biblical instruction would have provided them an understanding of the gifts of marriage and parenthood in the contexts of creation, corruption, and redemption introduced above.

In the context of creation, they could have learned about the beautiful one-flesh relationship of commitment and faithfulness in marriage that Averbeck discusses in chapter 1. Such a relationship not only takes physical form in the sexual intercourse that enables the conception of children and the joyful intimacy of the couple. God's design for marriage also provides a stable setting in which children can flourish.

Instead of such blessing, Betty, Tom, and their unborn child experience firsthand the world's corruption. For the fetus, a person created in God's image and precious in his sight, the corruption proves fatal. However, it also seriously damages Betty and Tom as they imbibe from their culture the destructive self-oriented way of viewing the world that Kevin Vanhoozer theologically critiques in chapter 5. They apparently have lost the joy of procreating a child together as a result. How helpful counseling could have been at an early stage to keep them from deciding to abort without the truly informed consent that Greggo and Parent discuss in chapter 3.

---

9. Charles Krauthammer, "Stem Cell Miracle?" *Washington Post* (January 12, 2007), A19. A fellow member of that President's Council, Princeton's Robert George, joins numerous others in voicing a similar concern. See Robert P. George and Christopher Tollefsen, *Embryo* (New York: Doubleday, 2008).

Thankfully, corruption is not the last word, according to biblical teaching, because of the possibility of redemption, which here could have included adoption. As Averbeck (chap. 1) explains, adoption is the very approach that God takes with human beings. Rather than allowing death to triumph, God redeems a fallen situation at great cost to himself by offering the blessing of adoption. Parents with unexpected and unwanted pregnancies can offer the alternative of adoption only if they too are willing to pay a price. It can be excruciating to know that one's child is alive but in someone else's care. The support of a church congregation is priceless in such situations.

THE ADULTS AND THE EMBRYOS

In light of how Betty and Tom previously handled the decision regarding their fetus, their approach to conceiving and supporting embryos is no surprise. Virtually any way they can bring new embryos into the world appears acceptable to them. They show little regard for what the different approaches will mean for their children. They need access to medical and other professionals to help them understand those implications (see Robert Orr and Susan Salladay, chap. 10). Again, relevant considerations can be grouped according to the illuminating biblical categories of creation, corruption, and redemption.

The very creation of children is a gift of God (Ps. 127:3–5), not the right of the parents. Refusing the first gift, and making themselves unavailable for ten more years to receive further gifts, may have rendered Tom and Betty unable to receive another gift in the way that God would normally provide one. The good news is that the God of creation is all-powerful and delights in bringing fertility where there was no fertility, as Averbeck (chap. 1) illustrates. That Betty and Tom have started attending a church in the midst of their struggle with infertility suggests that at some level they may recognize their need for their Creator. However, their attitude toward their church small group, where personal growth and accountability are most likely to occur, is telling. They participate only "whenever convenient." Apparently in their thinking, Christian faith — and implicitly the God of that faith — is there to serve them rather than the other way around. Whether they are true believers capable of the kind of "Genesis 4" trust in God that Averbeck describes is not clear.

As soon as their small group recognizes that they need help thinking through all that is involved here, group members would do well to facilitate communication between the couple and the congregation's pastor — if the couple needs more help than the group can provide. Pastoral ministry has much to contribute to bioethical challenges such as this. As Steven Roy explains in chapter 11, such ministry has two elements. It has a reactive element — it responds to situations after they arise — but it also has a proactive element. Pastors can equip couples, even before they are aware of their infertility, with the biblically sound understanding they need through teaching, preaching, counseling, and everyday conversations. That understanding includes not only matters immediately related to infertility but also the gospel itself, as D. A. Carson (chap. 9) reminds us. A godly life begins with a genuine personal commitment to God through Jesus Christ.

The primary problems embedded in the case before us, then, involve ways that people are thinking, acting, and relating contrary to the ways that God has created people and the world to flourish. It will be illuminating here to note some examples of how contradicting God's intentions can result in experiences that are "unblessed" (lit. "unhappy"). However, the presence of such complications is not the basis of the wrongness of thoughts, actions, and relationships; rather, it is the side effect of them.

Consider first the embryos, the children to be born via the reproductive techniques in view here. What are they missing because of the absence of genuinely believing parents who are living out their faith? When one parent contributes sperm, and the eggs come from a donor (or the eggs come from a parent and the sperm from a donor), the child does not emerge from the complete loving union of two parents, as God intends. The parents have different relationships with the child. There may be some shared dimensions, such as willingness to support the child. But people cannot easily set aside the physical dimension of their existence, as if that is insignificant. Witness the ardent efforts of many people born of donor sperm or eggs to find their biological parents and establish a relationship with them simply because of the biological bond they share.

If a child whom Laura and Tom produce and Betty and Tom raise knows of this arrangement, then she (if a girl) will lose some of the stability, peace, and support that God intends in the family as good gifts of creation. Whether the concern is warranted or not, the child will know that her genetic mother has given her away (or worse, sold her). She will have two mothers, in a sense, whom she can play off against each other, or who can potentially compete for her affection. Tom and Betty recognize this. They are adamant that no one in their family, including the child, should know about Laura's reproductive role here.

Even if the child and family do not know, Betty, Tom, and Laura will know. That alone will likely cause problems. Laura displays relatively little concern for the child, who is a mere "it" in her own words. Laura instead apparently wants recognition and appreciation for her genetic contribution.

Even without Laura's ongoing presence, though, using donor eggs can easily lead to problems between Betty and Tom. God's model at creation involves two parents who are roughly equally responsible for who their child is. For example, biologically (genetically) that is literally the case. In the present situation, with Betty not biologically responsible for the child, it will be tempting for her to shift responsibility solely to Tom's shoulders when convenient. Similarly, it will be tempting for Tom to claim that he has made the entire biological contribution that the couple has made to this child, so Betty should make most (if not virtually all) of the relational contribution that the child needs. Tom reportedly is ambivalent about parenthood to begin with and is going along with his wife only after "intense discussion" (likely quite an emotional one, if Averbeck's examples in chap. 1 are any indication). He may well feel he has done enough by going along with Betty's desires and contributing the sperm. This is a setup for problems in the marriage and the family.

Surrogacy, especially paid surrogacy, can introduce some similar relational dynamics, as Rae and Eckmann (chap. 2) remind us. So it is not hard to understand why God's model for parenthood in creation involves two rather than three parents, both with the same genetic and relational stake in their child's life. Tom and Betty would do well to pursue those avenues of parenthood that observe these parameters as closely as possible, for their own sake as well as (especially) the child's.

Instead they are seriously considering avenues that reflect more the corruption of the world. Their first thought is to ensure that only a healthy child is born, by employing genetic testing (amniocentesis) and abortion. They describe their actions in terms of pursuing health, but the means they have in mind involve pursuing death. They will dispose of any fetus who turns out to have a genetic defect. Betty and Tom have been down the abortion road before, and, to her credit, Betty is determined not to go down it again. Tom is still operating out of the same self-oriented mindset he had in earlier years, a mindset shared by Laura. Actually, Betty is still vulnerable to the same mindset. So Tom might persuade her to go along by shifting the focus away from doing the harm within her own body. If at the embryonic stage they dispose of any genetically disabled offspring conceived with Tom's sperm and Laura's eggs, then the harm can be done in the lab without Betty's having to participate genetically or relationally. The absence of any recorded response from Betty stands in marked contrast to her absolute refusal to abort.

The procedure that would facilitate identifying and disposing of genetically deficient embryos is preimplantation genetic diagnosis (PGD). The basic approach of PGD involves producing more human beings than are likely wanted, selecting those deemed best, and discarding the rest. Most often, the goal is to avoid passing on a genetic disease, though PGD is sometimes used for gender selection or selecting children with other traits as well. In the present situation, such selection would likely be an appealing way to further the interests of the parents. However, it would reinforce the idea that the children exist primarily for the satisfaction and convenience of the parents. It would encourage the illusion that technology is for removing all human limitations, which Vanhoozer theologically critiques in chapter 5.

Identifying serious problems such as genetic diseases is praiseworthy, and an eagerness to avoid them is even more laudable. However, allowing human beings to live only if they measure up genetically represents a profound shift in what it means to be a human being. It suggests that some human beings do not have enough value to justify their existence. Children who are the products of this technology enter the world only because they do not have some unwanted problem. Their parents would have terminated them had they not measured up to their parents' standards for them. Absent is the inspiring vision of all human beings created in the image of God (see Averbeck, chap. 1).

How different such conditional love is from the unconditional love that God has for people. God's love and life-sustaining provision do not depend on people being good or having certain desirable characteristics. Rather, "God demonstrates his own love for us in this: While we were still sinners, Christ died for us" (Rom. 5:8).[10] The contrast with the PGD approach to children could hardly be greater. Not only does God love people in the face of their greatest weaknesses and failings, but God himself bears the fatal brunt of the sacrifice required rather than destroying those who fall short.

The demise of the unconditional acceptance and love that usually exist when a parent has children does not bode well for Betty and Tom's children in the future. They are alive and receiving nurture from their parents only because they measure up to certain health standards—and perhaps other characteristics such as (someday) the height to excel at basketball the way Tom always wished he could. What happens when they develop unusually severe health problems or do not like basketball? The very basis for their receiving support disappears. Their siblings already failed the PGD test on these same criteria, and they were discarded (to put it nicely) as a result. In fact, the PGD world that Tom is asking Betty to embrace is worrisome for all people born with disabilities. After all, if several of Tom's embryonic children are not worth saving because of their health or disability, why should he (or ultimately society) provide any special accommodations or support for people who are born with disabilities because their parents decided not to discard them earlier?

Such is the way of corruption. But the way of redemption looks much different. As the model of God's provision in Christ noted above suggests, a redemptive approach to human embryos is not to subject any to harm but to provide them with the nurture they need. Once conceived, every embryonic human being needs the nurture of parents. So if Tom, Betty, and Laura end up producing and storing more embryos than they are willing to support until birth, what would a redemptive approach toward them look like?

It would not include selling them for stem cell research. Selling human beings for any purpose is unethical, as Rae and Eckmann (chap. 2) explain. But embryonic stem cell research itself is far from nurturing: it involves killing the embryos by taking them apart to obtain their embryonic stem cells (ESCs). Whether Tom and Laura understand this is not clear, since they refer to "stem cell research" as if it were a single enterprise that is helping many people today and warrants support for that reason. What they have in view is actually so-called adult stem cell (ASC) research, as we will see below. The need for better information in this regard underscores the importance of the counseling that Greggo and Parent commend in chapter 3.

The impulse to donate unwanted embryos for some worthy purpose is a good one, compared with the alternative of leaving them frozen in storage indefinitely. However, a redemptive approach to donation will seek the well-being of both the embryos and others who would benefit from the donation. The donation should therefore include

---

10. Similarly, God "sends rain on the righteous and the unrighteous" (Matt. 5:45) as a demonstration that his love and sustaining care extend to all whom he has created, even if they fall far short of what a human being should be.

identifying a recipient willing to provide the nurture that the embryos need. Embryonic children unwanted by their parents are very much wanted by women yearning to adopt them and carry them to term in their own wombs. Betty's sense of this is right on target. Even she may not realize, though, that there are so many such women that well over two hundred agencies are facilitating embryo donation for reproductive purposes.[11]

Some women wanting to adopt prefer embryo adoption to the adoption of children who are already born because of the opportunity to ensure the healthy development of their child before birth. Others are motivated by the opportunity to rescue a young one who otherwise would perish, perhaps inspired by the proverbial call to "rescue those being led away to death" (Prov. 24:11). These or other considerations could have been important, at least for Betty. So the clinic should have followed the suggestion of Rae and Eckmann (chap. 2) to explain the alternative of embryo donation or adoption.[12]

Learning that this alternative is such a redemptive act might tempt Tom and Betty to produce as many embryos as possible. They could thereby increase the likelihood both that attempts to implant embryos would eventually be successful and that there would be embryos left over to donate. However, were they to pursue this course, their lack of understanding about how in vitro fertilization (IVF) works would be leading them astray. If the infertility clinic staff produce more than two or so embryos, they cannot safely place them all into a woman's uterus. Were they all to implant, the health of the woman and children could be in serious jeopardy, necessitating the eventual abortion of some of the fetuses.

Therefore, the staff would normally freeze, for later IVF attempts, all but the number of embryos they can safely implant. They might well tell the woman (Betty or Laura in this case) that freezing embryos is common and represents a good alternative. What people may miss in such discussions is that, on average, only about two-thirds of human embryos survive the freezing and thawing process.[13] Producing more embryos than the clinic can safely implant right away, then, is far from redemptive for the embryos.

---

11. For a list of hundreds of such agencies and their contact information, see Miracles Waiting, Inc., "Clinics Directory," *http://www.miracleswaiting.org/clinics.html* (accessed April 15, 2010). See also Embryo Adoption Awareness Center, "Service Providers," *http://www.embryo-adoption.org/resources* (accessed April 15, 2010).

12. Technically, only so-called donation is necessary for the parents who want to give up their embryos, since the law does not presently recognize embryos as persons. Accordingly, one of the larger agencies is called the National Embryo Donation Center, based in Tennessee. (See "About the NEDC" at *http://www.embryodonation.org/about.html* [accessed April 15, 2010].) But other agencies, such as California's Snowflakes Program, go through a full adoption process as part of their affirmation of the personhood of the embryo. (See "General Information" at *http://www.nightlight* *.org/programs_SnowflakesFrozenEmbryoFaqs.html#General* [accessed April 15, 2010].) Snowflakes alone, as their website indicates, has provided well over three thousand embryos for adoption already, and those numbers are expected to escalate in the near future. See Natalie Lester, "Embryo Adoption Becoming the Rage," *Washington Times* (April 19, 2009), *http://www.washingtontimes.com/news/2009/apr/19/embryo-adoption-becoming-rage* (accessed April 15, 2010).

13. This well-established figure for embryos produced through in vitro fertilization has been confirmed for embryos produced through intracytoplasmic sperm injection as well (e.g., see Rita de Cassia Savio Figueira et al., "A Comparison of Post-Thaw Results between Embryos Arising from Intracytoplasmic Sperm Injection Using Surgically Retrieved or Ejaculated Spermatozoa," *Fertility and Sterility* 91 (March 2009): 727–32.

But what about the many sick people in the world who are in desperate need of the kind of cures that ESC research promises? Can a redemptive approach so easily protect one group (the embryos) while leaving another group (those who are sick) without hope? No, it cannot. A distinctly Christian approach to stem cell research needs to be inclusive of all stakeholders, as will be discussed below, for all are in God's image and are loved by God.[14]

BETTY, TOM, AND LAURA

At this point we would do well to take a step back from the misguided avenues that Betty, Tom, and Laura are initially inclined to pursue. Their needs are not for donated eggs, surrogate mothers, abortion, or the disposing of excess embryos. These are mere strategies to try to meet what their real needs are. Consider what their needs do include.

BETTY

Betty longs deeply for a child that her body appears unable to conceive. She shares this need with many women throughout history, as Averbeck (chap. 1) describes. She pursues virtually any avenue offered to her—first fertility drugs to stimulate egg production, then another source of eggs, then another uterus to carry the pregnancy. However, a better strategy would be the more careful routes of pastoral and mental-health counseling that Greggo and Parent discuss in chapter 3. They could help her not only to assess alternatives for having children but also to recognize other related needs that having children will not remove. Sadly, many women wrestling in secret with infertility would never think to turn to the church for help, considering fertility to be an exclusively medical matter. However, as is evident from the first four chapters of this book, there are many Christian resources available on this issue. How can congregations connect those resources with the people who need them?

It may be unrealistic for all congregational staff and leaders to become well versed in infertility and ways to address it. However, in most congregations there are one or more people, clergy or laypeople, who have that understanding or are willing to acquire it. Such people can gather the informational resources that people like Betty need and can communicate their availability periodically to the congregation.[15] They can also remind people of the relevant counseling resources present in the congregation[16] or available by referral to a Christian mental-health professional. They can even offer learning opportunities (sessions in adult education classes, freestanding speaker events, etc.) which can

---

14. For a fuller biblical and theological basis for such an inclusive approach, see Kilner, "Inclusive Ethics."

15. Much relevant biblically based information has been gathered in the BioBasics series of Q/A paperbacks developed by The Center for Bioethics and Human Dignity (*www.cbhd.org*)—e.g., the volume *Basic Questions on Reproductive Technology.*

16. A good example of this is the Crossings ministry at Winnetka Bible Church in Winnetka, Illinois (*http://www .wbc.org/crossings-ministry.asp*), which began by addressing the end-of-life issues covered in the third part of this book.

equip people to deal with or prepare for infertility, along the lines that Miriam Charter explains in chapter 14.

To reach more of the congregation, as Greg Scharf discusses in chapter 13, sermons and other parts of worship services (Scripture readings, baptisms, Mother's Day observances, etc.) need to alert people to the relevance of Christian faith for coping with infertility and for evaluating alternative ways to have children. Had Betty been present at such services, she might well have consulted both congregational and medical resources. Or if members of her church home-fellowship group had been present and later heard Betty make reference to her infertility in the privacy of their small-group setting, they could have pointed her to congregational resources. They also could have pointed her directly to God. She needs to learn to pour out her anguish to God in prayer, as Hannah (cf. Averbeck's discussion in chap. 1) models so compellingly.

However, the relevance of Christian teaching, preaching, and worship for Betty's current predicament is not limited to occasions when infertility is the explicit subject. Part of the way she is justifying pursuing virtually any option open to her, apparently without much reflection, is that she deserves a child, she has a right to a child, she is owed a child. This attitude surfaces in her claim that her sister, Laura, "owes her" some good eggs. Apparently Betty thinks that God has not given her what she deserves but has given her sister "all the good eggs."

The more Betty learns about how fortunate she is not to receive exactly what she deserves from God—which would be horrendous because of the sinfulness she shares with all humanity—the more open she will be to receiving whatever good gifts God intends for her blessing. She will be less likely to dictate to God requirements for the child through which God will bless her, and more likely to receive the unexpected blessings that God has for her. Rather than demanding "either a genetically related child or none," she may well become more open to the wonderful possibilities of adoption. Whether involving a child who is already born or who is yet to be born (i.e., an embryo), adoption could be a beautifully redemptive answer to infertility for Betty, and to abandonment or death for the child.

TOM

Betty's husband, Tom, is a conflicted person. On the one hand, he simply wants to go along with his wife; he "wants to make his wife happy." Their relationship has been stormy at times, and the stress of her trying to get pregnant threatens to undermine their marriage. Whatever options are available to move quickly beyond this state of tension and on to child-rearing appear to be very attractive. He is somewhat ambivalent about parenthood, but if having a child is a means to an enjoyable relationship with Betty, then so be it. The primary need he is trying to address, then, is his need for a better relationship with his wife. Tom may also be subject to the kind of cultural or familial expectations that Harold Netland, Bruce Fields, and Elizabeth Sung discuss in chapter 7 as "worldview assumptions" — specifically the expectation that he will have a child to carry on the family name. Entering into parenthood with the view that his family expects children, or that parenthood is "Betty's thing," not his, does not bode well ultimately for anyone in the family. As discussed earlier, Tom risks increasing rather than lessening the very marital tension and stress that he is so eager to avoid.

Tom's relationships with Betty and their child-to-be are not the only relationships that need counseling attention. Tom's relationship with Laura is also a matter of concern. Although they are not committing adultery, with the sexual infidelity that would entail, they are having a child together, even if Laura does not carry the child in her womb. But if she does, the intimacy involved is considerable. She and Tom would both know that Tom's sperm would be placed into her body, Tom's sperm and Laura's egg would join to conceive a child, and the child would spend most of his or her first year of life inside of Laura, being nurtured by her. Betty would even hand over to Laura responsibility for deciding if the child should live or be aborted if any genetic problems are detected later in the pregnancy.

As discussed earlier, God has intended such male-female intimacy and connectedness to be part of a marriage relationship, and establishing it outside of marriage invites trouble. Laura already refers to her involvement at one point as helping "him" have a child. There will likely be temptations to allow this intimacy to develop further. Even if it doesn't actually lead to more inappropriate intimacy between Tom and Laura, Betty could easily get jealous of Laura's bond with Tom, which she can never have. Simply embarking on this course could lead to a serious breakdown in the relationship between Betty and Tom, and between Betty and Laura.

Tom's internal justification for moving ahead with every technological option within reach may well involve a sense that this matter is in his, Betty's, and Laura's hands. They can do whatever they want. How badly they all need the preaching and teaching ministries of the church to ask them, "Do you not know that your bodies are temples of the Holy Spirit ...? You are not your own; you were bought at a price. Therefore honor God with your bodies" (1 Cor. 6:19 – 20). Whether their own efforts can produce a child is not the most important criterion of success. Whether they are honoring God with their bodies, including their sperm, eggs, and uteruses, is what matters most. As D. A. Carson reminds us regarding bodily decisions at the end of life (chap. 9), we do have the responsibility to make bodily decisions, but good decisions elevate God's priorities over what people (often mistakenly) think will secure their happiness. How sad if even Tom's, Betty's, and Laura's best efforts to do things their own way fail, and they lose treasured family relationships as well in the process.

LAURA

Laura's needs in the situation before us are rather different from those of Betty and Tom. She does not need another child; she needs money and needs to have strong family relationships. A financially irresponsible husband and costly divorce have left her with insufficient resources to support herself and two children. The absence of her husband may well have fostered the desire to have a closer relationship with her sister and brother-in-law, as well as to succeed as a mother. Like Betty and Tom, she needs the benefit of good counseling. The plan she is considering does not appear to be the best way to address her financial and relational needs.

Consider her relational needs first. Laura may think that she is strengthening her relationship with her sister and brother-in-law by helping them have a child. She may feel that she is satisfying the kind of cultural-familial obligation that Netland, Fields, and Sung characterize in chapter 7 as a "power issue." But as we have already seen, family relationships are just as likely to suffer instead. Apparently Tom and Betty are planning to "try to negotiate favorable terms with Laura," which means terms favorable not to Laura but to Betty and Tom at Laura's expense.

Laura is an adult, so financial negotiation might at first seem appropriate. However, as Debra Spar has described in *The Baby Business*, women in desperate financial straits are in a very vulnerable position. They need funds so badly that they will do things for money that they do not want to do.[17] They will take risks that people should not have to take, including the significant risks of hyperstimulation of the ovaries. These dangers have prompted the National Academy of Sciences to conclude that it is unethical for individuals or institutions needing eggs to make payments to donors, other than to reimburse them for actual out-of-pocket expenses.[18] Rae and Eckmann discuss such concerns related to both egg donation and surrogacy in chapter 2.

If Laura were able to solve her financial problems by taking the relational and physical risks in view here, that would be one thing. But her financial benefit from the course of action under consideration is relatively modest. If she merely sells her eggs, the payment is not likely to make much of a dent in her considerable financial problems. Even if she receives somewhat more from serving as a surrogate mother, she likely will remain in serious financial need.

A very different approach is needed in order to meet Laura's relational and financial needs. The transformative gospel, with values which are upside-down in the world's eyes, could make such a difference here. Instead of trying to negotiate the minimum payment possible to obtain valuable eggs, Tom and Betty could share some of their financial abundance with Laura without asking anything in return. Years ago, when Betty first began to experience a yearning for children, she could have offered to care for Laura's young children so that Laura could earn the income she and her children needed so badly. Both acts of giving may still be possible, to some degree, in this situation.

---

17. Deborah Spar, *The Baby Business: How Money, Science and Politics Drive the Commerce of Conception* (Cambridge, Mass.: Harvard Business School Press, 2006).

18. National Research Council, Committee on Guidelines for Human Embryonic Stem Cell Research, *Guidelines for Human Embryonic Stem Cell Research* (Washington, D.C.: National Academies Press, 2005), recommendation 16.

OTHERS

As noted throughout this chapter, there are many other people who have a lesser stake in what Betty, Tom, and Laura decide to do. One group identified earlier are the desperately ill patients who are waiting for the treatments that stem cell research is endeavoring to develop. We have noted Tom's and Laura's confusion regarding forms of stem cell research. They do not seem to realize that it is only *adult* (not embryonic) stem cell research that is already helping people with many different medical conditions[19] and is safe for those whose bodies produce the cells. In fact, ASCs are more specialized than ESCs, which can be an advantage if they are exactly the type needed for the medical problem in view, especially if they are the patient's own ASCs and so are a genetic match for the patient.[20]

The primary advantage traditionally touted for ESC research is that ESCs are so flexible ("pluripotent") that they can be coaxed in the lab to develop into any type of cell. However, select ASCs may be much more flexible than traditionally thought.[21] Even more promising is the comparatively recent discovery of induced pluripotent stem (iPS) cells. Like ESCs,[22] they are pluripotent, but producing them does not require destroying embryos. Instead, scientists turn on most of the genetic code of easily accessible cells like skin or hair cells, and the cells become genetically similar to ESCs.[23] This discovery has convinced some prominent stem cell researchers to abandon ESC research and focus on iPS cells instead.[24]

---

19. The list of seventy-three such conditions found in Michael Bellomo's *The Stem Cell Divide* (New York: Amacom, 2006) updates the documentation in the 2004 report of the US President's Council on Bioethics titled *Monitoring Stem Cell Research* (Washington, D.C.: President's Council, 2004) and is itself constantly being updated online (*http://www.stemcellresearch.org*) and in hundreds of research reports published or analyzed in the *Journal of the American Medical Association*—e.g., Richard Burt et al., "Clinical Applications of Blood-Derived and Marrow-Derived Stem Cells for Nonmalignant Diseases," *JAMA* 299 (February 27, 2008): 925–36.

20. As often happens in organ transplantation, the body may try to reject cells that are not a genetic match. Whereas ASCs can often come from the patient and so be a match, ESCs cannot unless a clone of the patient is produced and destroyed at the embryonic stage to obtain the ESCs. The United Nations ("Declaration on Human Cloning," March 8, 2005, *http://www.nrlc.org/UN/UN-GADeclaration-HumanCloning.pdf* [accessed June 30, 2010]) has called for the global prohibition of all forms of human cloning, including for stem cell and other research purposes, because they are "incompatible with human dignity and the protection of human life." For an elaboration of such ethical

problems, see David A. Prentice and Michael A. Palladino, *Stem Cells and Cloning* (San Francisco: Benjamin Cummings, 2002); and John F. Kilner, "Human Cloning," in *The Reproduction Revolution*, ed. Kilner et al., 124–39.

21. E.g., amniotic and placental cells (see Paolo De Coppi et al., "Isolation of Amniotic Stem Cell Lines with Potential for Therapy," *Nature Biotechnology* 25 [January 2007]: 100–106) and germline cells (Sabine Conrad et al., "Generation of Pluripotent Stem Cells from Adult Human Testis," *Nature* 456 [November 20, 2008]: 344–49).

22. A recent MIT study finds "little difference" between ESCs and iPSCs. See Matthew G. Guenther et al., "Chromatin Structure and Gene Expression Programs of Human Embryonic and Induced Pluripotent Stem Cells," *Cell Stem Cell* 7 (August 6, 2010): 249–57.

23. One of the most recent reports documenting a safer means of producing pluripotent stem cells very similar to embryonic stem cells is Luigi Warren et al., "Highly Efficient Reprogramming to Pluripotency and Directed Differentiation of Human Cells with Synthetic Modified mRNA," *Cell Stem Cell* 7 (November 5, 2010): 1–13.

24. E.g., Edinburgh University researcher Ian Wilmut, the cloning pioneer famous for "Dolly" the sheep. See Roger Highfield, "Dolly Creator Prof Ian Wilmut Shuns

So Tom, Laura, and Betty need not feel that they are leaving desperate patients in the lurch. A redemptive approach to their predicament would entail Betty and Tom pursuing ways to have a child which protect rather than jeopardize the lives of embryonic human beings, in the knowledge that alternatives to ESC research look promising for those who need stem cell treatments. "A better birth" is not one in which some people are seriously harmed without their consent so that others can benefit. Rather, it is one in which all people have the opportunity to benefit.

As we have seen, there are various responses to infertility that satisfy this standard. Infertile couples may use a technology such as IVF to bring their own sperm and eggs together in a way that ensures that more embryos than a woman can safely carry to term in her body cannot result.[25] Couples may instead decide to adopt an embryonic or already-born child. Or they may opt to pursue different opportunities that allow them to care for children and others apart from having another child. In the face of infertility, all such approaches are possibilities for a couple to pray and seek counsel about, so that they may discern God's good purposes for their particular situation. As Betty and Tom — as well as others in different circumstances — turn to the church for the help they need in the midst of their infertility, a wealth of experience and wisdom will accumulate to help the Bettys and Toms and Ebonys and Juans of tomorrow glorify God.

For further reading, see the annotated bibliography on "better birth" connected with this book at www.everydaybioethics.org.

Cloning," *London Telegraph* (November 10, 2008), *http://www.telegraph.co.uk/scienceandtechnology/science/sciencenews/3314696/Dolly-creator-Prof-Ian-Wilmut-shuns-cloning.html* (accessed April 16, 2010). Stem cell pioneer George Daley of Children's Hospital in Boston has also redirected his research, concluding that despite the limitations of current iPS cells, "there's no reason in my mind to think that we're not going to have iPS cells that function as well as embryonic stem cells." (See "Straight Talk with George Daley," *Nature Medicine* 16 [June 2010]: 624.)

25. Practically speaking, this entails not attempting to fertilize and implant more than two or so embryos, because of the risk to the mother of too many children developing within her simultaneously, and the risk to the embryos of too many embryos simultaneously trying to implant.

Part Two

BETTER
LIFE

CASE STUDY

GAINING EVERY ADVANTAGE

They had come to be known as "the Four" in the physics department at Highcastle University. Friends since they first met at the international physics competition in Berlin, they had all excelled during their undergraduate years and had even published mentored papers in the prestigious journal *Physics Applied*.

Now the Four had been selected to do their doctoral studies under the supervision of the famous chair of the Highcastle physics department, Dr. Oswald Bright. Working with Dr. Bright was an unparalleled opportunity. Dr. Bright's top students found it difficult to keep pace with him, including one postdoctoral fellow who had withdrawn last year — because of health issues, it was rumored. Following two years of course work, the Four had completed their qualifying exams and now would begin the research that would lead to their dissertations. Roberto, Paul, and Akira also taught as graduate assistants in Dr. Bright's undergraduate physics course, while Jill served instead as Dr. Bright's personal assistant.

Bright had coordinated their dissertation projects so that they would be poised to answer a fundamental question in physics. One evening he invited them over for dinner to "talk about their future plans." After dinner, Bright dismissed the caterers, pulled shut the doors to the elegant dining room, took his seat, and folded his hands. Gazing with piercing eyes at each in turn, he said, "I want you to know how pleased I am with the progress you are making. Your intellectual creativity has exceeded my expectations. Without question, you are the four most capable graduate students I have ever had the privilege to mentor. I have no hesitation in saying that, if you play the game right, together we will revolutionize nuclear physics to the amazement of all in the field. Few outside this room know it, but my plan, with your help, is to unlock the problem of cold fusion. Here lies the key to supplying affordable energy to the world."

As the Four listened intently, the professor refilled their glasses with the last of the wine and continued. "Now, we must get down to business. To go forward, I will need your cooperation on some basic matters. I trust that you enjoyed tonight's dinner. This was your final indulgence. After tonight, I expect you to pledge to forgo alcohol till we complete the project. I have learned how much alcohol can weaken the power of the intellect. What I propose is quite the opposite: taking a drug that will substantially boost your brain's capability.

"To explain, I will confide a secret. Twenty years ago, when I was a PhD student, my son Arnold was struggling in school. His pediatrician diagnosed him with ADD—attention deficit disorder—and prescribed methylphenidate—Ritalin. I was impressed that it helped him to focus his thoughts, study long hours, and communicate so much better. Then one night, I was under the gun in my dissertation research, exhausted, and just couldn't keep awake. I took one of Arnold's methylphenidate pills, and it absolutely transformed my work that night. I continued to use Arnold's until I talked my own physician, Dr. Bauble, into prescribing it for me.

"Years later as a faculty member, I was still taking methylphenidate when I read that pharmaceutical science had crafted more potent stimulants. I persuaded Dr. Bauble to prescribe amphetamine mixed with dextroamphetamine—Adderal—which sharpened my thinking even more. Dr. Bauble now writes prescriptions for an overseas pharmacy that ships monthly supplies of an improved tonic called Ginosko, which enhances mental focus and creativity beyond what any previous drug could do. You are clever enough by now to have made the connection. It was during the years I was taking Ginosko that I pushed forward with the research that won me the Nobel Prize at such a young age."

After an awkward silence, Paul asked, "Are these drugs legal for that purpose?" Surprised at his boldness, Jill blushed, while Roberto and Akira remained cautiously quiet.

"Of course they are legal," replied Bright, "at least in the country that supplies them, and in the United States they inevitably will become legal and ought to be now. Outdated policies still classify stimulants as controlled substances. Why, if not for bioethicists …"

Roberto quickly responded, "They're addictive, sir. Cocaine, too, is a stimulant, and I've seen what it can do. Back at my high school there was this kid who couldn't break free of a crack habit. It gave him high blood pressure and a heart condition, and he dropped out of school. That's why I went into science, to find ways to help people like him. Anyway, prescription drugs are supposed to be used to treat diseases."

The professor grinned. "Pharmaceuticals are a form of technology that helps us to flourish. Societies with the best technology have always outpaced more primitive societies. It's all about survival of the best fitted. Cocaine is a crude stimulant, but Ginosko is the Mercedes Benz of cognitive enhancers. Fender dents happen. Will you let that risk deter you from finding your personal destiny full speed down the exhilarating highway of science?

"And forget the quibbling over differences between medical treatment and enhancement. It's entirely arbitrary," said Bright, pausing to blot the sweat from his twitching brow. "What is normal, anyway? If a drug makes the brain work better, and people want it, in a free country they should have access to it."

Paul pushed a bit farther. "Okay, but is it really right? I mean, it doesn't seem fair to win a Nobel Prize when you're taking stimulants."

Bright chuckled. "That's an obsolete notion. Surely a progressive thinker such as yourself would not want to hold science hostage to an outdated moral grumble? In fact, Dr. Bauble regards his supplying me with Ginosko as his own contribution to the advancement of science. The proof is in the publishing. The success of my book sales alone shows that he is right. And I've thanked him with a share of the royalties.

"Ginosko, which only transiently boosts brain performance, is inadequate for the enormous challenge ahead. Drawing from recent discoveries of neurochemicals that govern the expression of genes for memory, Dr. Bauble has pioneered the next generation of cognitive-enhancement drugs. His new drug, Epiginosko, is an epigenetic neuropharmaceutical that permanently strengthens the synaptic connections underlying learning. Epiginosko alters the very structure of the brain to surpass normal human intelligence.

"I urge each of you to take this exciting new drug. With history as our witness, I set before you this night mental stimulation or staleness. Your decision will point you in a direction in which you will either succeed or stall. Therefore choose to be supercharged, that you and the students who follow you may thrive.

"Dr. Bauble has agreed to supply you with Epiginosko. I assure you that it is reasonably safe and that it will enhance your work considerably. I will also tell you that if you take the pills, it will enhance your stature with me, and I don't need to tell you what that will mean for your professional future."

The Four agreed to the plan.

But the next day, as they broke for lunch in the conference room, Paul expressed misgivings about their acquiescence. Paul, who had been reared in a devout Christian African-American home, had been thinking about the relationship between the moral principles of his upbringing and what is involved in becoming a successful scientist. Lacking the words to express fully his uneasiness, he said, "Even if taking the drug is not clearly illegal, it just doesn't seem right to gain an unfair advantage over others."

Akira, who was from a Buddhist family in Japan and had come to the West for doctoral studies, had a ready reply. "Success in research at this level is all about getting an advantage over others. There is nothing wrong with trying to get an edge that will help you be more successful than others." Like many families in Japan and Korea, where there is fierce competition for entrance into the best schools from an early age, Akira's parents had sent him to special tutorial schools for help in math and English from the age of four. "Besides, think of the potential global impact. This could be huge!"

Roberto then spoke up, with a hint of exasperation in his voice. "Paul, you sound like everyone should start from a level playing field and that no one should have any special advantages. You of all people should know that life is not like that." Roberto grew up in a single-parent home in a poor section of Los Angeles. But his mother sacrificed to ensure that he received a good education through high school, and Roberto was awarded a scholarship to the University of California at Berkeley. "Others have had plenty of advantages that give them an edge in life and in education. I see nothing wrong with using something that gives me a little edge."

Jill had been quiet, but now she spoke up with enthusiasm. "Roberto is right. Besides, what's the difference between using Epiginosko and drinking lots of coffee to focus the mind? In fact, if we do this properly, we could use Epiginosko to benefit a lot of students. For example, we might invite some disadvantaged undergraduates in Dr. Bright's physics course to do the menial tasks of our research in exchange for a brain boost at exam time. We could start by offering the drug to Hispanic and African-American students." Turning to Akira, she smiled as she said, "No offense, Akira, but we need to make sure that the Asian students learn nothing about this, since they are already an academic threat to their white classmates."

Suddenly, the Four were startled by a knock at the door. Peeking in, Dr. Bauble interrupted, saying, "Dr. Bright told me I'd probably find you here. I've got the Epiginosko and some forms for you to sign—just a slight formality. Are you ready?"

CHAPTER 5

WISDOM FROM THEOLOGY

Kevin J. Vanhoozer

Temporal power, to build a good world,
To keep order, as the world knows order.
Those who put their faith in worldly order
Not controlled by the order of God,
In confident ignorance, but arrest disorder,
Make it fast, breed fatal disease,
Degrade what they exalt.

—*T. S. Eliot,* Murder in the Cathedral, *part 1*

"POWER-KNOWLEDGE": AN OLD-NEW TEMPTATION NARRATIVE

As Francis Bacon observed centuries ago, *Scientia potentia est* ("Knowledge itself is power").[1] So it is not surprising that the quest for cognitive enhancement is as old as Adam. Our case study is another in a long line of temptation narratives that depict the lengths to which people go to acquire knowledge or other advantages. The primal fall resulted from Eve's desiring the forbidden fruit that would make her "like God, knowing good and evil" (Gen. 3:5).[2] What was sinful about Eve's act was primarily its means and motivation, not necessarily the knowledge itself but the manner in which she sought it. Something similar may pertain to the situation before us. Indeed, Dr. Bright cuts a compelling Satan figure, holding out the pharmaceutical fruit of scientific knowledge, urging his students to become, if not quite like God, then the next best thing: Nobel Prize–winning physicists.

---

1. Francis Bacon, *Religious Meditations* (1597). There are many reprint editions, including the 1924 London edition published by F. Etchells and H. Macdonald.

2. Unless otherwise noted, all biblical quotations in this chapter are from *The Holy Bible, English Standard Version* (Wheaton, Ill.: Crossway, 2001).

Why not, especially when it's all for a good cause (i.e., solving the energy crisis)? Moreover, the Proverbs urge people to "get wisdom; get insight" (Prov. 4:5). And if God has created humanity with the ingenuity to subdue the chemical world, might this not constitute permission, if not a mandate, for Christians to take drugs in order to memorize more Bible verses, focus their attention in prayer, or gain the stamina to minister even longer hours than would otherwise be the case if one did not partake of pharmaceuticals that enhance memory, attention, and wakefulness?

Our case study, upon careful reflection, challenges Christian thinkers to say why the use of cognitive-enhancement drugs by healthy persons counts as foolishness rather than wisdom. Specifically, it challenges theologians to draw the line that its four young protagonists are about to transgress, and to say why such an encroachment is not only an infraction of state law but a fracturing of one's sense of self and, at the limit, a refusal of both God's gift of life and the way of Jesus Christ. Make no mistake: though it may initially be difficult to see how, this temptation, like every other, ultimately concerns the human creature's denial of the Creator and the created order. Like Eve in her ur-temptation in the garden, the four students are on the verge of idolatry, desiring to be like God and hence willing to exchange God's glory for something less worthy of their devotion: power-knowledge.

To recognize what is at stake in pharmaceutical cognitive enhancement requires a discerning description of what is happening and a thick (i.e., theological) interpretation of what it means. What theology provides is not an abstract rule (e.g., "Thou shalt not injure thyself or another") as much as a large-scale interpretative framework with which to discern the meaning of things in relation to God. Otherwise put, theology helps people to distinguish the true story—the way the world really is—from its several counterfeit narrations. What then is the true story of this quest for power-knowledge? It is but one chapter of a much broader temptation narrative whose recurring theme is people's desire to achieve mastery of the world, the future, and hence their own fate.

The paradigmatic template of this broader temptation narrative is the story of Faust, the man who struck a deal with the devil in exchange for knowledge. Faust's willingness to trade his soul to satisfy his lust for knowledge is the stuff of literary and musical legend. The Latin *Faustus* originally meant "lucky," but thanks to the story, the adjective *Faustian* now describes a person whose stubborn pursuit of self-fulfillment leads to diabolical destruction.

There is something Faustian about the notion that human reasoning is autonomous and omnicompetent, as implied by Dr. Bright and his most like-minded disciples. To the extent that the modern university is predicated on this assumption, Christians should beware. What makes the temptation of cognitive enhancement attractive to the students in our case study is its intimation that by accepting its offer one will achieve something desirable, something *good*—for instance, the ability to help the human race.

Thomas, the eleventh-century Archbishop of Canterbury in T. S. Eliot's play *Murder in the Cathedral*, provides another pertinent example. Thomas has just returned from exile in France to Canterbury, where he is considered an enemy of the state. He must resist four tempters if he is to bear true witness to his vocation. The second tempter in Eliot's play holds out the prospect of the archbishop's collaborating with the king in order to protect the poor, serve justice, and rule for the good. Who has time for ethics, or theology, when there is so much good to do? In the tempter's words, "Power is present. Holiness hereafter." This is precisely the temptation in the cathedral of learning today: to wield power-knowledge or, in Eliot's words, to use technology "to build a good world."

Closer to home, Roger Corman's 1963 film *The Man with the X-Ray Eyes* features Ray Milland, who plays a scientist working on perceptual enhancement. He develops eye drops that give him X-ray vision. At first, he uses his power-knowledge to perform cheap tricks, telling people what they have in their pockets. Eventually, however, he loses the ability to see the world in human terms. The film ends with the hero in church, forcibly removing his perceptually enhanced organs in response to hearing a preacher repeat Jesus' words, "If thine eye offends thee, pluck it out."

On one level, there is nothing objectionable about seeking to improve one's world, others, or oneself. The devil, however, is in the definitions: to improve is to make or become better. Who decides, however, what criteria to use to distinguish better from worse? Moreover, even if people can agree on the goal—human flourishing—does it follow that Christians should use any means to arrive at this end? Those who regard cognitive-enhancement technology as inappropriate shall have to work hard to say what is immoral or satanic about it. This new temptation to become a little bit more like God, then, is a courtroom drama: the temptation narrative is in effect a trial of Christian wisdom, the ability to say and do in particular situations what glorifies God. Hence the goal of this essay: to achieve a measure of "theodramatic" wisdom, the ability to make right theological judgments about what to say and do in order to display in this particular case the mind of Christ.

"IN CONFIDENT IGNORANCE": IS ENHANCEMENT WITHOUT PRESUPPOSITIONS POSSIBLE?

Pursuing such wisdom includes locating the use of Epiginosko in the contemporary context of biotechnology in general, cognitive enhancement in particular, and the research program centered on the idea of radical human enhancement known as transhumanism. Since William Cheshire does that work for us in chapter 8, it need not be repeated here. Jacques Ellul saw this context developing decades ago and cautioned against making technique the ultimate concept with which to understand human existence (i.e., why people are the way they are): "Here man himself becomes the object of technique."[3] Technology tends to form users in the image of the tools they wield: to her with a hammer, everything is a nail; to him with neuroscience, everything is biochemical engineering. For champions of enhancement technologies, Epiginosko and its kin represent supporting proof of the claim that "bioengineers will likely control the future of humans as a species."[4] The tacit promise: people will be like God (Gen. 2:5).

It remains to be seen how society will conduct a rational debate over the merits and demerits of cognitive-enhancement techniques. The prevailing public discourse assumes a this-worldly framework in which happiness in this life is the supreme good, a good that is ever nearer humanity's technological grasp. Ethical questions are a part of the discussion, to be sure. But they tend to be the more obvious ones close to the surface, such as safety, coercion, and fairness, as illustrated in our case itself. For example, Roberto worries about the addictive nature of drugs like Epiginosko, though Dr. Bright is quick to reassure him that this particular drug is "reasonably safe." The professor also is less-than-subtly coercive in commenting, "I don't need to tell you what [taking] that [drug] will mean for your professional future." And the four students devote more time to pondering the matter of equitable access to cognitive-enhancing drugs than to any other ethical question.

Yet from the perspective of theology, the situation calls for a "thicker" description of what is happening, and of what is at stake. How, then, might one describe the project of cognitive enhancement in theological terms? What further concerns might Christians have in light of a theological interpretation of this and similar enhancement technologies? Before offering the view from theology, it is important to expose the countertheology, as it were, that undergirds the case for enhancement.

THE SOCIAL IMAGINATION

The underlying social imagination[5] of modernity goes a long way toward explaining the appeal of biotechnology, its claim to legitimacy, and its sense of entitlement. It is therefore important to clarify the presuppositions underlying the modern belief that cognitive enhancement is indeed a human good.

The Presumption of Physicalism. The presumption of physicalism—that the world can ultimately be explained in terms of physical matter and energy—has seeped into modern human self-understanding. If the processes and products of both mind (cognition) and heart (emotion) are ultimately a matter of brain chemistry, it is no surprise that neuroscience and psychopharmacology are increasingly the methods of choice of

---

3. Jacques Ellul, *The Technological Society* (New York: Vintage, 1964), 22.

4. Jane Bosveld, "Evolution by Intelligent Design," *Discover* (March 2009), *http://discovermagazine.com/2009/mar/02-evolution-by-intelligent-design* (accessed July 1, 2010).

5. The social imagination envisioned here is similar to the "social imaginary," Charles Taylor's term for that basic conception of the order of things (transmitted by stories and images) that generates and makes sense of the practices of a society. See Taylor's *Modern Social Imaginaries* (Durham, N.C., and London: Duke Univ. Press, 2004).

many psychologists. The enhancement of the body is the disenchantment of the soul. Is it really the case, however, that "soul care" is a misnomer, that the real problem is physical rather than spiritual?

The Authority of Scientism. If materialism is the preferred this-worldly metaphysic, then scientism—the belief that all properly grounded knowledge-claims should use the scientific method—is the authoritative this-worldly epistemology.[6] The modern social imagination has no room for an immaterial soul in the scientific inn. However, it is far from clear where, if scientism is true, authority with regard to values claims comes from. Those who profess biblical authority, however, have recourse to another source and norm for discerning the end of things and making value judgments: the created order.

The Premise of Consumerism. Modernity's Western inhabitants typically value individual freedom; many Americans believe that such freedom includes the right to buy arms (and armories). Enhancement technologies have a vested interest in marketing their wares to eager consumers. The President's Council on Bioethics rightly notes that biotechnology "is now intimately bound up with industry and commerce" and goes on to elaborate that desires (e.g., to be young again) can be manufactured (i.e., marketed) "almost as effectively as pills."[7] Proponents of free market economy argue that individuals have the right to purchase cognitive-enhancement technologies as much as anything else. The market is all-knowing, all-powerful, omnipresent, and brooks no argument.

The Promise of Medicalization. Cognitive-enhancement technology, then, assumes that the good for humans will be physical, approved by science, and something that people can purchase. If life's fundamental problems can be reduced to (and solved by) science, then there is less need to trust in or pray to God. In the modern social imagination, even hope has become this-worldly: medicalization is nothing less than the secularization of salvation. It is a way of conceiving life in medical terms, and hence in terms of phenomena that are susceptible to various kinds of technical intervention. In sum: a picture of human good as something essentially biological beguiles the modern imagination.

ESCHATOLOGY AND TECHNOLOGY: FOR WHAT MAY PEOPLE HOPE?

The social imagination of modernity comes complete with eschatology: a doctrine of last things and a vision of a possible future for which people can work and hope. "The unenhanced life is not worth living." This biotechnological revision of the wisdom of Socrates itself calls for careful examination. Specifically, what are the criteria for technological progress? What do proponents of cognitive-enhancement technologies presuppose counts as improvements and success? The prevailing social imagination

---

6. See Michael Stenmark, *Scientism: Science, Ethics and Religion* (Burlington, Vt.: Ashgate, 2001).

7. US President's Council on Bioethics, *Beyond Ther-*

apy: Biotechnology and the Pursuit of Happiness (New York: HarperCollins, 2003), 342–44.

encourages the McDonaldization of knowledge, so to speak—where the primary values are the fast-food values of convenience, quantification, efficiency, and control—and the authenticity of the self.[8] It is not enough to know how to do things, however; one must know what one should be doing, and why. What should people make of themselves with the newfound biotechnology? How do they know if they are there yet? Power-knowledge disconnected from right ends is not only blind but dangerous.

To speak of enhancement is to presuppose a certain conception of the human good, a desired end that justifies the chosen means. But all too often no such understanding of what a person is or is meant to be or do is involved. More commonly, cognitive-enhancement technologies do not presuppose an end that justifies means but a means that justifies ends.[9] The subtitle of Carl Elliott's book *Better Than Well* says it all: "American Medicine Meets the American Dream." Elliott worries that enhancement technologies cater to the consumerist temptation to reach fulfillment through acquisition of property or, in this case, personal properties, properties that can, moreover, be bought like other commodities (e.g., new car, new wrinkle-free face, new mental power). The new American dream is less about owning one's home than of "honing one's ownness," achieving authenticity through technological means. Yet is it really the case that the attainment of these superbiological ends, even if achievable, will be truly fulfilling? Is it possible that in wanting to enhance themselves, people risk despising who and what they are?

Essayist Wendell Berry astutely observes, "The question of human limits, of the proper definition and place of human beings within the order of Creation, finally rests upon our attitude toward our biological existence, the life of the body in this world. What value and respect do we give to our bodies? What uses do we have for them?"[10] As human bodies are "earthly," Berry notes that it is hardly surprising that there are "profound resemblances between our treatment of our bodies and our treatment of the earth."[11] People do the same thing to their bodies as they do to the land: they murder to dissect; they exploit to enhance. The real danger of "technological progress" is the tendency to look on the body and the natural world as millstones weighing down the self, combined with the arrogance that, in league with greed, sponsors "better living through biochemistry."

Faith in progress is a hallmark of the modern social imagination. The fundamental problem is pride: people's arrogant belief that they have the technical means of self-improvement—the power to reshape human nature, the ability to lift themselves up by their DNA strands—and the wisdom to use technology for good rather than ill. Human history makes only ambiguous progress; after all, world history, like the story of Faust, ends in judgment. There is no intrinsic necessity that more is always better.

8. See George Ritzer, *The McDonaldization of Society* (Los Angeles: Pine Forge Press, 2008).

9. I am indebted to Oliver O'Donovan for this way of putting the matter (personal correspondence).

10. Wendell Berry, *The Art of the Commonplace: The Agrarian Essays of Wendell Berry*, ed. Norman Wirzba (Washington, D.C.: Showmaker and Hoard, 2002), 93.

11. Ibid.

Simply to assume that all technological innovations are genuinely enhancements is to hold a naive optimism concerning the human tendency to do evil. It is misguided to equate advances in technology with genuine progress.

WHAT ARE PERSONS (AND THEIR COGNITIVE FACULTIES) FOR?

We now turn from the medicalized reduction of eschatology ("in pharmacology we trust") to anthropology. Indeed, the meaning of what it is to be human is the ultimate issue at stake in our case study.

Being

Oliver O'Donovan's *Begotten or Made? Human Procreation and Medical Technique*[12] rightly identifies what is ultimately at stake in the enhancement habit of mind: the concept, and dignity, of human personhood. Enhancement technologies are revolutionary—different in kind and not merely degree—inasmuch as their aim is not to restore but to transcend human health or wholeness. When "making" becomes the key category in society's interpretative framework, so that everything is fair game for technological makeovers, then there is no reason to let things "be." However, what people make is fundamentally unlike them—artificial—and is at their disposal, a thing to use rather than love: "when a bioengineer intervenes for non-therapeutic ends, he stands not as nature's servant but as her aspiring master, guided by nothing but his own will and serving ends of his own devising."[13] Cognitive-enhancement techniques resemble eugenics in at least one respect: "The problem with eugenics and genetic engineering is that they represent the one-sided triumph of willfulness over giftedness, of dominion over reverence, of molding over beholding."[14] By contrast, that which people beget comes into the world as a gift to be received, respected, and loved, for it is, amazingly, like them: not a thing to be manipulated but a person, with all the rights and privileges pertaining thereunto.

Christians confess that God has created everything that is or has being, including humans. God is the unauthored Author. To speak of creation is to acknowledge a divinely given, and authoritative, order of things: "The order of things that God has made is *there*.... Christian ethics, therefore, has an objective reference because it is concerned with man's life in accordance with this order."[15] Christians must therefore not participate in technologies that aim to revise or rewrite the created order. It is one thing to restore human being to its proper form—this way medicine lies—but quite another to reform it.

---

12. Oliver O'Donovan, *Begotten or Made? Human Procreation and Medical Technique* (Oxford and New York: Oxford Univ. Press, 1984).

13. US President's Council on Bioethics, *Beyond Therapy*, 324.

14. Michael J. Sandel, *The Case against Perfection: Ethics in the Age of Genetic Engineering* (Cambridge, Mass., and London: Harvard Univ. Press, 2007), 85.

15. Oliver O'Donovan, *Resurrection and Moral Order: An Outline for Evangelical Ethics* (Leicester, UK: InterVarsity; Grand Rapids, Mich.: Eerdmans, 1986), 17.

Doing

Enhancement technologies have an adverse effect on a person's sense of personal agency, one's sense of being oneself, a *doing* being. My agency is a function of my embodiedness, and I experience both as a given. I experience myself as free to act according to my nature. Indeed, to "be" human is to act according to my nature. Everything I do "communicates" my being. However, to suggest that I am a patient—a genetically programmed or biochemically enhanced person who merely responds to stimuli rather than an agent who initiates action—ultimately deprives me of the freedom that characterizes divine and human persons alike. By contrast, the Scriptures depict humans as free and responsible actors in a divinely authored drama of creation and redemption. Where other beings have a natural tendency to share themselves through action appropriate to their natures, human persons have a special capacity to engage in meaningful dialogue and so engage in properly communicative action (i.e., action oriented to understanding). To the extent that cognitive-enhancement technologies call into question the conviction that "this is *me* acting," they undermine personhood.[16]

Whereas O'Donovan worries about losing the notion of begetting, Jürgen Habermas examines the ways in which an enhancement mindset affects people's self-understanding as responsible agents. Specifically, biotechnology blurs the line between being an object and being a person (i.e., a communicative agent in covenantal relationship): "the boundary between the nature that we 'are' and organic endowments we 'give' to ourselves disappears."[17] Viewing bodily enhancements as commodities and persons as things that can be improved, however, makes people more likely to treat others strategically—that is, as things to manipulate rather than as persons with whom to communicate. Freedom and justice alike require people to engage one another communicatively, not strategically.

Relating

For people to understand their place in the created order is to understand their place in relation to everything else, to one another, and especially to God. Elsewhere I have argued that the Bible depicts God as a triune communicative agent who in love and freedom shares his life with human creatures in Jesus Christ through the Holy Spirit.[18] Human persons are communicative agents in God's image, able to respond to the call of God and others. What are persons for? With the persons of the Trinity in mind, one may answer "to know and love others." Human cognitive faculties allow people to relate to

---

16. Paul Ricoeur views the self as a person to whom actions can be ascribed, responsibility imputed, and stories told (Paul Ricoeur, *Oneself as Another*, trans. Kathleen Blamey [Chicago: Univ. of Chicago Press, 1992]).

17. Jürgen Habermas, *The Future of Human Nature* (Malden, Mass., and Cambridge, UK: Polity Press, 2003),

12. While O'Donovan draws on Trinitarian theology in his "begotten not made" contrast, Habermas distinguishes between the "grown" and the "made" (44).

18. Kevin J. Vanhoozer, *Remythologizing Theology: Divine Action, Passion, and Authorship* (Cambridge: Cambridge Univ. Press, 2010), esp. chap. 4.

God and others communicatively rather than merely strategically: "Come, let us reason together." To be a human person is to be a begotten communicative agent in covenantal relation with God and others, especially those human others who bear God's image (e.g., family members, fellow saints, neighbors). What are persons (and their cognitive faculties) for? In a word: communion.

"FOR WHAT DOES IT PROFIT ... ?": TOWARD WHICH GOOD, WHAT MEANS, WHOSE GOSPEL?

The students in the situation before us face essentially the same challenge that confronts Christians of every age and place: to embody the mind of Christ in new cultural and intellectual situations. The church's mission, and hence the preeminent equipping task of theology, is to demonstrate understanding by exhibiting the good news of Jesus Christ in terms that are both faithful to the Scriptures yet fit the situation: to embody in concrete forms of life one's theoretical and practical grasp of the drama of redemption.

The modern social imagination and newer enhancement technologies work together to support what is ultimately a different gospel: the good news that biochemistry gives humanity the means and mechanisms for self-improvement and self-transformation. The theology behind this gospel of enhancement comes complete with an alternative eschatology, anthropology, and doctrine of salvation. The best way to detect these deficient doctrines is, of course, to have a sure feel for the real thing. We turn, then, to consider the "performance-enhancing advantage" (so to speak) of union with Christ. Christology is far from being tangential to our topic for the simple reason that Jesus Christ is the paradigm of true humanity. Those who seek salvation would therefore do well to attend to his words: "For what does it profit ['benefit,' 'advantage'] a man if he gains the whole world and loses or forfeits himself?" (Luke 9:25). This is the issue underlying the decision to employ enhancement technologies.

To approach our case study from the perspective of the biblical imagination is to see that true progress in humanity is a matter not of mastering one's biochemistry but rather of growing up in every way—truth, goodness, and love—into Christ (Eph. 4:15). There is a natural order of things, but it is centered on and discerned in Jesus Christ, for "all things were created through him and for him" (Col. 1:16). In raising Jesus from the dead to a new bodily existence, God vindicates and completes his intention for the created order. Jesus is thus both means and end of the good life that God has prepared for human creatures.[19] What followers of Jesus ought to most want to improve is not their cognitive or muscular or sexual functions but their Christlikeness. Accordingly, this

---

19. See Eugene H. Peterson, "Introduction: 'The Purification of Means,'" in *The Jesus Way: A Conversation on the Ways That Jesus Is the Way* (Grand Rapids, Mich.: Eerdmans, 2007).

section reconsiders (1) the use of the Bible in bioethics, (2) the good of nature in terms of the created order, and (3) the nature of the good in terms of the ways in which the triune God restores the created order, and human nature, to humanity's great advantage.

THEODRAMATIC THEOLOGY: THE USE OF SCRIPTURE IN BIOETHICS

There are surprisingly few explicit treatments of the use of Scripture in bioethics. This is not the place for an extended survey. Suffice it to say that the way forward is to think not so much in terms of inserting isolated biblical verses into contemporary debates—though some texts do rise like mountain peaks out of the fog of conceptual confusion—as putting the whole debate into biblical perspective, into the drama of redemption for which the Bible is the authoritative script. Being biblical requires more (but not less) than appealing to Scripture here and there in the course of argumentation; it requires being apprenticed to the whole pattern of life that comprises Christian identity, the new creation already-not-yet inaugurated in Christ (2 Cor. 5:17). This is how people learn to make judgments about what to say and do today that accord with the reality of what yesterday the Father has done and tomorrow will do in the Son through the Spirit. The goal is so to enter into the story of the Bible that it becomes possible to indwell its dramatic plot, its ethos, and ultimately the divine *dramatis personae* themselves.[20]

Theology's aim is to direct the church to participate rightly in what God is doing—the theodrama (*theos* + *drao* = "God doing")—so that it can both speak, and do, the truth. Christians must indwell the strange new world of the biblical text to the point that they can almost spontaneously contextualize the main theodramatic action—the Father's making all things new in Christ through the Spirit—as they proclaim and practice the gospel in new cultural scenes. The understanding and obedience of faith, theology, and ethics are thus related: each in its own way is concerned with humanity's fitting participation in the redeemed order of creation.

Thanks to biblical revelation, the church knows what is most important: that God created and ordered everything in the world through his Word, that God is redeeming the world from the disorder into which it has fallen because of sin through this same Word (and Spirit). Being biblical in bioethics means making wise decisions about what actions and practices befit the theodrama. It is a matter of engaging in practical reasoning in light of the truth and *telos* of the gospel, the great story of what God has done, is doing, and will do to renew—not enhance—all things.[21]

---

20. This way of putting it draws upon my *The Drama of Doctrine: A Canonical-Linguistic Approach to Christian Theology* (Louisville: Westminster John Knox, 2005), as well as Brian Brock's *Singing the Ethos of God: On the Place of Christian Ethics in Scripture* (Grand Rapids, Mich.: Eerdmans, 2007).

21. Practical reasoning is reasoning about action: what to say or do. "'Authority' is a term of practical reason" (Oliver O'Donovan, "Scriptural Authority in Practice," unpublished lecture, April 2009).

Theology serves the church by setting forth God's "design plan" (see below) for his creatures and providing instructions for "proper functioning," directions for "doing the works of God" (John 6:28). The challenge for the company of Jesus Christ is to perform new life in the midst of the old, to put on scenes of God's kingdom in the public square. What is required is not simply a high view of Scripture but the wisdom to glean its rendering of reality and to conform to this reality in one's speech and life, even in unprecedented situations: "Scripture is the divine resource with which we may confront the indeterminacy of practical decision."[22]

Our case study ultimately is a test of the church's "performance" knowledge; obedience is a way of acting, and the church must study its script thoroughly in order to realize properly its true end. The decision of whether to use cognitive-enhancement technologies requires biblical reasoning, careful thought that does not simply repeat old formulations but devises courses of action that display sound practical understanding: the ability to stage the new self and its practices (Col. 3:9–10) by following the holy script into uncharted scenes.

PHARMACOLOGICAL COGNITIVE ENHANCEMENT AND THE DOCTRINE OF CREATION: TOWARD WHOSE SHALOM?

The doctrine of creation addresses two closely related issues concerning enhancement technologies that have proved to be among the most intractable: (1) whether one can distinguish the natural from the unnatural with respect to human being in order to respect the former as God-given, and (2) whether and how far one ought to improve what one finds in human nature if one is able to do so.

Nature: To (Let) Be or Not to (Let) Be? To restate the case for cognitive enhancement, not all that is natural (e.g., the bubonic plague) is good. No one is complaining about pharmacological technologies that combat infectious diseases, or about technological advances like jet propulsion, even though flying is hardly a natural form of human travel. In what sense is the pick-me-up from a cup of coffee more natural than a capsule of Epiginosko? So goes the "analogy of enhancement": if the one thing is not objectionable, then neither is the other. Herein lies the core of the present-day temptation to partake of this new form of power-knowledge: "In one sense, *all* technology can be viewed as an enhancement of our native human capacities."[23]

The core claim of the analogy of enhancement—that there is no significant difference between restoring or correcting and revising or improving nature—is fiendishly subtle. On one level, it suggests that the natural order of things is corrupt, tending to disorder and thus requiring technological intervention to put right. But this is to elide

22. Ibid.

23. Nick Bostrom and Julian Savulescu, "Human Enhancement Ethics: The State of the Debate," in *Human Enhancement*, ed. Nick Savulescu and Julian Bostrom (Oxford: Oxford Univ. Press, 2009), 2.

the distinction between creation and the fall. The natural—and this includes embodied human existence—is not simply what-is-there-to-be-overcome through technological means. The body is more than an obstacle course for the mind; it is the divinely intended enabling condition of human communicative action, knowing, and love. There is a divine design plan for human brains and bodies that enables people to identify a normative concept of health: *salus*, in the sense of "proper physical (and mental) functioning."[24] "A thing's design plan is the way the thing in question is 'supposed' to work."[25]

Technological interventions in the human body are natural (i.e., going with rather than against the grain of nature) when they intervene only in ways that respect and defer to the divine design plan. To restore proper function is one thing (i.e., therapy, healing); to revise proper function (i.e., enhancement in the strict sense of going beyond nature) is quite another. Technologies that aim to redraw those boundaries that define the created order are unnatural inasmuch as they refuse to align with the divine design plan. The analogy of enhancement ultimately breaks down, then, for there is a qualitative and not merely quantitative difference between restoring proper function and rewiring it. It is one thing to articulate this conceptual distinction, however, and another rightly to deploy it; hence the need to say more about the end for which humans were created.

My bodily limitations both partially define me and make possible a proper human existence. The givens of my existence (e.g., my height, IQ, gender, date of birth, ethnicity, etc.) do not constrain my freedom but are rather the condition of its possibility. Any attempt to transcend or transform these givens, except to restore health, is to reject my God-givenness. How much more tragic and self-defeating it is, then, to attempt to transcend the human condition itself. Martha Nussbaum illustrates the latter with the story, taken from Homer's *Odyssey*, of Odysseus's decision to refuse the gift of immortality. Odysseus saw that divine existence would deprive him of the very opportunities he needed in order to accomplish the peculiar excellences of human being. As Nussbaum puts it, "Human limits structure the human excellences, and give excellent action its significance."[26] To remove certain limits is to remove the whole point of certain activities; there would be no meaningful concept of athletic excellence, for example, "in the life of a being that is, by nature, capable of anything."[27] Why praise someone for jumping high hurdles if he is not subject to the laws of gravity?

Time is doubtless the most challenging limitation on human being, hence the concerted efforts to extend the human life span. Yet the prospect of time running out (i.e., death) is also an aid to character and spiritual formation. While death may be a consequence of sin, finitude per se is not, for God declared everything he created

---

24. I am borrowing the concept of a divine design plan—"a set of specifications for a well-formed, properly functioning human being"—from Alvin Plantinga's *Warrant and Proper Function* (New York and Oxford: Oxford Univ. Press, 1993), 14.

25. Ibid., 21.

26. Martha C. Nussbaum, *Love's Knowledge: Essays on Philosophy and Literature* (New York and Oxford: Oxford Univ. Press, 1990), 378.

27. Ibid., 372.

good—indeed, "very good" (Gen. 1:31). The space-time world is the proper context for interpersonal interaction and covenantal relations. People can become who God wants them to be only through bodily temporal existence. The good news is not that God saves people from their created existence but rather that, in Christ, he realizes their original design plan through it. The resurrection of Jesus Christ anticipates the future realization of God's design plan for creation.

It is vital to expose the lie behind the ancient Gnostic heresy that people's bodies are the fundamental problem. It is not physical existence but sin—rebellion against the creation and the created order (including the limitations of human finitude)—that is the problem. Nature as designed by the Creator is constitutionally open to transformation by grace. In Dietrich Bonhoeffer's words, "The natural is that which, after the Fall, is directed towards the coming of Christ. The unnatural is that which, after the Fall, closes its doors against the coming of Christ."[28] All things in nature were "created through him and for him [Jesus Christ]" (Col. 1:16). The final proof that bodily limitations are a matter of finitude rather than fallenness, and hence something to be received as a gift rather than rejected as an evil, is Jesus' own incarnation. Even Jesus "learned obedience" through his communicative action (i.e., prayer) to God during the "days of his flesh" (Heb. 5:7–8).

Playing God? On Enhancing the Created Order. As bearers of God's image, men and women enjoy the dignity of communicative agency; they are the actors, not producers (co-creators), of the drama of salvation history. Everything thus depends on playing one's part rightly, and on playing the right part.

Critics of enhancement technologies would be right to urge the four students in our case study not to "play God." The prospect of being "like God, knowing" (Gen. 3:5) is at the heart of the temptation to power-knowledge. Yet the Word of God clearly designates human creatures as stewards, not sovereigns, of the world. The meaning of stewardship is very much one of the key issues in the debate. How far should humanity seek to "subdue" the earth, to master its physical and biochemical processes? More pointedly: do people have dominion over their own being?

Many who subscribe to the analogy of enhancement opt for a third possibility, between the extremes of dominating nature (sovereignty) and preserving it (stewardship). Humans have already improved on the natural order, they say, by inventing things like aspirin and airplanes. The intent of the former is to restore health, but the intent of the latter is to enhance human existence. Why do people view antibiotics and airplanes as legitimate responses to the creation mandate rather than as rebellions against the created order? According to some advocates of enhancement, it is because aspirin and airplanes, together with Epiginosko, are examples of neither dominion nor stewardship

---

28. Dietrich Bonhoeffer, *Ethics* (New York: Macmillan, 1955), 143.

but co-creation. The idea is that God (if there is a God) invites humans into a creative partnership in the ongoing task of forming and transforming the world.[29]

Accordingly, some would say, the criticism that pharmaceutical enhancement is an example of playing God is ambiguous: Is it playing God to expose a pregnant mother to Bach's Brandenburg Concertos in the hope of enhancing the intellectual and artistic capacities of her child?[30] Is it playing God to insist that a child practice the piano even when he or she does not appear to be musically gifted? The pro-enhancement party would have people believe that cases like these soften the edge of the therapy-enhancement distinction. The analogy of enhancement suggests that there is no way to distinguish between the legitimate technological subduing of nature and supposedly illegitimate examples of enhancement. Who is in a position to judge which technological developments represent acceptable offerings and which unacceptable offerings that, by attempting to rewrite nature, usurp God's authorial rights?

The way forward, I submit, is to recover the Creator-creature distinction together with the concept of the divine design plan. The Genesis creation account or *mythos* ("plot") gives rise to a certain "ethos of the cosmos" that in turn suggests a certain way of responsible dwelling in the world.[31] The Bible depicts God's Word as world-shaping and creation as God's good speech act. Hence the key insights of the biblical imagination: that all things, including human beings, have been spoken into being; that God's Word sets the boundaries for human existence; that human beings were created to hear and respond to God in faith and obedience. To see God, people, and the rest of the world in light of the creation account is to grasp the significance of the fear of the Lord for bioethics, and for everything else. By contrast, to fail to respect the created order is to do violence to nature and ultimately to wreak havoc, if not chaos.

Humans are not co-creators (i.e., "authors") but stewards of creation, appointed as vice-regents to align creation, and themselves, to the Creator's design plan. It is one thing to use technology to cultivate the potential of the created order within its natural limits, quite another to use technology to transcend (i.e., transgress) the boundaries of human nature. Epiginosko is in very significant respects not like coffee, crutches, or computers. These latter helps do not set their users up as co-creators of humanity the way Epiginosko does. Drinking coffee may keep one awake (whether one wishes it or not), yet unless one willfully engages in caffeine substance abuse, there is a significant difference between a morning jolt of joe and technological interventions in the brain's biochemistry. The intent of the latter is to achieve a state of mental functioning that goes beyond the human species' natural limits and which aims at an end or *telos* other than the new humanity anticipated by the risen Christ.

---

29. See Ted Peters, *Playing God? Genetic Discrimination and Human Freedom*, 2nd ed. (New York: Routledge, 2002), 197.

30. For a development of this point, see C. A. J. Coady, "Playing God," in *Human Enhancement*, ed. Bostrom and Savulescu, 155–80.

31. I am indebted for this way of putting it to William P. Brown, *The Ethos of the Cosmos: The Genesis of Moral Imagination in the Bible* (Grand Rapids, Mich.: Eerdmans, 1999).

Supporters of enhancement technologies argue that human beings come into their own precisely by using their God-given potential to develop the resources of creation, including knowledge about people's genetic and biochemical makeup. Epiginosko is not a threat to authentic selfhood but a tool that allows humanity to bring one more part of nature under human dominion. By contrast, critics of enhancement technology worry that such attempts are ultimately self-defeating to the extent that they deny the kind of existence that God has given to humanity. In trying to gain an advantage in life, people may lose it altogether by exchanging the created form of the human creature for a manufactured lie.

God has designed human beings to grow physically, morally, and intellectually in certain natural ways. These have more to do with self-discipline than with self-mastery through biotechnology: "there is no mandate to exercise dominion over *oneself*."[32] Epiginosko may increase intellectual ability and help people more quickly to arrive at answers, but it cannot cultivate intellectual virtue. A drug that improves memory does not a scholar make. Human beings have the dignity of agency; they are able to take initiatives, to *do* rather than, as patients, merely be biochemically *done to*. Michael Sandel has argued at length that the net result of enhancement technologies is the diminished agency of the person whose achievement is artificially enhanced.[33]

Cognitive-enhancement technology is an insult to the Creator to the extent that it implies ungratefulness for one's divine design plan and impatience at the rate of its realization. It is a deeply poignant form of grumbling against God for not doing more than enabling proper cognitive functioning. To think of the good life in terms of maximal functioning only is to neglect the importance of another aspect of the created order: one's *salus* is ultimately a matter not of justification by work—even Nobel-Prize-winning work—but of entering into God's Sabbath rest (Heb. 4:9).

"To Work and to Keep": Biblical Reasoning, Wise Stewardship, and the Creation Mandate. The second creation account includes a lesser-known variation on the creation mandate. Whereas Genesis 1:28 speaks of "filling," "subduing," and "having dominion" over the things in creation, Genesis 2:15 depicts God putting Adam in the garden "to work it and keep it." To work something is to develop it, perhaps into a city; to keep something is to preserve it. Which action better leads to flourishing and *shalom*?

"To work and to keep." Is it possible that Genesis provides not just a single interpretive framework through which to reason biblically about technology but two? Both perspectives are on display in Genesis 30. In response to Rachel's complaint that she is barren—"Give me children!" (v. 1)—Jacob retorts, "Am I in the place of God?" (v. 2). Jacob here rightly expresses a perspective of gratitude for the mysterious gift of begotten life.[34] Later in the chapter, however, Jacob adopts an innovative selective-breeding

32. Brent Waters, *From Human to Posthuman: Christian Theology and Technology in a Postmodern World* (Aldershot, UK, and Burlington, Vt.: Ashgate, 2006), 144.

33. Sandel, *The Case against Perfection*, 25–27.

34. I owe this phrase, and the idea in this paragraph, to Erik Parens, "Toward a More Fruitful Debate about Enhancement," in *Human Enhancement*, ed. Bostrom and Savulescu, 181–97.

technique in order to obtain his rightful share of sheep and goats from Laban (Gen. 30:37–42). This Jacobean act expresses a "responsibility perspective," acknowledging that life sometimes puts people in situations where they must do or invent something to rectify or ameliorate their situation. There is no ultimate contradiction between the two perspectives, any more than there is between covenantal privileges and covenantal obligations: to work the earth is a privilege, to give thanks for it a permanent responsibility.

Advocates of cognitive enhancement, however, prefer to speak of creativity rather than responsibility: "As one side emphasizes our obligation to remember that life is a gift and that we need to learn to let things be, the other emphasizes our obligation to transform that gift and to exhibit our creativity."[35] There is a time technologically to intervene in nature, they say, and a time not to intervene; a time to enhance, and a time not to enhance. However, without a sure grasp of the design plan and final purpose for human beings, advocates of enhancement technology have no means of rightly telling time; the default assumption seems to be "can implies ought."[36] This way leads to madness and monsters.

Some readers at this point may find themselves still prone to lingering doubts: is it any more monstrous to want one's children to have keener memories or attention spans through pharmaceutical intervention than it is to want them to have straight teeth through orthodontic intervention? The analogy of enhancement is a slippery slope that lacks an obvious ledge or toehold. It invites people to accept a principle and to participate in a practice, a cooperative social activity ordered to certain goods that are really, in the light of the gospel, not goods. The problem with straightening teeth for purely cosmetic as opposed to health reasons is not that people violate a clear-cut moral rule but rather that they get caught up in a search for what are ultimately false goods and false gods. For the goods that enhancement technologies promise are culturally relative; they conform to society's arbitrary ideal, not to God's design plan. Moreover, once one accedes in principle to serving this god—the all-knowing, all-powerful voice of social fashion—where does one stop? What if breast augmentation were to become as common as straightening teeth? Acts of enhancement participate in enhancement practices that ultimately, though inadvertently, encourage spiritual vices (e.g., narcissism), not virtues. Such practices seem, moreover, to fall under the category of laying up your treasure on earth (Matt. 6:19–21).

The legitimate response to the creation mandate—the imperative to "work and keep" the garden—is to tend one's biochemical garden with reverence and respect for the Creator and the created order. Distinguishing between wise and foolish stewardship may be harder in some cases than others. Accordingly, Wendell Berry's words offer wise counsel: "It is plain to me that the line ought to be drawn without fail wherever it can be drawn easily."[37] What the company of the redeemed must always keep in mind

---

35. Parens, "Toward a More Fruitful Debate," 189.

36. Contrast this with O'Donovan's claim that morality and wisdom pertain to our willing participation in a created order that precedes us, such that "*is* implies *ought*" (O'Donovan, *Resurrection and Moral Order*, 17).

37. Berry, *Art of the Commonplace*, 79.

is whether what they say and do advances the main idea, and action, of the drama of redemption. Does it go with or against the grain of a creation groaning for transformation? Does it promote the practices of the kingdom of God? The line between grateful-responsible stewardship and irresponsible enhancement will be clearer if people keep in mind the reason for being here in the first place, the point of the whole play of creation. Hence it is to this matter that we now turn.

PHARMACOLOGICAL COGNITIVE ENHANCEMENT AND THE GOSPEL: TOWARD WHICH SALUS?

Science, medicine, and theology: each has an interest in saving lives, in *salus* ("health," "salvation"). Dr. Bright claims that using Epiginosko is instrumental to solving the world's energy crisis. The soteriological end justifies the pharmaceutical means. Increasingly, however, *salus* in a medicalized society means performing better than well for as long as possible. Berry puts the lie to this functional understanding of success: "The standard of performance tends to be set by the capacity of the technology rather than the individual nature of places and creatures."[38] The notion of "doing well" must relocate from the realm of psychopharmacology to theodrama. To perform well is to play one's part—to respond to one's vocation—in a way that pleases God: "well done, thou good and faithful servant." The question thus becomes, What are people trying to do in the world, and what can they use to improve their performance?

The Goal: Embodying the Mind of Christ. God's purpose in creating the world was to form persons with whom he can have fellowship and share his life—persons in his image, fully human (but not transhuman) persons who, like Jesus, know how to love God and others.[39] The aim of God's communicative action is ultimately self-communication: union and communion. This is *salus*: eternal life with, in, and through the triune God.

To see Jesus as the definition of true divinity and true humanity requires a reorientation of one's chief aim in life and a renovation of imagination. To view the world in light of the gospel is to see that the purpose of life is not merely to expand people's minds but to conform them, together with their whole lives, to the mind of Christ: to Jesus' way of thinking and acting. Jesus is "the way"; he is both means and end of truth and life (John 14:6). The problem is that too many adopt "the very ways and means that Jesus rejected" in order to pursue *salus* in a worldly fashion.[40] The aim must rather be to participate fittingly in what God is doing in Christ to renew all things: "For freedom Christ has set us free" (Gal. 5:1). The freedom to fit rightly into the created order is not achieved through enhancement; on the contrary, it is a gift of grace.

The Means of Grace: Word and Spirit as Means of Salus. If the end of life for human beings is to love God and neighbors as themselves—to live as people who are free

---

38. Wendell Berry, *The Way of Ignorance and Other Essays* (Berkeley, Calif.: Counterpoint, 2005), 87.

39. So C. Ben Mitchell et al., *Biotechnology and the Human Good* (Washington, D.C.: Georgetown Univ. Press, 2007), 150.

40. Peterson, *The Jesus Way*, 10.

(1 Peter 2:16) — how do they get there? What are the appropriate means by which people's natures may be redeemed, transformed, perfected? Put differently, What are the performance-enhancing means that enable people to realize their divine design plan? The question of means concerns the process by which something occurs, the mechanism that brings about some change. The Bible does indeed speak of an "advantage" that people need, but it is hardly biochemical.

Many have searched, like Faust, for that extra edge to give them an advantage over others. Some in the early church thought that Jews had a special advantage and that Christians had to avail themselves of this Jewish "technology" — namely, circumcision (as symbolic stand-in for the whole law). The apostle Paul puts the lie to this teaching: "Look: I, Paul, say to you that if you accept circumcision, Christ will be of no advantage to you" (Gal. 5:2). There is no other way to be right before God than the way of Jesus Christ.

Others in the church looked to "Greek" advantages. Certain Gentile Christians in the church at Colossae were apparently following a syncretistic philosophy that promised an ascetic way to gain power-knowledge over the body and the spirit world alike (Col. 2:16–23). Here, too, Paul responds that there is no other truly effective power-knowledge than the way and wisdom of the risen Christ. Once again, the key resides in the biblical imagination, the ability to see all things not only as created through and for Christ but as held together and reconciled in and through Christ (Col. 1:17–20).

To be sure, Jews and Christians have advantages: cognitive, moral, and spiritual. "Then what advantage has the Jew?" asks Paul in Romans 3:1. His reply: "the Jews were entrusted with the oracles of God" (Rom. 3:2). To have special access to the Word of God is no little thing. There is an additional advantage for the people of God. Jesus says to his disciples, "It is to your *advantage* that I go away" (John 16:7, emphasis added), referring to his death on the cross. Jesus' departure makes possible the performance-enhancing arrival of the Holy Spirit: "if I do not go away, the Helper will not come to you. But if I go, I will send him to you" (John 16:7).

In an era of biotechnological temptation, Christians must rededicate themselves to availing themselves of the distinctly Christian "advantage" of Jesus Christ, to wit, the triune "technology," as it were, of Word and Spirit. The Holy Spirit conforms disciples to the image of Jesus Christ by illumining and ministering the divine commands, promises, warnings, consolations, narratives, and so on that make up the canon. The Spirit uses the Scriptures to reprove, correct, and train his saints in righteousness (2 Tim. 3:16), to form in them the mind (including dispositions and desires) of Christ. What Christians need is not artificial enhancement but the "solid food" that improves their "powers of discernment" (Heb. 5:14). The word of Christ dwells in his followers richly (Col. 3:16), renewing their minds (Rom. 12:2). The peculiar "advantage" of Word and Spirit is nothing less than understanding and obedience. What Word and Spirit ultimately communicate is not merely information but a pattern of thinking and acting: the ability rightly to participate in the ongoing life of Christ through the Spirit.

Pharmaceutical cognitive enhancements are powerless to form the mind of Christ. How shortsighted Dr. Bright, Akira, Roberto, Jill, and Paul are to think that a drug can offer them an opportunity for "gaining every advantage," as the case study is titled. Epiginosko and other products of that ilk are no substitute for the bread and the wine that effect not enhancement but communion with the body of the risen Christ. In the final analysis, Christians must subscribe to the dis-analogy of enhancement: *this* (technological fittedness) is not *that* (theodramatic fittingness).

THE WAY OF COGNITIVE ENHANCEMENT VERSUS THE WAY OF TRUTH AND LIFE

The understanding that faith seeks is dramatic. The Christian actor-disciple must constantly improvise things to say and do that "fit" with the holy script and the theo-drama that defines his or her identity as one whose life is "hidden with Christ" (Col. 3:3). And this brings us back to our opening temptation narrative, and to the cathedral of modern learning: the university lab. What should the four students say and do—and, as we shall soon suggest, suffer—as concerns cognitive-enhancement technologies? How should Christians bear witness in the cathedral of learning?

Enhancement technology is first and foremost not a biochemical phenomenon but a philosophical and cultural ideal that is a peculiar yet distinctive by-product of modernity. The idea that technological advances will save humanity is a false hope proceeding from a false diagnosis. While some technologies (e.g., eyeglasses and aspirin) may be appropriate instances of wise stewardship (because they aim to restore rather than revise proper functioning), the *way* of pharmaceutical cognitive enhancement is mistaken, both as to end and means. To pursue *these* advantages is to preach a different *salus*, to march to the beat of a different gospel, to play scenes from some other drama than that of Jesus Christ.

The challenge for disciples of Jesus Christ is to speak and act in ways that bear witness to their faith in *God's* power-knowledge—the wisdom of the cross and resurrection—rather than their own. The church is the community whose vocation and mission is to communicate Christ, bearing witness by participating in the history of his covenantal effects. Soldiers are trained to snap to attention at the command "Present arms." The call to discipleship is even more urgent and demanding: "Present *bodies*" (as living sacrifices; Rom. 12:1). Discipleship begins with one person at a time leaving the advantages they enjoy in the world to take advantage of the way of Jesus Christ.

Among the four students in our case study, Paul is perhaps closest to following in his apostolic namesake's footsteps. Yet even he fails to see that the issue is not simply moral but martyrological. A martyr is one who suffers because of his or her witness. All Christians are called to bear witness to their identity in Christ, and this often means rejecting alternative ways of realizing one's identity or securing social status. In the face of temptations that promise a different kind of *salus*, martyrdom is a way of affirming the created order and of offering oneself up to the providence of God.[41] Specifically, it is a way of living that bears testimony to one's identification with the story of Jesus Christ by participating in practices whose ultimate aim is the power-in-weakness of the kingdom of God rather than the power-knowledge of earthly kingdoms.

Martyrdom is a communicative act, a costly countercultural expression of one's commitment to the truth of the gospel. Again, the issue is more than moral: what is ultimately at stake is the shape of the self, the very pattern of one's being as a person who hearkens above all to God's Word. Christians have been elected—cast in the divine drama—to be God's servants, not his masters: "thy will be done" (Matt. 26:42). It may be that Paul will suffer for his choice not to take Epiginosko. But it is in resisting this temptation to ill-gained power-knowledge that Paul can discover his proper part in the drama of redemption. For to surrender to Dr. Bright's temptation would mean compromising his true identity—the end for which he was created—and mistaking the true means of character and spiritual formation. It would be to aspire to some *salus* other than the one provided by Jesus Christ.

The test of the church today and in every age is whether it can bear true witness to the way of Jesus Christ. Like Paul (the student, not the apostle), Christians stand at a fateful crossroads. What they do next as concerns biotechnology will chart a course that cannot but leave a mark upon their souls. Like Paul (the apostle, not the student), Christians must be willing to suffer loss of status, and perhaps scorn, for living a theological life that understands its means and end in the light of the drama of creation and redemption. Those who are willing to do so would be in good company. For surely the apostle would count cognitive-enhancement technology too as loss, in view of the surpassing worth of another kind of cognition, aided by Word and Spirit—namely, "the surpassing worth of knowing Christ Jesus my Lord" (Phil. 3:8).

---

41. I am indebted for this way of putting it to Michael P. Jensen, *The Self on Trial: Martyrdom and Identity in Theological Perspective* (London: Continuum, 2010).

CHAPTER 6

WISDOM FROM LAW

Paige Comstock Cunningham

When people confront moral decisions, the first question they often ask is, What does the law say? Whether a question of first or last resort, it embodies the commonly held view that the law is the only standard that people can agree upon. In a culture of tolerance and letting all persons decide what is right for themselves, What does the law say? is the fallback position.

Some would acknowledge that the law embodies moral standards; others simply assert that the law represents enforceable standards of behavior that are socially desirable. Endless debates have addressed the purpose of enacted law. Its purpose may be to restrain evil behavior, to promote good behavior, to keep the peace. In any case, the "big stick" of governmental powers of enforcement presents a formidable first line of analysis in decisions about whether to pursue a morally troubling or ambiguous line of conduct. Thus, Paul's concern—"Are these drugs legal?"—is understandable. Lawfulness should not be the sum of a Christian's ethical analysis, but it is a consideration that could preclude further deliberation. If a law clearly prohibits the use of this drug, then people normally should not violate it.

THE SIGNIFICANCE OF LEGALITY
THE LAW AND MORALITY

Societies historically have understood the law to embody both moral and rational components. Lawmakers (legislators) and lawgivers (judges) have believed their mandate to involve discovering the law, rather than creating or shaping it. More recently, the theory of legal positivism has supplanted this "natural law" understanding. According to this theory, as long as the commands are knowable and consistent, law is whatever the reigning powers decide, without regard to its moral content. Legal positivism enabled the atrocities of totalitarian regimes in the twentieth century, such as Stalinist USSR and Hitler's Germany. The United States never fully embraced legal positivism, and largely rejected it after the Second World War. Since then, a variety of legal theories have waxed and waned.[1]

Nonetheless, there is still some sense that the law ought to have a normative aspect, and that the rule of law is binding on everyone. Justice is not to be capricious or sporadic but impartial, with the same rules for the president as for the pauper. The rules should be clear and known in advance. The law protects and promotes values such as individual liberty, equality, and social justice, values that contribute to the moral basis of the rule of law. The challenge for Paul and the other students is that, even though legal rules about drugs may be "clear and known in advance," their applicability to Epiginosko may be obscure.

How much moral weight does the law carry? There are at least three answers to this question. First, the law might embody moral conclusions, emerging from open and honest debate. In that case, the law points people in the direction of moral reasoning. The law acts as a moral teacher. Criminal statutes punishing murder are an example of clear moral mandates. A second possibility is that the law represents the minimum moral standard; it signals the outer limits of moral behavior but does not embody the highest virtues or a complete ethical framework. Regulations against embezzlement, for instance, do not also forbid greed. The third option is that the law represents no particular universal moral standard but simply the pragmatic conclusions of a legal authority as to what is expedient for the time being. Traffic laws—red means "stop"—illustrate this option. Under this option, the decision whether to follow the law—not the content of the law itself—is where the moral calculus occurs.

For many people, the moral inquiry begins and ends with the question of legality. Their thinking may follow a familiar pattern: "If it's legal, it must be right. If it's illegal, it may or may not be right, but I will think twice before doing it." This is not an entirely misguided approach, as a significant part of law is premised on moral considerations. In this line of thinking, "legal" equates with "morally acceptable," and "illegal" denotes "immoral," or at least "morally unacceptable." Considering the legality of something can involve both a positive and a negative inclination: (1) a desire to do what is right in the eyes of the law (for example, obtaining a building permit), and (2) an avoidance of negative consequences (for example, avoiding a speeding ticket). Thus, there are elements both of compliance, in obeying the law, and of self-protection, by avoiding punishment. The heart of the matter here is the motive of one's heart. Does compliance arise out of a conviction that we obey laws because they are right, or do we obey because obedience is right? Before we can answer that question in the case before us, we need to clarify some categories related to the legality of the drugs involved.

---

1. There have been a variety of theories of legal jurisprudence, including legal science, legal realism, law and economics, critical legal studies, feminist legal theory, and postmodern neopragmatic constitutional law. See Stephen B. Presser and Jamil S. Zainaldin, *Law and Jurisprudence in American History*, 3rd ed. (St. Paul, Minn.: West, 1995).

Criminal laws have a more obvious moral element than most regulations. People immediately recognize many of the prohibited behaviors as wrong, behaviors such as murder, assault, and theft. Lawyers characterize them as *malum in se*—that is, intrinsically evil or immoral. Of course, not every immoral act is also a criminal act. Regulations tend to deal with behavior that is not wrongful in and of itself but that impacts the public good, such as tax laws and parking regulations. Thus, conduct that is *malum prohibitum* is wrong because the law says so. We will need to determine here where drug use fits. Is it intrinsically wrong?

LAW, MORALITY, AND CHRISTIANS

When legality is the first question a Christian asks, we must pay attention to the reason behind the question. Does the person have a true desire to understand, know, and do what is right, and to avoid doing what is wrong? Is there a commitment to follow the law, regardless of the person's views about the wisdom of the particular law? Does the question reflect a desire to get by, to avoid running afoul of the law, or at least to know what the laws says and what the punishment is, to facilitate considering whether to risk breaking the law?

In the case study before us, by questioning whether Epiginosko is legal, Paul likely is contemplating enacted law, that vast body of federal and state statutes, regulations, and ordinances.[2] The Christian has a moral imperative to obey the law that may or may not occur to the nonbeliever. Paul ought to take into account the question of whether people have an obligation to obey all laws passed by those in authority over them, even if people do not agree that a particular law represents optimal, or even good, public policy.[3] Asserting that one knows better, that the law does not apply, or that ignoring it is inconsequential prepares a fertile bed for the seeds of antinomianism. *Antinomianism* means "against the law" (*anti* = against; *nomos* = law), or lawlessness. It usually refers to moral law but can also apply to human-generated or human-enacted law. Every time a person chooses to disobey the law, the antinomian tendency toward private judgment and self-rule grows.

DECISION-MAKING FLOW CHART

Since legal considerations play a role in the case before us, we would do well to clarify what a good legal analysis entails. A routine style of legal argument is to present a variety

---

2. *Legal* may also refer to judicial decisions about statutory and constitutional law, but these are of lesser relevance for the present case.

3. The apostle Paul reminded the church in Rome to obey the authority, regardless of how oppressive it was: "Let everyone be subject to the governing authorities, for there is no authority except that which God has established. The authorities that exist have been established by God" (Rom.

13:1 NIV). Nevertheless, there is no obligation to follow those laws that violate clear scriptural commands, and civil disobedience may even be necessary. In such cases, people may also be called to submit to the penalty for violating that law. An example might be a law that requires physicians to prescribe the morning after pill for thirteen- and fourteen-year-old girls.

of possibilities that could support one's position, beginning with the strongest point. Because the first argument may not settle the dispute, the advocate raises other grounds on which to win a legal victory, until he or she has exhausted all possibilities. The approach resembles a "just in case" argument. After all, a win on different legal grounds is still a win. The same approach may be helpful in examining our case from a legal perspective, but with a twist. This approach includes the additional context of paying attention to the moral questions and not simply the legal concerns. If the intended outcome is a legal win, then every possible legal argument should be evaluated. If the intended outcome is the best moral decision, then moral considerations should be explicit.

A useful decision-making flow chart concerning potential drug use would include both dimensions:

1. Is the drug use legal? If the answer is no,
   - the substance or activity should be avoided,
   - but if there are sufficient reasons to justify illegal activity, then the actor should accept the consequences of unlawful conduct, including punishment.
2. Is the drug use legal? If the answer is yes,
   - the actor may lawfully ingest the substance or engage in the conduct,
   - but this does not end the inquiry. Any of the following may also counsel against engaging in the conduct:
     It may not be lawful for all persons.
     It may not be lawful for every purpose.
     Not every lawful activity is necessarily moral.
     It may pose an undue risk.
     The actor might not be free from coercion.
     Use of the substance may violate principles of justice.
3. Is the drug use legal? If the answer is unknown,
   - the actor must exercise caution;
   - further inquiry is necessary prior to an affirmative decision.

The case study does not present a black-and-white factual situation that leads toward an easy analysis and quick decision. It is not clear whether Epiginosko is legal, although the facts certainly point toward illegality. It is not clear what type of drug Epiginosko is, although the facts certainly suggest it presents harms of the same magnitude as methylphenidate and dextroamphetamines. These are not insurmountable obstacles to good decision-making, as the flow chart can accommodate all of these variables. Difficulty does not excuse dodging the question.

Overall, the scenario is suspect, giving the impression that something rather fishy is going on. Additionally, Dr. Bright's behavior cues the reader that he is aware that his plan may be unethical or illegal. Even so, it is useful to examine all the possibilities, to give the widest possible latitude to consideration of the ethical and legal questions. Each decision point in the flow chart will receive due consideration.

IS EPIGINOSKO LEGAL? NOT LIKELY
REGULATION OF DRUGS

Congress has passed a number of laws that relate to the approval of drugs, such as the Food, Drug and Cosmetic Act of 1938, the Controlled Substances Act of 1970, and the Prescription Drug Marketing Act of 1987. The first of these delegates significant regulatory and rule-making authority to the Food and Drug Administration (FDA). Other agencies with enforcement power include the Department of Health and Human Services, and the Drug Enforcement Administration. The FDA approves prescription, over-the-counter, and generic drugs. The agency's enforcement power includes issuing warning letters and recalls, import bans, seizures, injunctions, civil money penalties, and criminal arrests (which can result in imprisonment).

The approval process for a new drug is lengthy and expensive, taking on average eight to twelve years and costing the manufacturer perhaps $350 million.[4] The FDA appoints expert review committees to evaluate the NDA (New Drug Application), data from clinical trials, and other evidence of the safety and efficacy of the drug. FDA approval implies that a drug is safe and effective for a specific medical use, under a particular dosage and regimen. In some cases, there may be age restrictions to prevent certain pediatric populations from using the drug. A drug approved for a specific use and dosage may not be marketed for other nonspecified purposes, or for different dosages or regimens—so-called off-label use. While pharmaceutical companies may not market their drugs for other uses, physicians are free to prescribe for off-label use.[5]

In fact, off-label use has led to the discovery of some additional beneficial applications. For example, modafinil (Provigil), a drug for treating sleep disorders—to help insomniacs sleep—can also help international travelers and physicians on night call, to enable them to stay awake and alert. Sometimes drug developers have one purpose in mind, yet the drug ends up being effective in treating another condition and the FDA reapproves it for that condition. The original intention for Adderall, an amphetamine-dextroamphetamine combination, was to promote weight loss, but it has since received approval for treatment of ADHD and narcolepsy.[6] Patients use Mifepristone (RU 486) primarily as an abortifacient, but also for breast cancer treatment.[7]

---

4. US Food and Drug Administration, US Department of Health and Human Services, "New Drug Approval Process," *http://www.drugs.com/fda-approval-process.html* (accessed January 28, 2010).

5. Randall S. Stafford, "Regulating Off-Label Drug Use: Rethinking the Role of the FDA," *New England Journal of Medicine* 358 (April 3, 2008): 1427–29.

6. K. Ullman, "Could an ADHD Med Double as a Weight Loss Drug?" *http://docnews.diabetesjournals.org/content/4/7/17.short* (accessed April 19, 2010); "Adderall," *http://www.drugs.com/adderall.html* (accessed April 19,

2010); Medline Plus, "Dextroamphetamine and Amphetamine," *http://www.nlm.nih.gov/medlineplus/druginfo/meds/a601234.html* (accessed January 10, 2010).

7. S. S. Kode, "Mifepristone: Auxiliary Therapeutic Use in Cancer and Related Disorders," *Journal of Reproductive Medicine* 43, no. 7 (July 1998): 551, *http://www.ncbi.nlm.nih.gov/pubmed/9693404* (accessed January 10, 2010); Medline Plus, "Dextroamphetamine and Amphetamine," *http://www.nlm.nih.gov/medlineplus/druginfo/meds/a601234.html* (accessed January 10, 2010).

Certain drugs have greater restrictions. These "controlled substances" are narcotics, or drugs with effects similar to narcotics, which have a high risk of abuse or addiction. The Drug Enforcement Administration sets schedules for regulating such drugs. Schedule I drugs are highly addictive and have no medical use. Schedule I includes drugs such as heroin and crack cocaine. Schedule II drugs do have legitimate medical uses but also carry a high risk of physical or psychological dependence. Examples are oxycodone, methylphenidate (Ritalin), and dextroamphetamine (Dexedrine and Adderall). Schedule III, IV, and V drugs may contain mixtures of narcotic and nonnarcotic drugs, such as Tylenol with codeine and diazepam (Valium).[8]

Ritalin, the first drug Dr. Bright used, has been a schedule II drug since 1971. It is illegal to use methylphenidate (Ritalin) without a prescription. Physicians prescribe Ritalin for patients with ADD or ADHD. It is easy to obtain a prescription for Ritalin,[9] and easy to sell individual pills to those who do not have ADD or ADHD. Students have discovered its cognitive-enhancing properties, creating a black market for Ritalin among students.[10] Nonprescription use has increased even among preadolescents.[11] One in five scientists has admitted to nonprescription use of drugs to enhance their cognitive performance, with Ritalin being the most common.[12]

Even though Ritalin is legal for medical reasons and with a properly authorized prescription, it is not legal for nonprescription, nonmedical use. This may be sufficient to end the Four's decision-making. If Epiginosko is a schedule II drug like Ritalin, they should decline Dr. Bright's offer.

EPIGINOSKO: EPIGENETIC NEUROPHARMACEUTICALS

The facts do not reveal whether Epiginosko is related to the drugs prescribed by Dr. Bauble for Dr. Bright. Although his first "cognitive enhancement" was an approved schedule II drug, the most recent formulation may not resemble any controlled substance. Thus, it is not clear what schedule, if any, applies. Its brain-altering design would seem to place Epiginosko in a separate class. If so, there are even fewer grounds for believing it is a legitimate drug.

8. Texas State Board of Pharmacy, "Controlled Drugs," http://www.tsbp.state.tx.us/consumer/broch2.htm (accessed January 10, 2010).

9. The website for Trapmusik.com links to a site purporting to offer "Ritalin without a prescription," http://www.trapmuzik.com/profiles/blog/list?user=0f34vsawfx96m, entry dated January 27, 2010.

10. Christiane Poulin, "From Attention-Deficit/Hyperactivity Disorder to Medical Stimulant Use to the Diversion of Prescribed Stimulants to Non-medical Stimulant Use: Connecting the Dots," Addiction 207, no. 5 (May 2007): 740–51; BBC News Health, "Brain Boost Drugs 'Growing Trend'" (October 13, 2008), http://news.bbc.co.uk/2/hi/7666722.stm (accessed January 27, 2010).

11. Josh Hamilton and Robert Ivker, "'Quick-Fix' Pills and Internet Peddling Condemned in World Narcotics Report," Lancet 349 (March 15, 1997): 784.

12. Marlowe Hood, "One in 5 Scientists Admits to Drug Use," http://www.theage.com.au/news/world/one-in-5-scientists-admits-to-drug-use/2008/04/10/1207420587015.html (accessed January 27, 2010).

In asking whether Epiginosko is legal, Paul vocalizes the surreptitious nature of the experiment. All facts point toward illegality: Dr. Bright held the after-dinner discussion behind closed doors. He confided "a secret" about his own experience with a cognitive-enhancing drug. The drug arrived in the United States from an undisclosed country. It is murky whether Epiginosko is legal in the country of manufacture. Legal approval by a foreign authority could at least suggest potential approval by the FDA. Dr. Bright, while not precisely admitting the illegality of Epiginosko, asserts that all the other drugs "inevitably will become legal and ought to be now." Unlike the methylphenidate (Ritalin), amphetamines (such as Adderall), and dextroamphetamines (such as Dexedrine) that Dr. Bright likely experimented with, Epiginosko — "an epigenetic neuropharmaceutical" — does not appear to be approved for any medical purpose.

The legal conclusion would seem clear: Epiginosko is not legal, and the Four should refuse to participate in Dr. Bright's experiment.

IS EPIGINOSKO LEGAL? FURTHER CONSIDERATIONS
LEGAL IN THE COUNTRY OF MANUFACTURE

Even though the facts seem to point toward a conclusion of illegality, it is possible that Dr. Bright is telling the truth, and that at least the precursor to Epiginosko, Ginosko, is authorized in Dr. Bauble's country of residence. If so, the Four may rationalize that Ginosko, and perhaps Epiginosko as well, is safe and okay to use because the appropriate agency in that country has authorized its manufacture and distribution in some form. They could also claim that the foreign manufacturer cannot afford the expensive new-drug approval process in the US, or that the FDA is dilatory in approving it.

The FDA at times permits travelers to bring back a drug they have purchased overseas legally, even if the FDA has not approved the drug; the importation must be exclusively for personal use. Additionally, during the approval process, the FDA may authorize use of an investigational drug for patients with a life-threatening illness, or for whom no other drug therapy is working, under the FDA's "compassionate use" exception. Clearly, the Four would not qualify for this kind of exception. Rationalizing the legality of Epiginosko, then, is based on the assumption that because Epiginosko and Ginosko have similar names, their clinical mechanism and legality are also similar. Nothing in Dr. Bright's description — nor the known legality of Ritalin — gives them a basis for that notion.

Nonetheless, the rationalizations above may be sufficiently attractive to draw them into experimenting with Epiginosko. The Four also have an incentive to see any delay in FDA approval as an encouragement rather than a caution: the rarity of the drug in the United States will give them a temporary competitive edge, at least until potential FDA approval. For the sake of argument, let us assume that Epiginosko is legal in the country of manufacture, and that it does not fit within established categories of controlled substances or banned imports. The Four might convince themselves that it is more like an herbal supplement or a nutritional additive, which is outside FDA jurisdiction. That would be rationalization and self-delusion of the highest order, as Dr. Bauble is manufacturing Epiginosko as a pharmacological, not herbal, potion to rewire the brain.

NOT ILLEGAL, BUT OTHER RULES MIGHT APPLY

The FDA is not the only governmental authority with power over drug distribution and use. Government authorities such as public schools and athletic associations have rule-making authority. They can prohibit the possession or use of drugs, steroids, cigarettes, and alcohol. Some schools have declared themselves to be free of nuclear weapons or firearms.[13] Private organizations and associations may also establish rules for their members, including private universities. Ethics codes, speech codes, and so on, can limit personal freedoms students might otherwise enjoy.

Whether it is a public university or private institution, Highcastle University may have legally enforceable policies that would impact the students' freedom to experiment with Epiginosko. However, these may not be applicable to graduate students. Institutions generally have greater authority and greater legal responsibility for minors, and may prohibit adult students under twenty-one from consuming alcoholic beverages. Certainly any university may prohibit the distribution or use of illegal substances on campus. Dr. Bright solicited, and is on the verge of distributing, a seemingly illegal substance. His conduct is suspicious and possibly criminal.

Even if Highcastle does not have an explicit code banning use of cognitive-enhancing or performance-enhancing drugs, its academic integrity policy might arguably cover drug-enhanced academic "cheating." Highcastle may be part of an accrediting or academic association that issues academic integrity policies, whether explicit or implicit, that would prevent recognition of achievement-by-Epiginosko. Just as in athletic competitions, there may be expectations of drug-free academic competition, a kind of clean Nobel Prize. A Nobel Prize winner in biology "was reprimanded because someone in his laboratory had falsified data in an experiment."[14] Using prohibited cognitive enhancements to make discoveries may simply be an ethical violation of a different but related sort, prompting admiration for the accomplishment but disdain for those who accomplish it.

Perhaps an increase in the use of such drugs will lead to random drug testing prior to final exams. Or the consequence of using drugs to achieve academic honors may be similar to the scenario in professional baseball: an explanatory footnote may have

13. "High School Forms Nuclear Free Zone," *Bangor Daily News* (November 10, 1982), *http://news.google.com/newspapers?nid=2457&dat=19821110&id=F1szAAAAIBAJ&sjid=qDgHAAAAIBAJ&pg=2843,3948836* (accessed April 14, 2010).

14. Brooklyn College Policy Council, "Statement on Academic Integrity for Brooklyn College Students," Brooklyn College, *http://academic.brooklyn.cuny.edu/core3/currah/acinteg.htm* (accessed January 21, 2010).

to accompany any accomplishment that a student achieves under the influence of a cognitive-enhancing drug, thereby undermining the prestige value of the achievement for the student. Epiginosko-aided discoveries would be tainted, depriving the students of the status and recognition they crave.

LEGAL IN THE US? MAYBE, BUT RISKY

Dr. Bright implies that all the drugs he uses are legal in the country of origin. Even though they are shipped from a pharmacy connected with Dr. Bauble, there is no guarantee that the manufacturing of these drugs takes place in this particular country, or that the manufacturing processes meet adequate standards of safety, purity, and consistency. Even if the Four can reasonably assume that Dr. Bright is telling the truth, their inquiry is not complete. The drugs could be narcotics, and therefore subject to international laws, conventions, or treaties.

Canadian pharmacies urge consumers to "buy cheaper drugs online" from them. The FDA does not recommend purchasing generic versions of FDA-approved drugs, because they may pose risk. The manufacturer may not meet standards of purity and may be marketing a drug with unidentified, counterfeit, or contaminated ingredients.[15] The students have no way of verifying the origin of the Epiginosko. If it was "home brewed," the possibility of contamination, improper dosage, or counterfeit ingredients may be even higher. Prudence counsels caution.

UNANTICIPATED ADVERSE SIDE EFFECTS

Even if the Four cannot discover what class of drug Epiginosko is, there are sufficient reasons to raise a red flag. Other drugs that Dr. Bauble has developed could be precursors to Epiginosko. Even legal drugs have side effects that are often serious. There are current safety concerns about methylphenidate (Ritalin), the first drug Dr. Bright "borrowed" from his son, and the patient must be carefully monitored. Methylphenidate can "aggravate mental illness, produce sleep disturbances and is associated with cerebrovascular complications."[16] Even if the drug successfully enhances memory in a "normal" person, there may be no limitation on the quality of those memories. Some evidence indicates that methylphenidate enhances one's "ability to recall aversive events."[17] After repeatedly ingesting Epiginosko, the students may wake up one day to find themselves living in the inverse of the "eternal sunshine of the spotless mind."[18] One of the authors

---

15. US Food and Drug Administration, "Importing Prescription Drugs," *http://www.fda.gov/Drugs/DrugSafety/ucm170594.htm* (accessed May 26, 2010).

16. V. Cakic, "Smart Drugs for Cognitive Enhancement: Ethical and Pragmatic Considerations in the Era of Cosmetic Neurology," *Journal of Medical Ethics* 35 (2009): 613.

17. Ibid.

18. The movie *Eternal Sunshine of the Spotless Mind* is the fable of a couple who undergo an experimental procedure to erase their memories of each other after their two-year relationship goes sour.

of a recent study of Ritalin concludes that nonmedical use of methylphenidate "can have structural and biochemical effects in some regions of the brain that can be even greater than those of cocaine."[19] Cocaine seems to change brain structure permanently. Part of withdrawal and healing from cocaine addiction may entail "rewiring" the parts of the brain that have been damaged.[20] Epiginosko could pose a similar risk, as it permanently alters synaptic connections, changing normal brain function. Part of that change could affect the users' ability to detect negative side effects.

Dr. Bright's alluring promises of a "substantial boost of brain capability," of "mental stimulation," and of being "supercharged" faintly echo writers and artists of the past who used drugs. LSD influenced their art; opium, morphine, or heroine influenced their writing. In the process, many became addicts.[21] Could Dr. Bright's hype reveal someone who is unable to detect the deluding impact of his own illicit drug use? It may have inflated his self-perception or blunted his assessment of his work.

There are deep concerns that some technological innovations might themselves impair the ability of the enhanced person to evaluate their impact. "The difficult question for regulators of various performance-enhancing neuropharmacological interventions is whether they have the potential to blunt users' perceptions of the deep changes they wreak in users themselves."[22] Thus, those who advocate most strongly for their approval may be doing so because they are dependent on the actual or promised benefits of the drug, yet unable to notice any adverse impact. For those considering whether to approve or use such drugs, "new neural performance enhancement addiction might work in a far subtler way [than substance addiction] by blunting the appeal of alternate sources of value and satisfaction."[23] People may not be aware of the possibility that they may eventually realize that they have lost or compromised their authentic or "real" selves.[24]

Could Paul and the others become dependent on Epiginosko and unable to function academically (or even nonacademically) without it? Would they be "more" of a student

19. "Ritalin May Change Brain in the Same Way Cocaine Does," *The Medical News* (February 5, 2009), *http://www.news-medical.net/news/2009/02/05/45622.aspx* (accessed January 10, 2010), reporting the following study: Y. Kim, M. A. Teylan, M. Baron, A. Sands, A. C. Nairn, and P. Greengard, "Methylphenidate-Induced Dendritic Spine Formation and ΔFosB Expression in Nucleus Accumbens," *Proceedings of the National Academy of Science* 106, no. 8 (February 24, 2009): 2915–20. See also National Institute on Drug Abuse, "NIDA Study Shows That Methylphenidate (Ritalin) Causes Neuronal Changes in Brain Reward Areas," *http://drugabuse.gov/newsroom/09/NR2-02.html* (accessed January 9, 2010).

20. S. Pendyam, A. Mohan, P. W. Kaliva, and S. S. Nair, "Computational Model of Extracellular Glutamate in the Nucleus Accumbens Incorporates Neuroadaptations by Chronic Cocaine," *Behavioural Neuroscience* 158, no. 4 (February 18, 2009): 1266–76.

21. Marcus Boon, *The Road of Excess: A History of Writers on Drugs* (Cambridge: Harvard Univ. Press, 2002). See also *http://www.cowboybooks.com.au/html/acidtrip1.html* (accessed May 26, 2010).

22. Frank Pasquale, "Technology, Competition, and Values," *Minnesota Journal of Law, Science and Technology* 8 (Spring 2007): 622. (This is part of a symposium: Toward a General Theory of Law and Technology.)

23. Ibid., 620.

24. Roberta M. Berry, "Genetic Enhancements in the Twenty-First Century: Three Problems in Legal Imagining," *Wake Forest Law Review* 34 (Fall 1999): 715–35, 730. See also the discussion of enhancement technologies and American life in Carl Elliott, *Better Than Well: American Medicine Meets the American Dream* (New York: Norton, 2003).

when under the influence of Epiginosko? Would dependence on the drug be any more serious than dependence on caffeine? These questions go beyond concerns about safety and legality, penetrating the deep issues of human identity.

Potential drug-induced changes are not merely physiological or temporary but may work in a subtler way by altering the user's attraction to other values and different satisfactions. Thus, unlike the heroin addict whose addiction is apparent when heroin is withdrawn, the "cogno-addict" may argue quite persuasively for the value of the new drug as a positive benefit all around, whether she is currently using or not. The danger is that she may be arguing on different grounds than she used to. Rather than pursuing cognitive development and academic excellence as one dimension of her life, she may come to see them as the primary value of her human existence, the *sine qua non* for all other human activity.

Gordijn raises similar concerns in his discussion of the convergence of various new technologies (nanotechnology, biotechnology, information technology, and cognitive enhancement, shorthanded as NBIC). The advocates of this convergence celebrate it as "something pivotal and highly positive."[25] Although Gordijn is primarily addressing computer-to-brain and brain-to-brain implant technologies, his concerns are apropos. NBIC technologies assume the "transform[ation of] our biological design for the purpose of enhancing performance."[26] A natural outcome might be a revised attitude toward the body, where people increasingly come to see the body as a kind of machine with replaceable parts (that may be superior to the original!) and an intertwining of flesh and technology to the extent that they cannot be distinguished. Thus, in the attempt to gain dominance and control via technology, the "cogno-addict" may indeed become a slave to technology. As C. S. Lewis prophetically warned us about presuming to retain ultimate control over the technologies we create, desire, and consume, "Man's conquest of Nature turns out, in the moment of its consummation, to be Nature's conquest of Man."[27]

OVERUSE AND LONG-TERM RISKS

Additionally, there is uncertainty regarding dose response or dosage abuse—using the drug more frequently or in a stronger dosage than clinical testing has demonstrated to be safe. The President's Council on Bioethics, in discussing potential adverse side effects of biotechnical agents, suggests that "until proven otherwise ... [n]o biological agent powerful enough to achieve major changes in body or mind is likely to be entirely safe or without side effects."[28] The report cites the well-documented adverse effects of

---

25. Bert Gordijn, "Converging NBIC Technologies for Improving Human Performance: A Critical Assessment of the Novelty and the Prospects of the Project," *Journal of Law, Medicine and Ethics* 34 (Winter 2006): 728.

26. Ibid., 730.

27. C. S. Lewis, *The Abolition of Man* (New York: Macmillan, 1965), 80.

28. US President's Council on Bioethics, *Beyond Therapy: Biotechnology and the Pursuit of Happiness* (New York: HarperCollins, 2003), 137.

anabolic steroids: "liver tumors, fluid retention, high blood pressure, infertility, premature cessation of growth in adolescents, and psychological effects from excessive mood swings to drug dependence."[29] One study suggests that use of methylphenidate (Ritalin) increases the rate of smoking among adults who already smoke.[30] Another study suggests that subjects who previously ingested methylphenidate may have higher sensitivity to amphetamines, regardless of their age when they took Ritalin.[31]

Should the Four be willing to accept similar long-term, possibly permanent risks? Athletes know they risk physical injury as an inevitable part of most sports. Academics have no expectation of bodily harm in their bookish pursuits. Research laboratories employ stringent safety precautions to prevent exposure to toxic chemical or biological agents. Requiring the Four to accept "voluntarily" a significant risk of bodily harm without safety precautions as a condition of their research with Dr. Bright appears to be inappropriate.

The students could be embarking on an experiment more dangerous than steroid overuse. The total range of adverse effects may not be evident for quite some time. There have been no comprehensive studies of the long-term health effects of the nonprescription use of drugs such as Ritalin, particularly among adolescents. Unapproved, novel drugs have not been evaluated for side effects on those who have a diagnosed medical need, much less those who use such substances for enhancement purposes.

Thankfully the Four are not engaged in the kind of work where drug use is prohibited for reasons of public safety. For example, train conductors may not take cocaine; airline pilots may not consume alcohol prior to flying.[32] Because alcohol and other drugs can impair judgment, thereby increasing the risk of an accident and significant loss of life, the government has enacted strict regulations on their consumption. Nevertheless, the interest these graduate students have in expanding the use of the drug to undergraduate students suggests that there may well be risks involved in this situation that are more than individual and private in nature. Not only may the manufacturer be liable for damage done if the drug proves to be harmful, but anyone using an enhancement drug such as Epiginosko might sue if it does not increase or it impairs their cognitive powers.[33]

29. Ibid.

30. C. R. Rush, S. T. Higgins, A. R. Vansickel, W. W. Stoops, J. A. Lile, and P. E. Glaser, "Methylphenidate Increases Cigarette Smoking," *Psychopharmacology* 181, no. 4 (2005): 781–89.

31. P. B. Yang, A. C. Swann, and N. Dafny, "Chronic Pretreatment with Methylphenidate Induces Cross-Sensitization with Amphetamine," *Life Sciences* 73, no. 22 (2003): 2899–911. Another study found no increase in sensitivity with long-term, low-dose use of Ritalin: R. Kuczenski and D. S. Segal, "Exposure of Adolescent Rats to Oral Methylphenidate: Preferential Effects on Extracellular Norepinephrine and Absence of Sensitization and Cross-Sensitization to Methamphetamine," *Journal of Neuroscience* 22, no. 16 (2002): 7264–71.

32. Federal Aviation Regulation CFR 91.17. The rationale for the ban on consuming alcoholic beverages less than eight hours prior to flight is outlined in "Alcohol and Flying: A Deadly Combination," *http://flightphysical.com/pilot/alcohol.htm* (accessed January 28, 2010).

33. See Berry, "Genetic Enhancements in the Twenty-First Century." Berry is referring to a hypothetical case of genetic enhancement and serious harms resulting from errors in the genetic enhancement. The legal issues she suggests might arise if the enhancement via a drug, or a device such as a computer-brain interface, goes awry.

BEYOND LEGALITY: AUTONOMY

The enhancement-seeker may claim that as an autonomous individual, she is free to take any substance or utilize any technology she wishes, as long as she is fully informed concerning safety considerations, risks to her health, and overall effectiveness. In fact, she might not care about risk, but only her "right to do as she pleases." The reliance on individual autonomy as a trump card that overcomes every kind of objection is a familiar one. "As long as it doesn't hurt anyone else, why can't I do what I wish with my own body?" Autonomy is not only a fundamental value in American law and public policy; it is a bedrock principle of biomedical ethics.

Autonomy presumes the freedom and ability to make an informed choice. The individual must have the legal capacity to consent, which the students do have, since they are legally adults. The individual must also have the mental capacity to understand information about a drug regimen, including its benefits and risks. Again, the talented physics students presumably understand what is at stake.

INFORMED CONSENT

However, no one may have provided the Four with all the relevant information about possible risks. Dr. Bright urged them not to "let that risk deter you from finding your personal destiny," casually dismissing the risks from cocaine, another brain-altering drug. When he rejected the notion that enhancement raises ethical concerns, Dr. Bright "[blotted] the sweat from his twitching brow." This might have signaled a side effect of twenty years of using Ginosko and possibly Epiginosko. If so, Dr. Bright has a duty to disclose. Roberto should have pressed his inquiry further, probing any ill effects Dr. Bright might have experienced and exploring why the postdoctoral fellow withdrew under mysterious circumstances. Was he damaged by drug use? Without substantially complete information, the Four could not give informed consent to using Epiginosko.

The law in many settings, such as the United States, is quite protective of informed consent. It sees informed consent as grounded in one of the basic principles of medical ethics, autonomy.[34] The overarching purpose of the informed-consent requirement is to ensure that no one medically treats people or subjects them to research without their voluntary agreement based on sufficient information. There are additional layers of protection for minors and others who presumably lack the legal capacity to give informed consent. In order to give truly informed consent, patients and research participants must understand the proposed procedure, including its potential benefits and harms and the alternatives to it, and must make a decision free from coercion or manipulation.

We have already observed that the Four do not appear genuinely to understand

---

34. Other basic principles in the commonly invoked "four-principles" approach include nonmaleficence, beneficence, and justice, as described in Tom L. Beauchamp and James F. Childress, *Principles of Biomedical Ethics*, 6th ed. (New York: Oxford Univ. Press, 2008).

what Dr. Bright is asking them to do. Nor do they acknowledge that they are aware of alternatives. They have not received the accurate or complete information required for informed consent. After dinner, the Four agree to Dr. Bright's plan, but they have not yet explicitly consented. The enthusiasm of the majority overrules the misgivings that Paul expresses the next morning. Dr. Bauble's startling appearance with, presumably, the drugs and a consent form curtails any further considerations. His role is not to facilitate full disclosure but simply to get their signatures. True informed consent is about a process, not a signature on a form. Although signatures will not protect Dr. Bauble from a lawsuit, they might suggest that these extremely bright students know just what they are doing. But are they genuinely free from coercion?

COERCION

Dr. Bright—through his careful manipulation of the setting, his wine that may have dulled their mental acuity and lowered their natural defenses, and his appeal to their pride—has curtailed any opportunity for genuinely free reflection and assessment of the potential benefits and harms. Coercion can take many forms, depending on the setting.

Coercion may be overt, implicit, or parental. Overt coercion occurs when military authorities or private employers require the use of a particular technology. More subtle coercion is the implicit coercion students may experience when they feel the need to take a drug in order to compete. Parental coercion can occur when parents select an enhancement for their children pursuant to their decision-making authority for their minor children. Parents can exercise informed consent on behalf of their children, and they can urge their children to succeed, encouragement which may push children to partake of a new technology they might not otherwise consider. (Of course, more often it is the child who is eager to try out new technologies and the parent who is reluctant.)

Soft or implicit coercion is commonly persuasive because of people's desire to get ahead both economically and socially. Pursuit of academic recognition, however, may be linked to desire for other kinds of gains. Academic excellence for its own sake may give way to the pressure to win a Nobel Prize or a plum teaching post. The Four may not be aware that this kind of coercive pressure has no upward limits. As Dr. Bright's own experience illustrates, one type of cognitive-enhancing drug leads to another, and then another, each a more potent combination than the previous one.

Not everyone shares this concern. Cakic notes that the pressure to use cognitive-enhancing drugs is likely to be higher at academically competitive colleges, where competition is already the norm. These students are already "wired" to compete, and they expect a serious contest to reach the top of the class. He argues that the better course is simply to disclose risks and allow the individual to decide, rather than limit their personal freedom based on a concern about indirect coercion.[35]

---

35. Cakic, "Smart Drugs," 612.

However, Dr. Bright's actions illustrate how easy it is for indirect coercion essentially to have the force of more direct coercion. His orchestration of the evening soiree, his closing the door, and his psychological manipulation are very powerful. The threats of exclusion from the elite group and possible loss of research opportunity are quite daunting. This level of coercion renders informed consent a virtual impossibility.

In fact, the Four may not be the only ones experiencing coercion here. Dr. Bauble may be as well. He has already benefited from his illicit procurement of the drug for Dr. Bright. Dr. Bright shared book royalties with Dr. Bauble; the incentive may be greater to share in the fruits of the anticipated Nobel Prize. Whether Dr. Bauble is acting purely of his own free will is not clear. There is only Dr. Bright's assertion that Dr. Bauble regards his role as drug procurer as "his own contribution to the advancement of science."

However, for someone supposedly so admirable, Dr. Bauble's professional judgment and integrity are suspect. Dr. Bauble intends to write prescriptions for the Four, this time for a drug that might or might not be similar to approved controlled substances. He does not have a physician-patient relationship with any of the students. He has never met them, and apparently prepared the Epiginosko for them before Dr. Bright even approached the students. Dr. Bauble likely cannot diagnose medical needs via long-distance assessment or effectively monitor patients for any signs of adverse effects. He has rendered his "virtual" medical judgment in this case remotely. In short, rather than a legitimate physician-patient relationship, there is a conflict of interest that prevents Dr. Bauble from acting on behalf of his "patients," Paul, Jill, Roberto, and Akira. At least indirect coercion appears to be at work.

BEYOND LEGALITY: JUSTICE

While issues of personal autonomy are important in the case before us, broader issues of social justice are also prominent. The concentration of public and private resources on the development of nontherapeutic technologies for the purpose of human enhancement may divert essential resources from legitimate medical research. These include human capital and innovative energy as well as monetary resources. For example, Americans spent around thirteen billion dollars on cosmetic surgery and Botox in 2007,[36] more than thirty times the amount spent worldwide on malaria research.[37] Personal and corporate resources today are devoted more to appearance, sensual pleasure, and entertainment than to the basic health needs of the world. There is little profit in malaria or

---

36. Plastic Surgery Research Info, "Cosmetic Plastic Surgery Research: Statistics and Trends for 2001–2008, 2007 ASAPS News Release," *http://www.cosmeticplasticsurgerystatistics.com/statistics.html* (accessed January 21, 2010).

37. Roll Back Malaria Partnership, "Global Malaria Action Plan," *http://www.rollbackmalaria.org/gmap/1-4*

.html (accessed May 26, 2010). In 2007 $422 million was spent in 2007 on malaria research and development, including drugs and vaccines. Forty percent of the total came from the US National Institutes of Health and the Bill and Melinda Gates Foundation.

tuberculosis research, but potentially great profitability in cognitive- and behavioral-enhancement technologies.

On the other hand, researching and developing technologies whose primary intention is to improve the capacities of those who are functionally normal could simultaneously or inadvertently lead to cures for human disease. For example, research for memory-enhancing drugs could contribute to the search for memory boosts for people with Alzheimer's and age-related memory loss. Discernment is necessary, then, when considering sweeping calls for a wholesale ban on the development or application of "enhancement technologies."

Enhancement is a moving target and not amenable to legal definition. Limitations on research dedicated to enhancement would be extremely difficult to draft with precision, even if they were politically feasible, a highly unlikely prospect. Many people would consider such bans imprudent, since prohibition would jeopardize breakthrough cures or treatments. It is even less likely that the state could limit physicians' freedom to prescribe therapies simply on the grounds that those therapies might also have the potential to increase certain bodily capacities.

The challenge before Paul and his colleagues, however, is much more focused. There apparently was no therapeutic purpose behind the development of Epiginosko. The proposed use, moreover, is explicitly to give its users a competitive edge—hardly the domain of "therapeutic purpose." Meanwhile, there are other fairness considerations that they must take into account.

FAIRNESS IN THE ACADEMIC ENVIRONMENT

Federal and state governments exercise significant control over educational institutions. Their authority to do so rests primarily on those institutions receiving government funding, whether directly through grants, indirectly through student aid, or via any other financial benefit. Through its "power of the purse," the state exercises its perceived responsibility to ensure that education is open to all students and that the academic environment is fair to all students. This is true whether the school is public or private (although private religious institutions may have the right to conduct their affairs according to their religious beliefs). The state has additional responsibilities for the education of minors, in its custodial role.

Public schools have the custodial responsibility to ensure a fair and safe environment for their students. In fulfillment of their responsibility, public high schools may ban smoking and conduct random drug testing as a constitutionally permitted "reasonable search and seizure." As mentioned above, regulations may be different for undergraduate institutions, where a significant number of all students are underage, as opposed to graduate schools, where students are presumed to be adults and the university is not acting in a parental role. Adult students have greater privacy interests than do minors. Do these students also have a reasonable expectation of a fair academic environment?

Or is it "survival of the fittest" at the graduate level, where students may pursue any and all measures to gain a competitive academic advantage over others?

Some would argue, in light of the impact of the current nonprescription use of drugs such as Ritalin and the potential impact of other cognitive-enhancing technologies, that competition among enhanced and nonenhanced students is inherently unfair. Not all would agree. For example, Cakic suggests that many factors other than "smart drugs" contribute to disparity in resources and opportunity—that is, "there never was an even playing field."[38]

In evaluating this debate, perhaps we can gain an insight by anticipating how the Four will talk about their future achievements. If they succeed in grasping the Nobel Prize, will they claim the achievement as entirely their own? Or will they give credit to Dr. Bauble and Epiginosko, "without whom this award would not have been possible"? Will they have so assimilated the drug that they cannot separate their performance from the chemical trigger? If questioned about their unusual leap forward over their previous academic performance, will they answer candidly that they used brain boosters? Or will they try to disguise the source of their unusual mental prowess?

FAIRNESS IN THE ALLOCATION OF RESOURCES

Even if they are legal, cognitive-enhancing drugs raise the justice issue of allocation of resources. Justice concerns here include (1) equal access to resources, (2) equal distribution, and (3) equal opportunity. Drugs which promise a competitive edge are prone to distribution in a discriminatory fashion. Students with economic resources can buy drugs; equally bright students who happen to be poor cannot. Various forms of unlawful discrimination can also easily arise, whether based on gender, ethnicity, or religious belief. For instance, Jill suggests that the Four should keep Epiginosko out of the hands of Asian students, despite the fact that the advantage it conveys may far outweigh any advantages many Asian students already have. Jill seems uninterested in this implication of equal access. Unequal access and unequal distribution drive unequal opportunity. Students who are equally as talented as the Four will become further disadvantaged by their inability to buy cognitive enhancements or by their disfavored social status. The academic enterprise is thus no longer about the pursuit of knowledge for the benefit of all, fostering instead a disproportionate, compounding advantage of the "haves" over the "have-nots."

The disparity in access to health care, quality education, and other factors that contribute to societal equality is well documented and a subject of national concern.[39] Most people would not respond favorably to a cognitive-enhancing drug as revolutionary as Epiginosko, should they learn that the Four have used it. Even if the drug

---

38. Cakic, "Smart Drugs," 612.
39. Kevin Fiscella, Peter Franks, Marthe R. Gold, and Carolyn M. Clancy, "Addressing Socioeconomic, Racial, and Ethnic Disparities in Health Care," *Journal of the American Medical Association* 283 (2000): 2579–84.

survives the FDA approval process—which presumes that Epiginosko has a legitimate medical application for which it is safe and effective—its distribution may be unjust. If insurance or health-care plans do not cover its costs, it will not be available in a racially neutral manner because of the connection between racial and economic inequities.

The rapidly exploding areas of biomedicine and biotechnology, with their array of boutique or designer enhancements, are further expanding the divide between the "haves" and "have-nots." Even if Epiginosko were widely available, concerns about fairness would not vanish. The distribution of natural intellectual abilities is uneven. An across-the-board increase in capacities would not erase these differences. While those with fewer abilities might proportionately benefit more, those who are already more gifted academically might instead soar proportionately higher. The outcome is uncertain and untested.

Unfair advantage for some means unfair disadvantage for others. What constitutes an unfair disadvantage? Is it merely that the drug is unavailable to most (in fact, it is available only to Dr. Bright and the Four) or that its monetary price is more than some can pay? There are likely other costs involved that are not economic but physical and psychological. Unlike external technological tools that people control and that enable them to perform work more efficiently, Dr. Bright's proposed drug changes the human body itself. It may alter the brain structure permanently, with unknown near-term and long-term effects. How fairly are the risks of those effects allocated? That depends on whether Dr. Bright is taking Epiginosko. His comments are vague, but it may be that he is using the Four as his guinea pigs. He could be experiencing some negative side effects of his long-term off-label use of Ritalin, Adderall, and Ginosko and wants to avoid further risks to himself.

FINAL OBSERVATIONS

Now that the Four are aware of Dr. Bright's use of an illegal or unapproved drug, do they have an affirmative obligation to report him? The duty to report falls on parties who have a particular responsibility—for example, teachers must report suspected instances of physical, emotional, or sexual abuse of a student. But there is no legal requirement that students act as "tattletales" on their professors. Whistleblower statutes offer protection in specific circumstances, such as the morality of corporate behavior, but there is no parallel for the situation the Four face. One option is the DEA hotline for anonymous tipsters to report the illegal sale and abuse of pharmaceutical drugs. Paul, Roberto, Jill, or Akira could turn in Dr. Bright but would risk exposure, since presumably only a few people know of the Epiginosko arrangement between Dr. Bauble and Dr. Bright.

Taking the drug, however, would involve this group of highly competitive students in a different sort of risk. It is possible that Epiginosko may benefit only one or two of them. As the familiar disclaimer goes, "individual results may vary." If, for example, Roberto and Akira achieve drug-boosted breakthrough research, while Paul and Jill continue to produce at their normal capacity, how will that affect both the team research and their individual sense of accomplishment? Roberto and Akira might resent sharing academic accolades with their lesser team members. The sense of inadequacy and inferiority that Paul and Jill experience could delay or impair their research. Cutthroat competition could spur the students on to new discoveries, or it could tempt them to undermine each other's work. Once they take the first step of accepting a morally questionable drug, it will be easier for them to violate other ethical boundaries, such as not falsifying data and not plagiarizing research. They could end up compromising rather than furthering Dr Bright's enticing enterprise. They may find themselves in a web of dependence, wanting to abandon the drug but fearful of falling behind the others.

In the end, then, the case before us is multifaceted. The law is but one lens through which to view an ethical dilemma. Enacted laws merely indicate society's determination of what conduct to prohibit, permit, or require for the common good. Fees, fines, imprisonment, or death are external tools to ensure compliance, but they cannot control powerful internal motivations. Citizens are free to decide whether to obey the law. Their decisions may have less to do with an ethical calculus than with the inconvenience to the pocketbook or person. Contemporary American law delineates legal and illegal but does not speak comprehensively about right and wrong.

For this latter distinction, Christians look to a higher law. Christ-followers may need to say yes when others say no, and "no, thank you" when others say "I'll have another." God may require this, reflecting a more complete view of the flourishing of individuals and communities. There *are* moral concerns; there *are* right and wrong answers; they *can* be found. While legal analysis alone will not reveal them, the law can play a role alongside other disciplines to help identify them.

CHAPTER 7

WISDOM FROM INTERCULTURAL MINISTRY

Harold A. Netland, Bruce L. Fields, and Elizabeth Y. Sung

Imagine that Paul comes to you for advice on whether he should take Epiginosko. Is it morally right to use the drug to enhance mental performance? What would you say?

Suppose that, contrary to what the case study suggests, use of Epiginosko is not illegal and that there are strong reasons to believe that by using it Dr. Bright and the students will achieve cold fusion. This technology would provide an inexpensive, widely accessible, and environmentally friendly source of energy for much of the world. The potential benefits of using Epiginosko are enormous. Assume also that the known risks of taking the drug are minimal, as Dr. Bright would have us believe. Other things being equal, it would seem that a strong case can be made for using Epiginosko.

Imagine a scenario, on the other hand, in which the benefits for humanity of taking Epiginosko are high but the known risks are also very high. (What is "reasonably safe" from Dr. Bright's self-interested perspective may not be so for the average person.) Would it then be right to take this drug? How do we calculate what are acceptable risks in light of potential benefits? Scientific breakthroughs which bring significant benefits to humanity sometimes have come at considerable personal cost. Consider the tragic accidents in the history of aviation or space exploration. There is often no agreed-upon formula for what would be an acceptable risk in such circumstances.

Some—such as Paul in the situation before us—might worry that *any* use of drugs to enhance cognitive performance is wrong. But even if correct, such categorical rejection is inconsistent with common practice. Acetaminophen can not only cure a splitting headache but is attractive to some students writing term papers as a way to transcend even normal minor bodily distractions. University students have long guzzled coffee to keep alert and focused during exam week. But as William Cheshire observes, many students today have graduated to more powerful mental stimulants. "University students in increasing numbers are turning to methylphenidate, in particular, as a convenient means to intensify mental focus, stay awake through the night to prolong studying, or otherwise gain a competitive edge."[1]

Is there a significant difference between using caffeine and methylphenidate? Is there a difference between either of these stimulants and the fictive Epiginosko? If so, at what point has one crossed the moral line? According to the case study, Epiginosko is "an epigenetic neuropharmaceutical that permanently strengthens the synaptic connections underlying learning. Epiginosko alters the very structure of the brain to surpass normal human intelligence." While it is not clear just how this works — contrary to Jill's suggestion that there is little difference between using Epiginosko and drinking coffee — presumably this places Epiginosko in a different category than stimulants such as caffeine or even methylphenidate. But exactly what is it about altering the structure of the brain in this manner that makes Epiginosko morally problematic?

What if use of Epiginosko not only greatly enhances one's cognitive performance but that one of its side effects is to change significantly aspects of one's personality or character? Imagine that its use results in loss of the capacity to feel compassion and love for others. Although one's cognitive function improves dramatically, one becomes insensitive to others. Does this affect the moral equation? That depends on how one regards compassion and love for others. With certain kinds of moral theory, this might not be a significant issue, but with others it would be. For Christians, for example, a fundamental moral principle is that they are to love God and to love others (Matt. 22:34 – 40), and they understand moral virtue in terms of developing the moral qualities found in Jesus Christ, the very epitome of loving compassion for others. A love-inhibiting effect, then, would make it much more difficult to justify use of Epiginosko from a Christian ethical perspective.

In considering whether it is right to use Epiginosko, we have now moved beyond a simple cost-benefit analysis to consider more fundamental questions, such as, What does it mean to be human? This, in turn, can be answered only by considering basic questions about human nature, the ultimate good, and how people are to align themselves with this good. Moral deliberation does not occur in a vacuum. Notoriously, there are disagreements over these issues. Everyone engaging in moral decision-making does so from within a particular conceptual framework or set of assumptions about the way things are and what is morally significant. Christians approach moral questions from within a framework shaped by the Bible as well as the heritage of Christian reflection on Scripture and life throughout the ages. Others will consider the issues from very different assumptions.

---

1. William P. Cheshire Jr., "Drugs for Enhancing Cognition and Their Ethical Implications: A Hot New Cup of Tea," *Expert Review of Neurotherapeutics* 6, no. 3 (2006): 263.

Moreover, moral dilemmas are not merely theoretical; they occur in connection with real people in specific historical and social contexts. People live at particular times and places and have specific identities and histories. They are the products of, among other things, the cumulative influences of ethnicity, gender, social institutions and patterns, culture, and religion. In this chapter, we will consider how social, cultural, and religious factors might affect understanding some of the ethical issues involved in the case study. Our concern is not merely determining the right thing for Dr. Bright or the students to do but also to explore how various contextual factors might shape the moral issues within the case study. Although there are many issues worth pursuing, we will focus on two in particular: (1) moral issues associated with power relations implicit in the case study, and (2) ways in which a religious and ethical framework very different from that of Christianity—Japanese Buddhism—might affect moral decision-making.

BIOETHICS AND SOCIOCULTURAL CONTEXTS

Individuals in modern societies participate simultaneously in a number of complex social and cultural "life-worlds." The institutional spheres associated with family, school, employment, government, leisure, and religion produce overlapping sets of relationships and a multiplicity of norms which, in any given situation, can result in unique opportunities as well as conflicting obligations. Moral reasoning takes place within such settings.

The sociology of knowledge reminds us that "social location"—one's historical context, gender, ethnicity, class, religion—affects how people understand and respond to the world around them.[2] One must not, of course, exaggerate the social and cultural influences on people's beliefs. Acknowledging that all people, to some extent, are products of their contexts does not mean that their beliefs are merely the result of social factors or that such contexts entirely determine what knowledge is. Such reductionism is self-defeating and untenable. We can accept that contextual factors affect our perception of reality without falling into a kind of relativism which maintains that truth and knowledge are simply products of particular contexts. Relativism is unacceptable for Christians who believe that truth—including truth in moral matters—transcends particular social or cultural contexts.[3]

Truth is not the same thing as plausibility. A statement is true if and only if the state of affairs to which it refers is as the statement asserts it to be. So truth does not vary from

2. The seminal work in this field is Peter L. Berger and Thomas Luckman, *The Social Construction of Reality: A Treatise in the Sociology of Knowledge* (New York: Doubleday, 1966).

3. The literature on relativism is enormous; e.g., see Paul K. Moser and Thomas L. Carson, eds., *Moral Relativism: A Reader* (New York: Oxford Univ. Press, 2001).

culture to culture.[4] Plausibility, on the other hand, varies by person and culture and thus does change with context. A belief or practice is plausible if it seems to a particular person or group to be reasonable or acceptable. For example, belief in reincarnation is very plausible to people in certain social, cultural, and religious contexts but is implausible elsewhere. Belief that all of reality consists of matter and energy is plausible to some people but not to others. Part of what explains the differences in plausibility is the very different social conditions that are in place in the different cases.

Because the world includes many different societies, cultures, and religious traditions, what is plausible concerning moral issues varies significantly among social groups. Akira is a Japanese Buddhist who comes from a culture heavily influenced by Buddhism and Confucianism. Paul, by contrast, is an African-American Christian. Some of the ways these differences might affect moral decision-making are noted below. Globalization makes the differences as well as linkages between particular peoples increasingly apparent. With today's technology, people can now travel virtually anywhere on earth within a matter of days and can communicate across the globe almost instantaneously. Globalization also means that advances in science, technology, and medicine are no longer confined to Europe and North America but are increasingly affecting societies worldwide, both for good and for ill. The implications for bioethics are substantial. As former chair of the US President's Council on Bioethics, Edmund Pellegrino, observes:

> In bioemedical ethics, this transcultural challenge is vastly complicated because medical science and technology, as well as the ethics designed to deal with its impact, currently are Western in origin. They are deeply ingrained with three sets of values distinctly Western—the values of empirical science, principle-based ethics, and the democratic political philosophy. Such values are often alien, and even antipathetic, to many non-Western worldviews.... Western values, however, may be strongly at odds with worldviews held by billions of other human beings.... Their ethical systems may be less dialectical, logical, or linguistic in character, less analytical, more synthetic, or more sensitive to family or community consensus than to individual autonomy, more virtue-based than principle-based. In turn, their political systems may be more attuned to authority, tradition, ritual, and religion; more comfortable with, and more responsive to, the centralization of decision-making; more tolerant of social stratification and inequality.[5]

Not surprisingly, then, ethicists from other religions such as Buddhism are also beginning to examine bioethical issues from within their own religious frameworks.[6]

---

4. This is a so-called ontological definition of truth. The degree to which, or the certainty with which, we actually apprehend truth is a separate issue. See William P. Alston, *A Realist Conception of Truth* (Ithaca, N.Y.: Cornell Univ. Press, 1996).

5. Edmund D. Pellegrino, "Prologue: Intersections of Western Biomedical Ethics and World Culture," in *Trans-cultural Dimensions in Medical Ethics*, ed. Edmund Pellegrino, Patricia Mazzarella, and Pietro Corsi (Frederick, Md.: University Publishing Group, 1992), 14.

6. See Damien Keown, *Buddhism and Bioethics* (New York: Palgrave, 2001); and Karma Lekshe Tsomo, *Into the Jaws of Yama, Lord of Death: Buddhism, Bioethics and Death* (Albany: State Univ. of New York Press, 2006).

The case study we are considering takes place in a Western university. But it would not be far-fetched to imagine a similar scenario taking place in a major research university in Tokyo or Bangkok. The dominant religious and cultural influences would then be Buddhist, and those might well affect deliberations over the use of Epiginosko.

ISSUES OF POWER

The case study is suffused with issues of power relations which raise significant moral questions. Power operates on both individual and institutional levels. On an individual level, power involves the capacity to influence states of affairs or the ability to accomplish desired ends even in the face of substantial opposition. Institutional power involves the capacity to define perceptions of reality within a particular domain (i.e., what is to be normative, cognitively and procedurally) and to allocate resources accordingly (tangible as well as intangible rewards and penalties). Mary Stewart Van Leeuwen defines power in this sense as "the ability to make ideas stick, to make them the dominant ideas, and to have the resources of doing so."[7]

When the exercise of power involves the manipulation or abuse of others, it is a moral issue. Power in and of itself, on either the individual or institutional level, is not necessarily problematic. However, it becomes a moral issue when its exercise or distribution involves morally unacceptable ways of treating people or achieving ends, or when power is directed toward immoral ends. We will consider several ways in which power relations in the situation before us introduce moral issues distinct from simply the question of whether to take Epiginosko. The broader context of the encounter, as well as specifics about the individuals and the nature of the conversation, reflects significant moral issues related to power.

INSTITUTIONAL SYMBOLS OF POWER

The case study takes place in a major research university located presumably in the United States. Few institutions in the modern world carry as much prestige and symbolic power as the research university. The West — and increasingly the world at large — has become what is sometimes called a "knowledge society," in which the creation, dissemination, and utilization of information and knowledge are the most important factors of production.[8] In knowledge societies, a large portion of the population attains higher education and much of the labor force includes specialized knowledge workers. Those who control the creation and utilization of knowledge exert considerable power throughout society. The prestige and power of the research university come from the

7. Mary Stewart Van Leeuwen, *After Eden: Facing the Challenge of Gender Reconciliation* (Grand Rapids, Mich.: Eerdmans, 1993), 234.

8. Arnost Vesely, "Knowledge Society," in *International Encyclopedia of the Social Sciences*, ed. William A. Darity Jr., 2nd ed., vol. 4 (Farmington Hills, Mich.: Macmillan References, 2008), 283.

university's central role in the production and dissemination of knowledge.[9] Such is especially the case regarding the physical sciences, due to their contribution to innovations in technology and medicine.

The case study concerns students in a physics department. Physics, perhaps the epitome of the hard sciences, is especially prestigious. When *Time* magazine identified its Person of the Century, it predictably chose Albert Einstein, a physicist who transformed human understanding of the universe.[10] The setting before us is hardly a neutral setting. The physics department of a major university is charged with social significance, so that positive responses to uses for technological innovation are much more likely than negative ones.

The research university is becoming increasingly influential in non-Western societies, especially in Asia. Akira is a student from Japan who (presumably) will return home upon completion of his doctoral studies. He is representative of a growing class of those who receive advanced education in Western universities — often in the physical sciences — and then return to their homelands, bearing with them not only the technical training but also the values and assumptions dominant in Western secular universities. Sociologist Peter Berger speaks of this class of highly educated international elites as comprising a growing global "faculty club culture" that "spreads its beliefs and values through the educational system, the legal system, various therapeutic institutions, think tanks, and at least some of the media of mass communication."[11] Thus, although the case study occurs within a Western university setting, the issues it raises are worldwide concerns.

POWER AND SOCIOCULTURAL LOCATION

The social location of individuals in the case study affects their relation to centers of power. Consider first Dr. Bright. As chair of the university's physics department and recipient of the Nobel Prize in physics — an honor which immediately makes him one of the most authoritative scientists on the planet — Dr. Bright embodies the social power that accompanies the highest level of success in science. Power is inherent in the relationship between Dr. Bright and the doctoral students. They do not come together as equals. As chair of the physics department and their dissertation mentor, Dr. Bright has considerable control over whether the students will complete the program successfully and their eventual placement after graduation. The pressure on the students to please their mentor is enormous, and each student would be subject to that in considering the use of Epiginosko.

---

9. The university, of course, does not stand alone in producing and utilizing knowledge. In many cases — especially in the physical sciences — funding for research within the university comes from sources in the corporate world with their own commercial interests in the results of the research. Thus, there are many different kinds of institutional interests — and conflicts of interests — at work in research such as Dr. Bright's efforts to solve the problem of cold fusion. These warrant further consideration.

10. See Frederic Golden, "Person of the Century: Albert Einstein," *Time* 154, no. 27 (December 31, 1999), 62–65.

11. Peter Berger, "Four Faces of Culture," *National Interest* 49 (Fall 1997): 24–25.

The doctoral students come from a variety of backgrounds. Three are male, while only one is female. Akira, Roberto, and Paul are ethnic minorities, whereas (presumably) Dr. Bright and Jill are white.[12] Roberto comes from a lower-income background. While Paul is a highly educated African-American, he would certainly be aware of what it means to be disadvantaged. So would Jill. Hispanics, African-Americans, and women alike often have been marginalized when it comes to the exercise of social power.

At one point Paul raises concerns about justice and fairness. Christians commonly maintain that all people are equal with respect to inherent value and dignity as human beings. Moreover, many Western Christians—especially Americans—like to think that when it comes to the actual treatment of people, their society is characterized by equality, justice, and fairness. The notion of justice or fairness operative in the West often includes the idea that no one should receive preferential treatment that enables him or her to benefit in ways not available to others. Success is to be a function simply of each person's capabilities and effort. From this perspective, Paul's concern is eminently reasonable: "Even if taking the drug is not clearly illegal, it just does not seem right to gain an unfair advantage over others." Those with access to Epiginosko have a significant advantage over those who do not, and this inequality raises questions about fairness in a highly competitive academic environment.

Such concerns, however, may derive much of their force from the assumption that people begin from roughly the same place. Although not all people are by nature equally gifted, all presumably have roughly the same opportunities for success. The sad reality is often quite different. Ethnic minorities are often victims of subtle discriminatory policies and practices that keep them from opportunities which their white counterparts take for granted. In many situations, whites tend to be the ones controlling and exercising social, economic, and political power. Roberto's sardonic reply to Paul reflects this inequity: "You sound like everyone should start from a level playing field and that no one should have any special advantages. You of all people should know that life is not like that."

There are many complicated issues here. In much of the West, one's social location—one's ethnicity, gender, class, and religion—does significantly influence access to goods like quality education, opportunities for employment, and bank loans. Quality of education is often directly related to the economic standing of the community, so that those from lower-income neighborhoods generally do not have access to the same quality of schools as those from middle-income or affluent neighborhoods. People of color often do not compete on a level playing field with whites but rather must overcome significant obstacles to achieve social success. Roberto and Paul are well aware of these issues and thus might understandably approach questions of fairness from a different perspective than, say, a white male reared in an upper-middle-class home.

---

12. There is a risk here of ethnic and racial stereotyping. The purpose of the following discussion is not to generalize about large groups of individuals in misleading ways but rather to put on the table certain observations to encourage reflection on ways in which ethnic, cultural, and religious factors can affect moral deliberations.

In light of these considerations, what exactly constitutes an unfair advantage over others? How does use of drugs such as Epiginosko relate to the issue of fairness in educational competition? Since the quality of education often is directly related to neighborhood income levels, what does justice or fairness in intellectual competition entail? If Epiginosko were legalized, would everyone have equal access to it, or only the wealthy and privileged? Is it more justified for those who have had to overcome significant social obstacles to benefit from other special advantages not available to all? Is there really a significant difference between using performance-enhancing drugs and other ways of enhancing cognitive performance, such as obtaining special tutoring, using sophisticated software programs or calculators, or attending elite private schools? Is Epiginosko different from a megadose of caffeine? Interestingly, Paul is not only an African-American but also a Christian. Despite the inequities that he has had to confront in his own struggle for success, he appears to have some ambivalence about doing something that would give him what he perceives as "an unfair advantage over others." Is Paul exercising sound moral judgment here, or is he being naive, as Roberto suggests?[13]

Cultural differences also affect how one might respond to Dr. Bright's "encouragement" to use Epiginosko. Dr. Bright presents the choice before the students in clear-cut, binary terms: "I set before you this night mental stimulation or staleness." Professional success or obscurity. Scientific progress or obsolescence. The professor treats the students as autonomous agents who can freely choose the best option simply by considering the potential benefits of using Epiginosko. He operates from within a framework that includes a highly individualistic view of the self in which professional achievement is one of the highest values.

Others might well see things differently. It has become customary to locate societies or cultures along a continuum, with individualism and collectivism at the extremes. The relation of the individual to "ingroups" — networks of relationships characterized by familiarity, intimacy, and a shared history (family, close friends, colleagues) — is different in individualistic and collectivistic societies. "On the one hand, individualistic cultures foster the needs, wishes, and desires of individuals over their ingroups." In individualistic societies competition, uniqueness, autonomy, and independence are valued. Collectivistic societies, on the other hand, "foster the needs, wishes, and desires of ingroups over individuals. They foster values such as cooperation, harmony, and conformity."[14] In individualistic societies, people tend to have independent self-concepts; the

---

13. As both an African-American and a Christian, Paul might well experience conflicting impulses. His awareness of social inequities and the history of discrimination against African-Americans could easily have fostered in him feelings of resentment and anger against whites. He might see becoming a top physicist as providing opportunities for him to exert power over others. At the same time, Paul might well be sensitive to the Christian values of justice, humility, forgiveness, and serving others. Thus, his moral deliberation likely occurs within the tension of these conflicting inclinations.

14. David Matsumoto, *The New Japan: Debunking Seven Cultural Stereotypes* (Boston: Intercultural Press, 2002), 37–38.

individual sees himself or herself as a distinct, separate, and autonomous entity. But in collectivistic cultures, one's self-concept is intimately connected to others in the ingroup.

In an influential study of values in the workplace in various nations, Geert Hofstede and Gert Jan Hofstede have introduced the notion of "power distance" as a mechanism for comparing cultural differences. Power distance is "the extent to which the less powerful members of institutions and organizations within a country expect and accept that power is distributed unequally."[15] In societies with less power distance, there are stronger commitments to egalitarianism, there is less distance between authority figures (teachers, bosses) and subordinates, and decision-making is more collegial and by consensus. In societies with greater power distance, those with less power are dependent on the powerful, there is a greater distance between authority figures and subordinates, and decision-making is more "top-down."

Dr. Bright reflects a context that is highly individualistic with a strong independent self-concept, and he expects the others to respond similarly. But he appears oblivious to the cultural differences between him and at least some of his prize students, such as Akira and Roberto. In more collectivistic societies, the individual is embedded in a host of familial and communal relationships and responsibilities. These relationships—and the privileges and responsibilities accompanying them—can take priority over individual considerations.

For example, the assumption in many communally oriented societies is that when children reach adulthood and attain some financial capability, they will "give back" to their parents and others who have enabled them to succeed. Such is especially the case if they have received opportunities and resources not available to others in the network. Parents raise young people with high hopes and expectations for their eventual vocational success, fostering a sense of filial obligation to reciprocate their parents' sacrificial investment in their education and development by providing assistance to their parents in their later years.

For Roberto, raised in a single-parent home and privy to education and potential earnings that far exceed that of any other of his relatives, participation in the proposed experiments may well entail assuming risks that go beyond Dr. Bright's rosy scenario. These risks affect not just Roberto but also his mother as well as others who may look to him for support once he is established. Despite Dr. Bright's assurances that the risks of taking the drug are limited, the unforeseeable hazards of taking Epiginosko—especially since it has not been tested and it "alters the very structure of the brain"—might compromise Roberto's mental and physical health. Significant negative and lasting effects on Roberto's mind and body, for instance, would affect Roberto's capacity for long-term employment and, with that, his income and stability over the course of his

---

15. Geert Hofstede and Gert Jan Hofstede, *Culture and Organizations: Software of the Mind*, 2nd ed. (New York: McGraw-Hill, 2005), 46.

life. Such developments could also adversely affect the security of his mother and others whose circumstances may require them to rely in part on his assistance. Since permanent impairment of the structure of the brain is a real though unintended risk of participating in the research project, and in light of the ethnocultural frameworks that inform the decision-making process, Roberto (or Akira or Paul) might well conclude that saying no to this opportunity constitutes the most reasonable and responsible decision.

To the degree that Japanese culture is more collectivistic than the individualistic culture of the United States, it could be very difficult for Akira to take a strong stand against Dr. Bright. Although not always the case, the individual in Japan tends to be subordinate to the group. Akira's family has probably supported him throughout his education, and his parents would have high expectations for him as a successful physicist. The power distance in Akira's case would be much greater than in the case of Dr. Bright. Reflecting the Confucian influence on Japanese society and education, Japanese students tend to be highly deferential to their teachers, rarely challenging them. As a foreign student, Akira would be even less likely to go against his mentor.

Similarly, Jill might well be especially sensitive to issues of power distance. In many social domains, men and women experience different treatment, and women need to work harder than men to succeed and gain respect. In the physical sciences, men far outnumber women; and Jill likely would be functioning in the physics department with a greater power distance than that of Dr. Bright. She would be acutely aware of the obstacles she has overcome to achieve this level of academic success. Knowing her vulnerability as a woman in an academic domain dominated by men, she would probably be reluctant to do anything to challenge her mentor and thus jeopardize her academic and professional future.[16]

LANGUAGE AND POWER

While people can use language in a dispassionate manner merely to communicate certain "facts," often one's choice of words reflects values or commitments that are far from neutral. Moreover, people can influence others, either positively or negatively, by their choice of terms and even by the tone of their voices. Such influence is not necessarily wrong. But legitimate influence can easily slip over into inappropriate manipulation of others through the use of language to distort what is the case or to exert unwarranted control over others.

Consider some examples of the morally problematic use of language in the situation before us. Dr. Bright uses his position of authority and power to pressure the students in inappropriate ways into taking Epiginosko. He suggests, for example, that the question of the legality of Epiginosko is a mere technicality which should not impede the progress of science. Speaking of such drugs, he maintains that "in the United States they inevi-

---

16. Cf. Anne M. Clifford, *Introducing Feminist Theology* (Maryknoll, N.Y.: Orbis, 2004), 16.

tably will become legal and *ought to be now*" (emphasis added). These last words suggest that other considerations—perhaps strictly pragmatic benefits—can and should override legal constraints in this case.

Dr. Bright states that "if you play the game right, together we will revolutionize nuclear physics." He concludes his pitch by saying, "if you take the pills, it will enhance your stature with me, and I don't need to tell you what that will mean for your professional future." The implication is clear: failure to take the drug could very well jeopardize their progress in the program and their future as scientists. The issue is no longer simply whether it is morally permissible to take the drug.

Dr. Bright also appeals to the prestige of science and its central role in human progress. He dismisses laws that prohibit the use of Epiginosko as "outdated policies" and rejects Paul's concern that the drug might give one an unfair advantage over others as "an obsolete notion." Dr. Bright challenges Paul by asking, "Surely a progressive thinker such as yourself would not want to hold science hostage to an outdated moral grumble?" No one—certainly no doctoral student in physics—wants to be identified as an impediment to the progress of science. In Dr. Bright's hands, moral scruples become inconvenient obstacles to science which prevent discoveries that could be of enormous benefit to humanity. Dr. Bright speaks of the "exhilarating highway of science" as if it were a morally neutral world of thought and activity for our benefit, free from concern about cost. What such language can obscure is that while certain experimental procedures in and of themselves might not be problematic, the individual scientists who conduct the science bring with them values, assumptions, and agendas. Then society at large utilizes the results of scientific research, both for good and for ill. Advances in science have brought about enormous benefits for humanity. But "advances" have also produced horrific evils when particular groups have allowed the possibility of lofty ends to justify destructive means.[17]

There is another sense in which language in the case study raises moral issues. Prejudices can lead to oppressing groups whose members are regarded as inferior or of little value. But prejudice can also result in denying certain groups opportunities when those in the group may constitute a threat. Jill's comment to Akira illustrates this outlook: "No offense, Akira, but we need to make sure that the Asian students learn nothing about this, since they are already an academic threat to their white classmates." Whereas Roberto had earlier expressed concern that minorities and whites do not begin on a level playing field, Jill's concern is that Asian students are already at a competitive advantage

---

17. The idea that an intellectual or scientific elite can and should subject vulnerable groups to experimentation, without their knowledge or consent, for the sake of science, has a long and sordid history in eugenics. In the mid-twentieth century, this took the form of the Tuskegee Study, sponsored by the United States Public Health Service and the Tuskegee Institute. For forty years, beginning in 1932, 399 black men with syphilis were studied, without their informed consent and without treatment for the disease, to determine the effects of syphilis. See "U.S. Public Health Service Syphilis Study at Tuskegee," *http://www.cdc.gov/tuskegee/timeline.htm* (accessed May 4, 2010).

with respect to white students and so should not have access to resources for cognitive enhancement. While such a statement might strike some as far-fetched, concerns about the numbers of Asians in certain sectors of higher education have prompted efforts to restrict their admission. Jill might simply be expressing what others think.

Jill's comment is an example of conventional racial stereotyping that conforms to, and perpetuates, inaccurate and reductionistic views of Asians and Americans of Asian descent. One common idealized image depicts Asian-Americans as a homogenous group and a "model minority." According to this myth, persons of Asian descent universally outperform other groups academically. Thus, they experience no disadvantages associated with discrimination; rather, they pose a threat both to the socioeconomic dominance Euro-Americans historically have enjoyed and to the ascent of other ethnic groups.

While we cannot explore the issues in depth here, this representation is misleading in several respects. First, "Asians" are not a homogenous group. There are significant differences among the South Asian, Southeast Asian, East Asian, and Pacific Islander populations in the United States. Moreover, socioeconomic disparities continue to obtain between Asian-American Pacific Islanders (AAPIs) and non-Hispanic whites. Recent government studies report that the percentages of AAPIs living both at and below the poverty line, and receiving public assistance, are higher than those of non-Hispanic whites.[18]

The level of educational attainment varies considerably among Asian-American ethnic groups, with some attaining considerably higher levels than others. Moreover, the assumption that achievement in one area indicates the absence of disadvantages and problems in other areas is mistaken. A growing body of research suggests that subdominant persons and groups — required not just to become competent but to excel in several divergent, conflicting social systems — experience great pressures to succeed. When internalized, these stressors often take a long-term toll on mental, emotional, and relational health. For first-generation, "1.5-generation," and second-generation immigrants and their intergenerational families, various factors frequently compound the pressures. Such factors include basic needs like language acquisition and other requirements for assimilation, subjection to racial aggression and other forms of emotional and physical abuse, and the traumatic experiences of war and displacement. More than thirty years of studies on mental health show that Asian-Americans exhibit high numbers of symptoms of depression. For example, in assessing the mental-health needs of different populations, the Surgeon General's report states that "Asian American/Pacific Islanders show higher levels of depressive symptoms than do white Americans. Furthermore, Chinese Americans are more likely to exhibit somatic complaints of depression than are African Americans or non-Hispanic whites."[19]

---

18. See US Department of Health and Human Services, Office of Minority Health, "Asian American/Pacific Islander Profile," 18, *http://raceandhealth.hhs.gov/templates/browse.aspx?lvl=2&lvlID=53* (accessed July 6, 2010).

19. US Department of Public Health, Publications and Reports of the Surgeon General, "Mental Health Care of Asian Americans and Pacific Islanders," in *Mental Health: Culture, Race and Ethnicity*, chap. 5, *http://www.ncbi.nlm.nih.gov/bookshelf/br.fcgi?book=hssurggen&part=A1898* (accessed July 2, 2010).

In other words, the common depiction of Asian-Americans as a homogenous "model minority" which is "taking over" US higher education—reflected in Jill's comment to Akira—is a false image. The perception of Asians (and Asian-Americans) that Jill articulates is not merely a matter of stereotyping; it is based on, and further perpetuates, misinformation that can be damaging. Even if boosting the cognitive ability of selected disadvantaged undergraduates by offering them Epiginosko were beneficial rather than exploitative, the exclusion of all Asians and Asian-Americans from participation would be misguided. It would be a disservice to deserving first-generation college students from low-income families—for example, those recently arriving from Southeast Asia.

IMPORTANCE OF WORLDVIEW ASSUMPTIONS

We noted earlier that moral questions about using Epiginosko cannot be settled apart from considering broader issues about the kind of universe we live in. Practical ethics presupposes metaphysics. Christians, for example, believe that there is a real distinction between right and wrong, good and evil, grounded in the way things are, that there are objective moral values and principles which apply to all people in all contexts. As such, Christian ethical thinking is a kind of moral realism.[20]

Many today, however, are moral nonrealists. Moral nonrealism denies the objectivity of moral values and principles, holding instead that they are merely expressions of personal or societal preferences; or they are products of biological or social evolution, or of particular cultures; or they may simply be the imposition of the views of the powerful on the rest. This view reduces what seem to be genuinely moral principles or values to natural nonmoral factors.

In the situation before us, Paul is a Christian who appears to believe that there are objective moral principles and that human beings are created by God in a way that has special significance. While other considerations are also relevant, part of the moral assessment of the use of Epiginosko from a Christian perspective must include the effect that doing so will have on what makes people distinctively human, as Kevin Vanhoozer discussed in chapter 5. Will such use enhance what gives human beings special dignity and value, or will it diminish or distort it?

As a Christian, Paul would also probably believe that there is a nonphysical component to the human person, often referred to as the soul. Although there are controversial and difficult issues involved here, most Christians believe that there is an enduring, substantial person who underlies the many changes that people undergo throughout life

---

20. See Michael Smith, "Moral Realism," in *The Blackwell Guide to Ethical Theory*, ed. Hugh LaFollette (Oxford: Blackwell, 2000), 15–16.

and who lives on after the death of the body. The human person is not reducible simply to physical properties. After death, the believer's soul becomes part of the new reality, which includes the resurrection body.

Needless to say, not all involved in bioethical debates share Paul's Christian assumptions. Suppose that Dr. Bright is an atheist, a moral nonrealist, and a physicalist, who believes that physical entities ultimately constitute whatever exists. There is then no nonphysical component (a soul) to the human organism; only physical elements make up so-called persons. Human beings have no special significance rooted in their creation by God. As a moral nonrealist, Dr. Bright would believe that there is no irreducible moral distinction between good and evil, right and wrong. Whether to take Epiginosko, then, becomes a strictly pragmatic question about the possible benefits of the use of the drug versus any potential negative effects.

Some might recognize in the disagreement between Dr. Bright and Paul the contrasting worldviews of naturalism and supernaturalism. They might assume that naturalistic worldviews, lacking a transcendent God, are inherently nonreligious. However, some religious perspectives, such as Buddhism, are also naturalistic in that they rule out the reality of a supernatural God. Akira is a Japanese Buddhist. How might that background affect how Akira approaches the issues?

As noted earlier, Buddhists are increasingly bringing their Buddhist perspectives to bear on bioethical issues. There is a growing need for those engaging in bioethical debate everywhere—and not only in Asia—to take account of these contributions. With the increasing religious and cultural diversity of Western societies, bioethicists in the West will also find themselves engaging ethicists from Buddhist and other traditions. It is estimated that there are three to four million Buddhists in the United States, with smaller numbers in Great Britain, Germany, and France.[21] Moreover, the social and cultural significance of Buddhism in the United States is disproportionate to the number of adherents, as American Buddhists are well represented in the universities, the media, and the entertainment industries, just as Buddhist influence is increasingly evident in popular culture.

BUDDHISM AND MORAL PRINCIPLES

Suppose that Akira is an informed Buddhist who takes the Buddhist worldview seriously. There are at least three significant implications of Buddhist metaphysics for how he might approach moral questions in the situation before us. First, classical Buddhism has no place for a creator God and thus is a form of religious atheism. It is common today in the West to think of Gautama (the Buddha, founder of Buddhism) as simply

---

21. See Robert Wuthnow and Wendy Cage, "Buddhists and Buddhism in the United States: The Scope and Influ-

ence," *Journal for the Scientific Study of Religion* 43, no. 3 (2004): 363–80.

agnostic about the reality of God. Nevertheless, classical Buddhism has consistently rejected the possibility of an omnipotent Creator.[22]

Since Buddhism has no doctrine of a Creator, it follows that human beings are not to be regarded as having special significance rooted in God's creation. Moreover, moral principles have no grounding in a moral being, a holy and righteous God. In these respects, Buddhism is closer to naturalism than it is to theism.

Second, Buddhism denies the reality of an enduring soul or self. This is a very counterintuitive notion. However, it lies at the heart of Buddhist teaching, which maintains that everything is characterized by impermanence and interdependence. Contrary to prevailing Hindu views, the Buddha and his followers denied the reality of a soul or *atman*. Not only is belief in an enduring soul false, but this mistaken belief leads to clinging or desire, thereby perpetuating the causes of rebirth. (One's present life is merely part of an unimaginably long series of past and future lives, in which one is continually being reborn on the basis of the principle of *karma*. According to this principle, the accumulated actions of all previous lives determine one's present existence, and past and present actions will determine future lives.)

What many think of as a person is merely the ever-changing combination of psychophysical forces, the "five aggregates" of matter, sensations, perceptions, mental formations, and consciousness, which produce the illusory sense of an enduring person. At death, what passes from this life to the next is not an enduring soul but simply the cumulative *karmic* effects of actions which then produce in the next life the mistaken perception of an enduring person.

A host of important questions arise at this point, including how there can be moral accountability across multiple rebirths (something presupposed by teachings on rebirth and karma) if there is no enduring person who passes from one life to another.[23] Furthermore, the teachings on no-self and the interdependence of everything raise questions about the moral significance of human beings. On Buddhist assumptions, is there any meaningful sense in which human beings differ from other forms of sentient life? Buddhism teaches that not only humans but also animals and insects are reborn. Do humans have a moral status that animals and insects lack? As a serious Buddhist, Akira might have some ambivalence on this issue. On the one hand, Buddhists insist that all living things, including human beings, are interconnected, and thus all "living beings are worthy of respect simply by virtue of the inherent dignity which is inalienably theirs as living beings."[24]

At the same time, many Buddhists wish to identify *something* about human beings as distinctive, but it is difficult to say what confers special moral status on humans. Thus,

---

22. See, e.g., Paul Williams, *The Unexpected Way: On Converting from Buddhism to Catholicism* (Edinburgh: T&T Clark, 2002), 25.

23. Karma Lekshe Tsomo acknowledges this problem and tries to respond to it in chapters 1–5 of *Into the Jaws*

of Yama. For a critical assessment of these Buddhist teachings, see Keith Yandell and Harold Netland, *Buddhism: A Christian Exploration and Appraisal* (Downers Grove, Ill.: InterVarsity, 2009), chaps. 4–5.

24. Damien Keown, *Buddhism and Bioethics*, 37.

Karma Lekshe Tsomo speaks of the capacity to make intelligent choices as what sets human beings apart from other living things, and Damien Keown suggests that "life has intrinsic value only when it possesses the capacity to attain *nirvana*."[25] (When the conditions producing rebirth are eliminated, nirvana, the only reality which is permanent and unconditioned, results.) Humans have intrinsic value because they, unlike lower animals or insects, have the capacity to attain nirvana. This, it seems, is a functional quality of human beings that makes them unique; it is not an inherent property of human nature itself that confers special moral status.

Third, the status of moral values and principles is ambiguous in Buddhism. Is Buddhism a form of moral realism or nonrealism? It is difficult to say. Moral values and principles are important in Buddhism, and many Buddhists are morally exemplary in their conduct.[26] Yet whether moral distinctions and principles in Buddhism have any real existence with necessarily binding force is not clear.

A dominant stream within Buddhism teaches that there are two levels of truth or reality, a provisional level and an ultimate level. Provisional or conventional truth applies to the ordinary world of experience, and moral values and principles are part of this dimension. But on the level of ultimate reality, the dualisms and distinctions—including moral distinctions—of our ordinary world of experience are transcended and no longer obtain. Mahayana Buddhism, and Zen in particular, emphasizes the nondual nature of ultimate reality (*sunyata* or emptiness).[27] Prominent Japanese Buddhist Masao Abe explains that although the distinction between good and evil is important on the level of provisional reality, as one awakens through enlightenment to the true nature of things, even this duality is abandoned.[28] Thus, even what has become for many the definitive symbol of evil, the Holocaust, becomes ultimately less significant. "While in a human, moral dimension the Holocaust should be condemned as an unpardonable, absolute evil, *from the ultimate religious point of view, even it should not be taken as an absolute but a relative evil.*"[29]

As a Buddhist, how might Akira respond to the moral issues raised by the use of Epiginosko? If he were faithful to classical Buddhist teachings, he would not think of

---

25. Tsomo, *Into the Jaws of Yama*, 205; Damien Keown, *Buddhism and Bioethics*, 46–47. Paradoxically, nirvana is not a place (it is not heaven); it is a state, and strictly speaking, there is no person to enter nirvana. Buddhists disagree on whether individual consciousness persists in nirvana, but even if it does, it is not the consciousness of an enduring individual person.

26. The Buddha's Noble Eightfold Path explicitly calls for cultivating moral virtues in right conduct, right speech, and right livelihood. See Peter Harvey, *An Introduction to Buddhist Ethics* (Cambridge: Cambridge Univ. Press, 2000).

27. On the two truths and the two levels of reality, see Yandell and Netland, *Buddhism*, 45–46, 111–16.

28. Masao Abe, "The Meaning of Life in Buddhism," in *The Meaning of Life in the World Religions*, ed. Joseph Runzo and Nancy M. Martin (Oxford: Oneworld, 2000), 160. See also Masao Abe, "The Problem of Evil in Christianity and Buddhism," in *Buddhist-Christian Dialogue: Mutual Renewal and Transformation*, ed. Paul Ingram and Frederick J. Streng (Honolulu: Univ. of Hawaii Press, 1986), 139–54.

29. Masao Abe, "Kenotic God and Dynamic *Sunyata*," in *The Emptying God: A Buddhist-Jewish-Christian Conversation*, ed. John B. Cobb Jr. and Christopher Ives (Maryknoll, N.Y.: Orbis, 1990), 53, emphasis added.

the human being as an enduring person, certainly not as a creature endowed with special significance by a Creator. Whatever special value human beings have would seem to be a consequence of their having certain capacities which place them in a superior position for attaining enlightenment and nirvana. Moreover, if Akira followed Abe's views, then the moral issues raised by the case study would have only a provisional status. While Akira could make moral judgments as part of this lower level of reality, he would do so with the realization that the moral principles on the basis of which such judgments are made are relative to our ordinary world of experience and do not obtain on the level of ultimate reality. This has the effect of trivializing such moral judgments.

It seems, then, that for Akira judgments about whether to use Epiginosko would be made on the basis of pragmatic considerations such as whether its use is likely to lead to higher levels of awareness, thus enabling enlightenment. So long as use does not obstruct one's own path to enlightenment or bring harm to others, it would seem acceptable. Indeed, if the drug actually enhances cognitive faculties and helps one to obtain the penetrating understanding of reality necessary for enlightenment, other things being equal, its use would seem the right thing to do.[30]

SOME MINISTRY IMPLICATIONS

Moral questions, such as whether the students in the case study should use Epiginosko, do not arise in a vacuum. We have seen how attention to the broader social context of the situation at hand sheds light on how individuals from different backgrounds might approach the moral questions as well as how such considerations can shape the nature of the issues. We also have seen how basic metaphysical assumptions can affect how one approaches such issues. So where does this leave us? What opportunities for ministry are there here, especially in light of the social and cultural issues discussed? This closing section will make two general observations and then consider two possible contexts in which moral deliberation might occur.

First, the preceding discussion alerts us to the importance of understanding the broader context within which a person is located as he or she engages in moral reflection. Paul, Roberto, Akira, and Jill come from different social, cultural, and religious frameworks which affect how each understands issues such as the nature of basic moral principles, justice, and power. If one is to advise, say, Roberto or Jill on whether to use Epiginosko, one should take into account the ways in which their respective backgrounds shape their assumptions and values. As a practical matter, for those who do not

---

30. When Buddhism, and especially Zen, became popular in the United States in the 1960s and '70s, many who were attracted to Buddhism also were experimenting with psychedelic drugs such as LSD. Many Westerners claimed that use of psychedelic drugs can assist in attaining desired states of consciousness in Buddhism, although this was controversial even among Western Buddhists. See James William Coleman, *The New Buddhism: The Western Transformation of an Ancient Tradition* (New York: Oxford Univ. Press, 2001), 64–65, 201–2.

share their backgrounds, this will require listening carefully and learning about their perspectives before launching into prescriptive advice.

Second, some undesirable features of the situation at hand are "givens" which are extremely difficult to alter. So moral deliberation must take place within these limitations. We have noted that there are significant issues of power at work in the relationships between Dr. Bright and the students, and that Dr. Bright uses his position to intimidate and coerce the students. It would be difficult for the students directly to challenge Dr. Bright's abuse of his position without jeopardizing their own standing in the doctoral program. (It would, of course, be a different matter if a faculty colleague or the dean of the university were to challenge Dr. Bright.) This places the question of the use of Epiginosko in a broader context of the unethical use of power.

If one were to offer advice to any of the four students, one should be sensitive to this context and the enormous pressure this places on them to acquiesce to Dr. Bright's wishes. Now it could be that Paul, as a Christian, would conclude that he simply cannot agree to Dr. Bright's plan and, after carefully considering the consequences, refuses to take Epiginosko. This would be a case of Paul's choosing to do what he regards as morally right and accepting the consequences, in spite of a context in which he is the victim of the unjust exercise of power.

Consider now two distinct contexts in which moral decision-making regarding Epiginosko might occur. First, what should a fellow Christian advise Paul to do? Many factors are relevant here, and we cannot answer this question definitively without knowing more about the effects of Epiginosko on those who use it, among other considerations. But several things can be noted. One consideration is whether there is anything in using Epiginosko that clearly is inconsistent with biblical teaching on what it means to be a disciple of Jesus Christ. If use of Epiginosko is illegal (see discussion in chap. 6), then unless there is a compelling reason why disobeying this particular law is permitted or obligatory for a Christian, Paul should not take the drug. If it is not illegal, then other factors are relevant, such as the effects of Epiginosko on users. If use of the drug were to impair or distort in a serious way God's creation of human beings or human community, then use of Epiginosko would be wrong (see discussion in chap. 5).

Paul's concern about the drug's providing an unfair advantage over others is an important consideration, but one must treat it with realism. Roberto is correct in pointing out that not everyone faces life's challenges and opportunities from a level playing field. There are many ways in which certain individuals and groups have advantages over others. Gaining an advantage over others from use of Epiginosko need not in and of itself be morally inappropriate; the injustice depends in part on the nature of the advantage and whether use of the drug is in principle something that is available to others as well.

Suppose that Paul (a Christian) is involved in a discussion about use of Epiginosko with Akira (a Buddhist) and James (another doctoral student who, like Dr. Bright, is an atheist, a physicalist, and a moral nonrealist). Suppose that Paul has come to the conclusion that as a Christian it would be wrong for him to use Epiginosko, but Akira and James both feel it is perfectly fine to do so. How might Paul persuade Akira and James to change their minds? Paul, Akira, and James have very different views about the nature of moral principles, the reality of the human person or soul, and the inherent dignity of persons. Paul would not be able to address the issue of Epiginosko without also dealing with these broader assumptions about morality and the human person. And if Paul is to be persuasive in challenging perspectives on that level, he cannot simply appeal to biblical teaching on morality and the person. He will need to raise in their minds some questions about the adequacy of their own beliefs. Moreover, he will need to find some common ground with Akira and James and draw on at least some beliefs or values that they share with Christians.

In Western societies that are becoming increasingly diverse on many levels, in which basic biblical assumptions about morality and the dignity of persons are not widely shared, Christians need to prepare in several ways to address moral issues in intercultural settings. They need to cultivate the ability to develop biblically faithful positions on contemporary ethical challenges. They should nurture both a genuinely loving interest in the different views that another person holds, and the ability to help that person recognize why his or her views are ultimately unsatisfying. In some cases this dissatisfaction will foster an openness to the gospel message itself and the liberating worldview that brings. Where it does not, Christians can learn to appeal to a vision of the common good and principles and values that diverse communities share with the church.

CHAPTER 8

BIOETHICS AND A BETTER LIFE

William P. Cheshire

Proposal for a well-lived day: The best days go fastest. Keep up.
—*Starbucks coffee advertisement, 2008*

Paul, Akira, Roberto, and Jill stand at the threshold of extraordinary opportunity. Their brisk academic climb has brought them within view of exciting prospects for scientific discovery and professional success. Laying hold of this opportunity entails a difficult choice. Should they swallow the pill that might make them smarter?

The four students face an ethical dilemma possible only in an age of neuroscience. Their professor offers them a tantalizing tonic to boost their brain capacity. Its alluring aroma promises enhanced mental power and the capability to gain every advantage. That advantage, we suspect, would come at a cost, for their conversations hint at potential risks, some of which may be predictable and measurable, while others may be more subtle, perhaps involving even the reshaping of personality, character, or personal identity. Their scientific education has taught them an impressive array of facts concerning things as large as galaxies and as small as quarks, but technical knowledge has not prepared them to answer the ethical question of whether it is right or good to use a drug to enhance cognitive performance.

The case before us concerns the means toward scientific progress. In regard to science, there is much that a Christian appraisal can affirm. The Belgic Confession declares that the "universe is before our eyes like a beautiful book in which all creatures, great and small, are as letters to make us ponder the invisible things of God."[1] To investigate nature through science is to discover the wonders of God's creation. In the words of

---

1. Belgic (Reformed) Confession of 1561, Article 2. Complete text available at *http://www.creeds.net/belgic/index.htm* (accessed August 9, 2010).

seventeenth-century astronomer Johannes Kepler, elucidating the principles that govern nature is a way of "thinking God's thoughts after him."[2] To study the human brain, with its one hundred billion neurons exchanging signals through 160 trillion synapses, is to glimpse the profoundly intricate handiwork of the Creator, who made us "fearfully and wonderfully" (Ps. 139:14).[3] We may be thankful that, by God's grace, scientific research has yielded knowledge that people can apply responsibly to alleviate suffering and diminish the burden of disease.

It is also important to keep in mind the limitations of science. As students of physics, the Four are accustomed to thinking about nature in terms of atoms and physical forces. It may be all too easy for them to imagine that thought, too, is reducible to chemical descriptions of brain events. Their penchant for scientific explanations may draw them toward Francis Crick's "astonishing hypothesis," which is "that 'You,' your joys and your sorrows, your memories and your ambitions, your sense of personal identity and free will, are in fact no more than the behaviour of a vast assembly of nerve cells and their associated molecules."[4]

The danger of thinking about this case in terms of physical reductionism is that if one believes the mind truly to be nothing more than molecules, and Epiginosko merely a neurochemical accessory for the brain, then the ethical decision of whether to use Epiginosko reduces to a discussion about technique. The technical analysis addresses questions of potency, safety, drug development, cost, and distribution. There are, of course, further questions crucial to human flourishing for which technology by itself provides no satisfying answers. From a model of human nature limited to churning aggregations of molecules and their physical interactions, one cannot derive, for example, the obligations to love one's neighbor (Lev. 19:18; Mark 12:31) or serve one another (Gal. 5:13),[5] which Roberto and Jill articulate.

The logical flaw in such reductionism is that it confuses correlation with causation. The contributions of neuroscience are necessary, but are not sufficient, to explain the mind. The scientific portrait of the brain, while accurate, yet is not the whole truth concerning human nature. In evaluating technologies such as Epiginosko that affect the brain, we must be careful not to fall into the trap of believing that moral principles, in the words of D. Gareth Jones, "are 'nothing but' a matter of neural organization, or 'nothing but' the outpouring of certain neurotransmitters."[6]

2. See *http://www.newworldencyclopedia.org/entry/Johannes_Kepler* (accessed July 21, 2010).

3. Some consider the human brain to be integral to human creation in the image and likeness of God (Gen. 1:26–27). See Frank Meshberger, "An Interpretation of Michelangelo's *Creation of Adam* Based on Neuroanatomy," *Journal of the American Medical Association* 264, no. 14 (1990): 1837–41.

4. Francis Crick, *The Astonishing Hypothesis: The Sci-* *entific Search for the Soul* (New York: Touchstone, 1994), 3. With James D. Watson, Crick codiscovered the DNA's double helix.

5. William P. Cheshire, "Till We Have Minds," *Ethics and Medicine* 25, no. 1 (2009): 11–16.

6. D. Gareth Jones, "Peering into People's Brains: Neuroscience's Intrusion into Our Inner Sanctum," *Perspectives on Science and Christian Faith* 62, no. 2 (2010): 122–32.

In wrestling with the tough questions this case raises, we need to draw from wisdom beyond what science alone can deduce. While science supplies concrete answers to the question, Can we do this? it cannot provide answers to the question, Should we do this? Admittedly, some scientists occasionally assert ethical claims under the guise of science. It is important to keep in mind that moral assertions concerning the values and implications of science are not based on the scientific method. Scientific research involves collecting objective, measurable, empirical data and performing experiments to test hypotheses. Scientific descriptions of natural phenomena elaborate questions of what and how but do not go so far as to ascertain what we should do or why.[7] One must look beyond the category of material things to discover the broader human landscape of value, obligation, meaning, and purpose. Questions of what we ought to do surpass the logic of science.[8] In recognition of this distinction, Einstein said that he had not derived a single ethical value from all his physics.[9]

There are several realms to which people may look for ethical insight. One is philosophy, which identifies methods of systematic reasoning that may or may not involve religious considerations. Philosophical reflection will vary according to cultural settings and assumptions, as Harold Netland, Bruce Fields, and Elizabeth Sung remind us in chapter 7. Everyone in today's pluralistic settings has much to learn from experiences and perspectives beyond their own. Another realm to which people sometimes turn for ethical insight is the law. Although good laws are useful and can demonstrate what justice looks like, laws governing the legitimate use of drugs develop over time. Notably, as Paige Cunningham reminds us in chapter 6, not all that is legal is morally right, especially for the Christian, whose allegiance is to a higher law.

Discerning that higher law and its particular applications requires wisdom and obedience, drawing from the revealed word of God in Scripture, the teachings of theological traditions, and personal time in prayer earnestly seeking the will of God. Accordingly, Kevin Vanhoozer (chap. 5) encourages looking beyond the prevalent yet narrow presumptions of physicalism, scientism, and consumerism to consider what it means to be a human person in covenantal relation with God and others who bear God's image. There are many resources, then, that we will need to draw on as we consider the case before us.

BACKGROUND ISSUES

However, before we will be in a position to consider the challenges each person in the case is facing, there are some background issues that first need clarification.

---

7. William P. Cheshire, "Can Grey Voxels Resolve Neuroethical Dilemmas?" *Ethics and Medicine* 23, no. 3 (2007): 135–40.

8. See Arthur S. Eddington, *The Nature of the Physical World* (New York: Macmillan, 1931), 345.

9. Stanley L. Jaki, "Beyond Science," in *The Limits of a Limitless Science and Other Essays* (Wilmington, Del.: ISI Books, 2000), 100.

WHAT'S IN A NAME?

The names of the drugs in this case derive from ancient classical languages, as do many drug names. *Ginosko* is Greek for "I know," and *Epiginosko* is Greek for "I know fully, exactly, or completely." The word *ginosko* occurs throughout the Greek New Testament. For example, in John 8:32, Jesus says, "Then you will know [*ginosko*] the truth, and the truth will set you free."[10] Jesus, of course, is speaking not of the drug Ginosko of our hypothetical case but rather of the liberating truth of believing and obeying his word. An author sometimes adds the prefix *epi* for emphasis, as in the beginning of Luke's gospel, when Luke writes that he wants his readers to "know the certainty" (1:4) of his account of the life of Jesus.

Dr. Bright would like to persuade his students to take, in lieu of Ginosko, the more invigorating drug Epiginosko to hurry their thought processes. The apostle Paul too looks to a brilliant future when he writes, "Now I know [*ginosko*] in part; then I shall know fully [*epiginosko*]" (1 Cor. 13:12). However, Paul in this context refers not to haste but to love, which he tells his readers is patient and kind (13:4). Dr. Bright wants to fathom all knowledge, be more than he is, and gain everything. The apostle Paul anticipates those desires and adds that if one has not love, one gains nothing (13:2–3).

THINKING ABOUT BETTER BRAINS

The prospect of cognitive-performance-enhancing drugs is a factual pharmaceutical iceberg of which the hypothetical drugs in this case are but a fictional tip.[11] An abundant selection of prescription drugs is now available for the treatment of impaired sleep, attention, mood, or memory. Legitimate (licensed and off-label) and illicit use of stimulants and other drugs that sustain wakefulness, increase alertness, and improve mental focus continues to increase. Healthy professionals as well as students may be tempted to use cognitive stimulants to compete or simply to keep up with their peers who are already using them.

Current research seeks to develop more effective "smart pills" which target the molecular basis of specific brain functions. Some of these drugs are now in clinical trials. There is also a sizable market of nonprescription nutritional supplements that are purported to enhance cognitive function. Despite marginal, if any, evidence of efficacy for many of them, their market volume indicates robust consumer demand for better mental functioning. Whether prescribing enhancement drugs should fall within the professional sphere of medicine is open to debate.

The goal of medicine is health. The protection and restoration of health involves attention to the proper functioning of the body as well as wholeness in relation to the spirit. Compassion for patients (see Orr and Salladay, chap. 10) and the scientific will to

---

10. Unless otherwise noted, all biblical quotations in this chapter are from *The Holy Bible, New International Version* (Grand Rapids, Mich.: Zondervan, 1985).

11. William P. Cheshire, "Drugs for Enhancing Cognition and Their Ethical Implications: A Hot New Cup of Tea," *Expert Review of Neurotherapeutics* 6 (2006): 263–66.

power (see Vanhoozer, chap. 5) have motivated medical research to explore the molecular, cellular, and organic structure of the human body. This research has yielded knowledge of how, albeit imperfectly and incompletely, to repair the body and heal patients.

Western medicine has traditionally understood its purpose to be treatment, which intervenes to restore lost bodily function or preserve failing health. Enhancement, by contrast, aims to exceed normal capacity. While both treatment and enhancement endeavor to make the body better, the goal of bodily enhancement lies beyond the primary professional mandate of medicine as physicians have understood and practiced it since the time of Hippocrates.

Ethical distinctions between treatment and enhancement are, nonetheless, sometimes blurred and contested, as we see in the comments of Dr. Bright to Roberto. The boundary between normal health and disease is not always clear. For example, would restoring mild forgetfulness in a healthy fifty-year-old count as therapy, or would it be enhancement? The answer depends on how one defines what is natural. Since natural capacities change over a lifetime, and people possess them to differing degrees, the concept of natural is contextual. Advocates of enhancement technology often argue that distinctions between the natural and the artificial lack conceptual precision. Echoing the postmodern skepticism that deems the natural order to be a cultural construction, Dr. Bright quips that they are arbitrary.[12]

Still, there does seem to be a substantive difference between the cognitive enhancements of restful sleep, disciplined study, healthy nutrition, and physical exercise on the one hand and pharmaceutical enhancements such as Epiginosko on the other. A group of prominent Christian bioethicists offers a cautionary perspective: "When enhancement is the sole intention of the use of biotechnology, when there is no disease present but only the desire to pursue perfection, immortality, super performance, a competitive edge, and so forth, there seems little justification for physician participation and good reasons for morally excluding it."[13]

These comments confirm Roberto's intuition concerning the appropriate relationship between drugs and the treatment of disease. Enhancement aspirations are misguided when they attempt to reduce fundamental human struggles to biological problems that medical technology can solve.

EVALUATING PROGRESS

While few readers may aspire to solve a seemingly impossible problem in physics, most can appreciate the unprecedented prosperity that inventions such as the electric

---

12. Brent Waters argues that the technology that "liberates" humanity from the constraints of nature is but the flip side of the postmodern ideology that what passes for nature is actually an arbitrary social construction—i.e., "culture." See Brent Waters, *From Human to Posthuman: Christian Theology and Technology in a Postmodern World* (Aldershot, UK, and Burlington, Vt.: Ashgate, 2006), 21–46.

13. C. Ben Mitchell, Edmund D. Pellegrino, Jean Bethke Elshtain, John F. Kilner, and Scott B. Rae, *Biotechnology and the Human Good* (Washington, D.C.: Georgetown Univ. Press, 2007), 135.

light, the telephone, the automobile, and the computer have afforded for modern life. Dr. Bright suggests that the next chapter in the story of human progress may be the discovery of an answer to the global problem of affordable energy.

Some scholars predict that "humanity's ability to alter its own brain function might well shape history as powerfully as the development of . . . mechanization in the Industrial Revolution."[14] The case before us probes this question of whether augmentation of the brain through technology is genuine human progress. If the measure of progress is human ability to manipulate nature, is it also progress to manipulate *human* nature, including the brain processes that underlie how people think?

Whether neuropharmacology could accelerate the speed of thought is a technical question. The related ethical question is whether faster thought would lead to a richer, more meaningful life. Admittedly, drinking more caffeine or taking stimulants stronger than caffeine might facilitate keeping up, but there are reasons to be cautious about emphasizing swiftness. If pushed to the extreme, augmenting the superficial aspects of cognition might detract from its more profound aspects. For example, James McClelland and colleagues, in researching the neurobiology of memory, warn that "selectively enhancing the durability of individual memories might come at the expense of less ability to generalize, to reflect deeply, to accumulate wisdom rather than mere information."[15] Increasing intellectual ability, as Vanhoozer points out in chapter 5, cannot by itself cultivate intellectual virtue.

Cognitive enhancement usually focuses on information processing, which is but one aspect of intelligence. Other aspects include the emotional qualities of interpersonal relationships, compassion, judgment, and spiritual reflection, which may not fit within a compressed timeframe. Gains in the speed of information processing might restrict the abilities to imagine, ponder, and experience awe and joy. The supercharged minds whizzing by one another in a hypercaffeinated world might overlook beauty and fail to see subtlety.[16] One wonders whether an overly revved brain could still pause to be reverent.

By analogy, gulping down a meal in one tenth the time may not enhance the experience of dining with friends. The conversation the Four are having over lunch requires time if they are to listen to one another and reach a thoughtful decision. As for the psalmist, whose "delight is in the law of the Lord" and who "meditates on his law day and night" (Ps. 1:2), the richest thoughts and the dearest relationships are best savored.

The challenge for Christians is how to honor God by applying biblical principles to the use of technology. Everything that is good about individuals, institutions, and

14. Martha J. Farah, Judy Illes, Robert Cook-Deegan, et al., "Neurocognitive Enhancement: What Can We Do and What Should We Do?" *Nature Reviews—Neuroscience* 5, no. 5 (2004): 421–25.

15. J. L. McClelland, B. L. McNaughton, and R. C. O'Reilly, "Why There Are Complementary Learning Systems in the Hippocampus and Neocortex: Insights from the Successes and Failures of Connectionist Models of Learning and Memory," *Psychological Review* 102 (1995): 419–57.

16. William P. Cheshire, "Accelerated Thought in the Fast Lane," *Ethics and Medicine* 25, no. 2 (2009): 75–78.

social structures comes from God, but all are severely flawed on account of the fall and are in need of redemption. To the extent that churches are local representations of the new order of Jesus Christ in the midst of the old, Christians must give serious thought as to how to live their technology-laden lives together. If they are to engage in thoughts and practices that are conducive to, rather than in competition with, the reality of the gospel, they need to be aware of increasingly influential cultural forces working against them, such as transhumanism.

REACHING BEYOND HUMAN

Pharmacologic cognitive enhancement is but one instrument in the toolbox of a relatively new philosophy today that seeks to enhance human nature. Transhumanism, urging a transition to a "posthuman" future, is an outlook centered on the idea of radical human enhancement. For transhumanists, trust in biotechnology is the key to overcoming fundamental human limitations.

According to Nick Bostrom, cofounder of the World Transhumanist Association, improvement in the human condition would be "a change that gives increased opportunity for individuals to shape themselves and their lives according to their informed wishes."[17] Bostrom considers human beings to be autonomous, a law unto themselves. In our case, Dr. Bright affirms very strong support for autonomy. Whereas the principle of autonomy in medical ethics has focused on preserving bodily integrity in terms of the right of patients to decide what may be done to their bodies, transhumanists go farther and appeal to autonomy to argue for the right to make of one's body what one wants.

Because the body to the transhumanist is an obstacle to humanity's will to power, overcoming it is essential. Transhumanist Simon Young promotes the ideology of "designer evolution," in which he believes that human beings have an innate will to evolve (i.e., a will to self-enhancement).[18] Enhancement technologies have, according to Young, brought near the moment when humans acquire the technology that permits them to take their evolution into their own hands, not only mastering nature but also mastering and even transforming human nature, if not overcoming death itself. The transhumanist hope is the anticipation that through technology, people eventually will become posthuman entities, superintelligences no longer bound by biological chains. Transhumanism outlines not a scientific program but an ethical position in proposing a vision for the good life. This vision concerns not the common human good but rather the empowerment of a biotechnologically elite class that aspires to leave humanity behind. Julian Savulescu, who also advocates for transhumanism, writes that "humans

17. Nick Bostrom, Transhumanist FAQ 3.7, *http://humanityplus.org/learn/transhumanist-faq* (accessed July 28, 2010).

18. Simon Young, *Designer Evolution: A Transhumanist Manifesto* (Amherst, N.Y.: Prometheus, 2006). See also Joel Garreau, *Radical Evolution: The Promise and Peril of Enhancing Our Minds, Our Bodies—and What It Means to be Human* (New York: Broadway, 2005).

may become extinct.... We might have reason to save or create such vastly superior lives, rather than continue the human line."[19]

The transhumanist vision contrasts sharply with that of Christians, who believe that the key to eternal life is to cultivate a right relationship with God. In place of "to glorify God and enjoy him forever,"[20] the transhumanist credo is to "seek out all possible information by which to transcend biological limitations."[21] The tacit promise of transhumanism, as Vanhoozer surmises in chapter 5, is that radically enhanced people will be like God (Gen. 3:5). The transhumanist dissatisfaction with given human nature differs strikingly from the value Christians recognize in humanity as bearing God's image (Gen. 1:27). Moreover, the Lord Jesus Christ supremely affirmed this special dignity by taking on human nature himself, entering into human history as one who is fully God and fully human in one person.[22] The upgraded version of cognitively enhanced humanity to which the transhumanism movement aspires, ironically and inevitably, falls short of the glorious state that redeemed humanity will experience in eternity, as glimpsed in the earthly appearances of the risen Christ.

PRIMARY STAKEHOLDERS

With a better appreciation of some of the challenges of technology-driven contemporary cultures, we are now in a better position to look more closely at the ethical dynamics of our case through the particular perspectives of each stakeholder.

ROBERTO

For Roberto, gaining advantages is about playing well the cards one has been dealt in the game of life. Coming from a single-parent home in a poor section of Los Angeles, he was able to pursue a university education against considerable socioeconomic odds, and only through his mother's sacrifices. He would understandably feel conflicted over whether to take Epiginosko. On one hand, he is loyal to his family, and if his mother (if he consults her) should express strong views against his gaining an advantage by taking a drug, he would likely heed her advice. On the other hand, he is pragmatic and has no moral qualms about "using something that gives me a little edge."

Roberto's experience has taught him to respect the potential risks and dangers of drugs that stimulate the brain. Signs of stimulant use, such as the sweat on Dr. Bright's

---

19. Julian Savulescu, "The Human Prejudice and the Moral Status of Enhanced Beings: What Do We Owe the Gods?" in *Human Enhancement*, ed. Julian Savulescu and Nick Bostrom (Oxford: Oxford Univ. Press, 2009), 244.

20. This is the answer to the question, "What is the chief end of man?" in the Westminster Catechism, available at *http://www.creeds.net/Westminster/shorter_catechism.html* (accessed July 13, 2010).

21. Young, *Designer Evolution*, 92–93.

22. The scriptural support of Jesus' combined humanity and deity is extensive. See Wayne Grudem, *Systematic Theology: An Introduction to Biblical Doctrine* (Leicester, UK: Inter-Varsity; Grand Rapids, Mich.: Zondervan, 1994), 529–67; Nigel M. de S. Cameron, *Complete in Christ: Rediscovering Jesus and Ourselves* (London: Paternoster, 1989).

twitching brow, may remind him of the destructive effects of cocaine on the health of his high school friend. We expect that Roberto would advocate for adequate and long-term studies of Epiginosko prior to its routine clinical use. He would recognize the importance of assessing the effects, beneficial and harmful, of the new drug on the brain and on society.

Roberto is likely to be sensitive to considerations of distributive justice. Suppose that, when he was in high school, Ginosko had been legal and available only to those with financial means. Unable to afford the drug himself, he might have felt academically disadvantaged in the same way he actually did growing up in relative poverty. Fast-forward to a possible future society in which health care takes on the responsibility not only for healing the sick but also for providing enhancement medications to the healthy. The advent of "cosmetic neurology" could, depending on demand, potentially strain the principle of distributive justice, which concerns the equitable allocation of limited resources. Sick people needing access to medical expertise would have to compete against healthy people seeking enhancements.[23] Since Roberto entered science "to find ways to help people," the prospect of diverting medical resources to the healthy may trouble him.

PAUL

For Paul, gaining advantages is a fruit of the good application of intelligence. His conception of what is right comes from the objective moral principles his parents impressed on him during his upbringing "in a devout Christian African-American home." Like many in the church today, Paul feels uncertain how to apply those principles to the realities of modern life and especially to the many challenges that the astonishing advance of science poses.

He has a sense that the wisdom of the Bible is relevant to his situation. Yet when discussing his ideas about spirituality, he lacks the precision of language that he has developed in the sciences. It does not help matters that the Bible has not provided him with explicit instructions telling him whether it is right to take a neuropharmaceutical cognitive-enhancing drug. So while his spiritual commitments may run strong, he is reserved in his efforts to explore the connections between his faith (defining who he is at the core of his person) and his science (defining where he is heading in a promising career).

Paul's understanding would benefit from D. A. Carson's discussion in chapter 9 about addressing issues unknown in the Bible. Carson's approach is to survey a variety of biblical-theological themes that are indisputably grounded in Scripture, teasing out principles relevant to modern questions. What makes an action right is not merely what one does but also why one ultimately does it.

---

23. William P. Cheshire, "Just Enhancement," *Ethics and Medicine* 26, no. 1 (2010): 7–10.

Paul's Christian assumptions, as Netland, Fields, and Sung point out in chapter 7, would include the belief that human persons are not reducible simply to physical properties. Accordingly, whether to take Epiginosko would be more than a pragmatic question for him. He would recognize Epiginosko's potential to magnify not only good but also evil human inclinations.

AKIRA

For Akira, gaining advantages is the cumulative result of mental perseverance. Taught to be studious from an early age, he has competed intensely and is not about to relax his efforts. He is ambitious and thinks globally. The world is his classroom. Large problems such as the international need for affordable energy intrigue him.

Netland, Fields, and Sung explain in chapter 7 that Akira's Buddhist worldview suggests to many that moral judgments about drugs such as Epiginosko affect only the lower or provisional level of reality and may have no consequence for the cycles of ultimate reality. As long as he does not harm others, then, he is free to enhance his cognitive functions, especially if that aids his path to enlightenment.

Akira is poised for a hypercaffeinated, digitally connected, multitasking life. In the near future, we may predict that the marketing division of the company that sells Epiginosko will organize focus groups to explore irresistible ways to present their product to potential customers like Akira. Within the licensing constraints of approved labeling, there is much that images can suggest. Artists in the company's graphic-design division, all of whom are using Epiginosko, will create shimmering digital images suggesting that Epiginosko accelerates the path to greater enlightenment. They will devise internet pop-up ads to show Akira why he should consider the next "improved" version of Epiginosko to enhance further his performance by clarifying his thought, strengthening his memory, and improving his self-confidence. New ads will appear each year. The ads will also show how, without the latest drug, potential customers such as Akira really are cognitively inadequate and falling behind. Finding satisfaction by chasing after the repeating cycle of drug promotion will prove ever elusive.

There is much that Akira and Paul might discuss together regarding their different religious upbringings. In seeking after a better world, Buddhists and Christians alike must wrestle with how their worldviews evaluate human effort in relation to progress in present and future reality. The writer of Ecclesiastes asks a universal question: "What does a man get for all the toil and anxious striving with which he labors under the sun?" (2:22). Both Akira and Paul could relate to the apostle Paul's advice, "Do you not know that in a race all the runners run, but only one gets the prize? Run in such a way as to get the prize" (1 Cor. 9:24). In his race onward to endless rebirths, Akira seeks after nirvana. If Paul has been faithful to run his race as Christ has directed, he knows that he will be able to say, "I have fought the good fight, I have finished the race, I have kept the faith," and will receive the victor's crown of eternal life (2 Tim. 4:7–8).

JILL

For Jill, gaining advantages involves transcending ordinary thought. She is already imagining applications of Epiginosko that had not occurred to the others. From the case description, we know less about Jill's origins. Perhaps she has been cautious not to confide many details about herself to the others. After all, she is the only woman in the group, and her special status as Dr. Bright's personal assistant distances her somewhat from the other students. Gender, as Netland, Fields, and Sung remind us, is relevant to the shape of personal values and the contour of interpersonal dynamics.

Cunningham (chap. 6) and Netland, Fields, and Sung (chap. 7) caution us not to underestimate the potential of relationships of unequal power to coerce decisions about whether to use Epiginosko. Accordingly, Jill might not feel free to decline the drug because of loyalty, attraction, or financial dependence resulting from her relationship with Dr. Bright as his personal assistant. (See also the parallel discussion of coercion by Scott Rae and Helen Eckmann in chap. 2.)

Among all the cognitive capacities subject to enhancement, the aspects a woman might value could differ considerably from those many men desire. For example, we see from Jill's comments that she appears to be less concerned with attaining a personal performance edge than she is with exploring potential altruistic applications of Epiginosko.

In Jill's final comment, we also glimpse the potential of Epiginosko, in the hands of imperfect human beings, to exacerbate rather than alleviate ethnic jealousies and other prejudices. Jill's startling comment raises serious questions about how, in a world plagued by racial prejudice and other forms of exclusion, disparities in access to a drug for enhancing human potential might play out. Would the enhanced come to despise those who, by choice or neglect, remained unenhanced? Would the enhanced come to stigmatize those who appeared exhausted, frustrated, or sleep-deprived as having a psychological deficiency in need of medication?

A Christian outlook, sensitive to the character of God, would be wary about proposals to provide a resource such as Epiginosko to certain types of people while excluding it from others. God rescues and provides for the poor and needy (e.g., Pss. 12:5; 109:31) and does not show favoritism. God's saving grace is for people of all ethnicities (Jonah 4:11; Rom. 2:11; 10:12–13; Eph. 2:14).

DR. BAUBLE

The first mention of Dr. Bauble finds him prescribing methylphenidate, a controlled substance, in a way that is ethically questionable if not illegal. It gets worse. He develops a shadowy relationship with an overseas pharmacy to supply Ginosko, which is not available (we may assume it is not approved) for medical use in the United States. Without taking a medical history or performing a physical examination, in the final paragraph of the case we find him not only prescribing but also dispensing his new drug, Epiginosko, and rushing the Four into a decision about treatment.

Before signing consent forms, which Dr. Bauble does not explain except as "just a slight formality," the students would be wise to ask questions. They might want to know something about the anticipated side effects and potential serious risks of the medication. They might inquire about Dr. Bauble's potential conflicts of interest, such as his share of publishing royalties which depends on the research to which the Four would be contributing.

They might inquire also about the postdoctoral fellow who withdrew because of health issues. Since, according to rumor, she had struggled to keep up with the program, she might have failed because she chose not to use Epiginosko, or else she may have developed adverse health effects from the drug. Some of the side effects from stimulant use can include anxiety, insomnia, headache, heart palpitations or rhythm disturbances, tremor, and depression. Greater health risks would be expected for higher doses. Even caffeine, if consumed to great excess, has been associated with an increased risk of suicide.[24]

While the Four need more information from Dr. Bauble, they would also benefit from counseling (involving someone other than Dr. Bauble) to help them appreciate the significance of that information. In chapter 3, Greggo and Parent discuss the value of counseling to help people consider the long-term implications of their decisions. In this case, such counseling could assist the students to weigh conflicting ethical considerations. It could also help them to envision how those who matter to them would view their winning the Nobel Prize, if it became known that they beat other researchers by gaining an unfair pharmaceutical advantage.

From the case study, we know nothing about Dr. Bauble as a person, but we do discover evidence of his style of medical practice. A physician who is so quick to take ethical shortcuts and fails to show concern for his patients' interests is not likely to be very admirable overall. Dr. Bauble is certainly not typical of physicians, who generally are dedicated to helping their patients. He hardly exemplifies the ideal of pastoral truthfulness that Steven Roy upholds in chapter 11. His actions are a caricature of the conduct of a few, for which reason professional standards exist.

Suppose that Dr. Bauble did not start out that way. Perhaps he began his medical career with the best of intentions. However, at some point he succumbed to the daunting challenge of keeping up with mounting volumes of medical literature,[25] the taxing time demands of a busy clinical practice, and the expectation of sustaining attention to respond on a moment's notice, day and night, to medical emergencies. He struck a Faustian bargain of the kind Vanhoozer describes in chapter 5 and began to take Epiginosko to augment his cognitive performance.

---

24. A. Tanskanen, J. Tuomilehto, H. Vilnamäki, et al., "Heavy Coffee Drinking and the Risk of Suicide," *European Journal of Epidemiology* 16 (2000): 789–91.

25. PubMed comprises twenty million citations from biomedical literature, with 680,000 citations added in 2009: *http://www.nlm.nih.gov/bsd/medline_cit_counts_yr_pub.html* (accessed July 13, 2010).

His initial motives may have been, for the most part, altruistic, with a genuine desire to practice excellent medicine. Perhaps he rationalized that taking a stimulant would be in the best interests of his patients because, if the drug made him more alert, it might decrease his risk of making errors when writing prescriptions. Perhaps he reasoned also that enhanced productivity during working hours would translate to more time left over for rest and to spend with his family. He found, instead, that he ended up using his boosted energy to accomplish even more work. When he missed a dose, he felt slow and ineffective. Epiginosko steepened the incline of his trajectory of professional performance expectations, and now the drug was no longer optional but necessary to maintain that trajectory. He feared falling behind. He became preoccupied with efficiency. Haste characterized all that he did. His creativity faded. Eventually, his relationships crumbled, he divorced, and his heart hardened.

In this hypothetical addendum to the case, we see that Dr. Bauble may have been the first casualty of Epiginosko and that his story could be a warning to others. Physicians by nature and by training are hardworking and frequently are perfectionists. The most conscientious physician is, at best, subject to human limitations and cannot meet all the needs of his patients perfectly all the time. Reliance on cognitive stimulants to enhance the performance of professionals could accelerate the risk of burnout.[26]

Although Dr. Bauble does not admit it, he knows that no drug is without side effects. For example, 1970s advertisements portrayed the supposed cultural attractiveness of cigarette smoking in appealing images such as the Marlboro Man and the Virginia Slims Lady. But we now know that the toxic health effects resulting from tobacco, in reality, paint an ugly picture. Drs. Bauble and Bright are alarming not because they represent portraits of where taking cognitive-performance-enhancing drugs must lead in every case but because they portray the deformation of character and spirit that results from yielding to the powerful temptations that do indeed constantly accompany such drugs.

PROFESSOR BRIGHT

The famous Professor Bright would like to think that he is the protagonist in this story. We find, however, that it is his students who engage our interest as they struggle to decide whether to pursue their careers with Epiginosko.

When disappointments have interrupted Dr. Bright's narcissistic quest, he has sought rescue in ever stronger enhancements. His academic ambition parallels the greed that drives some in the business world (which Rae and Eckmann discuss in chap. 2). There is an emptiness to Bright's overreliance on technology, the value of which he chooses to measure in articles published and books sold. The cautionary words of the author of

---

26. William P. Cheshire, "The Pharmacologically Enhanced Physician," *Virtual Mentor AMA Journal of Ethics* 10, no. 9 (2008): 594–98.

Ecclesiastes offer a rather different evaluation of such "success," noting that when "words grow many, there is vanity" (5:7 ESV).[27]

Dr. Bright correctly notes that "pharmaceuticals are a form of technology" and goes on to suggest that academic and other forms of social success are all about the "survival of the *best fitted*" (i.e., the biotechnologically outfitted, playing on Darwin's maxim of "survival of the fittest").[28] Nick Bostrom and Julian Savulescu would agree, finding no significant distinction between natural and enhanced human capacities. They argue that "*all* technology can be viewed as an enhancement of our native human capacities, enabling us to achieve certain effects that would otherwise require more effort or be altogether beyond our power."[29] In chapter 5, Vanhoozer dismantles that argument, pointing out the fallacy of equating technologies that aim to redraw the boundaries of the created order with those that align with the divine design plan. In a related vein, Richard Averbeck (chap. 1) illustrates how exerting willful human power without regard to God's original design leads to great difficulty.

Other champions of pharmaceutical cognitive enhancement appeal to the inevitability of use of drugs that will be "increasingly useful for improved quality of life and extended work productivity" and will thus "benefit both the individual and society."[30] Dr. Bright insists that all who want such drugs should have access to them. In support of widespread use, Martha Farah argues that "enhancement of mood, cognition and vegetative functions in healthy people is now a fact of life, and the only uncertainties concern the speed with which new and more appealing enhancement methods will become available and attract more users."[31] The appeal to inevitability, however, sidesteps the ethical question of whether each person should accept such practices or should resist them.

Dr. Bright aspires to a level of scientific discovery that he believes to be unreachable through ordinary human talent, even if combined with teamwork, funding, and sophisticated laboratory equipment. His ambitious objective lies, he insists, only within the grasp of the pharmacologically exalted intellect possible through Epiginosko, which permanently strengthens synaptic connections in a way that "alters the very structure of the brain." Such remodeling of the brain may not be unique, since neurobiology has

---

27. Note also the advice of Jesus, who said, "And when you pray, do not keep on babbling like pagans, for they think they will be heard because of their many words" (Matt. 6:7); cf. "When words are many, sin is not absent" (Prov. 10:19).

28. Compare also Bright's advice to choose mental stimulation over staleness to Moses' appeal to the people of Israel in Deut. 30:19–20.

29. Nick Bostrom and Julian Savulescu, "Human Enhancement Ethics: The State of the Debate," in Savulescu and Bostrom, *Human Enhancement*, 2.

30. Henry Greely, Barbara Sahakian, John Harris, Ronald C. Kessler, Michael Gazzaniga, Phillip Campbell, and Martha J. Farah, "Towards Responsible Use of Cognitive-Enhancing Drugs by the Healthy," *Nature* 456 (2008): 702–5; Anjan Chatterjee, "Cosmetic Neurology: The Controversy over Enhancing Movement, Mentation, and Mood," *Neurology* 63 (2004): 968–74.

31. Martha J. Farah, "Emerging Ethical Issues in Neuroscience," *Nature Neuroscience* 5, no. 11 (2002): 1123–29.

found that the brain is naturally plastic, meaning that learning and interactions with the environment themselves alter neural structure.[32]

What is noteworthy about this new technology is its potential to move beyond mastering human nature to rewiring it in a directed and invasive manner. Brent Waters summarizes, "If the modern project is to make humans better, then the postmodern goal is to make creatures that are better than human."[33] This new cognitive-enhancing technology is arriving just as postmodern thinkers are questioning whether human beings have natures and whether there is an objective order to the world as opposed to merely subjective versions of the world and the self.[34]

That many might choose to partake of the fruit of biomedical enhancement should not distract from its revolutionary significance.[35] While human beings have always used tools to cultivate the earth, neuroscience has discovered tools that potentially can rework the biological foundations of humanity in an unprecedented manner. Human tool users following the example of Dr. Bright risk being retooled by the very tools they made.

We find little in this story to admire about Dr. Bright. Even his prime achievement, the prestigious Nobel Prize, he won through considerable pharmaceutical assistance. Other scientists competing for the prize presumably lacked the advantage of cognitive-performance-enhancing medication to augment their scientific productivity. Full disclosure from Dr. Bright, which Rae and Eckmann in chapter 2 remind us is a paramount ethical obligation, might have acknowledged the contribution from Epiginosko and its manufacturer. Cunningham in chapter 6 has aptly drawn the analogy to fairness in athletic competition free of doping. Dr. Bright's appeal to financial success, while shrugging off any concerns about fairness as an "outdated moral grumble," comes across as crass. Moreover, Dr. Bright seems to be making an incorrect assumption that his students hold to his same values, which, as Greggo and Parent (chap. 3) emphasize, is problematic.

Dr. Bright's apparent lack of concern for the health and welfare of his students is troubling. His attitude is reminiscent of the tragic success of a cognitive-enhancement experiment in a 1963 television episode of *The Outer Limits*. In this science-fiction story, technology transforms an ordinary man into a superintellect. Having attained extreme intellect, he finds himself so far removed from human intelligence that he loses his compassion and, with it, his humanity.[36] In the end, we are uncertain whether Dr. Bright is a man of genius or merely the appearance of genius inflated by technology. To him, the distinction might not matter. His question, "What is normal?" echoes Pilate's question to Jesus, "What is truth?" (John 18:38).

---

32. Nancey Murphy, *Bodies and Souls, or Spirited Bodies?* (Cambridge, UK: Cambridge Univ. Press, 2006), 103; Normal Doidge, *The Brain That Changes Itself* (New York: Penguin, 2007).

33. Waters, *From Human to Posthuman*, 50.

34. See, e.g., Martha J. Farrah and Andrea S. Heberlein, "Personhood and Neuroscience: Naturalizing or Nihilating?" *American Journal of Bioethics* 7, no. 1 (2007): 37–48.

35. The widely traveled way may not be the better way (see Matt. 7:13).

36. David McCallum stars in "The Sixth Finger," *The Outer Limits*, season 1, episode 5, 1963.

RECOMMENDATIONS FOR THE CHURCH

Truth, as Pilate failed to recognize, has come into the world and has dwelt among us (John 1:1 – 17). The timeless words of Jesus, who said, "I am the way and the truth and the life" (John 14:6), remain an open invitation to the church in the twenty-first century. Jesus beckons us to a better way, which he thought best to illustrate in his ministry by healing rather than enhancing people.

The case before us focuses on a drug that enhances the intellectual abilities of normal, healthy people. It joins the pantheon of other pharmaceutical enhancers promising to improve one's strength, endurance, appearance, mood, and sex life. How we think about the cognitive enhancer in this case likely will shed considerable light on how we evaluate other forms of enhancement.

The purpose of this chapter is not to make a case that it would always be wrong to use cognitive-enhancing pharmaceuticals. People may enjoy coffee and tea, which contain caffeine, in gratitude to God who created the plants that produce them. Chocolate, likewise, has very mild stimulant properties due to theobromine, which is structurally similar to caffeine. Caffeine has health benefits as well as health risks; it can abolish a migraine headache, but if used to excess, it can also worsen headaches, and cause anxiety, insomnia, heart palpitations, and other undesirable effects. With stronger stimulants and drugs such as Epiginosko come weightier moral and spiritual concerns, and these call for responsible stewardship decisions.

To presume that Christians should decide to be for or against an entire set of technologies such as enhancement technologies would be to oversimplify a complex subject. In evaluating the consequences of enhancement biotechnologies, Christians would be wise to refrain from (or sometimes even proactively reject) those technologies that promise to enhance, yet in their application are found to erode human dignity, degrade human relationships, or divert attention from knowing and serving God. Discernment of the motives and aspirations of enhancement proposals is also crucial. A Christian perspective is careful not to mistakenly place ultimate hope in technology as the means to solve all human problems or save humanity by transforming it into something beyond human. With biblical assurance, people may trust completely in God's sovereign redemptive plan.

The principal aim of this book is Christian practical wisdom: knowing how to make good judgments about what the renewing of the mind (Rom. 12:2) entails and what the renewed mind can approve in an age of biological enhancement.

QUESTIONS TO ASK

When considering the option of taking a drug to improve mental functioning, there are various questions a Christian should ask. These include, What are one's motives for seeking enhancement? Is it only for one's own benefit, or is it to serve others better?

Medical and economic consequences are also important. Is the drug safe? What are the potential short-term and long-term side effects? What are the potential interactions with other medications? Is the expenditure a wise use of personal financial resources? Does it foster a better world or contribute to an unjust distribution of resources?

Life consequences matter as well. Would the drug enrich the quality as well as the amount of work that could be done? Would the drug truly ennoble, or would it more likely misrepresent or distort self-image? How would it influence one's evaluation of others? Would it enrich or impoverish relationships? Would the unenhanced eventually become jealous of those who seem more enhanced, or would the enhanced look down on those who seem less enhanced and unable to keep up?

Deeper questions of faith are central here. How would using the drug affect people's daily walk with God? Would the drug enhance or distract from their ability to be attentive to God and to the needs of others? Would using an enhancing drug lead others to stumble? (1 Cor. 8:9; Rom. 14:13). Would God's people want to use the drug in gratitude for what God, through science, has provided for their benefit, or would it as likely tempt them to rebel against the identity God has given them, seeking instead to remake themselves in our own image?

CHOOSING WELL

Miriam Charter asks in chapter 14, If the brain's design makes it capable of such a broad range of thinking skills, why do people not use it better? While human destiny is ultimately in God's sovereign hands, people's choices—including how they use their brains—shape the courses of their lives. Each day presents decisions about how to apply finite mental resources. People can choose from the thousands of sources of technological entertainment, so squandering their thinking on aimless and trivial distractions that they impoverish personal relationships and stunt their growth in the knowledge of God.[37] Having crowded out what is truly important, people might then find themselves more in need of using an enhancing drug simply to catch up and meet mounting routine obligations.

Or God's people can choose to apply their mental resources to what truly matters: acting justly, loving mercy, and walking humbly with God (Mic. 6:8). Achieving a proper balance of the mental ingredients of a well-lived life requires being intentional in making choices about how to spend time. Those who appreciate their finitude and the brevity of their lives will be less likely to waste mental effort on meaningless activities. They may join the psalmist in praying, "Teach us to number our days aright, that we may gain a heart of wisdom" (Ps. 90:12), for life is fleeting (Ps. 39:4).

Scripture offers helpful guidance for using one's brain effectively amid life's troubles.

---

37. Gary Small and Gigi Vorgan, *iBrain: Surviving the Technological Alteration of the Modern Mind* (New York: HarperCollins, 2008).

The apostle Paul writes, "Do not be anxious about anything, but in everything, by prayer and petition, with thanksgiving, present your requests to God. And the peace of God, which transcends all understanding, will guard your hearts and your minds in Christ Jesus" (Phil. 4:6–7). The secret to finding that peace begins with what Scharf in chapter 13 calls a "posture of gratitude," in contrast to the attitude of dissatisfaction that may motivate some to seek enhancements through biotechnology. In addition to gratitude, Paul emphasizes that where people choose to focus their thoughts affects their outlook on life: "Finally, brothers, whatever is true, whatever is noble, whatever is right, whatever is pure, whatever is lovely, whatever is admirable — if anything is excellent or praiseworthy — think about such things" (Phil. 4:8). Having a moral roadmap matters more than speed in living well and reaching life's goals.

LESS IS MORE

The following words exemplify the fashionable counsel for living well that confronts us daily through advertisements: "Supplement your performance with alertness, and alertness with information, and information with energy, and energy with sexual drive, and sexual drive with competitive edge, and competitive edge with something then to help you sleep, and better sleep with entertainment."

The wisdom of the gospel, by contrast, is foolishness to those with worldly notions of perfection. Jesus says in Matthew 23:12 that "whoever exalts himself will be humbled, and whoever humbles himself will be exalted." The New Testament recommends the following path to godly perfection: "Make every effort to add to your faith goodness; and to goodness, knowledge; and to knowledge, self-control; and to self-control, perseverance; and to perseverance, godliness; and to godliness, brotherly kindness; and to brotherly kindness, love. For if you possess these qualities in increasing measure, they will keep you from being ineffective and unproductive in your knowledge of our Lord Jesus Christ" (2 Peter 1:5–8).

With or without pharmaceutical assistance, people can do nothing ultimately meaningful if not in Christ (John 15:5), but in the strength of Christ, people can do all things (Phil. 4:13). Jesus' promise that, through him, we may "have life, and have it to the full" (John 10:10) does not depend on technological augmentation of human nature. God's refreshment surpasses psychopharmacology. Jesus holds out to us a hand, not with a pill but with the pierced scar of love. "Come to me," he says, "all you who are weary and burdened, and I will give you rest … for I am gentle and humble in heart, and you will find rest for your souls" (Matt. 11:28–29).

MY PACE IS SUFFICIENT FOR YOU

Part of what it means to be human is to be a limited creature. There is wisdom in limitations. Richard Swenson, a family physician, writes, "It is God the Creator who made limits, and it is the same God who placed them within us for our protection. We exceed them at our peril."[38] People think most clearly when they take time to pause and be still and know that the Lord is God (Ps. 46:10). Only in humility can one understand the words of Jesus: "My grace is sufficient for you, for my power is made perfect in weakness" (2 Cor. 12:9).

An informed-consent conversation would be incomplete without a discussion of the alternatives to the proposed treatment. There is abundant evidence that physical exercise, periodic rest, reading, and other forms of mental engagement all contribute to healthy cognitive function. Pursuing enhancements without regard for these readily available resources that God has provided would be unwise stewardship. Similarly imprudent would be engaging in activities that can be detrimental to mental acuity, such as taking illicit or recreational drugs, excessive use of alcohol, and risky behavior such as reckless driving that has the potential to cause head injury.

Further components of a constructively alternative lifestyle include not indulging in empty activities that steal from time with others, time with God, restorative rest, and work that is truly important. Moreover, exercising haste where necessary is appropriate, but taking care to cultivate an unhurried demeanor is important when it comes to the significant moments in human relationships. Freeing the mind requires also submitting the burdens of selfishness, unforgiveness, anger, and jealousy to the cross of Christ. Through confession and God's forgiveness come joy and the experience of God's love freely at work (see Carson, chap. 9, and Scharf, chap. 13).

ASK AND YOU SHALL RECEIVE

Placing all hope in pharmacology and other technologies ultimately fails to satisfy. If it were possible to solve all problems and achieve the highest goals through bioenhancements and other technologies (i.e., through human projects), there would be no need to trust in God. As Greggo and Parent observe in chapter 3, difficult questions that people formerly took to God in prayer they now take to medical science for answers. Medical science aspires to offer cognitive-enhancing drugs that will accelerate mental speed and the acquisition of knowledge. God, the author of knowledge, freely promises also the greater gift of wisdom. "If any of you lacks wisdom, he should ask God, who gives generously to all without finding fault, and it will be given to him" (James 1:5).

In the final paragraph of the case, Dr. Bauble knocks at the door, ready to supply Epiginosko, the drug that promises enhanced knowledge and power. There is another who knocks more quietly (1 Kings 19:12). Jesus stands at the door and knocks (Rev. 3:20), eager to provide true peace (Phil. 4:7) and the gift of eternal life (John 3:16; 5:24). Who offers the more trustworthy path to the ultimate renewing of the mind?

---

38. Richard A. Swenson, *Margin: Restoring Emotional, Physical, Financial, and Time Reserves to Overloaded Lives* (Colorado Springs: NavPress, 1992), 77. See also Richard A. Swenson, *The Overload Syndrome: Learning to Live within Your Limits* (Colorado Springs: NavPress, 1998).

Suppose that Paul in our story were to proceed without the benefits of Epiginosko. Trusting that God is at work in his life, he might mature in his Christian faith over time and come to reflect deeply on the questions that his former professor Dr. Bright had raised. Imagine also that, years later, Paul succeeds Professor Bright as chair of physics at Highcastle University. What advice might he give to his students? Perhaps he would stimulate their interest not with a drug but with words of understanding:

> Do not be anxious about your mental abilities, what pharmaceuticals you shall drink, nor about your brain, what you shall put it on. Is not the mind more than an object of neuroscience, and the brain more than neurochemicals?
>
> Therefore do not be anxious, saying, "What smart pill shall we synthesize?" or "What brain-boosting drug shall we take?" For the purveyors of cognitive enhancements sell stimulants promising greater capacity for attention, for learning, and for reasoning; and your heavenly Father knows that you need intelligent minds. But seek first the renewing of the mind of which the Bible speaks, and all these things shall be added to you in good measure.[39]

For further reading, see the annotated bibliography on "better life" connected with this book at www.everydaybioethics.org.

---

39. Cf. with Matt. 6:25–33 and Rom. 12:2.

Part Three

BETTER DEATH

CASE STUDY

A DIFFICULT DEATH

It was soon after Dave's fiftieth birthday that Mary noted something was wrong. He was often irritable and didn't have the energy for his regular Saturday morning basketball game. In fact, he had to push himself to go to his law office. This was not Dave. He had always been energetic and upbeat. As a wife, Mary thought the worst: Is his job in jeopardy? Is he having an affair? When she put on her professional hat as a clinical psychologist, she tried to be more objective: Is he depressed? Is this a midlife crisis? Is he ill? This change in Dave was very disturbing.

They had grown up in the same church and started dating as seniors in high school. They married twenty-seven years ago, soon after college, and postponed childbearing until they both finished professional schools and were established in their careers. During these years, they allowed their church attendance to lapse. After ten years of marriage, they had their first child. At that time, Mary suggested they go back to church, and it became the center of their social lives. Now their only child, Bethany, was in her midteenage years, and she was their pride and joy.

Since Mary could come up with no easy explanation, she asked Dave what was wrong. He said he had been having vague abdominal pain for a few weeks which was interfering with his sleep. In addition, he said he felt like a failure and was having trouble facing his daily responsibilities. She convinced him he needed to see a physician. He had been very healthy and didn't even have a primary physician, so she suggested they call Alex, an internist and one of the elders at their church.

Alex saw Dave in his office a few days later. His initial assessment was vague abdominal pain, slight weight loss, depression, and a hint of jaundice. He told Dave this could be serious. Blood tests done that same day and a scan of his abdomen a few days later confirmed Alex's suspicion — cancer of the pancreas that had already spread to his liver. Incurable! He asked both Dave and Mary to come in to discuss the results. He gently told them the bad news. After a few minutes of tears, anguish, and an emotional prayer, Alex suggested Dave see an oncologist to discuss chemotherapy. While it wouldn't cure the cancer, it might slow it down so that he could enjoy a few months of relatively good quality.

Dave and Mary decided together to tell Bethany that he had cancer that could be treated, withholding from her the dismal prognosis for a while.

They quickly developed a close relationship with Dr. Osgood, the oncologist, and asked him to be open and honest with them about the present and the future. He suggested a rather aggressive chemotherapy. Dave had a lot of misgivings. He had seen several of his parents' friends have a very difficult time with chemo, and he said, "I told myself years ago that I was not going to abuse my body with that horrible stuff." Dr. Osgood was the one who convinced him to at least give it a try. He told Dave that when the end came, he felt he would regret not at least giving chemo a chance.

Chemotherapy was miserable — loss of appetite, nausea, vomiting, complete lack of energy for several days. Dave said no way was he going to continue. Mary, Alex, and Dr. Osgood could not convince him otherwise, even by emphasizing their confidence that Dave's experience with further treatments would not be as negative.

Dave and Mary then sat down with Bethany, and Dave explained to her that he did not want to continue the treatments. He made it clear that he would not live much longer. Bethany was in shock. She started sobbing but then through her sobs said, "Daddy, don't you remember how I missed the cut for the volleyball team in my freshman year? You made me practice all summer and insisted I try out the next year. You wouldn't let me give up. But now that is just what you are doing. You're giving up!" With that, she stormed out of the room and locked herself in her bedroom. Dave would not change his mind. Mary talked to Bethany the next day to encourage her to respect her dad's decision. She warned her that anger would only make her last days with her dad miserable. Bethany responded, "Yes, I am angry; I have a right to be angry. I'm angry at Daddy for giving up, and I'm angry at God too. I still need my daddy and God should know that."

At this point Dr. Osgood discussed with Dave and Mary the importance of comfort becoming their primary goal, and the legitimacy of forgoing intensive life-extending measures, including cardiopulmonary resuscitation or a feeding tube. They all decided to pursue this course, and Dr. Osgood made a referral to hospice.

The hospice team provided excellent services. Dave's primary nurse worked with both Alex and the medical director of the hospice to address Dave's many physical symptoms, especially the pain that was rapidly overwhelming the entire family. Alex saw Dave at home every week or so. A social worker helped Mary with insurance forms. Volunteers came in to stay with Dave while Mary left the house to do errands and even provided some respite care so she could attend church. The folks from church were marvelous. Not only did the pastor and elders visit but women from their Sunday-school class organized and delivered one hot meal every day. During the several weeks of Dave's physical deterioration, Bethany withdrew even farther, spending hours on end in her room or at friends' homes.

Meanwhile, the pain was relentless. Increasing doses of sedation and morphine, both by mouth and by morphine pump, left Dave either asleep or uncomfortable and unable to sleep. He became exhausted. Mary became exhausted. One day as Alex was leaving, Mary asked him to sit down in the kitchen so they could talk. Realizing the end was near, they cried together. Alex prayed. Then, out of the blue, Mary said, "Alex, this is awful. It is pointless. Dave is suffering, and so are Bethany and I. The hospice social worker gave me this copy of *Final Exit*, and I agree with the author's concept of 'deliverance.' It seems to fit in our case. God can't want Dave to suffer any more. Bethany can hardly stand to be in the room with him. Won't you do something to speed this whole thing up?"

CHAPTER 9

WISDOM FROM THE NEW TESTAMENT

D. A. Carson

The case before us presents two primary bioethical questions: (1) Is it right to forgo reasonable medical treatment and thus die more quickly than would otherwise be the case (Dave)? (2) Is it ever right to take active steps to hasten death (Mary)?

The limitations of this essay must be recognized at the outset. This is not an attempt to provide well-balanced biblical and theological reflections on the many complex issues bound up with suicide, assisted suicide, and euthanasia, though such are available.[1] It cannot possibly treat all of the New Testament (let alone biblical) themes that bear on such questions. It cannot even address the different possible responses a patient might have when told the diagnosis is terminal pancreatic cancer; one thinks, for instance, of the decidedly different response of the late Randy Pausch, whose *The Last Lecture* circulated widely—deservedly so—in 2008.[2] Rather, this is a response to one case study, enriched by the reflections of a number of New Testament scholars.[3]

The Bible includes not only a lot of information about historical and theological matters but also a great deal of ethical reflection—one might say pastoral reflection. Because the focus in this chapter is on the bearing of biblical documents on the assigned case study, we cannot possibly avoid pastoral issues (even though they are taken up in greater detail in a later chapter), as that would betray the biblical documents themselves. For the same reason, we cannot responsibly ignore the bearing of the New Testament on related public policy, insofar as such concerns are raised explicitly or implicitly by the New Testament documents. These realities structure the rest of this chapter.

---

1. For a helpful introduction to these issues, see John F. Kilner and C. Ben Mitchell, *Does God Need Our Help? Cloning, Assisted Suicide, and Other Challenges in Bioethics* (Wheaton, Ill.: Tyndale, 2003), esp. chaps. 2, 5, 6.

2. For video and print versions, see *www.cmu.edu/ran*

dyslecture (accessed March 4, 2010).

3. Special thanks to Dana Harris, Te-Li Lau, Grant Osborne, David Pao, Eckhard Schnabel, and Robert Yarbrough.

SOME BIBLICAL PRIORITIES
THE BODY

It is not uncommon for contemporary Christians in the West to focus in practice on their bodily existence, with relatively little thought devoted to the eternal dimensions of their being, to the incorporeal nature of the intermediate state, or even to the looming resurrection existence in the new heaven and the new earth. When physical illness as serious as terminal pancreatic cancer hits, this foreshortening of the real horizons of existence taught and presupposed in the New Testament makes the threat seem even more disastrous than it is. Alternatively, some Christians seek comfort in "going to be with the Lord" in some incorporeal sense and may be tempted to depreciate the body, not only the present diseased body but its connection with the resurrection life to come.

There are many ways of demonstrating the importance of present bodily existence in New Testament theology, but perhaps it is enough to remind ourselves of the flow of argument in 1 Corinthians 5–16. Such a survey quickly convinces the reader that Paul utterly rules out every kind of "spirituality" that is detached from physical existence and personal interaction of a "real world" sort. First Corinthians 5 refuses to separate spirituality, including membership in the local church, from the sexual misconduct of incest. The first part of the next chapter sets out Christian expectations when Christians are tempted to sue other Christians, an action that takes place in the "real" world of space, time, and physicality, while the second half of the chapter instructs the Corinthians that because they are not their own but have been bought at the cost of Christ's death, therefore they are to honor, with their bodies, the God who redeemed them, and that excludes casual sexual liaisons. Chapter 7 wrestles with a range of ethical issues largely tied to matters of divorce, separation, and remarriage—all of which are necessarily tied to bodily existence. First Corinthians 8–10 focuses on how Christians should view idols, but more specifically food offered to idols. The possible pitfalls here are tied to the bodily function of eating, and the apostle's logic, as we shall see in a moment, is tied to Jesus' incarnation and death on the cross, both of which work themselves out in the matrix of history. First Corinthians 11 deals with male-female relationships grounded in creation, the very physical creation of Genesis, and then with the Lord's Supper, a very physical mediating of the grace of Christ in the cross. The relationships between the *charismata* and love take up chapters 12–14. However, as much as the work of the Spirit in some ways occupies center place in these chapters, love trumps all *charismata*, and this love is tied to the real world of human relationships and various gifts of speaking. The resurrection at the end of the age takes up 1 Corinthians 15, about which more will be said below. First Corinthians 16 reminds the Corinthian believers of their responsibility to continue gathering money to help poor Christians in Judea—a very physical, bodily demonstration of love.

None of this directly responds to the case study at hand, but it paints the sort of "whole life" vision of human existence that is everywhere presupposed or explicitly taught in the New Testament documents. This vision rules out any view of human life that treats the body as accidental, or merely temporary, or outside the orb of what makes us God's people, or removed from the structure of decisions in the ethical and relational realms. At the same time, there is another side to this matter: our present bodies are not so to be the focus of our attention that we are unable to think beyond the death of these bodies to our existence beyond death—but that trajectory of New Testament thought we will come to shortly.

A small but vocal group of Christian writers has in recent years argued strongly that human beings are *essentially* bodies, that there is no genuinely disembodied human being.[4] The various texts that seem to support the more traditional view are creatively reinterpreted to defend this stance. This is not the place to embark on a full-scale refutation. However, this view has a bearing on how we are to think of bodily life, so a few remarks are necessary.

The most obvious reading of a plethora of passages suggests that although embodied existence is the norm for human beings, disembodied existence is not impossible. The apostle Paul visited "paradise," "the third heaven," the abode of God—whether in the body, he neither knew nor cared (2 Cor. 12:1–10). That demonstrates that Paul did not consider embodied existence a requirement of ongoing human existence. That conclusion is most naturally in line with his insistence that to be away from the body is to be present with the Lord (2 Cor. 5:8); he does not say that to be away from this body is already to have adopted a resurrection body. Paul does not think disembodied existence is the ideal; he certainly is not pressing toward it, but is pressing toward being "clothed" again in resurrection existence (2 Cor. 5:1–10). Nevertheless, he happily avers that a martyr's death at present would in many respects be happier and better for him than his struggles in this life, and it is only his concern for fellow believers whom he helps by his ministry that draws him to the conclusion that it is better that he remain here (Philippians 1). Paul is adamant that the ultimate home of the Christian is resurrection existence (see esp. 1 Corinthians 15) in what other New Testament writers call the new heaven and the new earth (2 Peter 3:13; Rev. 21:1). He does not long for immortality, in a Greek sense, but longs for resurrection existence in line with the resurrection existence of the Lord Jesus. Jesus tells the repentant "thief" (more likely something like "guerrilla fighter" or "rebel") on the cross that he would join him in paradise that very day (Luke 23:43). But Jesus certainly was not equipped with his resurrection body that very day, and neither was the thief. Even if one argues that the thief received his resurrection body on that very day (as some have done), one must conclude that this ostensible resurrection body was not in any sense connected with his pre-death body, in the way that Jesus' resurrection body, which rose only on the third day, is necessarily tied to his pre-death body. (Jesus' tomb, after all, was empty on the third day, and his resurrection body retained the *stigmata*.)

---

4. See especially Joel B. Green, *Body, Soul, and Human Life: The Nature of Humanity in the Bible* (Grand Rapids, Mich.: Baker, 2006).

Most theologically informed Christians have concluded, rightly, that normal human existence is embodied. It is incorrect to speak of human beings "having" bodies, as if human beings were essentially nonmaterial entities that only accidentally possess bodies. Equally it is incorrect to think of human beings as "having" spirits or souls, if by that it is meant that we are essentially corporeal but happen to possess a nonmaterial component. Normal human existence is embodied, whether with the natural body that reflects the curse this side of the fall, a curse that inevitably ends in death, or with the resurrection body that awaits the end of the age.

THE INCARNATION, DEATH, AND RESURRECTION OF JESUS

The purpose of this section is not to summarize the biblical teaching on the incarnation, death, and resurrection of Jesus but to reflect briefly on the bearing of these enormous christological realities on how we are to think of embodied human beings and their sufferings. We may take two steps.

(1) When the Bible talks about the incarnation of the Son of God, whether in historical narrative (Matthew 1; Luke 2), in relatively abstract categories (John 1:1–18), or in hymnic praise (Phil. 2:5–11), the emphasis is on wonder, glory to God, God's kindness, the indescribable humiliation of the Son, and the like. Little if any emphasis is placed on how the incarnation elevates human existence or testifies to the importance of human embodied existence. Such inferences have often been drawn by later Christian theologians, but not by Scripture. It is useful to observe an analogy: when John tells us that "God so loved the world that he gave his Son" (John 3:16), not a few have leaped to the conclusion that this shows how important and valuable the "world" really is. John draws no such inference. For him, the world is the created moral order in horrible rebellion against its Creator and in wretched and culpable blindness with respect to the true identity of the Son. If "God so loved the world," this says a great deal about God and his love, and therefore about how incredibly privileged the world is, but nothing positive about the world itself. Similarly here: the in-fleshing (for that is what *incarnation* means) of the Word of God — his becoming a human being — does not in itself promote the importance of human beings but testifies to the immensity of God's grace. In the one passage (viz. Hebrews 2) that most prominently points out that the eternal Son became a human being to redeem fallen human beings and did *not* become an angel to redeem fallen angels (for no redeemer has arisen to save them), the author emphasizes the wonder of it all, the privilege of being among the redeemed, rather than the importance of being human.

Yet we cannot ignore the truth that to become a human being, the eternal Son judges it necessary to take on human flesh, to become "flesh and blood" (to adopt the language of Heb. 2:14). He dies a physical death; he gains a resurrection body that has some kind of continuity with his pre-death body. Physically, when Jesus was in Jericho, he was not in Galilee. This leads to the incredibly complex issues surrounding what it means to confess Jesus as the God-man. In fact, there are three kinds of difficulty at issue: (1) the commonly discussed christological issue: how one with the attributes of deity can also have the attributes of a human being as one person, not two; (2) the scarcely less commonly recognized truth that Jesus remains the God-man forever, with a body sufficiently physical that it could be touched and handled, that it bore the *stigmata*, that it could eat food—and yet "disappear" and "ascend" into glory; and (3) much less frequently discussed, what it might mean for Jesus to remain the God-man after his death and before his resurrection. Would those who insist that corporeality is essential to human existence stipulate that Jesus stopped being human between the cross and the empty tomb?

Once again, these sorts of reflections on the incarnation, death, and resurrection of Jesus do not speak directly to the case study before us, but they usefully corroborate the framework for thinking about bodily existence that we have already sketched out. Normal human existence is embodied; disembodied human existence is possible before death (witness Paul), but surely fadingly rare; disembodied existence is normal between death and the general resurrection; the ultimate hope is embodied resurrection existence in the new heaven and on the new earth. What that will be like lies at the very periphery of our vision, at the very edge of what revelation has disclosed. Nevertheless, the least we must infer is that we dare not treat the body as an optional extra or as something entirely extrinsic to our self-identity. But the present body is not simply to be identified with our resurrection bodily existence, either.

These fundamental assertions must be enriched by related reflections on sin, death, and eschatology. Before heading in those directions, we must pause for the promised second step in our consideration of Jesus' incarnation, death, and resurrection.

(2) Many of the passages that describe or refer to Jesus' incarnation, death, and resurrection have ethical implications built right into them. For instance, if Philippians 2:5–11 speaks movingly of the unimaginable condescension of the one who "did not consider equality with God something to be used to his own advantage" (2:6), verse 5 already establishes an ethical framework: "In your relationships with one another, have the same attitude of mind Christ Jesus had." This passage does not stop at the incarnation but descends to the shame and ignominy of the cross, all of it serving as the most telling ethical mandate toward resolute self-denial for the sake of others, a theme picked up in other New Testament passages (e.g., John 13:1–17; 1 Peter 2:11–25). In 1 Corinthians 6:12–20, the apostle Paul ties together the resurrection of Jesus with our own prospective resurrected bodies and draws an implication for our present bodies: it is unthinkable that Christians would want to join their bodies sexually with those of prostitutes. The same moral conclusion is drawn from the price Christ paid to redeem us: Christians "were bought at a price. Therefore honor God with your bodies" (6:20). Paul's long chapter on the resurrection (1 Corinthians 15) urges not only hope and steadfastness in the prospect of what is to come (15:58) but a thoughtful abandonment of mere hedonism ("Let us eat and drink, for tomorrow we die," 15:32). In other words, many lines are drawn from the resurrection to ethical conclusions.

More broadly, many strands of the New Testament tell us that Christians should expect to suffer. Very often, though not always, the suffering in view is the suffering that comes to Christians because they are Christians, because they follow Christ and pursue righteousness. This is bound up with inheriting the kingdom of heaven, and it aligns us with the prophets who lived and suffered before us (Matt. 5:10–12). Slaves of Jesus can scarcely pretend they have the right not to suffer at the hands of the "world" when the "world" has treated the Master himself so badly (John 15:18–25). The "great cloud of witnesses" who cheer on believers (Heb. 12:1) includes those who have suffered horribly before us (11:35–39), and "the world was not worthy of them" (11:38).

Once more, these sorts of christological and related considerations do not directly address the case study, but they are profoundly relevant to it. They ought to shape decisively how we as Christians think of human existence, life after death, suffering, following Jesus, and anticipating the resurrection. This broad sweep must now be supplemented, however succinctly, by four further themes.

SIN, SUFFERING, AND DEATH

On the broad canvas of Scripture, death is not normal. It is the result of sin. Sometimes individual deaths are the direct consequence of specific and individual sins (e.g., 1 Cor. 11:27ff.); sometimes mass deaths are the consequence of the judgment of God on national sins (e.g., the destruction of Jerusalem, Isa. 10:12; the judgment of God on many nations, e.g. Jer. 47–51); and sometimes suffering and death have no direct connection to any specific sin (e.g., John 9) but flow out of living in a sin-cursed universe.

The compelling sweep of the Bible's story line sets these stances in place. Several conclusions fall out of these realities, all of which have a bearing on how Christians ought to think of suffering and death, whether their own or others'.

First, there is a legitimate place for outrage. On the eternal scale, death is "not the way it's supposed to be" (to borrow the title of a book by Plantinga).[5] We rightly hunger to continue existing, because God made us for himself and for eternity. Death is the "last enemy" (1 Cor. 15:26), and a fearful enemy it is. When death snatches away a loved one, it is no part of Christian maturity to disown the grief under the mistaken impression that this somehow besmirches the promises of eternal life. To refer again to Paul, we too grieve, but not as those who have no hope (1 Thess. 4:13). Outrage in the face of the incalculably wretched results of sin is not only permissible; it is mandated. What we must carefully avoid, however, is viciously transforming righteous outrage, mingled with great distress at the horrible consequences of sin, into self-righteous outrage against God.

Second, death may be the last enemy, but it does not have the last word. Christ has already beaten it. When we die, though we will be away from the body, we will be

---

5. Cornelius Plantinga Jr., *Not the Way It's Supposed to Be: A Breviary of Sin* (Grand Rapids, Mich.: Eerdmans, 1994).

present with the Lord (2 Cor. 5:6–8), and beyond this we await the final transformation, the consummation of all things, ushered in by Christ's return. Hope, after all, is one of the three cardinal Christian virtues (1 Cor. 13:13), and Christian hope is as much grounded in the future, in what is yet to be, as it is in the past, in what Jesus has accomplished. As tragic as it is to lose a loved one, death is not the final goodbye, the cessation of existence, and believers must not only believe this truth (which belief turns, finally, on Jesus' resurrection) but also pass it on to the next generation. And that is done as much by our example as by anything else. In what way, if at all, is this virtue displayed by Dave and Mary in the case study? Is not the only alternative despair and bitterness?

Third, such confidence in joyful, God-centered, and fruitful life beyond death turns, in the New Testament, on being in union with Christ. This is not the place to contemplate the fearful prospects of those outside of Christ, since the case study affirms that Dave and Mary are Christians. But that means their approach to death ought to be transparently different from that of unbelievers.

Fourth, several passages go on at length about the absence of pain, sorrow, death, and suffering in the new heaven and new earth (not least Rev. 21:4), and of the exuberant joy around the one who sits on the throne, and the Lamb (e.g., Revelation 5). That means that as Christians face final suffering, they dare not think of it as the last *thing* but only as the final *suffering* they will face on the way to a triumphant transformation. Indeed, some Christians have been known to reject most or even all painkillers on their way into eternity, not because they were masochists but because they wanted to keep relatively clear heads to experience the sustaining power of Christ in the midst of weakness (2 Cor. 12:7–10), in anticipation of the glory still to come. That choice may be a personal one, depending on factors as diverse as the severity of the pain, the maturity of the believer, the boldness of the Christian's faith, and much more. But there is something spiritually myopic about not even thinking about these things and discussing them with fellow believers. We forget how much of our approach to suffering and death, here in the West, is of relatively recent vintage, the product of modern medicine. Such medicine can be a spectacularly wonderful boon; in my own case, I would have died at least three times had it not been for modern medicine. Yet that medicine, combined with the American way of death, which both sanitizes death and makes serious discussion of it taboo, constantly drags us toward the here and now and discourages thought about the end of life in this world, and of life beyond death.

GOD

Of all the things that could be said of God, four might usefully be mentioned here.

First, he is the God of creation. There is an unbridgeable chasm between Creator and created. Human beings are among the created; we have come from the dust, and to the dust we shall return (Gen. 3:19). Unlike God, who is uncreated and underived, our existence is derivative; it depends on Another. Nevertheless, only human beings are made in the image and likeness of God (Gen. 1:26–28). However complex and subtle such categories are, they certainly hint at our capacity for living in relationship with this God, reflecting him in some ways (as much as creatures can reflect their Creator), and marking our decisive difference from the rest of creation.

Second, God alone is God. He brooks no rivals because no one *can* compare with him (cf. Isaiah 40–45). The essence of human sin is the de-godding of God; human beings want to compete with God, assured that if they partake of what he forbids, they will become like God (Gen. 3:5). Anything and everything we use to establish our identity, our self-justification, our importance, apart from God, is an idol. It becomes what we ultimately cherish and pursue. That is one of the fundamental reasons why God insists he must be given all glory; it is not only because he alone is God and nothing and no one can compare with him but also because he knows full well that if his rebellious image-bearers are to return to him, they must acknowledge who he is. Our only hope is to be saved by him, and at the heart of that restoration will be abandoning our idols and loving him with heart and soul and mind and strength. He presents himself to us in all his glory, not only because his glory exposes our sin but also and more fundamentally because this sheer God-centeredness is what saves us.

Third, God is sovereign and rules with providential wisdom. He works out all things according to the counsel of his will (Ephesians 1). Because he is unqualifiedly good (James 1:13–15) as well as sovereign, he can be trusted. That means, among other things, we do not have the right to usurp functions that belong to him. We do not have the right to "play God." The principle is clear enough; the outworking of the principle demands, as we shall see, a very large degree of prudential wisdom.

Fourth, this same God, who stands over against us in judicial wrath because of our sin, pursues his wayward image-bearers, resolved to reverse the curse. His plan commissions the eternal Son to become a human being, live the life of a covenant-keeping Israelite, die the death of his people, and rise from the dead, vindicated. The kingdom of God has dawned. King Jesus reigns, vanquishing enemies until he has destroyed the last enemy, death itself.

In short, the Bible's narrative of redemptive history—from creation through the fall and the life and work of Christ to the consummation, all of it an expression of the character and purposes of God—constitutes the matrix in which Christians must think about life and death, the meaning of faith, even how to relate to God in the context of their own demise. This will be teased out a little further in the ensuing discussion.

THE HOLY SPIRIT, THE CHURCH, COMMUNAL HOPE, AND COMMON GRACE

At this juncture, we must avoid three mistakes.

1. It is a mistake so to focus on the forensic aspects of salvation, with its rich talk of the forgiveness of sin and of right standing with God, that the transforming

work of regeneration by the Holy Spirit is overlooked. When we think of the Christian's trials, including facing death, there is more to comfort and strengthen us than the prospect of resurrection existence, more than the confidence of acceptance with God: one must also reckon with the Spirit who has already been given to us as the down payment of the promised inheritance. He brings comfort, the manifest presence of God, an abundant grace and strength. This is not to deny that Christians face the vicissitudes shared by all people in facing death; rather, it is to assert that we must never overlook the help that the triune God affords.

2. It is a mistake so to focus on the individual's plight as he or she faces death that we overlook the communal nature of the people of God. The dying Christian will suffer, in many respects, like others. But dying Christians should not lack the support of loving brothers and sisters in Christ; they should not die alone and ignored; they should not die in deepest despair that no one will look after their children. The church has many faults, but even quite ordinary local churches are capable of providing the emotional, spiritual, and material support Christians need as they face the last enemy. The case study cannot be rightly thought through without reflecting on some of the communal dynamics that ought to be part of the process.

3. It is a mistake to think that the Christian's only resources in the crisis of dying and death are those provided directly by the new covenant community, those provided directly by the promises and graces of the gospel for the Lord's people. Those in the Reformed tradition speak rightly of "common grace," grace that God gives "commonly" to many people, believers or otherwise. It is in that framework that we should gladly receive the gifts and graces of God mediated through modern medicine, hospice, and a variety of social services.

INTERPRETIVE CLARIFICATIONS

People have often observed that the Bible can be used to "prove" almost anything. These ostensible proofs invariably deploy questionable hermeneutical tactics that sound plausible to some people, even though they do not stand up to close scrutiny. That is why the approach adopted in this essay does not finally resort to proof-texting to sort out complex bioethical matters. Rather, the aim here has been to survey a variety of biblical-theological themes that are indisputably grounded in Scripture, and then tease out, in the remainder of this piece, some of the bioethical implications most relevant to the case study.

Let's begin this last task by considering a couple of examples of illegitimate reasoning from Scripture:

1. Jesus' death was an act of self-sacrifice for the sake of others. Since Jesus' disciples are to imitate him, might it not be argued that by opting for assisted

suicide so as to spare his family further suffering, Dave is following Jesus? Initially the argument sounds plausible. But by dying, Jesus enables those he redeems to escape death, the second death. Had he not died, they would stand condemned; that was the alternative. At a comparatively miniscule scale, when a US marine flops down on a grenade to smother the blast so that his mates are spared (as marines are trained to do), it is an act of self-sacrifice for the sake of others when the alternative is that the other marines would die. But what is the alternative in Dave's situation? He is going to die in any case; his family members are not, regardless of whether he solicits help in committing suicide or opts for no treatment.

2. Paul speaks of finding it difficult to "choose" whether to die or to remain behind for the sake of others (Phil. 1:22–26), and this provides some with an ostensible warrant to make whatever choices they wish concerning forgoing life-sustaining medical treatment or more actively ending their lives. Paul's "choice," however, is purely rhetorical; in reality, the choice belongs to the imperial power under the hand of God's providence. Doubtless one can make a good case for people having the responsibility to make medical-treatment decisions that may affect how much longer they live. However, Philippians 1:22–26 does not establish such a responsibility. It may prepare us, though, to recognize that any such responsibility could never imply that whatever decisions people make are morally correct. The standard of rightness is beyond oneself, in the one to whom every person is accountable.

For those with deep love for the Bible and an equally deep desire to shape one's life by its revelation, it becomes important to admit the limits of our knowledge lest we unwittingly baptize every theory, justifiable or otherwise, with biblical authority. Alfred Lord Tennyson lost his dear Cambridge friend Arthur Henry Hallam in 1833. Swamped by the loss, he spent the next seventeen years composing the immortal poem *In Memoriam A. H. H.*, widely viewed as one of the most important poems of the nineteenth century. His wrestlings with the many facets of grief, loss, and guilt included the following reflections on what could not be known about Lazarus' experience of death (John 11):

Behold a man raised up by Christ!
   The rest remaineth unreveal'd;
   He told it not; or something seal'd
The lips of that Evangelist.[6]

We do well to remind ourselves of what we do not know.

---

6. Available in many locations online, including *http://theotherpages.org/poems/books/tennyson/tennyson03.html* (accessed April 29, 2010).

SOME PASTORAL REFLECTIONS IN THE LIGHT OF NEW TESTAMENT THEMES

EXPECTATIONS

The case study presents a man who is utterly surprised by the severe diagnosis of his condition. The man then becomes consumed by his wrestling with the disease, with no transparent horizons beyond the disease and his own suffering. The highest goal of his wife is to alleviate his suffering, to the point where she too considers assisted suicide. We are told that these two are Christians, but it is difficult to see how any of the transcendent Christian realities outlined in the first part of this paper exercise any controlling influence on their priorities, values, or conduct.

What should the expectations of Christians be? We should always be horrified by evil, but never surprised by it; similarly, we should always be horrified by suffering and death (it is not the way it's supposed to be), but never blindsided. Even as Christians view death as "the last enemy," they will also recognize not only that the foe has been defeated in principle by the Lord Jesus but also that our prospect of meeting Christ in our own deaths, our prospect of resurrection existence in the new heaven and the new earth, transforms the discussion, dissipates at least some of the fears, and removes one's eyes from an exclusive focus on the challenges of this world. Neither Dave nor Mary evinces any awareness of already enjoying eternal life, a life that expands in glory at death in anticipation of the consummation still to come.

None of this is meant to provide an escapist solution to suffering. I recall an aging and much-respected senior saint walking out of chapel at Trinity after listening to the last sermon that John Stott ever preached on our campus. In rather somber tones, he said, "It is so hard to adjust to the fact that all the decades of Christian experience bound up with this man, combined with his vast theological and spiritual insight, will shortly be lost to us." Inevitably I recognized that he was talking about his own impending death as much as about the death of another. What could I say? I told him that it was right to feel outraged. We were not designed for death. Sin and all its manifestations and entailments are simply appalling. But while it is important to keep acknowledging these brutal realities, it is no less important to insist that Christians strive to live now in the light of the "blessed hope" still to come. Because it may well be extraordinarily difficult to foster genuinely Christian expectations once the crisis of pancreatic cancer has already pirated all one's attention, it is essential to get these fundamental Christian perspectives into place in one's thinking and living before the onset of dreadful disease.

GOD AND THE IMAGE OF GOD

To think biblically about God and ourselves begins by acknowledging happily that we were created by God and for God—indeed, in the light of Colossians 1:15–20, by and for God's own dear Son. We are not our own. Both by creation and by adoption, we belong to another. While we seek to live out our lives with the kind of Christian expectations sketched in the preceding section, we confess that God is good, that he can be trusted, that embodied human beings are important, that God is the providential ruler who makes the gains and discoveries of medicine possible and among the gifts to be enjoyed, that God promises to give added grace where there is added weakness, that our greatest pleasure and joy are bound up with all that brings him greatest glory, and that because we are not our own, we do not have the right to destroy any of God's image-bearers, including ourselves.

This kind of God-centeredness does not preclude the wrestling of a Job in the face of personal loss, disaster, and chronic illness, but it is the kind of wrestling that still declares, "Though he slay me, yet will I hope in him" (Job 13:15). One must know something of God not only to trust in him but also to wrestle with him.

This side of the cross, genuine believers will find their self-identity not in belonging to the party of perfect health but in the joy of sins forgiven, of having one's name written in heaven (Luke 10:20). The fifteen-year-old daughter of a family I know lost her best friend to leukemia. By and large she handled it well, with time for frank discussion, open tears, genuine grief. Three months later, the father passed his daughter's room and heard his daughter quietly sobbing. He tapped on her door and quietly entered. He wrapped her in his arms, and she sobbed, "God could have saved my best friend, and he didn't, and I hate him!"

Her father held her and let her weep. Then he quietly said, "I'm so glad you've told me. God knows what you think before you speak it, so there is no use hiding it. Better to face it with honesty both toward me and toward God. But before you decide that God cannot be trusted or that he does not love you, I want you to answer two questions. First, do you really want a god whom you control? Do you want a god like the genie in Aladdin's lamp—very good at granting wishes but always under the control of whoever rubs the lamp? And second, how will you measure God's love? Will you measure it by assessing how much you get your own way? Or will the measure be a bloody cross on a little hill outside Jerusalem two thousand years ago? You lost your best friend; God lost his Son. In fact, he didn't lose him; he gave him, so that we might escape sin and death and all the ravages they bring. Are you quite sure that this God has abandoned you?"

The point is that when human beings, God's image-bearers, truly know God, the relationship may sometimes flash with hurt, misunderstanding, anger, questions, and doubt; it may sometimes be awash in hope, love, thankfulness, and joy. But the depiction of Dave and Mary casts up nothing of any of this. God is at most a tacit datum. If he is not hated, neither is he loved; if he is not feared, neither is he adored. It is next to futile to attempt to bring the consolations of the gospel, still less moral guidance, into a complex bioethical problem, unless people's knowledge of God and the Scriptures and their personal connection to God through Christ produce in them resources for consolation and wisdom in adversity—because they live daily in the light of who God is, what human beings are, what the cross achieved in answer to the fall, and so forth.

LEAVING A HERITAGE

Perhaps the most disheartening feature of the case study is the relationship between the parents and their daughter.

There were sins of commission and of omission. To take the former first: they lied to her, leaving her deceived and angry when the truth of the seriousness of her dad's illness could no longer be hidden. Perhaps their motives were good, but the lies were thoughtless, short-range, and immoral. When my own wife was desperately ill with cancer, early on we sat the children down and frankly told them of the disease and how serious it was. We told them that they could ask any questions they wanted, and we would answer truthfully. We also told them we would not burden them with every medical detail, or with ambiguous medical results or painful uncertainties, but we would never lie to them; and whenever there was reasonably clear news and direction, we would explain things to them as fully and faithfully as we could. We told them God could be trusted in every circumstance and loved us dearly, and we prayed with them. In that framework, they felt safe to ask not only medical questions but also questions of the type, "What will happen to me if . . . ?" They were treated with respect, felt they were participating in carrying the burden, and knew that if we were not telling them anything at the moment, it was because there was nothing to tell. There can be no substitute for truthful speech with one's children.

In a similar vein, consider the following passage from Werner Neuer's biography of the great twentieth-century biblical theologian Adolf Schlatter:

Already in childhood and youth Schlatter felt the "bitter severity" of nature: his oldest brother was severely handicapped both mentally and physically. His younger brother, the family's ninth child, was stillborn. His wonderfully gifted sister Monika died of typhoid fever at the age of nineteen, just after completing her education. Yet all these setbacks failed to thwart the grateful assessment of the natural order that reigned in the Schlatter household. Why? Because the parents convincingly modeled to their children a living faith in Jesus which centered on a hope that transcended, though did not denigrate, creation. Looking back Adolf Schlatter commended his parents' testimony by observing that they never succumbed to the temptation of "disparaging the natural order" or accusing God, even in the face of sickness and death in their family. Their travail triggered "no cry for God to justify his ways, no shaking or sundering of faith because of pessimism's ravages." Instead, Schlatter writes, "Over their view of nature stood the words, 'The Lord gave, and the Lord has taken away; blessed be the name of the Lord' [Job 1:21]."

His parents' basic attitude became especially clear to Schlatter at the death of his sister Monika in 1865. "We children were called into the bedroom. We stood encircling the bed of our deceased sister. Then our parents accompanied us to the living room, where Bibles were opened and we read Revelation 21 and 22. Our sister was dead: the first gap torn in our little family circle. Our pain was profound. But instead of lament our parents placed before us that word which sheds a ray of light on God's ultimate purposes. They did not just look back on a lost past, nor again gaze questioningly into an unknown future, but rather set their gaze and ours on God's eternal city. I encountered the incomparable hope that the New Testament mediates. Such hope detaches us from our pain and personal possessions, situates our lives in God's grand scheme, and shows us our place as members of the great fellowship he creates, a fellowship that is eternal because it is God's.[7]

If the sins of commission in the case study are bad, the sins of omission there are worse. The parents display no hint of the importance of passing on a godly heritage, no concern to use the passing days to build memories, to laugh and weep together, to long for eternity, to delight in Jesus' triumph over death, to face suffering with courage, to live with eternity's values in view, to learn better how to pray, to leave a heritage. The parents are so focused on Dave's suffering they cannot see what damage they are doing to their daughter, Bethany, by their self-absorption. The same observation could be adapted and extended beyond the family dynamics to the church. There is no sense in which Dave and Mary judge it important to use this suffering and death to help other believers. At least the church has gathered around them to help sustain them through their valley, surrounding them not only with prayers and presence but with concrete help. Yet who thought it wise to take their daughter to the zoo, to go for a walk and a chat, to look beyond the obviously hurting adults to the gradually withdrawing child?

HISTORICAL PERSPECTIVE

Those of us who have lived and served in parts of the world where there is far less medical help to alleviate pain than there is in the West cannot help but wonder if one of the unforeseen consequences of the countless benefits of modern medical science is the sense of entitlement it unwittingly engenders. We should not *have* to suffer; there *must* be medical answers to everything, even if the medical answer is assisted suicide. Similar dissonance arises in us when we read accounts of the deaths of serious Christians in the past. In many quarters (as part of the Puritan heritage), Christians were at one time recognized to be those who knew how to "die well." Believers prayed that they might "die well," by which they meant not that they would escape all suffering but that in their suffering, they would not say or do anything, even in extremity, that would bring any reproach on the name of Christ.

---

7. Werner Neuer, *Adolf Schlatter: A Biography of Germany's Premier Biblical Theologian*, trans. Robert Yarbrough (Grand Rapids, Mich.: Baker, 1996), 29–30.

Consider the following poem, written by Thomas Nashe (1567–1601). He chose to stay in London to help those who were suffering and dying from the plague. He contracted the disease himself, and when he knew he had at most a few days to live, he wrote:

> Adieu, farewell earth's bliss.
> This world uncertain is;
> Fond are life's lustful joys,
> Death proves them all but toys,
> None from his darts can fly.
> I am sick, I must die.
>   Lord, have mercy on us!
>
> Rich men, trust not in wealth.
> Gold cannot buy you health....
>
> Beauty is but a flower
> Which wrinkles will devour....
>
> Strength stoops unto the grave,
> Worms feed on Hector brave....
>
> Wit with his wantonness
> Tasteth death's bitterness....
>
> Haste, therefore, each degree,
> To welcome destiny.
> Heaven is our heritage,
> Earth but a player's stage;
> Mount we unto the sky.
> I am sick, I must die.
>   Lord, have mercy on us![8]

Doubtless one could quibble about a couple of thoughts in the poem. But it would be a very good exercise to run through the poem, line by line, and observe how many thoughts in the mind of the dying Nashe reflect the same themes outlined in this essay as fundamental to Christian maturity and New Testament teaching with respect to these matters, all of which are entirely absent from the minds of Dave and Mary.

PRUDENTIAL WISDOM

Nothing in this essay eliminates the need for substantial doses of prudential wisdom. The point, rather, is that prudential wisdom among Christians must be worked out within the givens of the biblical revelation.

---

8. Available in many locations online, including *http:// www.poemhunter.com/poem/adieu-farewell-earth-s-bliss* (accessed April 29, 2010).

Consider the oft-repeated distinction between prolonging life and hastening death. Is it right for Dave to forgo reasonable medical treatment? If "reasonable" is shaped by essentially secularist assumptions, it may well lead in one direction; if "reasonable" takes into account, say, the importance of leaving a godly heritage for the daughter, the importance of embodied human life, trust in God even in the midst of suffering, and related Christian stances, it may well lead in another. A woman with stage 4 breast cancer who has two teenage children may fight with every ounce of her being to remain alive for the sake of her children, knowing full well the damage frequently done to children in their teens when they lose parents. Consider, by comparison, a woman who has survived stage 2 breast cancer plus one return round seven years later, who is now fifty-nine years of age and whose physical reaction to chemotherapy (and thus the prospect of its "success") is extremely negative, made worse by the fact that she appears to suffer an allergic reaction of sorts to the anti-nauseants the doctors want to give her, leaving her with little choice other than steroids. She may well decide that this is unreasonable medical treatment and opt for hospice care. Her children are grown and mature, and she is ready to be away from the body and present with the Lord. Prudential wisdom must prevail, and in discussion with their respective families, in both cases in the matrix of mature Christian faith, the two women may rightly take opposite decisions. Simplistic formulae in such cases are not justified. "I would not give a fig for the simplicity this side of complexity, but I would give my life for the simplicity on the other side of complexity" (often attributed to Oliver Wendell Holmes, senior or junior).

It is difficult, however, to imagine any situation when Christian prudential wisdom could justify withholding food and water on the ground that this is withholding medical treatment, if that food and water is itself life-sustaining. Medically sanctioned starvation of a patient must not be glossed with words that make it less than a regimen of starvation.

In sum, if we are asked to establish some Christian bioethical guidelines in the dreadful situation in which Dave and Mary find themselves, we must surely first point out that (so far as the description in the case study goes) Dave and Mary think like secularists, without any of the values and expectations that ought to accompany normal Christian confession. We are told that they are Christians, but the study provides no evidence of genuine faith: the most we are told is that after a decade's hiatus, the church "became the center of their social lives." They are the very embodiment of, at best, nominal Christian faith. "Under the guise of 'social responsibility' a secular eschatology may have profoundly coercive implications."[9] It is impossible and even unwise to give ostensibly scriptural bioethical advice when the assumptions and priorities of Scripture and of the gospel are absent.

---

9. John Wyatt, "Bioethics and the Future," *Case 17* (March 2009): 6.

Someone may object that the case study is merely silent regarding the spiritual dynamics in the family, and so many of the concerns raised here may be irrelevant. But that is the point. If the case study does not think such material is relevant to bio-ethical choices, the response must be that bioethical choices boldly adopted absent the kinds of fundamental Christian truths, values, expectations, relationships, convictions, and priorities outlined here are bound to be, at best, shallow and unconvincing. Once those truths, values, expectations, relationships, convictions, and priorities are deeply cherished and lived out, the entire narrative is nudged in a different direction. It is not that we are enabled to formulate certain bioethical "laws" that address the exigencies of the case study but that the entire drama is reshaped. We do not thereby merely affirm the sanctity of human life and conclude that suicide and assisted suicide are morally questionable under the given conditions, but assert that in the light of the gospel, comprehensively understood, suicide and assisted suicide become unthinkable.

SOME PUBLIC POLICY REFLECTIONS IN THE LIGHT OF NEW TESTAMENT THEMES

The case study only indirectly and implicitly invites reflection on how New Testament morality might be worked out in terms of public policy. The issues are notoriously complex, tied as they are to the fact that the apostles worked out their faith under a dictatorship, not a democracy, and to the dominant emphasis on Christians being a people called out to be different from their surrounding culture.[10] Although in recent decades countless books have tried to reinterpret the New Testament documents to make them primarily political in thrust, sober-minded critics have reminded us how tiny the Christian movement was during the apostolic period, and how little evidence appears to justify the thesis that believers were vastly interested in influencing public policy.[11] By and large, the New Testament emphasizes the transformation of Christians, not the transformation of the Roman Empire.

Not least in the domain of suicide, New Testament approaches to the importance of human beings differed from what prevailed in Roman culture. Contrary to what has often been assumed, Roman law did not "punish" the successful suicide by the posthumous confiscation of his or her property.[12] The exception was the Roman soldier. If a soldier attempted suicide, he was punished by either death or dishonorable discharge.

---

10. Cf. D. A. Carson, *Christ and Culture Revisited* (Grand Rapids, Mich.: Eerdmans, 2008).

11. E.g., Seyoon Kim, *Christ and Caesar: The Gospel and the Roman Empire in the Writings of Paul and Luke* (Grand Rapids, Mich.: Eerdmans, 2008).

12. Gottfried Schiemann, "Suicide," in *Brill's New Pauly: Encyclopedia of the Ancient World: Antiquity*, vol. 13, ed. Hubert Cancik and Helmut Schneider (Leiden and Boston: Brill, 2008), 926.

Slaves were obligated to try to prevent their masters from committing suicide; masters were not similarly obligated to try to prevent their slaves from doing so. All of this contrasts with the apostle Paul, who insisted that in Christ there is neither slave nor free (Gal. 3:28).

Yet the mandate to love one's neighbor demands that we try to put in place laws and cultural norms that are good and healthy for society. Once again, large doses of prudential wisdom are required. Legislative "successes" built on nothing more than excellent organization and use of the media often invite a backlash that does long-term damage. (Witness Prohibition!) Mere articulation of moral goals without wise assessment of the steps needed to get there may elicit nothing more than anger from the broader culture. While it is good and right to devote time, energy, and imagination to influencing public policy on bioethical matters, we must not overlook how the structures of thought in the Bible that bear on the bioethical matters raised by our case study are essentially Christian structures. We must first of all articulate, promote, appropriate, personally embrace, and delight in them, within the Christian community that delights in the whole counsel of God.

CHAPTER 10

WISDOM FROM HEALTH CARE

Robert D. Orr and Susan Salladay

In our case study, Dave has been afflicted with a common and devastating malignancy. From the time of diagnosis, his life expectancy has been short. Clinical experience with pancreatic cancer suggests that his time remaining likely will be difficult. Our review of Dave's story will focus on the patient-doctor relationship, choosing goals of treatment, specific end-of-life treatments, and the question of hastening death.

Pancreatic cancer is the fourth leading cause of cancer deaths in the United States, accounting for more than thirty thousand deaths per year. People with this malignancy have a very poor prognosis, with fewer than 20 percent surviving for a year, and only 4 percent alive five years after diagnosis. The cause remains unknown. The anatomy of the pancreas is such that a cancer may grow within it for quite some time before causing any symptoms. The two most common symptoms that cause a person to seek medical attention are vague abdominal pain as the cancer invades the nerves behind the gland, and the onset of jaundice as the enlarging tumor compresses the adjacent bile duct. For some as yet unexplained reason, some patients with this malignancy develop symptoms of depression unrelated to social or spiritual circumstances.

Following a diagnosis of pancreatic cancer, treatment is difficult and not very effective. The type of treatment recommended depends on the location and extent of the tumor at the time of diagnosis. Surgery offers the only chance of cure, but in 85 percent of patients, the cancer has grown or spread beyond such surgical attempts by the time of diagnosis. Of those who do have curative surgical attempts, only a small number are actually cured. Radiation and chemotherapy are not curative, but they may in some cases slow the growth of the malignancy for a few months. Thus, most patients with pancreatic cancer achieve the greatest benefit from palliative and hospice care, treatment focused on both good symptom control and care for whole persons and their families.

THE PATIENT-PROFESSIONAL RELATIONSHIP

The relationship between patients and their health-care professionals is foundational to the healing enterprise. Prior to the 1970s, physicians played a dominant role in health care, making decisions about what was wrong and what should be done, often with little involvement of the patient in the decision-making process. This paternalistic approach to medical decision-making gradually changed in the 1970s and '80s with growing societal emphasis on individual rights leading to a dominance of patient autonomy in medicine and medical ethics. This change was manifested by the recognition that patients have a right to make their own decisions after being adequately informed of therapeutic options by their physicians.[1]

This power shift does not, however, change the professional's fundamental responsibility for the patient's well-being. The patient-professional relationship is a fiduciary relationship[2] in that the physician or nurse has greater knowledge, skill, and experience in the medical context than the patient. Because of this unequal partnering, the professional is expected to always act in the best interests of the patient.

The ideal situation is for people to have established a relationship with a physician while they are well, developing over time a sense of mutual trust. When a patient seeks a physician, what individual characteristics are important? Very often, location and convenience are the deciding factors, but some have described ideal characteristics for physicians. Edmund Pellegrino and David Thomasma, who have written extensively on the patient-physician relationship, highlight the following virtues of the ideal physician: fidelity to trust, compassion, practical wisdom, justice, fortitude, temperance, integrity, and self-effacement.[3] In a follow-up book, they focused on the three Christian virtues of faith, hope, and charity.[4] In looking back at the long history of Western medicine, medical historian Albert Jonsen concludes that the modern practice of medicine is a synthesis of the competence emphasized by Hippocrates and the compassion taught and modeled by Jesus.[5] From an analytic standpoint, we could add commitment to the patient to this synthesis. Thus, the modern practice of medicine consists of three C's: competence, compassion, and commitment.

People of faith often select a physician based on a belief system held in common. This is laudable and is particularly important in choosing a primary physician. Sometimes,

1. Jay Katz, *The Silent World of Doctor and Patient* (New York: Free Press, 1983).

2. Examples of other fiduciary relationships are attorney-client, banker-customer, accountant-client, clergy-parishioner, teacher-student.

3. Edmund D. Pellegrino and David C. Thomasma, *The Virtues in Medical Practice* (Oxford, UK: Oxford Univ. Press, 1993).

4. Edmund D. Pellegrino and David C. Thomasma, *The Christian Virtues in Medical Practice* (Washington: Georgetown Univ. Press, 1996).

5. Albert R. Jonsen, *The New Medicine and the Old Ethics* (Cambridge: Harvard Univ. Press, 1992).

however, a common faith is not sufficient for a working patient-physician relationship. Sometimes the patient needs expertise in a particular field of medicine, and in this case the competence of the physician may prove to be more important than the belief system or even more important than personal qualifications such as compassion. Rarely, patients may need to choose between competence and faith in their primary physician. While it is important, if possible, not to select a primary physician with a worldview that is in substantial disagreement with one's own, most people correctly choose competence as the deciding factor. That priority echoes the preference often attributed to Luther: "I would prefer to be ruled by a wise Turk than a foolish Christian."[6]

All health-care professionals should take a whole-person approach to patient care, considering and addressing the patient's physical, emotional, social, and spiritual dimensions. This broad approach is perhaps even more important in end-of-life care, and professionals who specialize in this field may be better situated to address this array of needs. All too often, however, health care becomes fragmented, with the physician attending to the disease process, the social worker looking at social concerns, the chaplain or pastor addressing spiritual matters, and the psychologist called in when emotional issues arise. It is the patient's nurse who often has the broadest perspective, looking at all four dimensions, addressing the issues as they arise, and/or providing the bridge between disciplines when needed. As patients and their families confront life-threatening illnesses, they will encounter nurses in the various physicians' offices, in the diagnostic activities, during therapy, and in the home setting. Unfortunately, while a patient has some degree of choice about what physician to see, there is rarely the opportunity to choose one's nurse.

In our case, Dave was previously healthy, had no established physician, and was perhaps unwilling to recognize that he was becoming ill. As so often happens, his wife encourages him to investigate his persistent symptoms and uncharacteristic mood. Fortunately, one of the elders in their church is a primary physician who is able to see him quickly. Alex proves to be competent, compassionate, and committed to Dave's well-being. He tells Dave that his symptoms could be serious, orders appropriate testing, confirms the diagnosis, gently and compassionately gives Dave and Mary the bad news, prays with them, refers Dave to an oncologist, and continues to be committed to their well-being.

GOALS OF TREATMENT

Once a condition is diagnosed, the patient and physician should discuss and decide together the goal of treatment. Speaking in broad terms, there are four possible goals. In some conditions, it is possible to achieve a *cure* (e.g., surgical removal of a gall bladder full of stones cures the problem). Many conditions can't be cured but can be *controlled* (e.g., hypertension and diabetes can be treated so that the blood pressure or blood sugar

---

6. Scholarly research by Richard John Neuhaus determined that this oft-repeated admonition cannot be found in Luther's writings. Its source remains unknown. See Richard John Neuhaus, "While We're at It," *First Things*, January 1997, 61–70.

is brought into normal range). Some progressive conditions can be slowed down through *palliation* (e.g., chemotherapy can slow the growth of some malignancies, often extending life for months or years). Sometimes none of these three goals is possible, and *maintenance of comfort and dignity* is the only feasible goal.

Occasionally pancreatic cancer is discovered when it still appears to be confined to the pancreas, and surgery aimed at cure is possible. In Dave's case, this is not possible because it has already spread into his liver. The oncologist, Dr. Osgood, suggests aggressive chemotherapy. He explains that this would be palliation, knowing that it would not lead to cure. Dave is reluctant, but is persuaded by Dr. Osgood to give it a try so that down the road when he is facing his inevitable death, he will not regret forgoing disease-abating treatment.

One has to wonder about the content and quality of this discussion. Is Dave able to adequately express his reservations? Is Dr. Osgood being too forceful and paternalistic? Is he pushing his own agenda rather than listening to Dave's values?

Choosing the goal of treatment should be a joint endeavor for the patient and physician. In most clinical situations, there is one course of therapy that is clearly preferable, and thus discussion about goals is easy and perhaps even perfunctory. In progressive or lethal conditions, however, the best treatment, or even the best goal, is not always so clear. These discussions are much more difficult, take much more time, and most often should include the views of other persons close to the patient. Physicians should lay out the benefits and burdens of various treatment options and may make recommendations, but patients should use this information and their own values to make a decision. The final decision should be the result of this shared decision-making model.

In most of these situations, there is not a right or wrong answer. Some patients may choose to forgo chemotherapy that has only a small chance of benefit in order to maintain a better quality of life for the time remaining. Others may choose to try the available chemotherapy with a goal of life extension, sacrificing some quality of life in the process.

Dave's initial response is to focus on the quality of his remaining life. He is persuaded by Dr. Osgood to accept a trial of chemotherapy, but this proves to be too burdensome to him. His values ultimately prevail. Does this mean that he was right and Dr. Osgood was wrong? The case does not tell us whether the doctor's advice had been merely a professional projection of values or he had a valid concern about Dave's possible regret if he had not tried chemotherapy.

Believers often get nervous when quality of life is discussed, maintaining that the scriptural precept of sanctity of life always trumps a subjective assessment of quality of life. Scripture does indeed undergird the sanctity of human life by revealing that all people (regardless of functional ability or chronic symptoms) are created in the image of God.[7] However, we are dealing in a temporal frame where each earthly life is finite.

---

7. See Gen. 1:27; 9:6.

Unless Jesus returns first, each of us will face death. In addition, we have been given the gift of life and the responsibility of stewardship. Thus, individuals may apply their God-given gifts and values in making end-of-life decisions about the level and duration of treatment in many circumstances, taking into consideration their physical, psychological, social, and spiritual burdens. Different believers may make different decisions about accepting or forgoing treatment in the face of an uncertain future, all within the will of God.

For believers, choosing a goal of treatment and even specific therapies should be an object of prayer, shared in most instances with other members of the body of Christ. In our story, Alex does share a time of prayer with Dave and Mary after giving them the bad news. One hopes that he also encouraged them to seek counsel in their decision from their pastor and Christian friends.

Dave tries one round of chemotherapy and finds the side effects intolerable. He feels that the small chance of temporarily slowing of his tumor growth does not adequately compensate for the anticipated misery of further chemotherapy. He would rather forgo this potential benefit in order to improve the quality of his remaining weeks. This is a very personal decision. His wife and two physicians encourage him to continue, but his choice is clear, and it is consistent with his initial response before beginning chemotherapy. Some might criticize Dave for stopping chemotherapy when there is "more that could be done." However, individual patients have the right to make their own decisions about treatment, even if those decisions are contrary to professional recommendations. They stand before God as responsible for their lives, and they must endure the consequences most intimately if further treatment makes a hard death even more difficult. In some instances of disagreement between patients and physicians, it is important for patients to have an advocate, someone to help them speak up for their values. This may be a nurse, social worker, pastor, spouse, or other. In this case, it appears that Dave is able to convince Mary, Alex, and Dr. Osgood that he has given chemotherapy a chance, but the burdens clearly outweigh the benefits by his assessment.

Some individuals might believe that Dave should have resisted Dr. Osgood's suggestion for no cardiopulmonary resuscitation or feeding tube at the time of referral to hospice.

Persons who are unwilling to "give up," instead insisting on all modalities of full treatment until the patient's heart does not respond to resuscitative efforts, are taking a stance often referred to as vitalism. This approach values biological life, regardless of quality or cost, and seems unwilling to accept the inevitability of death. When this stance is taken by a believer, it may be referred to as theological vitalism if it includes hope for miraculous intervention. Patients and their loved ones may well pray for a miracle but should conclude their prayer with "Thy will be done." It is not unbelief to recognize that miracles are distinctly uncommon, accept the limitations of the human condition, and rejoice in the life God has already given us, looking forward to eternal life with him.[8] Trusting oneself to God should be construed not as giving up but as trusting in whatever God wishes to do. This is easy enough to say when one is healthy, and immeasurably more difficult when confronted with a real decision for oneself or a loved one. It appears that at least his daughter, Bethany, is encouraging Dave to pursue treatment at all costs. As so often is the case, this stance seems to be based not on a deep theological conviction of the value of life but rather on the great difficulty she has in letting go.

PALLIATIVE AND HOSPICE CARE AT THE END OF LIFE

The modern hospice movement began in England in the 1960s, initiated by Dame Cecily Saunders, a woman of great faith. Prior to her innovations in end-of-life care, many Western physicians took a "never say die" approach to health care. They focused on treatment of diseases, not on patients' symptoms. Maximal treatments were recommended and used until the patient died in spite of such efforts. During that era, nurses were often more compassionate, recognizing that patients needed good symptoms management as well as treatment for their diseases. Using her background and experience in medical social work and nursing, Dame Saunders recognized the futility of such maximal efforts in patients who clearly were dying. She thus went to medical school and began a career of ministering to dying patients and their families. She started a revolution in health care that has slowly gained acceptance worldwide.[9] Hospice became an important addition to traditional disease-focused medicine. This approach is consistent with the ancient admonition of Hippocrates on the goals of medicine: "Doing away with the suffering of the sick, lessening the violence of their diseases, and refusing to treat those who are overmastered by their diseases, realizing that in such cases, medicine is powerless."[10] However, Dame Saunders updated the final phrase, demonstrating that even when the patient is overmastered by the disease, medicine is not powerless but is very capable of providing excellent whole-person care.

Though often thought of as a hospital or nursing home for terminally ill patients, hospice is not a building but a philosophy of care that can be utilized in any setting. This philosophy focuses on treatment of all symptoms, whether they are physical, psychological, social, or spiritual. Even though we think of hospice as being new in the late

---

8. See the December 2007 issue of the *Southern Medical Journal* (vol. 100, no. 12) for a thorough discussion of miracles, including scientific, philosophical, and theological perspectives.

9. Shirley Du Boulay, *Cecily Saunders, Founder of the Modern Hospice Movement* (London: Hodder and Stoughton, 1984).

10. This statement on the goals of medicine appears in that portion of the Hippocratic corpus called "The Art," quoted in Robert M. Veatch, *Cross Cultural Perspective in Medical Ethics* (Boston: Jones and Bartlett, 1989), 253.

twentieth century, its introduction actually represents the recovery of an approach to care that began during the Crusades, when people of compassion and faith would take in travelers who became seriously ill, addressing all of their needs. These services were provided in a place called a hospice. Sadly, this whole-person approach to health care was lost for the most part while medicine focused on great technological advances, being recaptured only in the last fifty years.

A hospice approach to care uses nurses, physicians, social workers, chaplains, and lots of volunteers. Volunteers enhance the professional care by doing routine household tasks, providing music or other diversions, and offering respite care for family members by being surrogate bedside caregivers. In most hospice settings, the patient's primary nurse establishes the closest relationship with the patient and family and is usually the professional who is present at the time of death. Many professionals and laypersons involved in hospice are motivated by their faith, while others look on this service as a noble humanitarian endeavor.

Hospice, in its beginnings, was often viewed skeptically by physicians as being a countercultural movement, outside the realm of traditional health care. But as physicians and families began to see and experience the successes and benefits of this whole-person care, the hospice philosophy became more mainstream. In the United Kingdom, where hospice was primarily an in-patient movement, there was a relatively smooth transition into a medical specialty called palliative care medicine. In the United States, where hospice was primarily an out-patient endeavor, this transition has been slower and less smooth. But gradually, palliative medicine has evolved, being recognized in the US in 2006 as an official specialty by the Board of Medical Specialties.

Palliative medicine is really an extension of the hospice approach into earlier phases of the disease process. Whereas ten or twenty years ago a hospice approach was utilized only in the last few weeks or days of life, now a palliative-care approach can be utilized earlier. When a patient is diagnosed with a life-threatening disease, or a progressively disabling disease, or even a chronic disease, therapy can begin with a primary focus on disease-modifying treatments, but with a component of symptoms management and whole-person care. As the disease progresses, the primary focus can gradually shift, with less emphasis on disease management and more focus on the needs of the whole person and his or her family. In most cases, there comes a point when disease-modifying treatment is no longer effective or desired, and the shift is then completed to hospice care.

In our case, Dr. Osgood refers Dave and Mary to hospice when Dave decides he no longer wants to receive chemotherapy. This suggests a more abrupt shift in focus than is optimal. Dave and Mary might have benefited from a referral to palliative care earlier in the illness.

At the point of referral to hospice, Dr. Osgood initiates a discussion of the goals of therapy, helping them to reach a decision to have a Do Not Resuscitate (DNR) order and to forgo any use of a feeding tube.

DO NOT RESUSCITATE (DNR) ORDERS

A Do Not Resuscitate order represents a decision that ought to be made jointly by a patient (or proxy if the patient has lost the capacity to participate in decision-making) and the physician that cardiopulmonary resuscitation (CPR) will not be used when the patient's heart stops. Absent this DNR order, the default in the United States and in much of Western society is for health-care professionals or even bystanders to use resuscitative measures when a patient loses consciousness from cardiac arrest, regardless of diagnosis, age, or situation. On television, CPR has a 75 percent success rate.[11] In reality, survival after CPR is about 15 percent, and most survivors are those who have a heart attack with a reversible disturbance of cardiac rhythm. When a patient is clearly dying of a specific illness, the survival rate if CPR is attempted is much, much lower, often close to zero. Some people think, "Why not just try CPR on everyone? If it works, everything is gained, and if it doesn't work, nothing is lost." This reasonable-sounding approach does not take into account that CPR is an invasive, traumatic, expensive series of procedures and that it carries a 20 percent chance of serious side effects, including broken ribs, ruptured organs, and more. The most dreaded outcome is survival with brain damage caused by lack of oxygen before or during the CPR attempt. This sad outcome can leave the person in a severely mentally disabled condition for the remainder of his or her life. Thus, discussion of patients' wishes about the use of CPR is critically important when they have a condition that will almost certainly lead to natural death in the foreseeable future.

Some healthy persons, perhaps fearing the brain damage described above, request a DNR order from their physician while they are still well. This is generally not wise because it precludes potential survival from a reversible condition such as a heart attack or choking while eating.

Dave and Dr. Osgood discuss the use of CPR after Dave decides to forgo further chemotherapy. Based on his poor overall prognosis, and the very small chance that CPR could even temporarily reverse his dying process, their joint decision seems well justified.

When a decision has been made by patient and physician to forgo CPR, that decision should be documented and available to emergency responders, though these steps are not mentioned in this case. This documentation may be on a physician's order sheet if the person is a patient in a hospital or nursing home. Even better is for that order to be engraved onto a bracelet or other jewelry that is worn by the patient at all times, perhaps a Medic-Alert bracelet or one provided by the state or local emergency medical services district. Such a bracelet will be checked by paramedics if the patient collapses among strangers or if the home caregivers call 911 when the patient is in the last moments of life.

---

11. Reported in S. J. Diem, J. D. Lantos, and J. A. Tulsky, "Cardiopulmonary Resuscitation on Television," *New Eng-* *land Journal of Medicine* 334 (1996): 1578, after review of all episodes of three medical television programs for one year.

Some people confuse DNR orders and advance directives. They are not the same.[12] An advance directive is a written legal document, signed by the patient, that may (a) record the patient's wishes regarding treatment (e.g., a living will) or (b) identify the person whom the patient would like to make treatment decisions when the patient loses the capacity to participate in such discussions (e.g., a Durable Power of Attorney for Health Care). Some advance directives do both. An advance directive is drawn up and signed by the patient, usually during a time of good health, anticipating future events.

A DNR order, on the other hand, is written by a physician. (The same goes for any other limitation of treatment order—e.g., a Do Not Intubate order, which forbids the insertion of a tube into the windpipe to assist breathing.) Such a medical order can be followed immediately in the applicable situation (cardiac arrest for a DNR order) without needing to be interpreted. This order may be based on the patient's written advance directive or on direct discussion between physician and patient. Having an advance directive does not per se ensure that a DNR order has been written, and an advance directive can address much more than resuscitation decisions. In many states a more comprehensive set of end-of-life medical orders is now being used. It includes documentation of decisions about more than cardiopulmonary resuscitation, usually including orders with regard to hospitalization, admission to an intensive care unit, antibiotics, and feeding tubes.[13] The goal of these immediately actionable transferable medical order forms is to ensure that patients' end-of-life treatment wishes are known and respected throughout the health-care system.

FEEDING TUBES

Feeding tubes have been in use for about a hundred years to give fluids and nutrition to patients who are unable to swallow an adequate volume by mouth. They are often used short-term for patients who are temporarily unable to swallow but are expected to recover this ability (e.g., after major surgery, or with acute trauma). These short-term goals are usually met by passing a tube through the nose or mouth and down into the stomach. Feeding tubes can also be used for longer-term goals (e.g., in patients who have permanently lost the ability to swallow from a stroke or dementia). In such cases, the tube is most often surgically inserted through the abdominal wall into the stomach or small intestine.

Short-term use of a feeding tube is pretty straightforward and rarely a point of conflict. There is less agreement about long-term use of feeding tubes. In some cases, a feeding tube is clearly appropriate. In some cases, it is clearly inappropriate. In more

12. For a broad discussion of advance health-care directives, the reader is referred to *http://www.nlm.nih.gov/medlineplus/advancedirectives.html* (accessed December 18, 2010).

13. They have been given various names: POLST (Physician Orders for Life-Sustaining Treatment, Oregon), MOLST (Medical Orders for Life-Sustaining Treatment, New York), POST (Physician Orders for Scope of Treatment, West Virginia), COLST (Community Orders for Life-Sustaining Treatment, Vermont).

than a few cases, there remains significant controversy. The most common point of controversy, especially for Christians, is about the use or non-use of a feeding tube for a person who is permanently unconscious. That discussion is beyond the scope of this chapter and does not pertain to Dave's situation.[14]

In most cases, there is agreement in medicine, society, and the church that even short-term use of a feeding tube for a patient who is imminently dying is inappropriate for a number of reasons cited below.[15] While there may be a temptation to "do something" for a person who is approaching death, there are many other beneficial things that can be done for the dying person.[16] One of the critically important things that can be done for Dave is to keep his mouth moist. The only place that dehydration is perceived in the body is in the mouth. So dying persons can well tolerate dryness in the rest of their bodies, but their mouths should receive frequent attention.

Dr. Osgood recommends to Dave that as his death approaches, he consider not allowing the use of CPR or a feeding tube. This is consistent with the goals of both palliative medicine and Christian compassion.

CARE AND COUNSEL FOR FAMILY

Hospice care is whole-person care for dying patients and also for their families. It is certainly incumbent on health-care professionals, friends, and volunteers to help the patient during the dying process in any way they can. But family members suffer during this difficult journey as well. They too may suffer physically, psychologically, socially, and spiritually. The entire hospice team should be available to assist those who are close to the patient. Mary was suffering from exhaustion. Was there more that could have been done to relieve her? Could volunteers have given her more respite from her bedside care of Dave? Maybe, but maybe not. Perhaps she needed help with sleep medication. Maybe she needed an ear to hear, a shoulder to lean on.

But of equal concern in this story is the interaction of family and professional caregivers with Bethany. Her teenage spirit has been crushed and her faith has been stretched, seemingly beyond the point she can bear. Mary is occupied full time with caring for Dave. Is Dave and Mary's initial deception of Bethany with regard to Dave's prognosis making it harder for her? There are lessons to be learned here about truth-telling. Bethany understandably feels she has a right to know, even if her father's intention

---

14. For a discussion of both sides of the issues by two Christian believers, interested readers are referred to Robert Orr and Gilbert Meilaender, "Ethics and Life's Ending," *First Things* (August–September 2004), 31–35.

15. E.g., fluid overload causing tissue swelling, excessive respiratory secretions causing coughing and choking, congestive heart failure, prevention of the release of natural endorphins which reduce pain, a requirement for restraints, infection at site of feeding tube (e.g., potential for sinusitis if a feeding tube remains in the nose), and bleeding from the stomach caused by erosion of the tube on the stomach wall.

16. Beneficial endeavors for the person close to death may include a quiet presence, holding a hand, wiping a brow, playing soft music, reading Scripture, etc.

is to protect her from bad news as long as possible. With the crushing truth out in the open, perhaps someone from hospice or from their church could have offered support and counsel for Bethany in the midst of her devastating suffering. Who were the key figures in her support system? What were her friends saying to her? What were her real needs? A more open approach to discussing the truth likely would have opened up the possibility of someone mediating the strained relationship between Dave and Bethany.

It is equally understandable that Bethany would be angry with God. He has failed her; he is taking away her earthly father. She is at a very vulnerable place. Support in her grief and counsel in her spiritual vacuum might save her years of unresolved issues and concerns.

OTHER CONCERNS

As implied above, there are many ways that hospice workers could have offered support for this family, and hopefully did, beyond what the case describes. Were their spiritual needs, hopes, and fears adequately addressed, if not by their pastor or friends, then by hospice staff themselves? Was there more that could have been done to muster spiritual support for this family as they walked through the valley of the shadow of death?

Families going through the anguish of terminal illness almost always have major financial concerns: loss of income, insurance, extra expenses. Was the hospice social worker able to address these with Dave and Mary and offer whatever help might be available?

Pain, insomnia, and exhaustion are all too common in the experience of a patient and his caregivers. Various members of Dave's hospice team have offered help in various ways. And then the hospice social worker gives Mary a copy of Derek Humphry's book, *Final Exit*,[17] a treatise that recommends hastened death when things get too difficult. In her desperation, Mary thinks maybe this is the only compassionate option left.

HASTENED DEATH

Dying is a process. Sometimes this process happens quickly—for example, as a result of trauma, a heart attack, or a ruptured aortic aneurysm. But more often in today's era of intensive medical care, dying happens slowly. When we consider the use of ventilator support to help a person breathe, dialysis to replace failed kidneys, transfusion to replace blood loss, antibiotics to fight infections, cardiopulmonary resuscitation to try to reverse cardiac arrest, we see that the timing of death can involve an element of choice. Whether a patient dies in a few minutes, or a few hours, or a few days, or a few weeks is often determined by a choice about whether to start, continue, or stop one or more of these or other treatments.

---

17. Derek Humphry, *Final Exit*, 3rd ed. (New York: Dell, 2002).

In the fairly recent past, there was a predominant focus on death-postponing treatment. Even today, many patients and families feel trapped by medical technology, such that natural death seems elusive. The shift in dominance of medical decision-making from physician to patient (or family), along with the development of more and better forms and settings of palliative care, has emphasized these medical choices that can dramatically influence the timing of death.

It is critically important in patient-physician discussions to recognize that when dying patients decide to limit treatment, knowing that the moment of death may come sooner as a result, it is still the disease that is taking the patient's life, even though there always remains some uncertainty about timing. It is not the patient or the family or the physician who is "killing the patient." The intent in making a decision to forgo life-sustaining treatment is not to cause death but to stop efforts to forestall death. Families often struggle with decisions about stopping artificial life-support for a loved one who is in the process of dying, fearing that such a decision will be the cause of death. Health-care professionals and others who counsel families should make it very clear, in explaining that the disease process is responsible for the death, that God's sovereign control is still operational. In his wisdom, grace, and sovereignty, God often allows a short span of time (minutes, hours, or days) between the discontinuation of life-support and the actual death. This may give time for closure for patient, family, and professional.

As we have gotten somewhat comfortable with this issue of choice and quasi-control over the dying process, many individuals have carried that thinking a step farther. Their reasoning is that if it is permissible to make treatment decisions with the intention of stopping the prolongation of the dying process, why is it not permissible to make similar decisions that hasten death and actually ensure the timing of death? Why not allow a dying person to take a lethal drug (assisted suicide) or even allow a physician to give a lethal injection (euthanasia)? If this were allowed, the reasoning continues, we would be able to avoid a prolonged dying process, prevent some of the patient's (and family's) end-of-life suffering, and at the same time eliminate the residual uncertainty about the anticipated time of death. This is often presented as the compassionate and practical thing to do.

This line of reasoning is very tempting, especially to people who are focused on compassion and a duty to eliminate suffering for the person who is dying and for their loved ones. How is the Christian believer, or the nonbeliever for that matter, to respond to this reasoning, to this temptation?[18]

Based on (a) the presence of God's image in each individual, (b) the scriptural command not to kill innocent persons, and (c) the sovereignty of God, most believers have concluded that the scope of human dominion does not include the authority to hasten

---

18. Readers who would like to study the topics of physician-assisted suicide and euthanasia are referred to the following websites: *www.internationaltaskforce.org* (International Task Force on Euthanasia and Assisted Suicide); *www.nightingalealliance.org/index.php* (The Nightingale Alliance); *www.cmda.org* (Christian Medical and Dental Associations); *www.cbhd.org* (Center for Bioethics and Human Dignity).

human death. Some believers reach a different conclusion based on (a) the admonition to be compassionate to those in need, and (b) an understanding that "thou shall not kill" means not to kill with malice.

Of course, many who debate this issue do not subscribe to scriptural teaching and make a different argument: some patients are suffering and the suffering cannot be relieved; patients have autonomy to act as they desire; if patients want to end their lives, it is permissible to allow them to do so, and we have an obligation to assist. The determining factor in this reasoning is patient autonomy. This freedom of choice leads many to want to exert near absolute control over the timing of death. The data from ten years of assisted suicide in Oregon documents that the primary reason for choosing a lethal drug is to control the timing of death, not to avoid unrelievable suffering.

The problems with exalting human autonomy and neglecting divine sovereignty are legion and are discussed elsewhere (see Carson, chap. 9). However, one need not invoke divine authority to point out that from an ethics perspective, choice is not always determinative. There are two aspects to autonomy: negative autonomy (the right to be left alone) and positive autonomy (an entitlement to one's wishes). In medical ethics, the right of negative autonomy is almost inviolable. It is very rarely justified to override a patient's choice against treatment, a choice to be left alone. Physicians and nurses may try to persuade patients otherwise, but if they consistently refuse a recommended treatment, that choice should almost always be honored.[19]

However, positive autonomy has much less force. Just because someone wants something, a health-care professional is not obligated to provide it if it is not in the patient's best interests. For example, a physician may justifiably decline to respond positively to a request for an antibiotic when the patient has a viral illness that will not respond to antibiotics, a request for a narcotic from a drug abuser, a request for unneeded surgery, or a request for a lethal prescription or lethal injection. There is no obligation to be complicit in a patient's autonomous demand for inappropriate or immoral treatment.

Since debate about legalization of physician-assisted suicide and euthanasia takes place primarily in the secular realm, proponents often ignore or criticize arguments that come from a theological perspective. But the believer who concludes that such practices are contrary to the will of God need not abandon the debate. There are many persuasive reasons to avoid such practices that are based on potential consequences rather than on theological principles: the possibility of misdiagnosis, the inaccuracy of prognosis, the issue of depression, the inadequacy of proposed safeguards, the danger of expansion of criteria (to situations involving children or mental illness), the danger of abuse of the practice, and concerns about complications.

---

19. It is beyond the scope of this chapter to give an exhaustive discussion of this point, but suffice it to observe that it may be justifiable to override a refusal of treatment if it is inconsistent with the patient's values and goals. E.g., if patients say they do not want to die, but also say they do not want antibiotics to treat their life-threatening meningitis, the treatment may be given over patient objection.

How does all this fit the situation of Dave and Mary? Dave's pain has been relentless and overwhelming, disturbing his sleep pattern. He has become exhausted, and so has Mary. This is not unanticipated. The pain of pancreatic cancer can in some cases be truly horrible when the tumor invades the numerous nerves just behind the gland, and it can sometimes be very resistant to standard forms of treatment. In such cases, it may often be relieved by a procedure called a celiac plexus block. The hospice team seems unable to control Dave's pain without using doses of medicine that make him stuporous. Perhaps more aggressive forms of pain control could have helped. Enrollment in hospice care does not mean that we cannot pursue aggressive measures to provide comfort.

In response to this situation, the hospice social worker, almost certainly motivated by genuine compassion but perhaps ignorant of other forms of treatment that might have brought Dave relief, gives Mary a copy of the book *Final Exit*. This book was written by Derek Humphry, a proponent of hastened death who says that he is an atheist. He argues for "delivering" dying patients from their suffering by allowing them to take a legally prescribed lethal drug or by allowing their physicians to give them a lethal injection. He admonishes religious people to neither request nor offer hastened death if doing so is against their conscience but to allow others to follow their own beliefs and wishes at the same time.

Mary asks Alex, her husband's primary physician through this terrible journey, to do something to speed up the dying process that is already nearly over. She longs to end the suffering of Dave, herself, and their daughter, Bethany. Is Mary wrong to ask this? How should Alex respond? It is easy enough to sit by the fireplace, reading this book, and pontificate on how assisted suicide and euthanasia are wrong. "Believers should not participate in hastened death. They should have more faith and courage. God's will be done." However, it is quite another thing to witness Dave's suffering sitting at his bedside, or sitting at the kitchen table in tears, searching for answers. Mary is terribly vulnerable. Let us not condemn her.

But what are we to do with this request? What about our duty of compassion? It would be immoral to leave the situation as it is, saying, "There's nothing more that can be done." The first thing is to step back and review the situation to see if something has been overlooked that might relieve Dave's suffering. The suffering in this case is from pain, but there might be other physical, psychological, social, or spiritual issues in another case. In fact, some of the distress in this case may have a spiritual component; perhaps Dave, Mary, and Bethany feel abandoned by God. A prayerful response to this possibility may help. Spiritual inquiry and counsel should be offered about each person's relationship with God, their personal feelings of abandonment by God (each story will be different), and their understanding of God's promises.

But that is not sufficient. At the same time, Alex needs to look at the drugs used to treat the pain, the dosing schedule, the route of administration. Would any change here be helpful? Would consultation from a pain specialist bring some new ideas for relief? Pain at the end of life can be controlled adequately without undue sedation 97 to 99 percent of the time.

However, if there are no other options to relieve Dave's pain — if he falls into that 1 to 3 percent of patients whose pain cannot be adequately controlled — there is another option called palliative sedation. This is a modality of treatment reserved for a patient who is imminently dying and has intolerable physical symptoms, when all possible treatments have been tried, but they have proven to be unsuccessful. The symptoms that most often lead to this intolerable situation are pain and shortness of breath. In those rare circumstances, it is ethically justifiable to give patients sufficient sedating medication to render them unconscious in order to relieve their suffering. This sedation may need to be continued for several hours or a few days. The physician does not give enough medication to cause death but gives enough to relieve suffering, even if this causes unconsciousness. The intention is to relieve suffering that is otherwise uncontrollable. Such relief of bodily distress may occasionally hasten death by a few hours or even days. However, that relief of distress sometimes allows the body to relax so that death may actually be postponed for a short period. It is impossible to predict whether palliative sedation will hasten, postpone, or have no effect on the timing of death. Even if death is hastened, that is acceptable as an unintended side effect. The moral justification for this is "the rule of double effect."

The rule of double effect is an ancient concept developed by St. Thomas Aquinas in the thirteenth century.[20] Though this rule originated during Aquinas's discussion of justifiable homicide, it has had wider application in situations where an action may lead to both good and bad effects. Aquinas asserts that it is morally acceptable to do an act that has both good and bad effects if:

- the act is inherently good, or at least morally neutral;
- the agent intends the good effect; the bad effect is not intended even if it is foreseeable;
- the good effect is not achieved by means of the bad effect; and
- there is a morally grave reason to allow the bad effect.

The paradigm most often used for teaching this rule is that of morphine, which if given in high enough doses may cause respiratory depression, which can lead to death. Using the rule of double effect, it is found to be justifiable to give increasing doses of morphine until pain relief is achieved, even if this causes respiratory depression and an earlier death. Though commonly used, this example is very poor. Pain is a powerful

20. Though widely used in discussions of end-of-life care for decades, the rule of double effect has been criticized as inapplicable by some (e.g., Timothy E. Quill, "The Rule of Double Effect: A Critique of Its Role in End-of-Life Decision Making," New England Journal of Medicine 337 [1997]: 1768–71). For an excellent defense of its use, see Daniel P. Sulmasy and Edmund Pellegrino, "The Rule of Double Effect: Clearing Up the Double Talk," Archives of Internal Medicine 159 (1999): 545–50.

respiratory stimulant, and it is very rare indeed that the dose of morphine needed to relieve severe pain will cause sufficient respiratory depression to cause death (though it is not impossible).

Palliative sedation, when needed to relieve intolerable physical symptoms, is a better illustration of the justified use of the rule of double effect. Palliative sedation is good end-of-life care, professionally, ethically, and legally allowed, even praised.[21] However, there is a potential moral problem here as well. The use of palliative sedation requires intellectual honesty. Otherwise, a physician or nurse may rapidly increase the dose of morphine, not waiting for it to have its full effect, leading to premature respiratory depression and hastened death. Or this method may be used inappropriately in some instances when less consciousness-impairing methods of pain relief have not been tried.

Dave's pain and Mary's desperation lead to a request for something that most Christian believers find morally unacceptable—hastened death. Instead, Alex would be on solid ground to offer and provide palliative sedation for Dave when all other efforts have failed and Dave remains in intolerable pain. This could bring him relief from his intense suffering for his remaining hours or days. If palliative sedation is to be considered, it should not be initiated without discussion with Dave and Mary, allowing them to make the decision about its use, and allowing time for goodbyes if it is to be used.

This morally acceptable form of treatment is not without its controversies, however. In most instances when palliative sedation is applied, the patient has only a few hours or a couple of days to live before he will die from the progressive disease. In some cases, the intensity of symptoms occurs when the patient still has several days or a few weeks (or more) of natural life. This raises two questions about how best to care for sedated patients who may well continue to live more than a couple of days.

First, should such patients necessarily remain sedated until death? The answer is a matter of medical judgment. It depends on whether there is a reasonable possibility that, after a period of sedation-induced rest, patients may be better able to cope with their pain without continued sedation. If so, then they should periodically be restored to consciousness in order to ascertain their level of pain and their need for continued sedation.

Second, should sedated patients be given fluids and nutrition during their final days or weeks if a dying process is under way? Most often, supplemental fluids and nutrition are not given in such circumstances, because patients have chosen to forgo any treatment that will postpone death and there is no longer an option to be awake and free of intolerable symptoms. A dying process is unavoidably under way, and so most believe that any form of technological intervention, even fluids and nutrition, is no longer morally obligatory. However, those who want to avoid even the possibility of dying from dehydration can request that fluids and nutrition be administered. The more likely it is that

---

21. To see the position statement of the American Academy of Hospice and Palliative Care Physicians on palliative sedation, visit *http://www.aahpm.org/positions/sedation.html* (accessed March 9, 2010).

death will not occur soon and that the patient will be restored to consciousness again, the more understandable is the request that supplemental fluids and nutrition continue.

CONCLUSION

In reviewing the difficult death experienced by Dave, Mary, and Bethany, we have emphasized the moral obligation to treat suffering, the importance of whole-person care for patients and their families, the scope of morally acceptable forms of treatment, and the thin line that separates these from the morally unacceptable practice of hastened death. Excellent hospice and palliative care are a ministry, to fellow believers and to others. But there is more.

The church has multiple roles to play in this endeavor—roles in service, education, and counseling.

- The church should encourage members to become involved in hospice ministry, by training them to become volunteers, provide music, or give pastoral support. Perhaps the local church could offer space for hospice training classes or a hospice volunteer office.
- The church should provide education for adults on end-of-life issues, encouraging discussions among families and urging completion of advance directives. Thinking about the moral precepts before being confronted with difficult situations can lay a common foundation that makes such decisions less problematic. Sadly, many believers develop a poor theology suggesting that God will always provide miraculous cure in response to earnest and heartfelt prayer.
- The church should offer counsel for parishioners who themselves—or whose loved ones—are facing life-threatening illness. This should involve more than visits to read Scripture and pray, as important as those are. It should include helping people to understand the stresses on them and providing them with whatever supports they need on their difficult paths to natural death. A reminder that death opens the future to a painless eternity[22] with a loving God can be a great source of comfort to people as they struggle with the difficulties of today.

Let us all learn from the painful experiences of Dave, Mary, Bethany, and their church family.

---

22. "'He will wipe every tear from their eyes. There will be no more death' or mourning or crying or pain, for the old order of things has passed away" (Rev. 21:4).

CHAPTER 11

WISDOM FROM PASTORAL CARE

Steven C. Roy

Death is, at the same time, the most universal and the most unnatural of all human experiences. Understanding this can give us great insight into the struggles of Dave, Mary, Bethany, and others in the case before us.

Our common human experience testifies to the universality of death. And this is confirmed by the biblical record. In the garden of Eden, the good and gracious Creator provided bountifully for our first parents, giving them permission to eat of every tree in the garden (Gen. 2:16). But there was one prohibition as well, and with God's prohibition came a warning of penalty for disobedience. "You must not eat from the tree of the knowledge of good and evil, for when you eat of it you will certainly die" (Gen. 2:17). And in spite of the serpent's false assertion that such eating would not result in death (Gen. 3:4), our first parents did in fact experience what Paul later described as "the wages of sin"—death (cf. Rom. 6:23).

When they disobeyed God and ate the forbidden fruit, Adam and Eve immediately began to experience what we might call spiritual death—alienation and estrangement within their own persons, from each other, and ultimately from God himself. In God's merciful patience, they did not experience physical death immediately. But from the moment of their rebellion, it became inevitable. The principle of death was implanted in their bodies, and they began the process of deterioration. We read in Genesis 3:17–19 that the ground itself became cursed because of Adam's sin. As a result, his labor would be hard, painful, and often frustrating throughout his life—or, as God put it, "until you return to the ground, since from it you were taken; for dust you are and to dust you will return" (Gen. 3:19).

So God promised, and so in time, it came to pass. In Genesis 5:5, we read, "Altogether, Adam lived a total of 930 years, and then he died." And physical death was passed on to all of Adam's descendents. In Genesis 5, there is a genealogy listing ten generations from Adam to Noah. In every case, except for Enoch, who was a remarkable and unprecedented exception, the account of each person ends with the terse and chilling words "and then he died" (Gen. 5:5, 8, 11, 14, 17, 20, 27, 31). And the rest of the biblical record demonstrates that this spread of physical death is indeed universal. This side of the fall, death is every bit as universal as birth. As Ecclesiastes 3:2 states, there is for every person "a time to be born and a time to die."

In the New Testament, Paul reflects on the universal experience of the wages of sin in Romans 5:12: "Therefore, just as sin entered the world through one man, and death through sin, and in this way death came to all people, because all sinned." The author of Hebrews also affirms this sober reality, asserting in Hebrews 9:27 that all people "are destined to die once, and after that to face judgment."

The biblical record confirms the facts of our own human experience—death is the most universal of all human experiences.[1]

But death is also very unnatural. It was not part of God's intention for his human creation. Rather, as we have seen, it is the result of sin. That is why Paul calls death an "enemy," the last enemy to be destroyed by the risen, reigning Christ (1 Cor. 15:26).

Windows into this reality come not only from the theological reflections of Paul on death as the wages of sin and the last enemy to be destroyed by Christ, but also from the incarnate experience of Jesus himself. His powerful emotions at the grave of his beloved friend Lazarus (John 11:33–36) give evidence to his conviction that death is a foreign intrusion into God's good creation, one that he will in fact overcome through his own subsequent death and resurrection.

While there is much more that can, and will, be said here about a biblical view of death, its reality as a foreign intruder and a powerful enemy makes death (and the process of dying) a fearful prospect (Heb. 2:15). This is true even in the case of a "good" death (which for most Americans would be pain-free and unexpected; e.g., the painless heart attack while one is sleeping at the end of a long, rich, and full life).[2] How much more is this true in the very difficult case before us. The task of this chapter is to discern how faithful pastoral ministry, following in the footsteps of the Good Shepherd, Jesus Christ, can help Dave and his family navigate this very difficult season of dying and grieving.

Pastoral ministry always involves human beings—pastors themselves and those they are called on to shepherd. And since death is a universal human experience, pastoral ministry is unavoidably concerned with death. This was particularly true in the pastoral theology of the Puritans. One of the primary goals of pastoral ministry for them was to help one's people die well.[3] This is an extraordinarily wise and helpful perspective. It

1. According to Scripture, the only exceptions to the universal experience of death are the rare and exceptional cases of Enoch (Gen. 5:23–24), Elijah (2 Kings 2:11), and the generation that will be alive when Christ returns (1 Thess. 4:15–17).

2. The concept of what makes for a "good death" is highly cultural and reflects diverse cultural values. See Kathryn L. Braun, James H. Pietsch, and Patricia L. Blanchette, eds., *Cultural Issues in End-of Life Decision Making* (Thousand Oaks, Calif.: Sage Publications, 2000).

3. One writer in this tradition is Puritan Jeremy Taylor (1609–1667). In his book, *The Rules and Exercises of Holy Dying* (written in 1651, the year of his wife's death), he observes, "It is a great art to die well." He understood that "dying well" for a Christian involves dying with dignity and peace, filled with faith and the hope of the resurrection in Christ. Another Puritan resource on the topic of dying well is James Durham, *Blessed Death of Those Who Die in the Lord* (Grand Rapids, Mich.: Soli Deo Gloria, 2003).

gives to pastors an important set of priorities and a valuable way to evaluate the effectiveness of their ministries.

So how can pastoral shepherds, both vocational and lay, help people in the process of dying well? It will be helpful to divide pastoral responses into two categories: reactive pastoral care (care given once the crisis has arrived) and proactive pastoral care (the regular and ongoing care that pastors give to their flock before the crisis comes). Logically and temporally, proactive pastoral care needs to come first. But life is not always so orderly. When we meet Dave and his family in the case before us, they need reactive pastoral care, so we will consider that first here. But some of the most important wisdom to be gained from a consideration of such a case is the proactive care that the church could have provided. That will be the focus of the final section of this chapter.

REACTIVE PASTORAL CARE

Dave's is an example of a slow death, as opposed to a sudden death. While the vast majority of contemporary Americans would indicate a preference for a sudden death (no doubt out of fear of prolonged suffering and the impact of medical technologies that would be utilized during a prolonged process of dying),[4] there are distinct advantages of a slow death. Central among these advantages is the opportunity it provides for one to prepare for death, to be intentional about living the final phase of life wisely and well, to strengthen relational bonds with family and friends, and to leave a godly legacy to those closest at hand. One of the primary privileges and responsibilities of pastoral care to those who are terminally ill is the opportunity to help them accomplish these goals.

In his majestic prayer of Psalm 90, Moses prays, "Teach us to number our days, that we may gain a heart of wisdom" (Ps. 90:12). In other words, wisdom demands that we recognize that our lives will not go on forever. Only as we live in light of the finiteness of our days can we truly live lives of wisdom. If this is true for all people at all stages of their lives, how much more is it true when one has received a terminal diagnosis.[5] Recognizing that we are going to die can give us a whole new perspective on the days we have left. Different priorities rise in importance. The goal of finishing life well sharpens the focus of the remaining days.

A heart of wisdom, rooted in the fear of the Lord (Job 28:28; Prov. 1:7), would have us seek to die a good death, a death consistent with the faith and hope and love that are in Christ. It involves our living to the very end of our days in ways that affirm our faith in Christ and that rest in his love. Among other things, this involves the opportunity

---

4. This preference for sudden death is historically relatively recent. Earlier views are reflected in the petition found in the Book of Common Prayer, "Lord, prevent us from sudden death." See John Dunlop, *Finishing Well to the Glory of God: Strategies from a Christian Physician* (Wheaton, Ill.: Crossway, 2011), 74.

5. Augustine's wisdom is worth reflecting on: "It is only in the face of death that man's self is born" (quoted in Dunlop, *Finishing Well*, 76).

to reflect on our lives. Knowledge of our impending deaths can free us to look honestly at those things we have accomplished and those things we have failed to accomplish, at areas of faithfulness and areas of sin in our lives. No doubt memories of past sin will be painful, but the comfort of the forgiving grace of God in Christ will be very precious in these days. Our hearts can be filled with gratitude to God for all the good gifts he has given us, and we can recognize that all the good things we have accomplished have been done by God's grace working in and through us. In these reflective moments, we will be able to see much of how God has used past struggles and pain and failure in accomplishing his good purposes in our lives. To be sure, we will not be able to see everything clearly (in this life we always and only see through a mirror dimly; 1 Cor. 13:12). But our memories of God's faithfulness can strengthen us to trust him to the very end.[6]

FINISHING WELL

A frequent biblical metaphor for life is the race (e.g., 1 Cor. 9:24; Heb. 12:1; 2 Tim. 4:7). Implicit in this metaphor is the need to finish well. In a race, it does not matter how far ahead runners are at the beginning or in the middle of the race. It matters how they finish. Endurance matters. Enduring to the very end of our lives in faith, hope, and love is indeed one of the most important parts of a life that truly honors God.[7] As we have seen, one of the key ways God can strengthen us for this task is through honest, grateful reflection on our lives.

The last portion of our earthly lives can also afford us time to pray. Especially as a terminal illness progresses and physical strength becomes less and less, the opportunity to pray is so valuable. We can pray as an expression of our love for God — prayers of praise and thanksgiving. We can pray as an expression of our love for our neighbors — prayers of petition and intercession.

Seeking to finish our lives well will have significant and crucial relational components. Thomas Oden has wisely said, "Death is eminently a social event. It breaks in on a community like an echoing, ricocheting sound reminding us all of our finitude. It rearranges relationships in families.... Ministry and death is best understood, not just individualistically as care for a single person, but also interpersonally for the family, friends, and wider community."[8]

Those who seek to die well will give thought and effort to loving their families. Many have prioritized the strengthening of family bonds as one of their key goals in this last season of their lives.[9] Reconciliation, wherever needed, becomes crucial, along with enriching family relationships.

---

6. Ibid., 76–77.

7. Recognizing the difficulty of patient endurance, Paul prays for the Colossians that they would be "strengthened with all power according to his glorious might so that you may have great endurance and patience" (Col. 1:11).

8. Thomas C. Oden, *Pastoral Theology: Essentials of Ministry* (San Francisco: HarperSanFrancisco, 1983), 296.

9. Dunlop, *Finishing Well*, 80.

Dr. Ira Byock, a palliative care physician and past president of the American Academy of Hospice and Palliative Medicine, encourages those who are in the final stages of their lives to say and to hear four things frequently:

- I love you.
- Thank you.
- Forgive me.
- I forgive you.[10]

Byock speaks of how often he has seen people come to a significant sense of peace and closure in their lives by saying these four things.

While Byock does not write from an explicitly Christian perspective, his counsel certainly reflects biblical wisdom.[11] Love that is verbally expressed and heard is a vital part of obeying the Second Great Commandment (Matt. 22:37–39). Gratitude to God and to those people he has put into our lives is appropriate and needs to be expressed regularly. Forgiveness, freely given and received, is appropriate only in light of the great forgiveness given to us by God through Christ (Matt. 18:21–35). These four things are important for all of us throughout our lives. But no doubt a great advantage of a gradual death is the opportunity to make sure that we say and hear these four things as we seek to bring closure to our lives.

One additional aspect of dying well is passing on a good legacy to family and friends. Consideration of how one can pass on a legacy of faith and godliness is crucial. The Psalms regularly speak of the crucial importance of telling the next generation about God. For example, in Psalm 71:18 the psalmist prays, "Even when I am old and gray, do not forsake me, my God, till I declare your power to the next generation, your mighty acts to all who are to come." In Psalm 78, Asaph speaks of the things that his ancestors have told to his generation, vowing, "We will not hide them from their descendants; we will tell the next generation the praiseworthy deeds of the LORD, his power, and the wonders he has done" (Ps. 78:4). This should be an ongoing practice among the people of God, even as Psalm 145:4 says, "One generation commends your works to another; they tell of your mighty acts."

It can be so valuable to give expression not only to the events of one's life but also to one's faith. This can be done in group settings with loved ones or in one-on-one contexts. Recording these reflections, in writing and/or electronically, can preserve this legacy and give it enduring power in others' lives. Even as the patriarch Jacob called each of his twelve sons to him prior to his death so that he could give them a word of blessing (Genesis 49), so a gradual process of dying provides the opportunity for cherished times of blessing, as well as of love, gratitude, and forgiveness.

---

10. Ira Byock, *Dying Well: The Prospect for Growth at the End of Life* (New York: Riverhead, 1997), and Ira Byock, *The Four Things That Matter Most: A Book about Living* (New York: Free Press, 2004).

11. Dunlop gives an appreciative reflection on these four things in *Finishing Well*, 82–83.

All of these are crucial elements of what it means to live wisely in the final stages of one's life. They are the kinds of things that enable one to die well in ways consistent with faith in Christ. These elements were all possible for Dave after he received his diagnosis of terminal pancreatic cancer. Admittedly the progress of Dave's disease and the onset of his pain made the window of opportunity for him fairly short. But there was time for reflection and prayer, there was time for strengthening of relationships with Mary and Bethany, there was time for saying and hearing the four crucial things, there was time for legacy and closure. Effective pastoral care will seek to ensure that Dave and Mary are reminded of these goals and priorities and will help them to strategize how they can best be carried out.[12]

Dave's decision to discontinue his chemotherapy was no doubt made to increase the quality of his life in his final days. This was a legitimate decision in Dave's case, given his terminal diagnosis and his sense that the costs of continued treatment were far greater than any potential gains. It is a good thing to seek to enhance the quality of the life one has left, though the goal should be to use those remaining days wisely and well. Tragically this did not happen for Dave.

HURDLES IN THE WAY

From what we can read in the case, Dave's final days were not spent in the kind of intentional activities that would bring peaceful and faith-filled closure to his life and that would strengthen the bonds of his family and leave a godly legacy to his wife, daughter, and friends. There were hurdles hindering his way that kept Dave from fulfilling these strategically important priorities. At least three stand out.

The first is *depression*. Elizabeth Kübler-Ross, in her groundbreaking study of terminally ill patients and their responses in the process of dying, identifies five stages of response that patients typically go through: denial and isolation, anger, bargaining, depression, and acceptance.[13] Dave, it appears, is stuck at the stage of depression. To be sure, he seemed to be showing signs of depression even before his diagnosis. This can be a presenting symptom of pancreatic cancer. Medical treatment for depression is certainly warranted, particularly after the cessation of his chemotherapy.

However, depression may well be a significant component in Dave's decision to discontinue his chemotherapy despite the expectations voiced by Mary, Alex, and Dr. Osgood that future chemotherapy treatments would be more bearable. In addition,

---

12. It may be helpful for pastors to compile a kind of checklist of crucial priorities for the last stage of life. Thus in ministering to the dying, they would have a set of questions they could ask that would help to set the agenda: e.g., Have you done a "life review"? How are you doing with family closure? Are there any relationships in special need of reconciliation? Who do you need to say the "four things" to?

13. Elizabeth Kübler-Ross, *On Death and Dying: What the Dying Have to Teach Doctors, Nurses, Clergy, and Their Own Families* (New York: Scribner, 1969). For Kübler-Ross's further reflections on the ways we experience the process of grief, written just prior to her own death, see Elizabeth Kübler-Ross and David Kessler, *On Grief and Grieving: Finding the Meaning of Grief through the Five Stages of Loss* (New York: Scribner, 2005).

depression may be involved in Dave's apparent inability or unwillingness to reach out to his daughter, Bethany, in her grief and anger. It seems very surprising that Dave was not more intentional to take advantage of the time he had left to be with her and to work through their doubts and fears and anger together. But depression can often lead people to make unexpected choices that are not helpful in the end.

In addition to the medical treatment for depression that Alex could have ordered, pastoral caregivers have an important role to play at this point. Kübler-Ross helpfully distinguishes what she calls reactive depression from preparatory depression.[14] Reactive depression comes in response to losses a patient has already experienced — in Dave's case, the loss of his career and especially the loss of his quality of life through his responses to chemotherapy. Preparatory depression, on the other hand, is a response to anticipated future losses — David's loss of his relationships and ultimately his life on this earth. Many of the causes of Dave's reactive depression could have been addressed especially by Alex and Dr. Osgood as they discussed the prospects of future chemotherapy and options for end-of-life medical care. But Dave's preparatory depression is best addressed by family, friends, and pastoral caregivers.

This latter form of care will most likely need to begin at the pastor's initiative. The same depression that contributed to Dave's unwillingness or inability to reach out to Bethany would also make Dave less inclined to seek help from his pastor and other church leaders. They need to come to Dave, rather than wait for him to request their presence.

Effective pastoral care does not come through a denial of depression or a simplistic "keep a positive outlook" approach. Kübler-Ross says that preparatory depression and grief are what "a terminally ill patient has to undergo in order to prepare himself for his final separation from this world."[15] Time spent with Dave is far more important than words in helping him navigate this preparatory grief and depression. The value of the ministry of presence cannot be overstated. Just sitting with Dave, Mary, and Bethany and crying together is an important way to begin the process of grieving for this family. It is crucial for pastoral caregivers to listen to Dave — carefully and well.

Oden points out the crucially important fact that living pastors are not on equal footing with Dave with respect to the experience of terminal illness. Dave experientially knows far more of this reality than any shepherd. Thus, all who seek to minister the grace of Christ in these days must remember to listen carefully to the unparalleled expertise of the one who is dying.[16] In time, there will be opportunity to remind Dave of the strategic importance of these days and the enriching possibilities that can come

---

14. Kübler-Ross, *On Death and Dying*, 98. These forms of depression are in addition to the possibility of a clinical or disease-induced depression that Dave might be experiencing.

15. Ibid.

16. Oden, *Pastoral Theology*, 301 – 2. Oden describes this kind of pastoral ministry as one in which "the dying 'learner' is experientially ahead of the pastoral 'guide.'"

from living them wisely and well. There will also be opportunity to remind Dave of all the grace he has been given in Christ that cannot be lost, even in death.

Dave, however, may not be the only one depressed in this situation. Mary certainly is fatigued and likely is depressed as well in her role as caregiver and grieving wife. Many resources could be directed her way. For instance, medical personnel could provide any medication needed for depression and to help her sleep. The church community could provide respite care for Dave and enable Mary to have some time to rest and to process things on her own. Members of her church family could connect with her relationally in rich ways that would strengthen her soul. And pastoral shepherds could also help connect her with the spiritual resources she needs to sustain her in this trying time.

A second hindrance to the process of Dave's ending his life well is the *lack of truthfulness* that Dave and Mary exhibit. They initially tell Bethany that he has a cancer that can be treated, withholding from her the true prognosis that has been given to them. Whatever their motivation was, this lack of honesty has the effect of withholding from Bethany the very truth that would eventually make Dave's decision to discontinue treatment a legitimate one. No doubt, Bethany would have experienced intense grief and anger, even had her mom and dad been honest with her from the start. But honesty and truthfulness could have laid a foundation for them to navigate these difficult days together rather than being alienated and isolated from one another.

Had Dave and Mary sought the counsel of their pastor prior to their initial conversation with Bethany, the pastor could have counseled the value of honesty. It's one thing not to tell her everything. It's another thing to deliberately give a false impression. Once the deception had transpired, a pastoral caregiver could have encouraged Dave and Mary to come clean with Bethany and to apologize and ask for forgiveness while there was still time.

A third hindrance involves a *lack of intentional wisdom* on the part of Dave and Mary with respect to Bethany. She is clearly hurting greatly. She needs friends who can help her process and who can do "normal" things with her, even when everything else in her life is decidedly not normal. She needs other support people in her life from school and church. But she also needs her mom and dad.

Mary's encouragement to Bethany to respect her Dad's decision is appropriate to a point. However, her ongoing efforts to get her not to feel and express her anger are not at all helpful. Yes, her anger would be uncomfortable for Dave, since it is directed at him as well as at God. But the way to cope with anger productively is to work through it rather than to deny or hide it. Pastoral guidance and support in the process of feeling and expressing anger, as well as other doubts, fears, and questions, could be very helpful for this family as a whole.

While the progress of Dave's disease meant that he had a relatively short window of opportunity with Bethany, he needed to be encouraged (by his pastor as well as family and friends) to make the most of the time he did have with her. He needed to be encouraged to seek out opportunities to be with her and to talk about the important things of life and death, of love and gratitude and forgiveness, rather than to allow her to withdraw and to retreat into isolation. The legacy of faith, hope, and love that he would leave with her would depend in large measure on the intentionality he exhibited in reaching out to her.

Not all is problematic, however. There are many very encouraging dimensions to this case from a pastoral care perspective. Dave received excellent medical care from Alex and from the hospice team. Mary received the help she needed with insurance forms. Church members pitched in to provide care for Dave and Mary in tangible ways, including meals and respite care so that Mary could attend worship services at church and do other needed errands. This is as it should be and is a sign of the body of Christ functioning as Christ would have it.

This kind of tangible, practical care can free up a whole variety of family, friends, and pastoral caregivers to attend to the spiritual concerns of Dave and Mary. The case says that the pastor and elders of the church visited them regularly. That is wonderful. In the context of genuine love and careful, empathetic listening, God can use these pastoral caregivers as means of his grace. They and the family can cherish Scripture together as the word of their Creator and Redeemer that offers assurance and hope, even in the midst of life's final challenges. They can offer prayer to their sympathetic high priest (Heb. 4:15), who experienced death so that he can give grace to all in time of need.[17] They can share the Lord's Supper as a visible and tangible reminder of God's grace in Christ and as a means of spiritual nourishment.[18] Pastoral caregivers can encourage and help to facilitate important conversations that need to happen for the sake of reconciliation, relational enhancement, legacy, and closure. Moreover, Dave, Mary, and Bethany need to know that this kind of support will continue after Dave's death.[19]

The Christian life is a life to be lived by faith (2 Cor. 5:7; Gal. 2:20). This is true even in the darkest days of terminal illness. By the grace of God, and with the help of various means of grace, including pastoral caregivers, Dave and Mary can be strengthened to trust in Christ and to rest in him even to the end.

---

17. Prayer can certainly be offered for healing. God can and at times does heal miraculously, even from otherwise terminal illness. However, as discussed above regarding suffering, God alone is wise enough to know when to heal in this life and when he will defer physical healing until the resurrection. In no way should pastoral caregivers imply that it is always God's will to heal physically if only we have enough faith. Paul's experience with his thorn in the flesh (2 Corinthians 12) dispels that idea. It is always and eminently appropriate, though, to pray for wisdom and

strength to live well in one's final days, and for grace to continue to trust God throughout.

18. My mother-in-law's pastor brought her the Lord's Supper less than a week before she died in the rehab center where she was staying. Susan and I will be forever grateful for the wonderful expression of pastoral love and care.

19. Oden's chapter "Pastoral Care of the Dying" is an excellent resource on the broad range of forms that loving, gracious pastoral care can take in these difficult days (Oden, *Pastoral Theology*, 293–310).

PROACTIVE PASTORAL CARE

As noted earlier, however, much of this strengthening should have taken place long before Dave's health crisis arose. Because suffering and death will be experienced by all people, one of the key pastoral priorities must be to help people get ready for them. Central to this preparatory process are the tasks of preaching (see chap. 13), teaching (see chap. 14), and counseling (see chap. 3). But every conversation with other people is an opportunity to help them develop the kind of understanding and outlook they need in order to face something like Dave's dying when they encounter it.

Pastors have the unspeakable privilege of communicating the inspired, God-breathed Scriptures. And Paul is very clear about the value of the Word of God. "All Scripture is God-breathed and is useful for teaching, rebuking, correcting and training in righteousness, so that all God's people may be thoroughly equipped for every good work" (2 Tim. 3:16–17). Certainly included in the good works for which Scripture will equip God's people are the works of suffering and dying well. To be prepared to suffer and to die in faith, in peace, and in the hope of the gospel, we need Scripture to equip us. A deep and true and God-honoring biblical and theological foundation is essential to dealing well with issues of life and death, of sickness and suffering over the long run. As a result, this must be an ongoing focus of a pastor's equipping ministry.

One of the greatest privileges of an extended pastoral ministry with the same flock is the opportunity to build this biblical and theological foundation in advance.[20] The most effective time for all of us to grapple with the deep and thorny and mysterious truths of Scripture is now, before the suffering is the most intense. Thus, when Dave's diagnosis comes back revealing incurable and terminal pancreatic cancer, the biblical foundation would not need to be built from scratch. Dave, Mary, and Bethany, along with Alex and other pastoral caregivers from their church, could just hold each other and cry, knowing that in all of their questions, doubts, and fears, they were standing on firm footing.

To be sure, there would be some time for Dave and Mary's pastor to explore Scripture more fully with them after the initial shock of the diagnosis wears off. But Dave's initial chemotherapy treatments and the pain he so rapidly started to experience would no doubt make this very difficult. All of this points to the great advantage of preparing the foundation in advance.

So what should a pastor be communicating in all of these varied ways? The following strands of biblical teaching, among many others, are particularly important for a deep and solid foundation.[21] (See also chap. 9 for a fuller development of New Testament perspectives.)

---

20. See D. A. Carson, *How Long, O Lord? Reflections on Suffering and Evil* (Grand Rapids, Mich.: Baker, 1990), 110; and Oden, *Pastoral Theology*, 302.

21. The descriptions of each of these central strands of biblical thought are of necessity brief and incomplete. Faithful pastoral ministry of the Word can and should fill in each of these areas of biblical revelation richly and deeply.

THE CHARACTER OF GOD

One of the central and most important biblical reflections on the mysteries of suffering and pain is the book of Job. The agony that this righteous man endured is intense and prolonged. Throughout, Job pleads with God, and at times he angrily demands from God answers as to why he is suffering. The book is clear that the answer of Job's friends (all suffering is the result of sin; Job is suffering; therefore Job must have sinned and needs to repent in order to be freed from his suffering) is dangerously wrong. But if Job's suffering is not the result of sin, why does he suffer? In the end, God never gives Job the answers he is seeking. What he does give him is in the end far better. God gives to Job a revelation of himself. One of the central truths of the book of Job is that answers to the mystery of suffering are incomplete at best,[22] and people need to content themselves with what he is pleased to reveal.[23] But in the final analysis, the agonies of suffering are best navigated through faith in and worship of the true and living God.[24]

This makes it imperative that people are growing in their understanding of the character of God. Biblical truths of God's holiness and love, his sovereignty and power, his knowledge and wisdom, and the ways these are all supremely demonstrated through the cross of Christ are essential building blocks of the kind of foundation that can enable people to endure and to suffer and die well.[25]

This theological foundation ultimately provides a way to navigate the waters of suffering with a focus on faith in and worship of God. It would not have spared Dave, Mary, and Bethany the agonizing questions, doubts, and pain that they experienced. But it could have been very helpful in keeping their focus on God as their ultimate source of hope. Reminding themselves and being reminded of God's great love and faithfulness would greatly serve to strengthen their ability to walk by faith through the darkness of this valley of the shadow of death. Such faith greatly honors God and would enhance the godly legacy Dave could leave to Mary, Bethany, and many others.

LIFE AND DEATH[26]

The God of the Bible is the true and living God (Deut. 5:26; Heb. 10:31). He exists and is self-existent (Exod. 3:14) and alone has "life in himself" (John 5:26). As such,

---

22. See John F. Kilner, *Life on the Line: Ethics, Aging, Ending Patients' Lives, and Allocating Vital Resources* (Grand Rapids, Mich.: Eerdmans, 1992), 103.

23. Christopher Wright (*The God I Don't Understand: Reflections on Tough Questions of Faith* [Grand Rapids, Mich.: Zondervan, 2008], 42) helpfully argues that with infinite wisdom and for reasons known only to himself, God has determined not to reveal any ultimate answers to the origin of evil and suffering.

24. A helpful treatment of key themes from the book of

Job that relate to suffering is found in Carson, *How Long, O Lord?* 153–78.

25. On the character and attributes of God, see John Feinberg, *No One Like Him* (Wheaton, Ill.: Crossway, 2001).

26. On this topic, see the helpful essay by David J. Atkinson, "Life, Health and Death," in *New Dictionary of Christian Ethics and Pastoral Theology*, ed. David J. Atkinson, David F. Field, Arthur Holmes, and Oliver O'Donovan (Downers Grove, Ill.: InterVarsity, 1995), 87–92.

he is the giver of all life. It is he who gives to all people "life and breath and everything else" (Acts 17:25). All life (physical and spiritual) is a gift from God. As a result, it is to be cherished gratefully, and as children of God we are to seek to preserve and enhance this good gift for ourselves and for others.

As we have seen, death is not a part of God's original intention. It seems from the Genesis account that if our first parents had not sinned, they would have been permitted to eat from the tree of life and live forever.[27] But because of human sin, death entered the world and has spread to all people. It is, in fact, the judgment of God against our sin.[28] Yet in his grace, God has determined not to allow death to have the last word. He sent his one and only Son into the world to overcome death through his own atoning death on the cross and triumphant resurrection. Through his death, Jesus has broken "the power of him who holds the power of death—that is, the devil," thereby freeing his people from the enslaving fear of death (Heb. 2:14–15). Christ has taken away the sting of divine judgment from death (1 Cor. 15:54–56), for "there is now no condemnation for those who are in Christ Jesus" (Rom. 8:1). As a result, not even death can separate those who belong to Christ from the love of God in Christ (Rom. 8:38–39). Rather, it serves God's redemptive purposes and ushers believers into the very presence of their Creator and Redeemer (Luke 23:43; 2 Cor. 5:8; Phil. 1:23). This is why Scripture can pronounce the death of God's people to be "precious" (Ps. 116:15) and "blessed" (Rev. 14:13) and a great "gain" (Phil. 1:21).

Such is the profound ambiguity we as Christians experience in the face of death. It is and remains an enemy, yet in Christ it is a conquered enemy. Thus, as Christians we refuse to accept physical death as something normal or good. But we also refuse to view it as the ultimate disaster. John Kilner expresses this ambiguity well when he writes, "Death is both enemy and destiny, both penalty and promise, both cross and resurrection. It is necessarily a real evil, the result of rebellion against God, but it is something over which God's love did, does, and will triumph."[29]

A deep appreciation of this ambiguity would be helpful to Dave. Honest reflection on the reality that death is an enemy, an intruder into God's good and gracious order, would help to give Dave permission to feel his own anger and grief and to share them honestly with Mary and Bethany. It would have helped Mary encourage Bethany to be honest with her father. But knowing that death is a *conquered* enemy in Christ would foster the kind of hope that could have enabled Dave to attend to what should be his most important priorities in this final season of life.

---

27. Millard Erickson, *Christian Theology*, 2nd ed. (Grand Rapids, Mich.: Baker, 1998), 1177.

28. However, it is not the case that every individual human death is the direct and immediate judgment of God against his or her individual sins. The teaching of Jesus in John 9:3 and Luke 13:1–5 confirms this fact. See the discussion in Wright, *The God I Don't Understand*, 44–55.

29. Kilner, *Life on the Line*, 103. For a helpful treatment of the biblical view of death from a Christian physician who specializes in geriatrics, see Dunlop, *Finishing Well*, 65–70.

SORROW AND GRIEF

Even though in Christ death is a conquered enemy, it remains an enemy nonetheless. Physical death is the ending of one's life on this earth. It separates us from those we love, and the reality of such separation is indeed painful. Even the Son of God knew the reality of such painful grief, as reflected in his tears at the grave of Lazarus (John 11:36). Paul's desire that Christians might not grieve over the death of their fellow believers "like the rest, who have no hope" (1 Thess. 4:13) should not be understood to deny the reality and indeed the value of grief. No, Paul's goal was to discourage hopeless grief and to ensure that in the midst of their grief, these Thessalonian believers were filled with the hope of the gospel. In Philippians 2, when Paul is reflecting on the mercy of God to spare his coworker Epaphroditus from death, he says that such grace has spared him "sorrow upon sorrow" (Phil. 2:27). When we encounter those who grieve and mourn, Paul's counsel is not to discourage such grief but rather to "mourn with those who mourn" (Rom. 12:15). Grief in the face of death, whether one's own death or the death of a loved one, is normal, natural, right, and healthy.[30]

Not only is grief experienced but there is also fear. It is true that Christ came to deliver his people from their slavery to the fear of death (Heb. 2:14–15). Yet this deliverance from fear is not yet fully completed in any of us. In this life, we face the very real enemy of death.[31] Even those who are confident in Christ of what they will experience after death often fear the process of dying. We worry about the welfare of those we will leave behind. We experience sadness at the prospect of leaving our life on earth. Doubts can and often will come.

It is crucial to note that doubts, fears, sadness, and disappointments are not necessarily signs of spiritual weakness.[32] Remember that our Lord himself did not look forward to his own death. In the garden of Gethsemane, Jesus told Peter, James, and John, "My soul is overwhelmed with sorrow to the point of death" (Matt. 26:38). And he prayed, "My Father, if it is possible, may this cup be taken from me. Yet not as I will, but as you will" (Matt. 26:39). While fully acknowledging his own sorrow and anguish at his impending death, in the end Jesus submitted all of his pain to the will of his Father in heaven.

Acknowledging the reality of questions, doubts, and fears can set us free to be open about them. This would have been so helpful for Dave and Mary. Were they able to do that, they could have derived strength from one another and from others in the community of faith. This in turn would greatly help them grow in their experience of resting in the grace of God even to the point of death.[33]

---

30. Biblical examples of grief are abundant (Gen. 37:34–35; Job 1:20; 2:13; Luke 7:11–13; etc.). The presence of the lament psalms and the book of Lamentations in the biblical canon shows that responses of grief, mourning, and lament in the midst of suffering and death are appropriate for the people of God.

31. Karl Barth (*Church Dogmatics* III/2, quoted by Atkinson, "Life, Health, and Death," 91) suggests that because death is a sign of God's judgment against sin, fear is an appropriate response.

32. Dunlop, *Finishing Well*, 131, is very helpful at this point.

33. When we turn our attention to the specifics of the case before us, we will see some of the heartache and sorrow that come from Dave and Mary's unwillingness to be open and honest, especially with Bethany.

SUFFERING AND PAIN[34]

The Bible is clear that God is morally holy and free from every taint of evil (Ps. 5:4; Hab. 1:13; James 1:13). But Scripture also teaches that God does ordain and use suffering to accomplish his good purposes. In other words, suffering is not an *essential* good. It is not a part of the very nature of God or the world he initially created (Gen. 1:31) or the new heavens and the new earth that is his ultimate goal (Rev. 21:3–4). But in this life, suffering is used by God as an *instrumental* good. In his divine wisdom, God uses suffering to accomplish his good purposes.[35] While in the vast majority of cases the specifics of how any particular experience of suffering fits into God's good purposes are shrouded in mystery (cf. Deut. 29:29), Scripture does give some examples of the kind of instrumental goods God wills to accomplish through suffering.

For example, while God ordains that some suffering (not all) is a punishment for sin and God's means of bringing judgment on those who oppose him (e.g., Isa. 10:5–19; 2 Thess. 1:6), on other occasions pain and suffering can be part of God's good and gracious purposes for his children. Suffering can be an expression of his loving fatherly discipline that he uses to mold his children in holiness (Heb. 12:5–11). At times God can allow suffering for the strengthening and purification of his children and their growth in faith (Rom. 5:3–5; James 1:2–4). In fact, suffering can draw us into a deeper intimacy with Christ as we participate in the *koinonia* of his sufferings (Phil. 3:10).[36] Suffering and pain can expose human weakness and frailty, thereby weaning us away from self-reliance and allowing the strength of God to shine all the more gloriously (2 Cor. 1:9; 4:8–12; 12:8–10). Moreover, suffering can equip believers to care more effectively for others in their own pain (2 Cor. 1:3–7), and it can allow opportunities for growth in caregivers as they love and serve those who suffer. What Jesus said of the man born blind — "this happened so that the works of God might be displayed" (John 9:3) — is true of other forms of suffering as well. This list is by no means comprehensive, but it does demonstrate that God is at work in and through our suffering to bring about a variety of instrumental goods for his glory and for our eternal joy.[37]

Such realities about suffering should serve to counteract one of our culture's dominant beliefs about suffering — that it is an unqualified evil that should be removed at all costs.[38] While suffering is not intrinsically good in and of itself, this does not mean

---

34. See Carson, *How Long, O Lord?* Also very helpful are John Feinberg's personal reflections on the journey he and his wife have traveled through suffering: John S. Feinberg, *Deceived by God? A Journey through Suffering* (Wheaton, Ill.: Crossway, 1997).

35. Steven C. Roy, *How Much Does God Foreknow? A Comprehensive Biblical Study* (Downers Grove, Ill.: InterVarsity, 2006), 265.

36. See Richard B. Hayes, *The Moral Vision of the New Testament: A Contemporary Introduction to New Testament*

Ethics (San Francisco: HarperSanFrancisco, 1996), 16–59.

37. The way Paul looked at and experienced his great sufferings (2 Cor. 11:23–28) was radically transformed by seeing them in light of eternity. As he writes in 2 Cor. 4:16–18, "We do not lose heart. Though outwardly we are wasting away, yet inwardly we are being renewed day by day. For our light and momentary troubles are achieving for us an eternal glory that far outweighs them all."

38. On this dominant cultural belief and the ways that biblical truths counter it, see Kilner, *Life on the Line*, 103–8.

it has no value and that God cannot use it powerfully for good in the lives of his people. While suffering is not something that is to be sought for its own sake, neither is it to be avoided at all costs. Jesus in the garden of Gethsemane demonstrates that once and for all.

Rather than avoiding it at all costs, believers are to endure suffering in submission to God's will (Matt. 26:39; 1 Peter 2:17), while growing in fellowship with Christ (Phil. 3:9; Col. 1:24; 1 Peter 4:13), trusting in God's providential ordering of their lives (Rom. 9:28–29; Heb. 12:5–11), rejoicing in his all-sufficient grace (Rom. 5:3–5; James 1:2–4), and hoping in the eternal consummation of all of God's purposes (2 Cor. 4:16–18).

When we suffer, it is natural and appropriate for us to ask God to take it away. Jesus did that, as we've seen, in the garden. Paul asked God three times to take away his thorn in the flesh (2 Cor. 12:8), and it was only after God explicitly told him that his purpose was to help Paul grow in humility by allowing the thorn to remain and to strengthen him as he endured that Paul was able to contentedly accept his sufferings and even to delight in them (2 Cor. 12:9–10). At times, God is pleased to intervene and to take away our suffering as firstfruits of the fullness of our salvation (Rom. 8:22–23)—but not always. In the end, only God is wise enough to know when his purposes of grace are best served by taking away our suffering now and when to give us grace to endure before finally and fully removing all of our suffering forever in eternity.

It is this biblical foundation that can enable Alex to respond appropriately and in a God-honoring way to Mary's request at the end of the case to "do something to speed this whole thing up." Don Carson (chap. 9), Robert Orr (chap. 10), and John Dunlop (chap. 12) have addressed elsewhere in this book the biblical-ethical dimensions of actions to hasten death. Suffice it to note here that God is the giver of all life, the one who sovereignly controls all dimensions of life and death (Job 1:21), including issues of timing (Ps. 139:16). This reality challenges all who seek to follow God to pursue and to nourish life. We are to align ourselves with the Lord's gift of life. Thus, we are not to choose death, our own or that of another,[39] nor are we to intentionally seek to cause it.[40]

At the same time, the fact that suffering is not an essential good makes it legitimate to seek to relieve pain. This is true even if a physician foresees that such palliative care

---

39. Atkinson ("Life, Health, and Death," 88) writes, "To choose death, whether one's own or another's, is not an option open to the Christian. It is a denial that the Lord of life is trustworthy in trusting us with life, and it is an assertion of human autonomy which cannot be justified in the light of the biblical view that human life is dependent on God."

40. Kilner helpfully focuses the question on the issue of intention rather than the more traditional categories of active and passive euthanasia (Kilner, *Life on the Line*, 79–80, 118). Taking steps to end the life of another always intends death, whereas various forms of withholding or discontinuing medical treatment so that the medical condition runs its course and death ensues may or may not intend death. See also the discussion on the centrality of the issue of intent in ethical decision-making in Kenneth P. Mottram, *Caring for Those in Crisis: Facing Ethical Dilemmas with Patients and Families* (Grand Rapids, Mich.: Brazos, 2007), 131–32.

could shorten life in the end. Such action is morally justified because of the principle of double effect, in which a treatment with a potential (and foreseen) negative effect (hastening death) can be utilized if certain conditions are met, including the direct and primary intent being to help the patient (relieving pain).[41] In our case study, since the intended outcome was to relieve pain rather than shorten life, administering pain-relief medications did not require Alex or others to align themselves with death in a way that would dishonor the Lord of life. Such actions here seem compassionate and wise.

We conclude our discussion of proactive pastoral ministry in the face of suffering and death with the reminder that more is needed than preaching and teaching. Pastors must seek to model healthy attitudes toward life, death, and suffering. In their own lives and ministries, they need to celebrate the mysteries of the faith, to recognize the reality of unanswered and incompletely answered questions, to acknowledge the reality of doubt and struggle. They need to teach and model spiritual practices of prayer. And they need to encourage an atmosphere of mutual care in which the people of God travel together in faith, along with all their doubts and fears and questions, through the valley of the shadow of death.

As the title of this case indicates, this is indeed a very difficult death. It is not the kind of death that Dave or Mary would have chosen. The challenges and pain are real and intense. But God is there, his love endures forever, and his grace is sufficient even in this tragic and difficult situation. Faithful and loving pastoral care—both reactive and proactive—can help Dave, Mary, and Bethany live out this very difficult season wisely and well, in ways that honor God.

---

41. See Robert Orr's discussion of the principle of double effect in chap. 10 of this volume.

CHAPTER 12

BIOETHICS AND A BETTER DEATH

John T. Dunlop

Many of the choices that people make in the case before us are both morally sound and prudentially wise. Roy (chap. 11) comments on the value of Dave and Mary choosing to give their home a spiritual foundation on which to raise Bethany. Dave's attempt to prolong life when it seems that he has a reasonable chance of succeeding is consistent with a biblical view of the body that Carson develops in chapter 9. At the same time, Orr and Salladay (chap. 10) observe that it is morally acceptable for Dave to choose to limit aggressive treatment for his pancreatic cancer in the face of insurmountable odds. Roy comments that this decision not only opens the door for more comfort care in the face of imminent death but also creates the potential for more quality time and closure with his family. Orr and Salladay affirm the value of hospice care, appreciating the legion of services provided through the dedicated caregivers who serve this family so well. In a similar vein, Roy commends the church congregation for providing lay and pastoral support to the family during these difficult days.

Still, this was a difficult death. It reminds us that even for Christians, death can be nasty and messy. Had the Lord himself been present at Dave's bedside, he likely would have shed tears as at the grave of Lazarus (John 11:35). Death was not a part of his originally good creation. It came as the result of sin. Although God can redeem and use death to accomplish his greater purposes and glory, it is fundamentally alien to his holy character. A fifty-year-old man dying a painful death, taken away from a loving wife and teenage daughter, would be tragic enough. But the legitimate questions Scharf (chap. 13) and Carson raise make it potentially even more tragic: Is Dave truly a believer? Has he repented of sin and trusted the crucified Savior for eternal life? Does this tragic death lead to eternal peace or to fearful judgment? The latter would infinitely compound the tragedy. As we read this case study, we too may weep.

It is incumbent on us to look at this difficult death and ask, How could it have been perhaps not good but better? What could those in the story have done differently? To answer this question, we will first consider some of the ingredients of a good death. Then we will look at the three major characters and ask how things could have been better for each of them. We will conclude the essay by giving similar consideration to the church and the broader society.

A GOOD DEATH

Dying well is not the default; it requires intentionality.[1] Some people in previous generations took this very seriously, particularly the Puritans. They wanted to die peacefully, with a sense of completion to their lives. However, as Carson observes, above all else they did not want to bring reproach to the name of Christ. Coming to life's end in this way requires a clear understanding of what it means to die well. As suggested in part by the previous three chapters, there are at least ten characteristics of a good death.

1. *A good death is the culmination of a life lived well.* Those who die well do so in large part because they have lived well. They can identify with the apostle Paul when he says, "I have fought the good fight, I have finished the race, I have kept the faith" (2 Tim. 4:7). There are, in one sense, only two groups of people—those who are living and those who are dead. We must remember that even though we may say someone is dying, that person is still very much alive. No matter how close people are to death, there are almost always things they can do to help someone else, and lessons they can learn to mature their character.

2. *A good death affirms the values of the person.* As the end of life approaches, there are many values which distinguish individuals. Some people may value their cognitive abilities and choose to endure more pain to preserve them.[2] Some may have a very strong preference to die at home; others may prefer a hospital. Some will prioritize quality of life over burdensome treatment that may or may not prolong life, while others will think that the sanctity of life requires the use of all possible treatments until death intervenes. The medical team should seek to understand and honor such values. For Christians, the gospel should have

---

1. In medieval times, death commonly struck early and quickly. Christians had to be prepared for it at any time, and this became a focus of their lives. To assist even the illiterate, there was created in the fifteenth century a series of woodblocks called the *Ars Moriendi* (*Art of Dying*) that illustrated five temptations that would often distract from dying well and five Christian graces that could answer them. This later developed into a literary genre that eventuated in the preaching and writing of Puritan John Donne. A most helpful discussion of *Ars Moriendi* is found in Rob Moll's *The Art of Dying* (Downers Grove, Ill.: InterVarsity, 2010).

2. There appears to be a swing in the world of palliative care and hospice away from controlling pain at all costs to being sensitive to the desires of the patient who may prefer to maintain mental acuity. See Ronan McGreevy, "What Makes a 'Good Death'?" *Irish Times* (March 2, 2010), *http://www.irishtimes.com/newspaper/health/2010/0302/1224265424874.html* (accessed July 8, 2010).

preeminent value. Believers should consider carefully what responses near the end of life are consistent with the gospel and which are inconsistent with it. If it is true that people generally die the way they live,[3] how much more should that be the case for followers of Christ. There should be no discontinuity between the faith they live by and the faith they die by.

3. *A good death follows a change in longings from earth to heaven.* As people come closer to the end of life, particularly as they deal with the difficulties that so often accompany their later days, they will become less enamored with this life. If at the same time they are able to experience in their inner being the great love which God has for them, they will be better prepared to slip into his visible presence. They will have a greater desire to be with God, they will long for freedom from the sin that is in and around them, and they will want to experience a resurrected body.

4. *A good death minimizes suffering when possible and affirms dignity.* No one wants a painful death. Suffering was not a part of God's original good creation. Along with disease and death, suffering came as the result of the fall. These difficulties are not welcome. Nevertheless, God can use them to accomplish his greater purpose. As Job learned, suffering can make possible a deeper experience with God. This necessitates seeing God as big enough to allow people to go through times of great difficulty with a confidence that he knows what is best. Steven Roy (chap. 11) reminds us that suffering is an instrumental, not an essential, good. Therefore, while suffering can have some beneficial results, its alleviation affords an opportunity to glorify God by reversing one of the results of the fall. In addition, the ability to benefit from suffering affirms human dignity, and we should never consider it undignified to suffer well.[4]

5. *A good death comes after closure with family and loved ones.* The days between receiving a terminal diagnosis and death can be very rich. Here is an opportunity for quality family time to talk about the most important things in life. It is appropriate to review together the major events of life, thank God for the good times, and rejoice in his forgiveness for the wrongs done. It is a time to

---

3. Stephen Kiernan, *Last Rights: Rescuing the End of Life from the Medical System* (New York: St. Martin's, 2006), 67.

4. Dignity is a "sounds good" term that is often ill defined and used in various ways to support a variety of positions. E.g., the Oregon statute legalizing physician-assisted suicide is the Death with Dignity Act, whereas a bioethics organization headquartered at Trinity International University in Illinois that opposes the practice is the Center for Bioethics and Human Dignity. For many, dignity is primarily about being in control; for others it implies freedom from pain and suffering. Still others con-sider dignity to involve being held in high regard by others or maintaining their own self-esteem. None of these are the primary concerns of a biblical view of human beings. In Scripture, human dignity is rooted in the fact that people are made in the image of God. Though Christians have fallen into sin, the transforming and sanctifying work of Christ is in the process of restoring them. Human dignity is therefore found in being in proper creature-Creator relationship with God, by submission to him and allowing him to accomplish his purposes by whatever way he chooses.

say and hear the four statements that Roy quotes from Ira Byock: "I love you. Thank you. Forgive me. I forgive you." The family can draw closer together and become stronger as they minister to a dying member who does not fight dependence but gives loved ones the opportunity to serve in very personal ways.[5]

6. *A good death uses medical technology appropriately.* Modern medicine is a gift with which God allows people to defeat many diseases and at times even delay physical death. It may restore full health; but on those occasions when it does not, it can enable a quality of life that is still rich and fulfilling. Employing medical technology can honor life and allow people to be good stewards of God's gifts. Yet there comes a time when technology only adds more burdens to an unavoidable death. Then it is appropriate to forgo technology, seek comfort care, and not make it a fight to the finish. Patients understandably resist aggressive life support that people all too often push on them "despite their desire to be allowed to die a 'normal' death."[6] Medical professionals may initiate overly aggressive medical care, or it may come at the request of well-meaning family members who are struggling with letting go.[7]

7. *A good death does not involve euthanasia or assisted suicide.* D. A. Carson (chap. 9) argues that euthanasia, by seeking to control death, is fundamentally incompatible with the gospel. The gospel is not about controlling but about the freedom that comes from entrusting one's life to another. Surrendering control is antithetical to the motives which commonly drive assisted suicide and euthanasia. As Averbeck (chap. 1) has explained, humanity's creation "in the image of God" (Gen. 1:27) places a unique protection on human life. God will "demand an accounting" from "whoever sheds human blood, . . . for in the image of God has God made humankind" (Gen. 9:5–6).

8. *A good death involves resting in Jesus.* Human beings spend much of their lives seeking to be in control. Even after coming to faith, they are in a constant tug-of-war, wanting to surrender control to God but still trying to pick it back up and go their own way. Carson has reminded us that in the face of death, "God alone is God." People must not compete but rather surrender themselves to him. There is no more fitting time for people once and for all to give that control to God than when death is imminent. Death then has the potential to become a quiet resting in Jesus.[8]

---

5. Ira Byock, *Dying Well* (New York: Riverhead, 1997), 22.

6. William M. Lammers, "Autonomy, Consent, and Advance Directives," in *Ethical Dilemmas at the End of Life*, ed. Kenneth J. Doka, Bruce Jennings, and Charles A. Corr (Washington, D.C.: Hospice Foundation of America, 2005), 105.

7. Hank Dunn, *Hard Choices for Loving People* (Lands-downe, Va.: A&A Publishers, 2001), 53ff., provides an excellent discussion regarding the dynamics of letting go of a family member.

8. The New Testament does not generally speak of believers in Jesus as dying. Rather it uses metaphors such as "falling asleep" (Acts 7:60; 1 Cor. 15:6, 18, 20, 51; 1 Thess. 4:15; 5:10).

9. *A good death brings people to God.* The ultimate purpose of the good news that Christ died for sins, was buried, and was raised from the dead is that people might be brought to God (1 Peter 3:18). Scripture teaches that Christ has defeated the enemy of death (1 Cor. 15:26). Believers do not ultimately fear death, because Jesus' resurrection gives them hope and takes the sting out of death (1 Cor. 15:54–57). When believers die, it opens the way for them to begin a more direct personal and eternal relationship with the God who made them and who is the fulfillment of their deepest longings. This understanding contrasts directly with the Buddhist view as described by Netland, Fields, and Sung (chap. 7). In that view, people experience the ultimate state in nirvana not because desire is fulfilled but because it is absent. Those who have rejected God's offer of forgiveness in Christ can still go through a dying process that is good in many ways. However, anything good about their death stops there. Upon death, they will experience not God's blessing but rather his judgment.

10. *A good death brings glory to God.* God created human life for his own glory (Isa. 43:7). It is common to think of living to the glory of God, but it is less common to associate death with the glory of God. Yet this is a theme that is repeated in the New Testament. Paul speaks of exalting Christ in his body either by his life or by his death (Phil. 1:20). Jesus speaks of Peter's dying in a way that will glorify God (John 21:19). In fact, the glory of God is especially central in the way that Jesus himself dies. Anticipating his death, he prays, "Glorify your Son, that your Son may glorify you" (John 17:1).

It is instructive—and conducive to worship—to appreciate how the death of Jesus Christ illustrates many of these principles. First, there is the godly character and dignity he demonstrates even while enduring excruciating pain. Then there is the closure he brings with his family by entrusting the care of his mother to John. Particularly impressive are his willingness to forgive his persecutors and, as death approaches, his surrender of full control to his heavenly Father.[9]

We have developed here a sense of what a good death is, partly by recognizing that the case before us is at odds with a truly good death in many ways. We now ask, How could Dave's death have been better for those involved?

First, consider Dave himself.

BETTER FOR DAVE

Dave decided not to pursue aggressive treatment when there was little or no hope of meaningful survival. Greggo and Parent (chap. 3) write about the danger when

---

9. These illustrations largely come from Rob Moll, "Jesus' Last Words as *Ars Moriendi*," *Christianity Today* (April 5, 2007), *http://www.christianitytoday.com/ct/2007/ aprilweb-only/114-42.0.html* (accessed July 8, 2010).

medicalizing infertility prompts people to ignore important human values. The same can be true at the other end of life. Dave did not want to "medicalize" the last days of his life. He takes a significant step when he chooses to forgo not only chemotherapy but also a feeding tube and resuscitation. The reason for those decisions includes avoiding further pain and suffering. However, as Roy observes, the rationale also involves giving Dave quality time to come to closure with his family and leave behind a legacy of strength and faith.

Dr. Osgood, Alex, Mary, and Bethany did not make this choice easy for him. They apparently worked together to convince Dave at least to try the chemotherapy he did not want. Then, after a very negative experience with the first course of treatment, Dr. Osgood sought to convince him that future ones would not be so bad, even though such optimism is contrary to most patients' experience. Cunningham (chap. 6) discusses the bioethical principle of autonomy and observes how it requires truly informed consent and freedom from coercion. Though Dave was able to resist certain pressures and decide to discontinue chemotherapy, it is questionable whether this was a truly informed choice free from coercion. Nevertheless, in making this choice, Dave succeeds in minimizing the danger of spending his last days focused on his treatment and aspirations for long-term survival.

As it turns out, before Dave can gain the quality time he anticipates at the end of his life, the pain quickly takes over and limits those opportunities. Emily Dickinson captures the all-consuming nature of pain in her poem "The Mystery of Pain":

Pain—has an Element of Blank—
It cannot recollect
When it began—or if there were
A time when it was not—

It has no Future—but itself—
Its Infinite realms contain
Its Past—enlightened to perceive
New Periods—of Pain

C. S. Lewis has written of pain being a megaphone that God uses to speak into people's lives.[10] That may be true, but Dave's pain is more than a megaphone. It is a great outdoor speaker that, when it is right next to the ear, leaves nothing but a garbled blast of noise. What could anyone have done to prevent this assault? First, there may have been a failure on the part of the medical team. In situations like this, it is customary to use high doses of opiates. They usually are effective and well tolerated, yet still allow reasonable alertness.

---

10. C. S. Lewis, *The Problem of Pain* (New York: Harper Collins, 1940), 91.

The challenge comes when they do not work. Then the medical team must think outside the box of standard care. To do so necessitates time, energy, and creativity, all of which are too often in short supply. Alex, as the primary-care physician, has the chief responsibility here. Did he consider, as Orr and Salladay (chap. 10) suggest, a celiac plexus block to numb the nerves carrying the painful signals to the brain? Could he have put in a call to a palliative-care specialist, perhaps at an academic medical center, to get another opinion? Any one of these additional steps could have made a huge difference for Dave. Not only could better pain management have been possible, but it may have given him the chance to attain better closure with his family, especially with Bethany.

The case history does not refer at all to the cost of Dave's care. Rae and Eckmann (chap. 2) would be very interested in that. Perhaps Dave and Mary had the foresight to assure good medical insurance and adequate savings to pay for the noncovered expenses. That would have allowed the physicians to make their recommendations without undue concern for the financial implications of the treatments. It would have helped Dave and Mary to make the wisest choices they could without financial constraints. Unfortunately, many even in the affluent United States do not have such freedom. Medical care, particularly end-of-life care, can be prohibitively expensive. Christians should be in the forefront of efforts to obtain needed end-of-life care for those who cannot afford it.[11]

Meanwhile, what about Dave's relationship with God? What is Dave's true spiritual condition? It seems that his involvement in church is primarily to meet social needs. The case study gives no assurance that he has saving faith. We do not know the content of the discussions he has with the pastor. Has the pastor taken time with Dave early in his illness to explain God's plan of salvation and encourage Dave to repent of sin and accept Christ as Savior? Robert Orr writes elsewhere of the priesthood of all believers.[12] A pastor is not necessary in order for this spiritual ministry to take place. A lay minister or elder, possibly someone like Alex, can do it well. Yet it seems incumbent on the pastor to ensure that someone does it.

After addressing the question of Dave's eternal destiny, his spiritual mentors should discuss a number of other pastoral issues while his mind is still functional. It would be appropriate to speak with Dave of the glories of God, the joy of his presence, and the anticipation of a resurrected body free from disease and death. D. A. Carson rightly observes that if Dave is trusting in Christ, his suffering during the dying process will be his final suffering. Reflecting with Dave on the comforting role of the Holy Spirit could provide another resource to help him find some peace in the midst of this tragedy. Perhaps he would be open to discuss God's purposes in suffering and where he is in his own character development. At the same time, pastors must also be listeners and

---

11. For a discussion of such matters, see part 3, "Allocating Vital Resources," in John F. Kilner, *Life on the Line* (Grand Rapids, Mich.: Eerdmans, 1992).

12. Robert D. Orr, *Medical Ethics and the Faith Factor* (Grand Rapids, Mich.: Eerdmans, 2009), 451ff.

consolers. Dave needs to talk honestly about his fears, his anger at what he perceives is an early death, and his depression.

Did Dave have a truly biblical understanding of God's love for him? Had he experienced God's love in a way similar to what Paul prays for the Ephesian believers when he asks God to allow them to "know this love that surpasses knowledge" (Eph. 3:19)? How did Dave measure God's love? Was it by his circumstances? If so, one can understand why he would be depressed and feel forsaken by God. Carson has observed that all Christians must learn to appreciate God's love not on the basis of their circumstances but on the basis of the cross of Jesus. One wonders if Dave would have responded differently to his death had he embraced a true understanding of the cross. By meditating on the cross, perhaps by regularly celebrating the Lord's Supper, he may have seen that God's love can effectively work through suffering and that part of being an embodied soul in God's image is the capacity to gain strength by suffering.

Perhaps Dave could have experienced true fellowship with Christ in his sufferings (Phil. 3:10). Fellowship, after all, is a two-way street. Suffering is in some ways a sharable commodity, for when suffering is shared, it can diminish. The more believers are able to appreciate the profound nature of the sufferings of Jesus, the more they will be able to share their suffering with him. Dave may have suffered less if he had a deeper appreciation of what Jesus endured to allow him the hope of eternal life. That is fellowship in suffering.

BETTER FOR MARY

Mary is suffering along with Dave. It is natural that Dave receive much attention in his suffering. However, what about Mary? The church and the entire hospice team are of major help. But is it enough? Can it ever be enough? They *do* things for her, but are they *listening* to her? One critical factor for a primary caregiver like Mary is sleep. Is she sleeping, or lying awake listening for Dave? Among the army of helpers she has during the day, could three of them each spend one night a week with Dave, to give Mary a good rest at least for those nights? Perhaps Alex could prescribe a sleeping pill for use on her "nights off."

It is not uncommon for well-meaning people to say or do very thoughtless things in demanding situations like this. Did someone ever say to Mary, "If you need any help, just let me know"? John Feinberg, a veteran of battles with severe illness, writes about how unhelpful that is.[13] He observes that in a sense it is saying, "You need to look at all of the things you need done, match them up with my time, interests and abilities, and then take the initiative to swallow your pride, call me, and ask for my help." How

---

13. John S. Feinberg, *Where Is God? A Personal Story of Finding God in Grief and Suffering* (Nashville: Broadman and Holman, 2004), 55.

much better it is to watch for things that need doing, initiate a call, ask for permission, and do them.

Perhaps the most telling evidence of Mary's emotional state is in her request that Alex do something to "speed this whole thing up." If we are to help Mary deal better with Dave's death, it may be of value to speculate some on what motivates her to make such a request.

Consider both the spiritual and psychological dimensions. Spiritually, Mary's desire to control the time and circumstance of death may be a part of the "power-knowledge" struggle that Vanhoozer discusses in chapter 5. This struggle has been present in the human race since the fall in the garden of Eden, and people continue to evidence it in part by their sinful desire to be like God rather than submit to his authority. At times, people's desire to be in control may represent not so much a desire to push their own agenda as disappointment or even anger with God.

Psychologically, it is good to understand Mary's core values. In pursuing her graduate degree, she has been an achiever. She and Dave took control of their reproductive capacity and delayed starting a family. Then they took steps to ensure that Bethany was raised in a church. They are used to getting things done the way they want. Another core value for Mary is to relieve pain. As a psychologist, she helps people through painful situations. Fellow counselors Greggo and Parent (chap. 3) would note that in light of these values, her request for something like assisted suicide is not surprising. Rather than simply shaming her for the request, one should review with her all of the ways her family has been blessed by those values.

Though it is helpful to understand the psychological dynamics of Mary's request, it is equally important to understand the psychological consequences of her proposed action. Were there time, it would be good for Mary to embark on the "implication counseling" that Greggo and Parent refer to in chapter 3. It may be very difficult for Mary down the road—and even more so for Bethany if she ever finds out—if something Mary had initiated intentionally shortened Dave's life.

As with Dave, it would have been better for Mary to have a deep theological understanding and experience of God's love and power. She needs to understand what the Bible says about suffering. Averbeck (chap. 1) reminds us that part of life in a fallen world is groaning. As difficult as it is to acknowledge, Mary's statement that "God can't want Dave to suffer any more" does not fit with the reality Scripture presents. End-of-life suffering is a result of fallenness and manifests how catastrophic the fall really was (Genesis 3; Romans 8). It would be so helpful for Mary to see in the cross a model of suffering that encompasses a trusting obedience allowing a surrender of control to God.

These are not lessons that people best learn "in the heat of battle." One can wish that Mary and Dave were in a church that faithfully taught all of the Scriptures, including those that deal with such unpopular subjects as suffering and death. Such teaching is a part of what Roy describes as "proactive" pastoral care. Had Mary been consistently under the type of preaching that Scharf (chap. 13) recommends, she may have found in God's Word a greater sense of contentment and the ability to view her situation with an eschatological perspective. Complementing this type of preaching should have been the consistent teaching in an adult educational setting that Charter (chap. 14) advocates. There the normative guidance of Scripture would prepare Mary and Dave for wise responses to difficult situations.

While it is surprising in this case that Mary would demonstrate an interest in "speeding this whole thing up," it is equally surprising that it is the hospice nurse who plants the thought in Mary's mind. Most hospice programs and workers would never mention assisted suicide as an option for consideration. Nevertheless, as Netland, Fields, and Sung (chap. 7) would remind us, norms and values are constantly shifting in the pluralism of today's world.

Rae and Eckmann (chap. 2) would want us to inquire if there could be any potential financial conflict of interest prompting the nurse to voice this option. They point out the potential conflict in the ethics of the business of health-care providers and the ethics of patient care. Most insurances reimburse hospices a daily amount for the services they provide each patient. That arrangement creates no financial incentive to promote an early death. However, there is a cap on the annual amount of expenses for which a hospice can receive reimbursement. Although the presence of the cap provides a potential conflict of interest between the business of hospice and the well-being of the patient,[14] the financial incentives for hospice in general do not promote premature death.

BETTER FOR BETHANY

After Dave dies and all of the activity dissipates, the most lasting tragedy in this case may involve Bethany. Her situation should have shown up on the 911 screen in the church office. This is a crisis demanding immediate intervention.

Yet Bethany's storming away from her dad and expressing all of her anger has its roots too. It should not be that surprising. Dave and Mary make a grave mistake when they choose to belittle the seriousness of his cancer to protect her. It is possible that in not telling the full truth, Dave and Mary are simply expressing their own denial. Their approach may be understandable, but that does not justify it. In retrospect, it would be easy to say that they should have consulted with their spiritual mentors on how to present this tragic news to their daughter, assuming that these mentors would have advised them to speak truthfully. Such was not their approach, and now Bethany is paying for their error. Bethany may need a professional counselor. At the very least she needs a mature believer a few years older than her (but not likely her parents' age) to befriend

14. See *http://www.hospicepatients.org/hospreimburse.html* (accessed July 11, 2010).

her, enjoy some fun things together, and do a lot of listening. Roy has observed how detrimental Mary's advice is: to deny her anger instead of trying to work through it.

Dave needs strong urging to seek reconciliation with Bethany. He needs to confess his wrong, tell her he loves her, and ask her forgiveness. They need to embrace and cry together. Dave's pain and sedating analgesics are hindering all of this from happening. It may have been appropriate for someone to initiate a call to Alex, arrange a time to gather the family, stop the morphine temporarily, return Dave to his senses, and facilitate closure between him and Bethany.

Alex also could spend more time with Bethany. She needs to understand Dave's medical situation better. As Orr and Salladay observe, she needs to appreciate that choosing not to pursue aggressive care while trusting God to do what is right is not suicide and is not even the same thing as giving up.

BETTER FOR THE CHURCH

Experiencing a tragic death like Dave's can have a beneficial and sobering effect on any body of believers. Members of the congregation need to be there to experience firsthand his suffering and possibly even his dying. Before the pain becomes overwhelming, Dave needs to teach them what it is like to face the end of life. They need to learn that some of the trite responses that people throw around in difficult situations like this may not be helpful. Christian friends need to sit and wonder at the tragedy that is unfolding. They must resist the temptation to be too quick to try to explain it.

The church needs to assure Dave that they will be there in the future to help Mary and Bethany, that they will not evaporate after the funeral luncheon. The best way for them to do that is to point to a track record of others in the church who are receiving ongoing help through their grief. That awareness will help Dave feel more comfortable as death approaches.

The church must realize that Dave is not likely the last tragic death they will deal with, and they should review their response in this case to ensure that next time they will do better. After Dave dies, some of the church volunteers who were there to help may find that they want to become hospice volunteers. This type of ministry to the dying is a wonderful way to express Christian love and compassion. There may even be an opportunity to establish in the community explicitly Christian hospices that demonstrate God's love for all people.

One measure of the quality of a church's ministry is how her people die. Church leadership will want to ensure that the ongoing ministry of the church has a healthy balance between a celebratory, victorious view of life and one that prepares the congregation to suffer and die well. The church is to pray for healing in situations of desperate need such as Dave's. However, they should add to that prayer a request that when God chooses not to heal, he will grant the grace to die well in a way that brings glory to

God. Pastors need to know about death and dying. For many it will be a large part of their ministry, yet most seminary curricula devote very little time to this critical area. Seminaries should better equip future pastors and other church leaders for this ministry.

A thoughtful pastor will have in mind an entire list of things that dying parishioners need to work through in order to die well. This will include questions that are:

1. Medical
   - What do patients understand regarding their disease, the likelihood that it is terminal, and its expected time course?
   - Do they clearly understand the goal of their treatment (e.g., cure, stabilization of the condition, or comfort care)?
   - Do they have an advance directive?

2. Spiritual
   - Are they able to articulate a saving faith in Jesus?
   - Do they have unrepented sin?
   - Are they longing for God's presence?
   - Do they have any anger or disappointment with God?
   - What is their view of heaven and of the resurrected body?
   - If they are in pain or suffering, is God using it in their spiritual transformation?
   - How do they view losing the good things of this life?
   - Are they yielding control to God?
   - What are their prayer requests?

3. Social
   - Are there spiritual and relational tensions among their family members?
   - To whom do they need to say, "I love you, thank you, forgive me, and I forgive you"?
   - How can the church mobilize to meet the practical needs of their family?
   - Do they have concerns for their loved ones' well-being after they are gone?
   - Can they be confident that the church will continue to help their family after they die?

4. Ceremonial
   - Are there specific things they want at the funeral or memorial service?

Death as a consequence of sin is not good by its very nature. It leads to unnatural separations and is often rather messy. Yet dying in the midst of community, particularly a church body, can also be a great blessing because of the abundant practical help and emotional support that can be available. It must be a team effort, with all participants providing help in the area of their own passion and expertise. Through the body of Christ functioning as a team, a difficult death can become a better death, to the glory of God.

BETTER FOR SOCIETY

In rather dramatic fashion, this case raises the questions of the morality of physician-assisted suicide and euthanasia. Such statements as "It's my body, isn't it? Can't I do with it as I please?" are not unusual today. Some will speak of "meaningless suffering" and say something like, "They shoot horses, don't they?" Others will fail to see a significant difference between Dave's choosing not to pursue aggressive medical care and Mary's asking that something be done to hasten death. Physician-assisted suicide is legal in several countries of the world, as well as in several US states, and there are initiatives in many other states and countries to move in this direction.

Accordingly, it is imperative that thoughtful people, Christians and non-Christians alike, reflect carefully on this issue. To approach this subject, we will organize our thoughts around four widely acknowledged principles of bioethics: autonomy, beneficence, nonmaleficence, and justice.[15] Because such principles, rightly understood, reflect certain biblical concerns to a significant degree, as well as receive wide affirmation in secular society, they provide useful headings for our thinking.

AUTONOMY

"It's my body, isn't it?" This is an affirmation of autonomy. It was not that long ago when medical choices were very limited. Medicine was paternalistic, and the physician alone made the decisions. The pendulum has swung decidedly the other way now, and patients expect to make many of their own health-care decisions.[16] But few would support a capricious autonomy where individuals can do whatever they please. Most people allow limits to their freedom based on values of the past, present virtues, and future consequences of a particular action.[17]

Allen Verhey observes that legitimizing the option of suicide may increase some options. However, it also effectively eliminates an option — namely, staying alive without having to justify one's existence.[18] So assisted suicide is not a clear affirmation of autonomy. Many people with disabilities are understandably worried about the growing openness toward the option of assisted suicide. They fear that a right to die may subtly become a duty to die. One British study shows 65 percent of respondents maintaining that if assisted suicide were legalized, "vulnerable people could feel under pressure to opt for suicide."[19]

---

15. These are the four principles of biomedical ethics codified by Tom Beauchamp and James Childress and later supplemented by the concepts of veracity, privacy, confidentiality, and fidelity. See Tom Beauchamp and James Childress, *Principles of Biomedical Ethics*, part 2 (Oxford: Oxford Univ. Press, 2001), 57–282.

16. This is one of the major points of Paul Ramsey's *The Patient as Person* (New Haven, Conn.: Yale Univ. Press, 1970).

17. James Thobaben, *Health-Care Ethics* (Downers Grove, Ill.: IVP Academic, 2009), 293.

18. Allen Verhey, *Reading the Bible in the Strange World of Medicine* (Grand Rapids, Mich.: Eerdmans, 2003), 333.

19. Dutch Euthanasia Stats, *Care Not Killing*, September 27, 2007, *http://www.carenotkilling.org.uk/?show=435* (accessed July 8, 2010).

Assisted suicide and euthanasia present other threats to freedom as well. The slippery-slope argument predicted what has actually transpired in the Dutch experience with euthanasia: once society removes the legal prohibition against euthanasia in the case of adults with severe physical pain, pressures will eventually mount to allow the killing of children under similar circumstances, to allow the killing of patients who have no physical pain but are stressed in other ways,[20] and even to kill patients against their will.[21] Furthermore, people may interpret a so-called right to die to include the right to have someone else assist their deaths. In political environments like the present in the United States, where the traditional protection of physicians from being forced to act against their consciences is under assault, the danger of this development multiplies.

Closely linked to autonomy is the desire to be in control. Orr and Salladay have observed that we live in a culture of choice. Dave and Mary had taken control of many aspects of their lives, and it was only natural that they would want to do so at the end of life. The Oregon experience under the Death with Dignity Act is illuminating at this point. The published records from that state show that 460 persons died under the Death with Dignity Act between 1998 and 2009. Of those, 414 (91%) listed on a questionnaire that a contributing reason for their decision was losing autonomy. By comparison, only 101 (22%) listed inadequate control of pain, including both present pain and possible pain in the future.[22]

Christians must be wary of appeals to autonomy and control, for they acknowledge that God, their Creator and Redeemer, actually owns them. "You are not your own; you were bought at a price," Paul reminds believers (1 Cor. 6:19–20). In Christ, people have great freedom, but that freedom is the freedom to choose what will bring glory to God. Thus, Paul concludes the 1 Corinthians 6 passage by saying, "Therefore honor God with your bodies" (v. 20).

BENEFICENCE

One of the most common arguments for assisted suicide is that it is an act of mercy. Mercy is a virtue Christians should value. Therefore, it would seem natural for them to support such behavior. But most end-of-life pain and other noxious symptoms are controllable with excellent palliative care. It is actually uncommon for a patient to expe-

20. For a review of these developments, see Joe Carter, "Sympathectomy of the Soul," On the Square, *FirstThings.com*, March 10, 2010, *http://www.firstthings.com/onthesquare/2010/03/sympathectomy-of-the-soul* (accessed July 8, 2010).

21. Herbert Hendin, professor of psychiatry at New York Medical College, recounts a case presented to him from the Netherlands of a nun dying of breast cancer whose physician performed euthanasia on her without telling her because he "felt her religion prevented her from agreeing to euthanasia so he felt both justified and compassionate in ending her life." See *Palliative Medicine* 17 (2003): 178–79, *http://www.eapcnet.org/download/forEuthanasia/hendin.pdf* (accessed July 8, 2010). There is a legitimate concern that the equal protection clause of the fourteenth amendment to the United States Constitution could be interpreted to require involuntary killing of individuals incapable of making that decision for themselves.

22. See *http://www.oregon.gov/DHS/ph/pas/docs/yr12-tbl-1.pdf* (accessed December 23, 2010).

rience an excruciating death. Admittedly, the occasional deaths that are very difficult for physical, emotional, spiritual, or social reasons raise the possibility that assisted suicide could sometimes be beneficent. Before we can assess the goodness of such an act, we must take a more careful look at the situation of the patient as well as consider the impact of the act on all of the stakeholders in the death.

The Patient

Human beings have a remarkable capacity to grow through adversity. They choose to climb Mount Everest, or to run Ironman triathlons. Auschwitz survivor Viktor Frankl observed how often people found life's true meaning at a time of great suffering, as death approached in a concentration camp. It is not uncommon that as the attractions of life on earth are less powerful, the dying are more inclined to search for a larger meaning than they have previously experienced. It may not be truly beneficent to limit the time available for that quest. Natural-law ethicist J. Daryl Charles observes that suffering does not diminish what it means to be truly human,[23] even if one is physically or mentally disabled. Part of the intrinsic dignity of human beings made in God's image is the ability to benefit from suffering. God can use suffering to accomplish his greater purpose in the life of the one who is enduring it.[24]

Arthur Dyck begins his book *Life's Worth* by telling the following story: "After being diagnosed with cancer and given less than three months to live Mr. Cohen described himself as 'bed bound by pain and weakness, having been able to drink only water for six weeks ... desperate, isolated and frightened' and wishing for euthanasia. Eight months later he wrote: 'I now know that only death is inevitable and since coming under the care of the MacMillan Service my pain has been relieved completely, my ability to enjoy life restored and my fears of an agonizing end allayed.... My experiences have served to convince me that euthanasia even if voluntary is fundamentally wrong and I'm now staunchly against it on religious, moral, intellectual and spiritual grounds."[25]

Beneficence for Mr. Cohen entailed excellent palliative care, not assisted suicide. To be sure, no matter how beautiful the theory and proper the theology, death may be challenging. In such situations, the need is for the best palliative care possible, immense amounts of time providing human presence and compassion, tears of anguished sorrow, and prayers crying out to God for his mercy. Compassionate care like this is beneficence at its best.

---

23. J. Daryl Charles, *Retrieving the Natural Law* (Grand Rapids, Mich.: Eerdmans, 2008), 271.

24. Scripture affirms that God has purposes in allowing suffering. These may include teaching lessons to those observing suffering (1 Peter 5:9), equipping some to help others (2 Cor. 1:4), demonstrating God's work (John 9:2–3), transforming character (Heb. 12:7–8; Rom.

5:3–5; James 1:2–4), fortifying the denial of sinful desires (1 Peter 4:1–2; 2 Cor. 12:7), preparing believers for future glory (Rom. 8:17–18; 1 Peter 4:13), and allowing a richer fellowship with Jesus (Phil. 3:10–11).

25. Arthur J. Dyck, *Life's Worth* (Grand Rapids, Mich.: Eerdmans, 2002), 2.

The Survivors

How anyone dies has a significant impact on the survivors—family members, friends, and others. Heroes are those who finish well, not those who have the "courage" to drop out when the race gets difficult. In most families, the soldier who was killed on the beach at Normandy is reverenced, while the one who committed suicide is an embarrassment. Perhaps the starkest evidence that suicide impacts the survivors is the research that shows an elevated rate of suicide among the survivors of suicide victims.[26]

The Caregivers

Caring for the dying can be enriching for the caregivers themselves. It can help bring the type of closure to a relationship where nothing is left unsaid, and it helps initiate the grieving process.[27] It may promote family unity as never before. Being able to comfort the suffering is a great blessing. Recall what Portia says in Shakespeare's *Merchant of Venice*:

> The quality of mercy is not strain'd
> It droppeth as the gentle rain from heaven
> Upon the place beneath; it is twice bless'd;
> It blesseth him that gives and him that takes.

Watching someone suffer is very difficult. Caring for the dying can lead to exhaustion, as in the case of Mary. In that state, it is all too easy to become self-centered and utter comments such as "I can't stand to see him suffering any longer." James Goodwin insightfully wonders if the wrong person's suffering is taking precedence.[28] That is a question worth pondering in the case before us.

The Medical Team

The medical team is a stakeholder here as well. They need to be confident that they are giving the best care at the end of life. In ancient Greece, it was the norm for the medical profession to hasten death. Hippocrates and those who followed were a minority group of physicians who took a stand against this practice.[29] Over the last few millennia, the medical profession has assumed the role of healer and eschewed that of killer. Joni Eareckson Tada decries the situation where it becomes "easier to kill than to cure or even to care."[30] Legalizing physician-assisted suicide pushes society in that direction.

26. Ping Qin, "The Relationship of Suicide Risk to Family History of Suicide and Psychiatric Disorders," *Psychiatric Times* 20, no. 13 (December 1, 2003), *http://www.psychiatrictimes.com/display/article/10168/48641* (accessed July 12, 2010).

27. Byock, *Dying Well*, 231.

28. James Goodwin, "Mercy Killing: Mercy for Whom?" *Journal of the American Medical Association* 265, no. 3 (January 16, 1991): 326.

29. Nigel M. de S. Cameron, *The New Medicine* (Wheaton, Ill.: Crossway, 1991), 37.

30. Joni Eareckson Tada, *The Life and Death Dilemma* (Grand Rapids, Mich.: Zondervan, 1992), 79.

NONMALEFICENCE

At face value, killing someone is contradictory to the principle of "do no harm." Admittedly, suffering and the inability to make it go away are harms. But no one is inflicting those on the person; they are the product of the illness or injury. Christians would define harm as doing something that is outside of the will of God and not contributing to his glory. As Carson and Roy have reminded us, the full scope of biblical teaching affirms that killing a patient is against God's will.

JUSTICE

Justice likewise needs discerning application. In the context of civil democracy, justice has a broad meaning relevant to living within the civil law. Allen Verhey writes that justice minimally "insists on respect for the autonomy of each person, demands the protection of individual rights, and attempts to guarantee a space for each one to act in ways that suit one's preferences as long as such actions do not violate the autonomy of another."[31] As attorney Cunningham (chap. 6) reminds us, euthanasia and assisted suicide are largely illegal worldwide. Christians bring God's authority into the equation and so widen the scope of legal justice to include (and prioritize) God's law, which says, "You shall not murder" (Exod. 20:13).

Some would view justice in terms of fair distribution of the vast amount of resources that are spent on end-of-life care. They are concerned that such expenditures ultimately limit the resources available for the care of younger people who are more likely to get well and return to the workforce. Resorting to euthanasia or assisted suicide, however, is not the only way to address this situation.

Another approach without the ethical problems already noted is to take informed consent more seriously. The vast database available could enable the medical profession to do a much better job of predicting the outcome of potential interventions. A physician may say to a patient with pancreatic cancer, "There is one more thing we could try if you do not want to die." How much better it would be to say, "You could undergo this chemotherapy, but it has a zero percent chance of curing the cancer, a seventy-five percent chance of making you very sick, and a twenty percent chance of allowing you to live six months longer. Another option would be to enroll you in hospice and allow you to live out your days comfortably at home." If patients could have the freedom to make their own choices on the basis of truly informed consent, much of the cost of end-of-life care could be reduced, resulting in more equitable distribution of resources.

KILLING VERSUS LETTING DIE

Some in contemporary society would argue there is no substantive difference between killing and letting die, or between the omission and commission of an act.[32] They would

---

31. Verhey, *Reading the Bible*, 317.
32. This controversy moved to the forefront when James Rachels published "Active and Passive Euthanasia" in *New England Journal of Medicine* 292, no. 2 (January 9, 1975): 78–80.

say that the result is the same—the patient is dead—and there is, therefore, no difference. Why would it be right for Dave to forgo chemotherapy, with little chance of affecting the outcome, but wrong for Alex to give Mary a prescription to hasten Dave's death?

The answer to this question must begin with consideration of agency and intent. In the case of forgoing a treatment, it is the disease that is responsible for the death. However, in assisted suicide, it is the drug as prescribed by the physician and the patient who ingests it that causes the death. If Dave takes the former route, his death certificate will read cancer of the pancreas. If Alex gives in to Mary's request, the cause of death will be self-inflicted drug overdose. In the former case, the intention is not to prolong the dying process. In the latter, it is to cause the death. Daniel Callahan writes, "Since death is biologically inevitable, sooner or later, and not the consequence of human action per se, we can hardly be said to intend death when we admit that we can no longer stop it."[33] This recognition does not imply that very ill patients should always forgo further treatment; it only implies that it can be acceptable to do so.

Intentionally causing death, however, is something different. John Kilner writes, "Ethically the key question is ... whether anything is done or left undone with the intention of causing the patient's death."[34] Killing someone is wrong even if the intention is good. It is never right to appeal to beneficial consequences and do wrong in order that good may come. That is what people slanderously accused Paul of, and in Romans 3:6, he emphatically responded, "Certainly not."

If dying a natural death is best for a believer who looks forward to an eternal future in God's presence—as opposed to a death induced via euthanasia or assisted suicide—is that still what is best as public policy in a pluralistic society? Many of the above considerations are relevant to people from any religious background and would argue that it is.

VIRTUOUS DYING

Autonomy, beneficence, nonmaleficence, and justice are important virtues. G. K. Chesterton has observed how gravely we err when we emphasize one virtue above another.[35] Those who argue for assisted suicide typically choose autonomy and beneficence above nonmaleficence. Allen Verhey wisely speaks to this tension, referring to the Old Testament prophet Micah to locate the integrating principle:

He has shown all you people what is good.
And what does the LORD require of you?
To act justly and to love mercy
and to walk humbly with your God.
—Micah 6:8

33. Charles, *Retrieving the Natural Law*, 290.

34. Kilner, *Life on the Line*, 118.

35. G. K. Chesterton, *Orthodoxy* (1908; Chicago: Moody, 2009), 50. Chesterton writes, "The modern world is full of old Christian virtues gone mad. The virtues have gone mad because they have been isolated from each other and are wandering alone." That is as true today as it was in the first decade of the twentieth century.

Justice and mercy frequently lead to different conclusions. How are people to know the good, what God requires of them? The answer is they are to walk humbly with God. They are not to claim omniscience—not to play God—but are to pursue his way of thinking. They are to, as Carson says, "survey a variety of biblical-theological themes that are indisputably grounded in Scripture" and then make a decision. Verhey observes why "suicide, assisted suicide, and euthanasia are forbidden. They do not fit the story of God's grace and faithful human response. They cohere rather with the story of betrayal and denial."[36]

When facing a difficult death, there are two basic options. The first is to insist on control to the very end. The other is to recognize God's love and power, acknowledge his control, trust him, and in that trust experience peace. That may lead to the decision not to pursue aggressive medical care to the very end. Comfort care becomes the priority. Death comes with Christ-honoring humility and God-endowed dignity. God is glorified as God when his people surrender final control and rest in his goodness.

For further reading, see the annotated bibliography on "better death" connected with this book at www.everydaybioethics.org.

---

36. Verhey, *Reading the Bible*, 315.

Part Four

BETTER LEARNING

CHAPTER 13

WISDOM FROM PREACHING

Greg R. Scharf

What wisdom can the fields of homiletics and liturgics provide for addressing the three cases central to this book? The insights offered here build on earlier chapters. For instance, Averbeck (chap. 1) reminds us of Jacob's complaint to Rachel, "Am I in the place of God?" That question calls for a negative answer, as sound preaching and rich worship repeatedly emphasize. In the first case, we learn that Tom wants to make Betty happy. A balanced diet of carefully expounded Scripture redefines happiness and does so in a context in which the glory of God is the focus and aim of the gathering, and the good of his people flows from that.

Other examples abound. Those preachers who grasp Kilner's (chap. 4) distinction between the development of a human being and his or her status at any moment in time will courageously preach those texts such as Luke 1 which offer insights into the status of a young human still in the womb. Moreover, well-read preachers will notice teachings of biblical texts that are relevant to bioethical issues, as Kilner's handling of Genesis 1 illustrates. Learning from Vanhoozer's insights (chap. 5), good preachers will see particular instances of sin as examples of various categories of sin, such as denial of the Creator as flagrant idolatry. They will notice how the Bible routinely dethrones autonomous human reason, critiques this-worldly epistemologies, and provides a valid basis for discerning what has true value.

These and many other insights will furnish what the Puritans called "matter" for preaching. Whether the occasion is a special Sanctity of Life Sunday conducive to preaching a topical message, or a sermon or a series from a book of Scripture, the preacher has plenty of material from which to draw.

With our theological cupboard stocked with the provisions that previous chapters have provided, our aim here is to ask a focused question: What might have been different had those in all three cases been listening over a period of time to sound preaching in the context of liturgically rich corporate worship? How might Betty and Tom have dealt with their childlessness? What alarm bells might have sounded in the minds of

God-honoring graduate students, or for that matter in Dr. Bright himself or Dr. Bauble, who conspired with him? What might Dave, Mary, Bethany, Alex, and Dr. Osgood have done differently if they had joined their hearts and voices in corporate worship weekly and there heard the Word of God clearly expounded and sensitively applied?

To answer these questions we must first ask, What do we mean by sound preaching in the context of liturgically rich corporate worship? The definitions of preaching and liturgically rich worship offered here intentionally set forth an ideal. No single church can do everything it might possibly do in public worship or in its preaching ministry. However, setting forth an ideal underscores what preaching in the context of worship uniquely contributes to good ethical behavior. Nor would we countenance the thought that preaching and worship are magic; they do not automatically transform those in attendance. Even if Roberto, Paul, Akira, and Jill went to a church every Sunday, it does not follow that temptation would go away or that the wise discernment they need would be theirs. The following definitions, together with certain qualifying assumptions, will further sharpen the image of how God may, should he choose to do so, graciously use this facet of church life to equip his people to behave wisely.

WHAT IS PREACHING?

Definitions abound.[1] For our purposes, J. I. Packer provides a helpful definition: "Christian preaching is the event of God himself bringing to an audience a Bible-based, Christ-related, life-impacting message of instruction and direction through the words of a spokesperson."[2] Donald Miller also emphasizes God's role when he refers to the partnership of text and Spirit as "an act wherein the living truth of some portion of Holy Scripture, understood in the light of solid exegetical and historical study and made a living reality to the preacher by the Holy Spirit, comes alive to the hearer as he is confronted by God in Christ through the Holy Spirit in judgment and redemption."[3]

None of these definitions specify the length of the text the preacher is expounding, nor whether the sermon is part of a series of consecutive expositions from a book of the Bible or the faithful opening of various Scripture portions that address a subject. The assumption here is that a text or texts of Scripture shape both the content and the aim of the sermon. Considered from this angle, preaching is not identical with teaching. What helps shape ethical decisions and actions is not merely *what* preachers preach but *that* they preach. Preaching is not only descriptive and informative; it is also hortatory. Paul

---

1. A good review of the landscape before 1995 is chap. 1 of Harold T. Bryson, *Expository Preaching: The Art of Preaching Through a Book of the Bible* (Nashville: Broadman and Holman, 1995). For an update, see Greg R. Scharf, "Were the Apostles Expository Preachers?" *Trinity Journal* 31, no. 1 (Spring 2010): 85 – 89.

2. J. I. Packer, "Some Perspectives on Preaching," in Evangelical Ministry Assembly, *Preaching the Living Word* (Fearn, Ross-shire, Scotland: Christian Focus, 1999), 28.

3. Donald, Miller, *The Way to Biblical Preaching* (New York: Abingdon, 1957), 26, cited in Jim Shaddix, *The Passion-Driven Sermon* (Nashville: B&H Academic, 2003), 147.

told Timothy to "point these things out to the brothers and sisters" (1 Tim. 4:6),[4] but he did not stop there. He told him to "command and teach these things" (v. 11), and to "teach and insist on" certain things (6:2).

At the same time, there is more going on in preaching than one human being—the preacher—urging others to act or even the preacher faithfully relaying God's commands "with all authority" (Titus 2:15). Peter counsels, "If anyone speaks, he should do it as one speaking the very words of God" (1 Peter 4:11). Not only are preachers to expect people to hear God's voice when they speak to the church in God's name, but listeners should expect it too and respond accordingly. That is how Paul and his team understood what happened in Thessalonica as 1 Thessalonians 2:13 explains: "And we also thank God continually because, when you received the word of God, which you heard from us, you accepted it not as the word of men, but as it actually is, the word of God, which is at work in you who believe."

Heinrich Bullinger saw preaching this way. A heading in his Second Helvetic Confession captures the idea: "The Preaching of the Word of God Is the Word of God." This lofty claim should be taken to assert not that preaching is the Word of God normatively but rather that it is so functionally.[5] That is why John Stott writes that "to preach is to open up the inspired text with such faithfulness and sensitivity that God's voice is heard and God's people obey Him."[6] Those who are confident they have heard the voice of God, albeit mediated through a preacher, instinctively understand that the message is to be heard *and* heeded.

WHAT IS LITURGICALLY RICH CORPORATE WORSHIP?

"For worship is to quicken the conscience by the holiness of God, to feed the mind with the truth of God, to purge the imagination by the beauty of God, to open the heart to the love of God, to devote the will to the purpose of God. All this is gathered up in that emotion which most cleanses us from selfishness because it is the most selfless of all emotions—adoration."[7] So, famously, wrote Archbishop William Temple. His definition, while interpretable as portraying worship too individualistically or as a utilitarian undertaking, nevertheless highlights the way worship does indeed transform worshipers.

Worship and wisdom go together in both New and Old Testaments. Romans 12:1–2 defines spiritual worship as offering ourselves to God to *do* what our renewed minds have come to discern is good, acceptable, and perfect as God himself defines it.

---

4. Unless otherwise noted, all biblical quotations in this chapter are from *The Holy Bible, New International Version* (Grand Rapids, Mich.: Zondervan, 1985).

5. See Greg R. Scharf, "Was Bullinger Right about the Preached Word?" *Trinity Journal* 26 (2005): 3–10.

6. John Stott, *The Contemporary Christian: Applying God's Word to Today's World* (Downers Grove, Ill.: InterVarsity, 1992), 208.

7. William Temple, *The Hope of a New World* (New York: Macmillan, 1942), 30.

Nevertheless, "the idea that acceptable worship is a total-life orientation is not a new discovery by the writers of the New Testament!"[8] Walter McConnell argues that since "the fear of the Lord is the beginning of wisdom" and *fear* is one of the major Old Testament words for worship, "fearing God parallels knowing him experientially (Prov. 9:10). It thus becomes virtually synonymous with righteous living or religious piety."[9]

In this chapter, we have a somewhat narrower form of worship in view: liturgically rich *corporate* worship. This involves public gatherings for worship where, whatever the historical tradition or other distinctives of the assembly, someone has carefully thought through how all the elements of the service proclaim the gospel and help worshipers draw near to God. Bryan Chapell makes an impressive case that throughout church history, with surprising continuity, the liturgical elements of a well-crafted worship service retell the gospel story. Those elements are adoration, confession, assurance, thanksgiving, petition and intercession, instruction, communion/fellowship, charge, and blessing.[10] Whether a spoken, sung, or enacted word represents them, these elements make the service "liturgically rich."[11]

Corporate worship, needless to say, is participatory. God is seeking neither spectators nor consumers (see Vanhoozer, chap. 5) but worshipers (John 4:23). Worshipers of old were cautioned, "Guard your steps when you go to the house of God. Go near to listen rather than to offer the sacrifice of fools, who do not know that they do wrong" (Eccl. 5:1). This is still wise counsel. Corporate worship includes occasions when people participate in baptisms and the Lord's Supper. Though not weekly events in every tradition, they are part of what shapes ethical behavior. By offering visual testimony to the gospel and an opportunity for self-examination and submission to God's will, they call worshipers into engagement with God and resurrection life in Christ. Such engagement and empowering sets the stage for countercultural obedience that is "worthy of the gospel" (Phil. 1:27) as opposed to being out of step with the truth of the gospel (Gal. 2:14).

With these limited, focused definitions as a starting point, we must now clarify some working assumptions. Doing so will keep us from expecting too much or too little from preaching in the context of public worship as a resource for understanding and engaging the situations that the three case studies portray.

WORKING ASSUMPTIONS

First, the congregation assembled for worship includes a wide range of participants. There will be unbelievers, as well as those who profess faith but are either immature

---

8. David Peterson, *Engaging with God: A Biblical Theology of Worship* (Grand Rapids, Mich.: Eerdmans, 1992), 29.

9. Walter L. McConnell III, "Worship," in *Dictionary of the Old Testament Wisdom, Poetry and Writings*, ed. Tremper Longman III and Peter Enns (Downers Grove, Ill.: InterVarsity, 2008), 933, 930.

10. Bryan Chapell, *Christ-Centered Worship: Letting the Gospel Shape Our Practice* (Grand Rapids, Mich.: Baker, 2009), 148–49.

11. Ibid., 99–100.

Christians or not yet regenerate, and there will be genuine believers who manifest various degrees of sanctification. Here the preacher proclaims the gospel and people come to true faith, grow in Christ, and get equipped for ministry. Common grace notwithstanding, those who simply attend public worship cannot presume consistently to make good bioethical decisions and act on them without the sanctifying work of the Word (John 17:17) and the Spirit (Gal. 5:16–26).

It is in the assembly that the preached Word does this good work, as Scripture frequently attests. "He chose to give us birth through the word of truth, that we might be a kind of firstfruits of all he created" (James 1:18). "For you have been born again, not of perishable seed, but of imperishable, through the living and enduring word of God. For, 'All people are like grass, and all their glory is like the flowers of the field; the grass withers and the flowers fall, but the word of the Lord endures forever.' And this is the word that was preached to you" (1 Peter 1:23–25 TNIV). "Consequently, faith comes from hearing the message, and the message is heard through the word of Christ" (Rom. 10:17). In other words, "Word and Spirit. They are always together. A word cannot be separated from the breath that carries it."[12]

Second, preaching is not the only ministry of the Word.[13] Much of the renewal of the mind that Christians need happens in private Bible reading and meditation, small-group Bible studies, edifying conversation, reading good Christian books, and by other direct and indirect ministries of the Word. In fact, coming to grips with weighty bioethical issues is often more readily facilitated in settings where there is give and take—where people can raise and discuss questions and where others can provide missing factual information. Public worship, including the reading and preaching of Scripture, cannot replace other facets of congregational life involving the ministry of the Word. Nevertheless, preaching in public worship underscores that what the church affirms is "public truth," to use Lesslie Newbigin's expression.[14] The proclaimed message is not merely the subjective conviction of an ingroup. Rather, it is an announcement of the public appearance of the kingdom of God and of the implications of that historical event.

Third, Christian worship can happen in settings other than the public gathering of the whole assembly. Individuals, families, roommates, and fellowship groups can worship. These private or smaller gatherings may well have some of the same benefits described below. Normally, baptisms and celebrations of the Lord's Supper will take place in public gatherings for worship.

Fourth, corporate worship includes public prayer, which is more than someone reciting the perceived needs of those in the congregation. God hears and answers. Beyond

12. Darrell W. Johnson, *The Glory of Preaching: Participating in God's Transformation of the World* (Downers Grove, Ill.: InterVarsity, 2009), 31.

13. Peter Adam, *Speaking God's Words: A Practical Theology of Expository Preaching* (Downers Grove, Ill.: InterVarsity, 1996), 59–60.

14. See Lesslie Newbigin, *Foolishness to the Greeks: The Gospel and Western Culture* (Grand Rapids, Mich.: Eerdmans, 1986), 115, 117, and Lesslie Newbigin, *Truth to Tell: The Gospel as Public Truth* (Grand Rapids, Mich.: Eerdmans, 1991), where this idea is developed.

that foundational truth, the apostle Paul's recording of prayers in his epistles indicates the teaching value of prayer. He wants his listeners to know what is closest to his heart. Scriptural prayers also reinforce the biblical conviction that obedience is never merely a matter of someone deciding to do the right thing and following through with action. The Holy Spirit must be involved. Furthermore, confession of sin in public worship — especially in conjunction with the charge and benediction to go forth in faithful obedience — helps worshipers understand that grace does not excuse ethical indifference and disobedience.[15]

Fifth, God himself promises to be present when two or three people gather in his name (Matt. 18:20). We may even think of him presiding over the assembly (Ps. 82:1). God himself historically delivered ethical instruction rooted in his nature, through his spokesman, in and to the assembly (Lev. 19:1–4). And those who gather today for worship and instruction share some responsibility for doctrinal purity in that context.[16] The ideal for corporate worship happens when all the participants, including the preacher, are physically present in the same room. Moreover, ideally the preacher is the pastor of the worshipers and knows many, if not all, of them by name.

Sixth, the corporate worship experience is multigenerational, draws people from across the socioeconomic and ethnic spectrums, and includes those in the fellowship who have physical, emotional, and mental limitations. The children present warrant respect as full human beings, as Kilner (chap. 4) reminds us. This gathering is a visual aid of the truth that people are not "giving units" in the church, functional units of production in society, sources of status or fulfillment for others, or anything else that smacks of *using* as opposed to *being*. They are people and are members of one another (Eph. 4:25). In this ideal congregation, preaching and worship are not merely means to an end. Worship is an end in itself and never merely a tool to move people to do something.

Nevertheless, biblical worship, including the exposition of God's Word, *is* a God-ordained means of grace for transforming listeners individually and corporately (1 Peter 4:10–12). Indeed, Paul invokes the language of worship to say that God has given him grace "to be a minister of Christ Jesus to the Gentiles with the priestly duty of proclaiming the gospel of God, so that the Gentiles might become an offering acceptable to God, sanctified by the Holy Spirit" (Rom. 15:16). Through the ministry of the Word, the triune God does in fact transform hearers of that gospel into acceptable worshipers of himself.

With these definitions and assumptions in place as qualifiers, we may now state and explore the central claim of this essay. *Biblical preaching in the context of liturgically rich corporate worship favorably influences ethical behavior toward gospel obedience in specific*

---

15. See Chapell, *Christ-Centered Worship*, 182.

16. See, for instance, 1 Cor. 14:29; 1 Thess. 5:21; 1 John 4:1; possibly Eph. 3:18. Leaders have a responsibility in this regard, as Titus 1:5–16 makes plain.

ways: (a) before ethical decisions are made, (b) at the point of decision, and (c) afterward, when those decisions lead to righteous behavior. This influence is not merely upon the decision-makers and actors themselves but also upon those whom their decisions affect, and other fellow members of the body of Christ as well.

INFLUENCES BEFORE THE POINT OF DECISION

Steven Roy in chapter 11 has already mentioned the value of preaching as part of proactive pastoral care. Here we offer some examples of how things might have been different—what people in the three case studies might have received—had they heard the Word in the assembly.

REGENERATION

Tom and Betty ("Having a Baby the New-Fashioned Way") have a heightened interest in spirituality, attend an active Christian church, and participate in a small home-fellowship group "whenever convenient." These words describe many who one day wake up to the realization that they are not in fact children of God (John 1:10–13). As D. A. Carson notes, Dave and Mary ("A Difficult Death") do not show evidence of "enjoying eternal life." Of the characters in "Gaining Every Advantage," only Paul has had noteworthy exposure to Christian preaching and worship. His functioning conscience is perhaps one bit of evidence that regeneration has taken place.

Among many other things that happen with rebirth, converts turn from idols to serve the living and true God (1 Thess. 1:9). Babies and scientific achievements can be idols. The Holy Spirit who grants us new life comes to live within us and gives us the mind of Christ (i.e., the capacity to accept and discern spiritual truth from God). Otherwise, what is foolish will often appear to be wise and vice versa (1 Cor. 2:12–16; cf. James 3:15–18). God is at work within the regenerate person "to will and to act according to his good purpose" (Phil. 2:13). Without this internal work of God, people are more or less at the mercy of their rebellious natures and various external pressures. Regeneration is the foundational event that opens the door for all that follows.

A GROWING KNOWLEDGE OF GOD

Because God himself meets us in worship and speaks to us through the preached Word, regular public worship is a forceful reminder that he is alive and active. Liturgically rich affirmations of his triune nature help worshipers resist the temptation to reduce God to someone who helps us get what we want. There appears to be very little fear of God in any of the characters portrayed in the cases, with the possible exception of Paul. When scriptural readings recite God's saving works—when the preacher with appropriate gravitas holds forth God's majesty, holiness, searching righteousness, and awful judgment—worshipers should find it much more difficult to practice functional atheism (i.e., to act as if there is no Creator, Redeemer, and Judge). When they apprehend God's gracious power on their behalf, indeed within them, they more likely will incline toward the obedience of faith (Rom. 1:5; 16:25–27). Those who not only witness but participate in the ordinances of baptism and the Lord's Supper have two powerful visual aids to remind them that God takes sin very seriously but also graciously cleanses, forgives, and nourishes repentant sinners.

It is striking that in the Epiginosko case, even Paul, who has the most exposure to Christian teaching, defines morality largely in terms of what is fair. This reveals that his categories are fundamentally human. In other words, he defines good and evil as basically human constructs as opposed to what pleases God, on the one hand, or rightly invites his wrath, on the other. Sound preaching in the context of liturgically rich worship could, over time, change that.

A GOSPEL LENS

"As revelation and response, worship provides a perspective that informs and shapes our perception of the world and our responsibilities."[17] A Christian worldview entails an accurate understanding of many things, such as humanity as made in God's image; God himself, to whom all people are accountable; the human predicament resulting from the fall; the nature and extent of evil; the groaning of all creation until the day of its restoration; the necessity of calling on God for grace and mercy, as well as for wisdom; and the goal and end of history. At the heart of a Christian worldview is the gospel itself, and at the heart of the gospel is the cross of Christ.

This cruciform perspective changed everything for the apostle Paul, including how he viewed himself.[18] The liturgy restores the worshiper's gospel focus by means of confession, adoration, instruction, and benediction. Had Dr. Bright ("Gaining Every Advantage") been a regenerate worshiper, he might have tempered his philosophy of science by a judicious submission to Genesis 1:26–28, read in the light of Romans 8:18–27 and Revelation 21. Enthroning God dethrones self, and vice versa. A valid understanding of history, and one's place in it, tends to tame selfishly grandiose ambitions. Bright might have become grateful *not* to get the judgment he deserved (cf. Kilner's discussion of Betty in chap. 4).

MODEL HANDLING OF SCRIPTURE

Good preaching not only gives human voice to divine words; it models how to handle the Bible so that we do not mistake our ideas for God's. Good preachers equip

---

17. Roland Chia et al., *Bioethics: Obstacle or Opportunity for the Gospel?* Lausanne Movement Occasional Paper No. 58, 16, *http://www.lausanne.org/documents/2004forum/LOP58_IG29.pdf* (accessed December 30, 2010).

18. Andre Resner Jr. skillfully explores how the cross of

Christ transforms Paul's criteria for success as a preacher in Andre Resner Jr., *Preacher and Cross: Person and Message in Theology and Rhetoric* (Grand Rapids, Mich.: Eerdmans, 1999), 83–131. In 2 Cor. 5:11–21 and Phil. 3:3–4:1, Paul summarizes this transformed vision.

careful listeners to handle the Word rightly when ethical decisions arise. Scripture itself urges people to have the right kind of critical mind, one that tests all things and holds fast to that which is good (1 Thess. 5:21). Good preaching, over time, fosters this God-ordained capacity. Significantly, none of the people in the three situations before us turns to Scripture for guidance. Had these people heard it capably expounded in a context where they could hear God's voice through that exposition, they might well have looked to it for wisdom and known how to interpret it.

Dr. Bright uses emotional reasoning and loaded vocabulary to counter objections. The way he sets before his students the choice of "stimulation or staleness," "succeed or stall," is a secular parody of the blessings and curses set before Israel as they prepared to enter the Promised Land (Deut. 27:9–28:68). The unspoken difference, which Bright fails to recognize, is that God is able to deliver what he promises or threatens; Dr. Bright is not. Good preaching uncovers faulty thinking at the level of its assumptions and models taking every thought captive to Christ (2 Cor. 10:3–5). Just seeing this modeled by a thoughtful expositor can help even the brightest listeners, like the graduate students, gain confidence that they can find truth in God's Word and can pursue righteousness, even if at the time these younger listeners are unsure of their abilities to do either. When preachers illustrate sermons with judicious reference to contemporary ethical issues, listeners will be more likely to search the Scriptures for wisdom when tough ethical dilemmas arise.

ALERTNESS TO TEMPTATION AND SIN

Good preaching reinforces biblical realism. It helps listeners place themselves in the flow of salvation history between the fall of humanity and the return of Christ to judge and to save. People are to resist the devil, who prowls around like a roaring lion (1 Peter 5:8–9). Those who belong to Christ are no longer under obligation to what biblical writers call "the flesh," with all its temptations (Rom. 8:12). The gravitational pull of secular society loses some of its attraction. Christians are, to use Paul's wording, crucified to the world and the world to them (Gal. 6:14). None of these sinister influences has given up trying to lure Christians back into bondage by means of temptation to sin. Good preaching alerts us to these dangers and the consequences of giving in to them.

Most of the characters in our cases seem oblivious to temptation, as we would expect from unbelievers. They appear — and seem to see themselves — as more or less autonomous actors who are weighing observable factors to do what seems in their self-interest or, occasionally, for the greater good. The thought that they might already be under the wrath of God and slaves to sin does not apparently enter their minds; nor does any way of escaping the wrath to come. While one certainly can ignore good preaching in the context of gospel-rich liturgy, it is nevertheless a recurrent reminder of the real world. And because God's Word is powerful, it can speak to and awaken those who resist and ignore it.

OPPORTUNITY FOR RECONCILIATION

When Christians come to the Lord's Table, a meaningful liturgy bids them to examine themselves, confess their sins, and be reconciled to those with whom they have broken relationships. When these spiritual disciplines happen in conjunction with the exposition of Scripture, Christians are in a position to test themselves on the basis of external criteria as opposed to their own subjective preferences. Moreover, in those traditions which link the Lord's Supper to church discipline, elders or others in authority may participate in this process.[19] Consider the potential difference if Tom, Betty, and Laura had been in the habit of regular communion, at which time they examined their relationships. They could have recognized the nascent jealousies, resentments, profiteering, sense of indebtedness or entitlement, and unhealthy attractions (among other relational temptations), confessed them, and become free of their lure before ungodly desires gave birth to sin that leads to death (James 1:14–15).

GROWING FAITH

Since the preaching of Jesus Christ establishes Christians as well as wins them (Rom. 16:25–26), being present for worship can serve as a reminder that God-given spiritual growth—the outcome of remaining connected with Christ—is the norm, not the exception (Col. 2:19; John 15:1–8). Baptisms, testimonies, reports from ministries, and even funerals can all reinforce this awareness. The cross shapes the trajectory of the Christian life. Humility is the way to glory; taking up one's cross is the path to resurrection power. Divine discontent with anything less than Christlikeness puts all ethical decisions in a different light than if people made them without reference to God's purposes (Rom. 8:26–29). Any of the characters tempted to radically enhance their intellectual capacity pharmacologically would have trouble justifying doing so if at least weekly, in a worship service, they faced the cross and the Christian paradigm of true growth that it represents.

SUPPORTIVE RELATIONSHIPS

Although interpersonal relationships are unlikely to reach their fullest expression in meetings for corporate worship, they nevertheless can grow there. Those who confess their sins publicly and corporately, who together hear a preacher expound the biblical text, who pray and break bread together, have a measure of life in common. There a word from the Lord can prompt one listener to speak to another—and the other to accept it—in a way that would not occur otherwise (Prov. 24:25; 25:12; Heb. 10:24–25). Alex is an elder in the church Dave, Mary, and Bethany attend. He is also an internist who

---

19. See Edmund Clowney, "Presbyterian Worship," in *Worship: Adoration and Action*, ed. D. A. Carson (Grand Rapids, Mich.: Baker, 1993), 119–29. See also Jonathan Leeman, *The Church and the Surprising Offense of God's Love: Reinforcing the Doctrines of Church Membership and Discipline* (Wheaton, Ill.: Crossway, 2010), for additional wisdom on how church discipline helps the church bear witness to the gospel.

functions as Dave's default primary-care physician. Had they worshiped side by side frequently and been to the Lord's Table together again and again, might not Alex have felt the freedom to confront Dave's stubbornness and duplicity, taken a stronger pastoral interest in Bethany, and been able to help Mary persevere?

In the Epiginosko case, Jill affirms Roberto's assessment of the situation ("Roberto is right") but then adds, "We could actually use Epiginosko to do good for others." Her comments both support and influence him, but not in a constructive direction. One thinks of Priscilla and Aquila, who heard Apollos preach in the synagogue but who then took him aside, inviting him to their home, where they "explained to him the way of God more adequately" (Acts 18:26). It seems unlikely that they did so without judiciously affirming his learning, his thorough knowledge of the Scriptures, his fervor, and his boldness. Just how much godly older people could legitimately affirm in Roberto and Jill's assessment of the opportunity before them is open to question. But such relationships that start with looking for something to affirm often begin at public worship.[20]

A POSTURE OF GRATITUDE

By reminding us of the basis of our access to God and our hope of eternal life (Rom. 5:1–5), worship not only expresses our gratitude to God; it fosters it. Colossians 3:12–17 is a good description of the transformative influence that corporate worship can have on worshipers: "Therefore, as God's chosen people, holy and dearly loved, clothe yourselves with compassion, kindness, humility, gentleness and patience. Bear with each other and forgive whatever grievances you may have against one another. Forgive as the Lord forgave you. And over all these virtues put on love, which binds them all together in perfect unity. Let the peace of Christ rule in your hearts, since as members of one body you were called to peace. And be thankful. Let the word of Christ dwell in you richly as you teach and admonish one another with all wisdom, and as you sing psalms, hymns and spiritual songs with gratitude in your hearts to God. And whatever you do, whether in word or deed, do it all in the name of the Lord Jesus, giving thanks to God the Father through him."

It is difficult to imagine Dr. Bright doing and advocating the actions in the Epiginosko case "in the name of the Lord Jesus" if he had listened attentively and obediently to good preaching. What a difference it would have made had the word of Christ dwelled richly within him and overflowed in songs of gratitude to the living God.

GOOD EXAMPLES

Assemblies for worship, even the most unstructured gatherings, have visible leaders. When their selection has been according to scriptural standards, when they do what

---

20. I think of Judge Paul Pressler, who met me at church when I was an undergraduate, befriended me, and in just a few conversations had a profound impact on the direction of my life.

Scripture mandates them to do, and when they receive public admonishing when necessary (1 Timothy 3–5), they provide powerful models for all parishioners. Indeed, their roles as examples are evident in the biblical requirements for their selection (1 Tim. 3:2, 7), their lives and ministries (1 Tim. 4:12–16), and cases involving discipline (1 Tim. 5:20). Had Roberto, Paul, Akira, and Jill observed leaders with integrity, leaders who were not a law unto themselves but were accountable to others, the enormous power Dr. Bright had over them just might have been less. People succumb to temptation sometimes because they do not have compelling alternative models.

GROWING CONTENTMENT

What all the people in the three situations before us have in common is that they lack contentment. Some discontent is appropriate; it is of God. On the other hand, some behavior that people label contentment is actually complacency. It is possible to learn true contentment, as the apostle Paul testifies in Philippians 4:11–13. When combined with godliness, it is great gain (1 Tim. 6:16–18). One of the secrets of contentment is existentially embracing the truth that God is with us (Heb. 13:5). Corporate worship not only reaffirms this truth; it provides a context and culture in which people can experience it.

Recall the absent student in the Epiginosko case, the postdoctoral fellow who withdrew—allegedly for health reasons—before Dr. Bright made his tempting offer. This person, if a faithful worshiper, might have been able to sense God's presence and to see his providential hand in the midst of what must have looked and felt like failure. God's specialty is bringing life out of death. The biblical writers' pervasive use of the cross and resurrection as a paradigm for the Christian life shapes the consciousness of the worshiper when sermons and liturgy work together to proclaim these gospel events. Significantly, even before the incarnation, it was when Asaph "entered the sanctuary of God" that he was enabled to say from the heart, "Whom have I in heaven but you? And earth has nothing I desire besides you" (Ps. 73:17, 25).

AN ESCHATOLOGICAL PERSPECTIVE

Asaph also gained this eternal perspective: "My flesh and my heart may fail, but God is the strength of my heart and my portion forever" (Ps. 73:26). New Testament worship provides the same. At the Lord's Table, believers "proclaim the Lord's death until he comes" (1 Cor. 11:26). Worship helps people fix their eyes "not on what is seen, but on what is unseen. For what is seen is temporary, but what is unseen is eternal" (2 Cor. 4:18). Tom and Betty's childlessness, Dave's suffering, and the graduate students' cognitive normality are all, for the believer, temporary when viewed in light of eternity. Christians need not deny present limitations; they can endure them with dignity in light of the incomparably glorious freedom of the children of God that will be theirs at the redemption of their bodies (Rom. 8:18–25).

Worship puts the present in perspective. It chastens human ambitions. Moreover, by praying for those who suffer, worship leaders reinforce the truth that suffering is part of this fallen world and will not be eliminated until the parousia. A preacher who wisely handles, for instance, 2 Timothy 4:20 ("I left Trophimus sick in Miletus") could help Mary and Bethany put Dave's terminal illness in a realistic perspective. God does not heal on demand. Preaching that mentions Hansen's disease sufferers could describe how pain plays an important role now—with disastrous results when pain is *not* felt—and could also point with great anticipation to that day when there will be no more pain, tears, or mourning (Rev. 21:4).

INTEGRATION OF KNOWLEDGE AND OBEDIENCE

Whenever the preaching of the Word takes place, a response is mandatory. Paul does not hesitate to say to the Thessalonians, "We instructed you how to live in order to please God, as in fact you are living. Now we ask you and urge you in the Lord Jesus to do this more and more. For you know what instructions we gave you by the authority of the Lord Jesus" (1 Thess. 4:1–2). When preaching comes as a word from God, it comes with the authority of Jesus, who intends for people to hear and to heed literally "how it is necessary for you to walk." Good preaching in the context of rich worship creates the anticipation that when situations arise which call for ethical wisdom, Jesus can and does speak to such challenges, and when he does so, he requires growing obedience. It is possible that the churchgoing people in the three cases before us see religious ideas as optional propositions to be weighed and adopted or dismissed as it suits them. This faulty approach is more difficult to maintain where people hear faithful preaching of the Word in the context of genuine worship.

BETTER UNDERSTANDING OF STEWARDSHIP

Whenever a congregation collects offerings as part of corporate worship, the worshipers remind themselves of God's grace (2 Cor. 8:1–9:15). We have nothing that we have not received (1 Cor. 4:7). When the people gave abundantly for the building of the temple, David, in the presence of the whole assembly, not only exalted God but humbled himself and saw the assembly as stewards: "David praised the LORD in the presence of the whole assembly, saying, "... But who am I, and who are my people, that we should be able to give as generously as this? Everything comes from you, and we have given you only what comes from your hand" (1 Chron. 29:10–14).

Habitually seeing oneself as a recipient of lavish provision and a steward of what one has received—not of what one has not received—frees the worshiper, at least potentially, from unwarranted ambition and brings in its place genuine joy. Every character in the three cases would have profited from the liberating limitation of stewardship. No graduate student should feel guilty for failure to do more than he or she can do, based on the abilities God has given. Life is God's to give and God's to take; all people are stewards of each day that God entrusts to them, no more, and no less.

GODLY IMAGINATION

Not all decisions are rational. Not all the influences God supplies to move people toward Christlikeness are simply cognitive. Habitual worship that is richly liturgical draws on a storehouse of spiritual wisdom and experience set to music for people's benefit. The Psalter and other poetic oracles in Scripture are intentionally memorable, concrete, and vivid. Their recitation and the physical involvement of using one's voice as a worshiper ingrains truth into the mind, where it can influence thought, feelings, and behavior. For instance, the lament of Psalm 39 reinforces the reality of human fallenness and the shortness of life, but it puts this reality into perspective for those who cry out to God. Preachers who preach this psalm enrich congregational singing every time psalms reappear in the liturgy.

Thomas Long wisely observes, "A psalm ... aims at creating a shift in the basic moral perception of the reader. Psalms operate at the level of the imagination, often swiveling the universe on the hinges of a single image. Sermons based on psalms should also seek to work their way into the deep recesses of the hearer's imagination."[21] Preaching, in the context of worship, can and does change moral perception, because God has built into his Word structures and images he has designed to do just that.

INFLUENCES AT THE TIME OF THE DECISION

In addition to those cumulative influences that incline people toward wisdom, there are some decisions that they make in the assembly, in the very act of worship when they hear the voice of God. How does being present at worship and hearing God's Word expounded immediately evoke wise bioethical decisions, decisions that lead to wise living?

BELIEVERS SUPPORT ONE ANOTHER

Being "together with all the saints" (Eph. 3:18) provides a "plausibility structure," to use Peter Berger's term[22] — an alternative "life-world" as Netland, Fields, and Sung (chap. 7) call it. To resist cultural pressure and take a courageous and costly stand seems not so strange in the company of others who think and act the same way. Peer pressure is a prominent theme in the case "Gaining Every Advantage." Ideally, the fellowship of the saints counters ungodly pressures with more sanctified ones. An unusual instance of this, but one that has a clear ethical component, occurs when Paul exercises apostolic authority from a distance, as recorded in 1 Corinthians 5:3–5: "Even though I am not

---

21. Thomas G. Long, *Preaching and the Literary Forms of the Bible* (Philadelphia: Fortress, 1989), 47.

22. Peter L. Berger, *The Sacred Canopy: Elements of a* *Sociological Theory of Religion* (Garden City, N.Y.: Anchor, 1967), 45–47.

physically present, I am with you in spirit. And I have already passed judgment on the one who did this, just as if I were present. When you are assembled in the name of our Lord Jesus and I am with you in spirit, and the power of our Lord Jesus is present, hand this man over to Satan, so that the sinful nature may be destroyed and his spirit saved on the day of the Lord."

Notice here the importance of the church's being assembled in the name of the Lord with his power present. The gathered church can exert constructive ethical pressure.

Although Paul certainly exercised authority, his life and ministry stand in stark contrast to the "power relationships" that Netland, Fields, and Sung highlight between Dr. Bright and his graduate students. The apostle Paul learned from Jesus that true power, the power of God, manifests itself in weakness and that whoever wants to be the greatest must be the servant of all (2 Cor. 12:9; 13:10; Mark 9:35). Preaching and worship that exalt Christ significantly relativize differences of social location for the benefit of all concerned. James sets forth this ideal in James 2:1–7 as he criticizes those who show favoritism in the gathered fellowship. God himself has already exalted the lowly and humbled the proud. When human practice reflects God's values, people become less susceptible to the worldly pressures to exalt the learned, such as Dr. Bright, over "mere students."[23]

WORSHIPERS PRAY AND GOD HEARS

Prayer may include the intercessions of others for the person facing a tough ethical decision or the supplications of the person facing the decision. Upon hearing Dr. Alex's diagnosis and prognosis, there were "a few minutes of tears, anguish, and an emotional prayer." We do not know what Dave and Mary asked of God then. In corporate worship, though, they would be joining their hearts in supplication and intercession with leaders who could help them pray according to the will of God at the same time as they pray in faith. Bethany could pour out her heart to God on such occasions and experience the support of her friends and others. Their encouragement might even have enabled her to pray, as the Lord Jesus did in the garden of Gethsemane, a prayer of submission: "Not my will but yours."

GOD SPEAKS

God's Word impresses itself on a worshiper and not only calls for response but evokes and enables it. The writer to the Hebrews understands this, making a great deal of the word "today" in his repeated citation of the words "today, if you hear his voice" (Heb. 3:7, 13, 15; 4:7; drawing on Ps. 95:7–11). He expects Scripture to speak to his readers then and there as he expounds God's Word to them. Specifically, he urges those facing persecution to enter God's rest by faith. As Dunlop (chap. 12) notes, Dave could have accepted this word of invitation and died a good death, resting in Jesus.

---

23. I served churches in three settings where there were many students and professors. Again and again I saw the two groups interact as equals, as brothers and sisters in worship and at the Lord's Table.

Sometimes God speaks more indirectly. Consider the potential impact of a good exposition of Jonah 4 on Bethany ("A Difficult Death"). Examining God's question, "Do you have a right to be angry?" (4:4, 9), along with Jonah's defiant actions and words in response, might remind Bethany of her action—storming out of the room—and her words to her mother, "Yes, I am angry; I have a right to be angry. I'm angry at Daddy for giving up, and I'm angry at God too." Yes, as Carson notes (chap. 9), there is a legitimate place for outrage, but not all anger is warranted. In her youthfulness and in the difficulty of the situation, Bethany needs help to face her anger and yet not sin (Eph. 4:26). God speaks not only through the preached Word but in the benediction of the worship service that reminds participants that the triune God is with them as they go forth in faith and obedience.

HUMILITY HAPPENS

In the presence of God, with a palpable sense of his glory, worshipers feel undone, like Isaiah (Isa. 6:5). Like Peter they know themselves to be sinners (Luke 5:8), and resistance to God's will melts in the presence of his holy love. Worshipers do not remain in despair but gain a sense of wonder at having become recipients of God's grace. "Brothers and sisters, think of what you were when you were called. Not many of you were wise by human standards; not many were influential; not many were of noble birth. But God chose the foolish things of the world to shame the wise; God chose the weak things of the world to shame the strong. God chose the lowly things of this world and the despised things—and the things that are not—to nullify the things that are, so that no one may boast before him" (1 Cor. 1:26–29 TNIV).

Humility is indispensable to ethical thought and action. Virtually every character in the cases before us is guilty of thinking too highly of self in the sense critiqued by Philippians 2:1–11. No one is really looking out for the interests of others in the genuinely self-sacrificial way that the Lord Jesus models in this passage, and that Timothy, Epaphroditus, and Paul emulate there.

FAITH COMES BY HEARING

In a worship service, people can make a decision and perhaps with it a public commitment to take a step of obedience. Not all worship services include an "altar call," but even those that do not can encourage postures such as bowing and kneeling to reinforce the obedience of faith that lies ahead. Even if Dave ("A Difficult Death") was too weak to kneel, his presence in a wheelchair might not only have strengthened his faith to persevere—as he receives, perhaps, a challenging word from Hebrews—but could well have immeasurably encouraged others, including his family members.

"DENIAL" DISSOLVES

Truth is a hallmark of the people of God (Eph. 4:15–25). The tempted find no place to hide from God in their midst. All those we meet in the three cases, true to Romans 1, to greater or lesser degrees suppressed the truth. That is a temptation every person faces. Dave and Mary suppress the truth of Dave's prognosis and as a consequence lie about it to Bethany. Gathering for worship with the people of God to hear a word from God, who does not lie (Titus 1:2), is to come into the light to let one's deeds be exposed (John 3:16–21). There is nothing quite like the freedom that comes from knowing that one has nothing to hide, and no reason to do so anyway, for God is ready to forgive everything that his people confess (1 John 1:9).

INFLUENCES SUBSEQUENT TO THE DECISION

When people make good ethical decisions as a consequence of hearing God's Word and responding in worship—whether in a church or elsewhere—the fact that the very same people will meet again next week for corporate worship and teaching is pivotal. Those who opt for obedience as they understand it in light of Scripture, when facing an ethical dilemma, are in a very different place than before. As Jesus has observed, people who do evil hate the light and stay away from it. "But those who live by the truth come into the light, so that it may be seen plainly that what they have done has been done in the sight of God" (John 3:21 TNIV). People like this have done an about-face, turned one hundred and eighty degrees, and are moving toward the light instead of toward darkness. Such a person now has the capacity to hear more truth and to grow in the knowledge of God and in gratitude (Col. 1:9–14). What this person needs now is prayer, support, and accountability.

Admittedly, prayer partners and small-group members can supply all three of these, but corporate worship settings function this way too. Paul publicly expresses gratitude for God's work in new converts (Col. 1:3; Phil. 1:3; 1 Thess. 1:2; 2 Thess. 1:3) and in seasoned fellow workers (cf. Phil. 2:20; 1 Cor. 16:15–18). Affirmation of obedience is an important part of how Paul urges the Thessalonians toward further obedience (1 Thess. 4:1, 10). Acknowledging this is not to put people on some sort of inescapable treadmill of escalating responsibilities; it is to recognize that God himself has been at work making new creatures (1 Thess. 1:1–2:13) and that what he has begun he will complete (Phil. 1:6). Every part of the worship service will now speak reassurance, reinforcing the message of each sermon, now received as life-giving manna from heaven.

How important is God's Word, then, for each person in this book's case studies, particularly as Peter articulates it in 1 Peter 5:6–11: "Humble yourselves, therefore, under God's mighty hand, that he may lift you up in due time. Cast all your anxiety on him because he cares for you. Be self-controlled and alert. Your enemy the devil prowls around like a roaring lion looking for someone to devour. Resist him, standing firm in the faith, because you know that your brothers throughout the world are undergoing the same kind of sufferings. And the God of all grace, who called you to his eternal glory in Christ, after you have suffered a little while, will himself restore you and make you strong, firm and steadfast. To him be the power for ever and ever. Amen."

Preachers should preach the Word being faithful not only to its content and intent but also in the sense of trusting God to speak through them in the assembly. They should preach the Word "with great patience and careful instruction," not presuming immediate impact (2 Tim. 4:2), since they know that much of their work will bear fruit only later. Worship leaders should work hard to let the elements of the worship service work with the sermon to preach the gospel to converted and unconverted alike. Those not facing immediate ethical temptations or dilemmas will benefit from learning not to resist the sanctifying work of the Word and the Spirit, so that when circumstances arise that call for wisdom, God will have worked in them what they need. In fact, just their presence at worship, their posture, their eagerness to hear from God, their joy and contentment, may be what nudges a fellow worshiper into the path of gospel obedience, the obedience of faith.

CHAPTER 14

WISDOM FROM EDUCATION

Miriam L. Charter

Nearly seventy years ago, Professor Charles Gragg of Harvard University questioned a common assumption. Teachers in particular often think that by providing information and general principles that have taken others a lifetime to acquire and develop, they can give learners a head start over less-informed contemporaries. In his estimation, this assumption flows from another decidedly questionable assumption: that it is possible, by a simple process of telling, to pass on knowledge in a useful form. In an article titled "Because Wisdom Can't Be Told",[1] Gragg introduced the truism that telling is not teaching. He suggested that if the learning process is to result in wisdom, something dynamic must take place within the learner. That dynamic process is the concern of every teacher in the church who seeks to develop men and women whose lives and decision-making are characterized by godly wisdom.

The chapters in this book bring together the insights of outstanding Christian scholars of our day, as each approaches a very complex bioethical case from the perspective of their own discipline. The intent of the book is not to attempt to provide right answers to complex questions. Its purpose is to serve church practitioners and other Christian leaders whose task it is to help men and women in the pew to deal with the increasingly complex bioethical issues of the twenty-first century, leading them in the way of wisdom.

A biblical perspective of wisdom suggests far more than possessing knowledge that godly people and others have accumulated through the ages. Biblical wisdom speaks of an alternative approach in which experience is the context of learning, and active engagement by learners in situations of puzzlement is its motor.[2] This concluding chap-

---

1. Charles I. Gragg, "Because Wisdom Can't Be Told," *Harvard Alumni Bulletin* 43, no. 2 (1940): 78. The article suggests a pedagogical tool and educational methodology followed by the design of this book—learning by the use of case studies.

2. Doug Blomberg, "A Problem-Posing Pedagogy: 'Paths of Pleasantness and Peace,'" *Journal of Education and Christian Belief* 3, no. 2 (1999): 97.

ter is especially for those involved in teaching men and women of God who, when faced with difficult life-and-death decisions, will be able "to say and do ... what glorifies God" (Vanhoozer, chap. 5).[3] Obedience to truth in all its expressions—not merely the description of it—is what godly wisdom strives to produce.

The bioethical questions God's people will face in coming years will become increasingly complex, never replicating exactly the three case studies that serve as templates in this book. The speed with which technology and information change means that no single book, regardless of the wisdom of the contributors, can adequately prepare Christians to deal with the complex issues of the next generation. In a climate of rapid change and proliferating knowledge, the role of educational leaders in the church will no longer be one of dispensing answers. Answers to medical ethics issues are typically obsolete in six months. The scientific database doubles every twenty months. New technologies, new discoveries, and shifting cultural perspectives on health and healing mean that people can rarely approach ethical issues with packaged answers in books.

As new bioethical issues continue to arise, church leaders and educators must commit to a never-ending task of learning—lifelong learning. People need help to develop their capacity to think, rather than merely receiving instructions about what they should think. Of necessity, this will require a shift in outlook, from viewing education within a teaching-telling paradigm to developing a learning paradigm for all educational settings in the church. Thus, education in the church will help the people of God retool their knowledge and learning skills, even as knowledge expands and evolves.

The task before us is multidisciplinary, enriched in part by the work and resources of those who have gone before us. The perplexing challenge is how to nurture a godly community of people who truly know God, know the Scriptures, and know themselves, thus bringing together a composite of wisdom to effectively deal with the issues that they confront in this messy world. From an educational perspective, the challenge of integrating the increasing mass of knowledge is, at times, overwhelming.

THE PURPOSE OF TEACHING IN THE CHURCH

The three case studies central to this book place readers in scenarios that people in the pews might well encounter in the third millennium. Most readers will naturally wonder, "How might a pastor prepare the Bettys and Toms of today's congregations to know and live truth and love as they deal with issues of infertility and alternatives to old-fashioned ways of having children?" ("Having a Baby the New-Fashioned Way"). They will ask, "How can we assist the burgeoning student population in our churches

---

3. Cf. Richard Averbeck (chap. 1), who speaks of wise living as living within God's design.

to deal truthfully with the kinds of decisions that Roberto, Paul, Akira, and Jill face about using mind-enhancing stimulants?" ("Gaining Every Advantage"). Any pastor or church educator in touch with mortal human beings will naturally ask, after reading "A Difficult Death," "What is the role of my church in preparing people like Dave and Mary who will deal with difficult end-of-life decisions?"

One way of envisioning the task of educators in the church, particularly as it relates to preparing the people of God to deal with complex bioethical issues, is to speak of nurturing in them a *wisdom worldview*.[4] This would involve developing within them, over time, an understanding of both the interpretive framework provided by Scripture and the way the world really is—and how the two present a "picture of the whole within which knowledge is to be sought."[5] Since, as Scripture affirms, the fear of God is the beginning of knowledge or wisdom[6] (Prov. 1:7; 9:10), wisdom is "not a rationalistic or empiricist project of assembling scientific facts or helpful information. Rather it is a theological search for meaning which reacts responsively ... to a religious encounter with Yahweh. Wisdom acts after, and because of, a divine encounter—not before it."[7] The fear of God is the sphere within which wisdom is possible; it is the precondition for both wisdom and ethical behavior.[8]

D. A. Carson (chap. 9) reminds us that the first task of Christian educators is to shape the personal connection people have with God through Christ, which in turn will produce within them the resources for consolation and wisdom in adversity. Indeed, to use Carson's words, "It is next to futile to attempt to bring the consolations of the gospel, still less moral guidance, into a complex bioethical problem, unless people's knowledge of God and the Scriptures and their personal connection to God through Christ produce in them resources for consolation and wisdom in adversity—because they live daily in the light of who God is, what human beings are, what the cross achieved in answer to the fall."

While the book of Proverbs is about knowing, it is just as surely about doing. It is an "ethical and religious message."[9] Vanhoozer (chap. 5) suggests that the educator's passion and longing is for men and women of God who are learning to make right theological judgments about what to say and what to do in order to display the mind of Christ.

Approaching this formidable educational task requires that we consider two foundational issues, closely related but distinct: "What does it mean to know?" and "How do people learn?"[10] How we view knowledge will affect our understanding of learning,

---

4. Ryan P. O'Dowd, "A Cord of Three Strands: Epistemology in Job, Proverbs, and Ecclesiastes," in *The Bible and Epistemology: Biblical Soundings on the Knowledge of God*, ed. Mary Healy and Robin Parry (Colorado Springs, Colo.: Paternoster, 2007), 66.

5. Ibid.

6. In most of Proverbs 1–9, *wisdom* and *knowledge* are used synonymously.

7. O'Dowd, "A Cord of Three Strands," 67.

8. M. V. Fox, *Proverbs 1–9: A New Translation with Introduction and Commentary* (New York: Doubleday, 2000), 69.

9. M. V. Fox, "Ideas of Wisdom in Proverbs 1–9," *Journal of Biblical Literature* 116 (1997): 613.

10. The two questions are not necessarily to be answered sequentially but considered coterminously.

and hence our approach to educational tasks. To begin: When I say that the people in my church know God, know the Scriptures, and know themselves, what do I mean?

WHAT DOES IT MEAN TO KNOW?

The approach that John Frame has developed can help us to think about what it means to know truth and then teach God's people to think wisely about complex ethical problems. His model will also be particularly helpful in addressing the much talked about but little understood task of integration. Educators often pose the question, How does one faithfully integrate the truths revealed in Scripture with the reality found in the world and the reality that exists within oneself? In the context of this book, how might the educators in Dave and Mary's church have proactively prepared God's people (including Dave and Mary) to integrate the truths of Scripture (faithfully taught over time) with the realities of the end-of-life crisis they encounter and the realities that exist within each person in their complex situations? Frame's model of Christian ethics provides for the educator a potential bridge between theory and practice; indeed, it can provide a legitimate way of thinking about what biblical wisdom is and about the structure of a wisdom worldview.

Frame's model (see fig. 1) highlights three perspectives on human knowledge: (1) knowledge of the normative (*rationalism* or *a priorism*, the view that human knowledge presupposes certain principles that people know independently of sense-experience, principles which govern knowledge of sense-experience); (2) knowledge of the situation (*subjectivism* or, as we shall rename it, the *situational-contextual*, the view that criteria external to people — in the social situation or context — often shape what they perceive as true and how they perceive it to be true); and (3) knowledge of oneself (*empiricism* or, as we shall call it, the *existential-personal*, the view that the data of sense-experience, the human condition, ground human knowledge).[11]

A strong case can be made for each perspective. For the insightful pastor or church educator, all three are in evidence in Christian apologetics today. Many have used the traditional normative-rational arguments in refuting skepticism and in defense of the objectivity of truth.[12] Existential-personal arguments are also evident in the work of many evangelical apologists.[13] It is more difficult to find situational-contextual appeals in the works of evangelical apologists, because of the evangelical emphasis on the truth-falsehood antithesis. Frame, however, in referencing Edward J. Carnell's writing, suggests that there may be a kind of situational element there which is compatible with the other epistemological principles.[14] His analysis affirms and demonstrates that all three perspectives can be found in the work of evangelical apologists today.

---

11. John M. Frame, "Epistemological Perspectives and Evangelical Apologetics," *Bulletin of the Evangelical Philosophical Society* 7 (1984): 1.

12. Ibid., 3.

13. John W. Montgomery is a case in point, one among many.

14. Frame, "Epistemological Perspectives," 3.

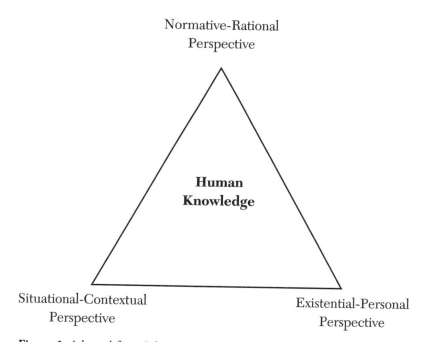

Normative-Rational
Perspective

**Human
Knowledge**

Situational-Contextual
Perspective

Existential-Personal
Perspective

Figure 1. Adapted from John M. Frame, *The Doctrine of the Knowledge of God* (Phillipsburg, N.J.: Presbyterian and Reformed, 1987), 75, with permission from the publisher.

Frame refers to these three perspectives on knowing as three "tendencies" that have exerted influence on Christian and non-Christian thinking alike. None of these perspectives exists completely independently from the others. Each includes the others, but historically each has taken a dim view of the others. Each, therefore, is a "perspective" on the whole of human knowledge, suggesting a model of integrative thought that may be helpful for a Christian educator who, with feet firmly planted in biblical revelation (the normative perspective), seeks to learn and teach prudential wisdom.[15] For example, a pastor or church educator dealing with end-of-life issues such as Dave and Mary face ("A Difficult Death") cannot expose people to the truths of Scripture (the normative perspective) without also developing within them an understanding of the human condition (the existential perspective) and a growing facility to understand biblically the social context, the situation in which the crisis is happening (the situational perspective).

The temptation is to seek a standard in only the existential, situational, or normative realm. Seeking truth in any of those locations is not entirely wrong, for whoever looks

---

15. Carson (chap. 9) speaks of the "integrative task" as "transcendent Christian realities ... [exercising] controlling influence on their priorities, values, or conduct," and in so saying alludes to the multiple perspectives which must be brought to the integrative process.

faithfully in those places *will* find the word of God, which *is* an adequate ethical standard.[16] Indeed, God's word *is* in the self, in the world, and in the realm of norms (Rom. 1:32). Hence, Frame would affirm that a fully Christian ethic accepts as final only God's word. "That word is found pre-eminently in Scripture, the covenant constitution of the people of God (Deut. 6:6–9; Matt. 5:17–20; 2 Tim. 3:15–17; 2 Peter 1:21) but is also revealed in the world (Ps. 19:1ff; Rom. 1:18ff), and in the self (Gen. 1:27ff; 9:6; Eph. 4:24; Col. 3:10)."[17]

A wisdom worldview such as this suggests a picture of the whole within which to seek knowledge. An educator with integrity will search for truth in all three realms, presupposing their coherence, seeking at each point to integrate each source of knowledge with the other two while finding ways to teach from each perspective.

TEACHING FROM THE EXISTENTIAL PERSPECTIVE

Teaching from the existential perspective attempts, through the lens of Scripture, to judge what in human nature—in the human condition—is the result of sin and what expresses God's image. Within the existential perspective, the self is seen as the perspective from which to view the full range of ethical norms and data. It does justice to the experiential side of human life, particularly people's sense of the direct presence of God's Spirit. This perspective will not lead to skepticism, if the objectivity of God's word anchors it.

There is no suggestion here that it is possible to learn to act wisely only from experience—in the "school of hard knocks," as some would suggest. From a practical perspective, strict adherence to the literal meaning of "learning from experience" would harmfully impact the task of teaching. For generations the church has followed the model of 2 Timothy 2:2, which instructs pastors and teachers to pass along to students what they as experts in their field know (or have been taught to believe they know). Indeed, the question for every pastor and church educator—yes, and for every Christian parent—is, "If I *tell* them, has learning occurred?"

Reflecting on the case "Having a Baby the New-Fashioned Way," one might, for example, ask how the decision-making of Betty and Tom would have improved had their pastor been courageous enough to lovingly help them reflect on how much of their crisis was because of the cumulative result of their selfishness in earlier decision-making, the result of past sinfulness. John Kilner (chap. 4) suggests a carefully reasoned and biblical response to the abortion issue that, even after the fact, might have lovingly helped Betty and Tom to understand the contribution of their past decisions and sin to the complex

---

16. Frame, "Epistemological Perspectives," 3. Frame also suggests that there are problems with any simple identification between the Bible and the word of God; Frame speaks of the word of God as God's "self-expression" and then carefully specifies the various forms of self-expression that

Scripture uses to refer to such divine speech (pp. 10–16).

17. John M. Frame, *Perspectives on the Word of God: An Introduction to Christian Ethics* (Phillipsburg, N.J.: Presbyterian and Reformed, 1990), 52.

decision they now are attempting to make. Teachers in the church often neglect the existential perspective (enabling people to judge, through the lens of Scripture, what in the situation is the result of the human propensity to sin), because it requires courage to help people acknowledge and "own" their sinfulness and its implications.

TEACHING FROM THE SITUATIONAL PERSPECTIVE

From the situational perspective, an educator will teach people to acknowledge human pain and pleasure. Christ has called people to love others as they love God. Teaching and learning within the situational perspective acknowledges the scriptural norms and the impact, positive or negative, that people's context has in shaping what they perceive as truth. The learner examines the situation as a milieu into which to apply God's norms, understanding at the same time the "situatedness" of human knowing. Is the way one's context has shaped perceptions of truth in line with scriptural norms? Within the structures of a wisdom worldview, Proverbs declares the learner's identity as being a subject of and within the Creator's world. As products of creation, learners share historical and geographic space with the object (that which is known) and find that object shaping their knowledge.[18]

Had the people in Dave and Mary's church ("A Difficult Death") benefited from consistent preparation to help them understand and enter with compassion into the pain Dave and Mary and their daughter, Bethany, faced in a time of enormous crisis and decision-making, Dave's death process might have been a triumphant experience for all. Steven Roy (chap. 11) and Greg Scharf (chap. 13) have emphasized the critical importance of proclaiming God's Word consistently over time to build up and proactively prepare God's people for unexpected crises. That proactive teaching and preparation seems to be so sadly lacking in the church bodies with which the two couples, Dave and Mary, and Tom and Betty, identify.

TEACHING FROM THE NORMATIVE PERSPECTIVE

Teaching from the normative perspective involves the educator's focus on Scripture. The scriptural word is primary, but learners cannot properly use the Scriptures without the personal illumination of God's Spirit and a deep awareness that the Spirit is leading them into truth. Likewise, Scripture is meaningless unless it is applicable to situations, which implies that people must understand the social context in which they are living. No one of these perspectives, rightly understood, can exist without the other two, because each includes the other two.[19] God's word stands firm; there is no need of fear that it will disappoint us.

Authors contributing to this volume speak of the normative perspective in different ways. D. A. Carson (chap. 9) speaks of developing the "matrix" within which Chris-

---

18. O'Dowd, "A Cord of Three Strands," 73.

19. Frame, *Perspectives on the Word*, 56.

tians will think about "life and death, the meaning of faith, even how to relate to God in the context of their own demise." Offering a New Testament scholar's reflections on a troubling case, Carson presents the biblical framework as a "way of thinking." The realities that the biblical text posits have structured his thinking as a believer attempting to find solutions in the midst of a very complex situation for which there is no one comprehensive and easy answer. He is careful to emphasize that the challenge is a matter not of "proof-texting to sort out complex bioethical matters" but of instilling in people the "biblical-theological themes that are indisputably grounded in Scripture." People need to be in command of those resources when attempting to make sense of the bioethical issues in what life has handed them. In so saying, Carson acknowledges the multiple perspectives which must be brought to the learning process.

In a similar manner, Richard Averbeck (chap. 1) speaks of living within the design of God from a bioethical point of view. His chapter is a graphic demonstration of how biblical principles form the framework within which decision-making must take place. Nevertheless, he also acknowledges that people cannot fully understand the normative in isolation from the existential and the situational. Pain may lead people to attempt to escape in any way they can, even if it knowingly violates God's design. The task for those who seek to nurture problem-solvers among God's people, as he explains, is to help people understand from Scripture what is God's design and take that into consideration as they seek to resolve complex problems.

Harold Netland, Bruce Fields, and Elizabeth Sung (chap. 7) speak of approaching moral questions within a framework shaped by the Bible as well as by the heritage of Christian reflection on Scripture and life throughout the ages. They suggest that other disciplines beyond those highlighted in this book also have contributions to make. The people of God should not ignore such disciplines when approaching bioethical issues. For example, Netland, Fields, and Sung call for an understanding of contextual (sociocultural) contexts that emerge from a religious framework that is not Christian, which they suggest Christians must also explore and understand. These authors would say that contextual (situational) factors affect our perception of reality. They call God's people to seek to understand the "social location" of those among whom they minister,[20] the "life worlds" within which others live.[21] Regarding the case study "Gaining Every Advantage," one might ask how a believer like Paul, one of the young scholars deciding whether to use Epiginosko, should have been prepared to think through issues such as the use of mind-enhancing drugs within a framework shaped by Scripture and by the heritage of Christian reflection on Scripture and life. He grew up in a devout Southern

---

20. Not that this would lead to what Netland, Fields, and Sung (chap. 7) refer to as a "kind of relativism which maintains that truth and knowledge are simply products of particular contexts." As they demonstrate, such an outlook is not acceptable for Christians, who believe that "truth— including truth in moral matters—transcends particular social or cultural contexts."

21. Frame reminds us, "A fully Christian ethic accepts as final only God's Word" (Frame, *Perspectives on the Word*, 51).

Baptist home, and his Christian family was committed to high moral principles. Yet when needing to make a critical, ethical, life-impacting decision, Paul is uncertain as to what all is at stake. He seems to lack a framework, shaped by Scripture, for the moment when a decision of such magnitude stares him in the face.

DESIGNING LEARNING FROM ALL THREE PERSPECTIVES

If the church is to prepare its people to respond to complex bioethical issues, the task of pastors and educators is to design approaches that will ensure that knowing (learning) and understanding occur from each perspective, from all the data available, from all the revelation of God. This is not to suggest that people study some data from an existential perspective, other data from a situational perspective, and yet other data from a normative perspective. When dealing with a complex bioethical question or when counseling God's people, three questions are central, each of which forces people to think of the problem from a different perspective within the integrative model:

1. What is the problem? (the situational perspective)
2. What does the Scripture say about it? (the normative perspective)
3. What changes are needed in the person involved so that he or she will do the right thing? (the existential perspective)[22]

People must ask and seriously answer each question with care, always mindful that a conclusive answer to any of the three questions will remain elusive unless they have an answer to the others. The model helps us to understand why contemporary bioethical questions often appear to be so complex and difficult. Their solution calls for so many kinds of knowledge—exegetical, empirical, psychological—which in turn calls for the use of logic and other types of thinking. A wise teacher will realize that simply dispensing the answer to any one of the three questions without engaging the minds of the learners in addressing the other two does not constitute learning. A teacher's breadth of knowledge affects how well that teacher understands and appreciates what is required for effective teaching and consequential learning.

HOW DO PEOPLE LEARN?

A second perplexing question that educators of God's people will need to consider in addressing complex bioethical issues is, How do people learn? The prevailing tendency among those who teach is to tell, assuming that what people need most, in order to learn, is information. This tendency is rooted in a modernist paradigm of schooling in which the task of one who teaches is to provide answers and to reward the amassing

---

22. Ibid., 54.

of information. People often perceive pastors and church educators as "the ones who know," "officials" who have the right answers. Their books are the sources for these right answers. However, as men and women in the pews face increasingly complex questions, collecting right answers is not an effective long-term solution. Nor does this approach honor God's people as rational human beings, made in the image of God, capable of sorting out complex and vital issues.

It is important to equip God's people to think, to think critically, to think for themselves.[23] Greggo and Parent (chap. 3) remind us that consumer-oriented medicine has shifted the weight of responsibility from informed and detached medical providers, who make the decisions, to the patients themselves or to the loved ones with the greatest stake in the decisions and their aftermath. The burden of knowing will fall increasingly on people who may not have easy access to Christian bioethicists, Christian counselors, or resources such as the present book. How will they find the pathway of wisdom—God's path of peace (Prov. 3:17)[24] as they encounter complex problems?

Stephen Brookfield, in his seminal work on developing critical thinking in adult learners, suggests that critical thinkers must develop an awareness of the assumptions under which they (and others) think and act. Critical thinking, in Brookfield's definition, comprises two interrelated processes: (1) identifying and challenging assumptions, and (2) imagining and exploring alternative ways of looking at and behaving in the world.[25]

Netland, Fields, and Sung (chap. 7) model for church educators facing complex bioethical issues how to move beyond what at face value appears to be the problem, to consider more fundamental questions about who people are supposed to be and the kind of universe in which they live. Critical thinkers are to consider more basic questions about human nature, the ultimate good, and how people are to align themselves with this good. Moral deliberation does not occur in a vacuum. Each person and group brings to the task a particular conceptual framework (or set of assumptions) about the way things are and what is morally significant. Kilner (chap. 4) approaches the challenges of the case study "Having a Baby the New-Fashioned Way" by asking the reader to consider the dilemma from the perspectives of the various stakeholders, even that of the developing embryo. Behind his approach is the profound and essential question, Do embryos have the full moral status that other human stakeholders have? As learners answer that question, their conceptual framework as to the way things are and what is morally significant becomes more visible.

---

23. When speaking of teaching God's people to think critically (especially in Western contexts), the implication is that people learn to "think for themselves," a suggestion that, for some, smacks of Western individualism. Such a suggestion, in this context, is tempered by the reality of community hermeneutics to be addressed in the closing section of this chapter.

24. Unless otherwise noted, all biblical references in this chapter are from *The Holy Bible, New International Version* (Grand Rapids, Mich.: Zondervan, 1985).

25. Stephen D. Brookfield, *Developing Critical Thinkers: Challenging Adults to Explore Alternative Ways of Thinking and Acting* (San Francisco: Jossey-Bass, 1987), ix.

Netland, Fields, and Sung also remind us that one of the foundational tasks of church educators is to assist God's people to develop a trustworthy conceptual framework within which they will make decisions, a framework shaped by the Scriptures and by the rich heritage of Christian reflection on Scripture and life throughout the ages. Developing the framework is the lifelong, proactive task of church education, a task that cannot be postponed until the crisis happens and those involved are inaccessible.

A key challenge here is how to develop the conceptual framework that is so necessary for critical thinking. If educators think only in terms of a teaching-telling paradigm, they will think of delivering the framework over time, usually in neatly packaged units. Their primary expectation will be that learners will listen passively, hopefully recording their teacher's wisdom in a notebook for future reference and memorizing the well-ordered propositions that have been taught. The expert may teach (deliver the facts), perhaps even with outstanding ability. The question remains, Has learning taken place? Can the learners, using what they know, generate solutions that arise from the word of God revealed in Scripture? Will the learners recognize God's word, which is so often obscured in the messiness of the world in which they live, the still, small voice of the Spirit who promises to lead his people "into all truth" (John 16:13)?

LEVELS OF LEARNING

For decades educators have tried to describe the dimensions of thinking and levels of complexity in human thought, seeking to understand what kind of thinking happens when it is of the critical kind described above. Models they have generated divide thinking into two categories: convergent (lower-order) thinking, and divergent (higher-order) thinking. Educators have asked intriguing questions as to how the human brain is organized to think with increasing complexity, from lower-order, convergent thinking (basic processes such as observing, finding patterns and generalizing, forming conclusions based on patterns, and assessing conclusions) to higher-order, divergent thinking that might be described as critical thinking,[26] creative thinking,[27] and metacognition.[28]

If, indeed, the brain is designed for and capable of such a broad range of thinking skills, including higher-order thinking, why is relatively little of it evident in the normal course of discussions with people in the pews? Could it be that many people do not think critically because they have never had models or experienced situations that required them to do so? Those skills, latent within the human brain, are still relatively

---

26. David A. Sousa, *How the Brain Learns*, 3rd ed. (Thousand Oaks, Calif.: Corwin, 2006), 246. Critical thinking is a complex process based on objective standards and consistency; it includes making judgments using objective criteria and offering opinions with compelling reasons.

27. Ibid. Creative thinking involves synthesizing information to arrive at a whole new concept, idea, or understanding.

28. Ibid. Metacognition is the awareness one has of one's own thinking processes, knowing when and why one uses basic processes and how these functions relate to the content being learned. Sousa points out that there are two processes that occur simultaneously in metacognition: monitoring progress while learning and making appropriate changes when problems occur during learning.

undeveloped. Teaching and preaching, for the most part, are unilateral, demanding primarily the lower levels of convergent thinking—content acquisition through rote rehearsal, rather than the process of thinking for analysis and synthesis. If the primary focus is the transmission of content, which makes demands primarily in terms of recall and application, the right answer is seen as more valuable than the process used to arrive at the answer. Consequently, in the church context, teachers as well as learners gravitate to practicing the least demanding thought processes, perhaps because it is easier to anticipate and manage what happens when engaging lower levels of learning.

One of the most helpful models of thinking and learning that some teachers use to promote higher-order thinking in the church is Bloom's Taxonomy (fig. 2).[29] Although there are six levels, each increasing the complexity of the process, educators recognize that an individual may move easily among all levels during extended processing of information. Because some people are never challenged to move to higher levels of thinking, they consistently, perhaps even exclusively, operate at the lower levels of the taxonomy.

The educational challenge for those who want to nurture thinking people in the church is to develop teaching skills and methods that will train and require learners to move beyond lower-level (convergent) types of thinking to higher-level (divergent) types of thinking. Discerning educators search diligently for such methods. Higher-level types of thinking are necessary for making complex bioethical decisions. How can the church become a learning environment that helps the people of God to move beyond convergent thinking, where learners merely recall or focus on what they already comprehend to solve a problem? A more worthy goal is to encourage and require them to operate at the upper levels of divergent thinking, where the learners' processing results in new insights that were not part of the original information. They will now have engaged in critical thinking about the issue.

The differences in levels and types of thinking raise challenging questions for the cognitive-enhancement initiative that Dr. Bright offers to his top students ("Gaining Every Advantage"). Issues of cognitive enhancement confront Roberto, Paul, Akira, and Jill in the same way they will increasingly arise for all who compete in the academic world. Definitions of cognitive enhancement need clarification. Dr. Bright suggests that the mental ability of those taking Epiginosko will "surpass normal human intelligence." But exactly what improvements in thinking will the new drug Epiginosko generate? To some degree, an increase in information and memory can be helpful. But how would a massive increase in lower-level capacities affect one's ability to engage in upper-level thinking? Wisdom is not the same thing as information, and a preoccupation with the latter could conceivably be an obstacle to the former. How is a Christian, who treasures

29. Bloom's original taxonomy (published in 1956 as *Taxonomy of Educational Objectives: The Classification of Educational Goals; Handbook I: Cognitive Domain* [New York: David McKay]), has seen significant revisions by educators in recent years (Lorin W. Anderson and David R. Krathwohl, eds., *A Taxonomy for Learning, Teaching, and Assessing: A Revision of Bloom's Taxonomy of Educational Objectives* [New York: Longman, 2001]).

↑↑	**Creating**	Ability to put parts together to form an idea that is new to learner; this level stresses creativity with major emphasis on forming new patterns or structures; learner uses divergent thinking but draws on learning at all the other levels (imagine, compose, design, infer)
↑↑	**Evaluating**	Ability to judge the value of material based on specific criteria and standards; learner may determine criteria or be given them; examines criteria from several categories and selects those most relevant to the situation; conscious judgments based on definite criteria (appraise, assess, critique, judge)
↑↑	**Analyzing**	Ability to break material into its component parts so that its structure can be understood; includes identifying parts, examining relationships to the whole, and recognizing organizational principles involved; learner can organize and reorganize information into categories (analyze, contrast, distinguish, deduce)
↑↑	**Applying**	Ability to use learned material in new situations with a minimum of direction; ability to apply rules, concepts, methods, and theories to solve problems; select, transfer, and apply data to complete a new task (practice, calculate, apply, execute)
↑	**Understanding**	Ability to make sense of the material; rather than merely recalling, the material is available for future use to solve problems and make decisions (summarize, discuss, explain, outline)
↑↑	**Remembering**	Recall, recognition of previously learned material, using it in the form in which it was learned (define, label, recall, recognize)

Figure 2. Levels of Bloom's Taxonomy of Educational Objectives, revised version, based on Lorin W. Anderson and David R. Krathwohl, eds., *A Taxonomy for Learning, Teaching, and Assessing: A Revision of Bloom's Taxonomy of Educational Objectives* (New York: Longman, 2001), 66–89, and David A. Sousa, *How the Brain Learns*, 3rd ed. (Thousand Oaks, Calif.: Corwin, 2006), 250–52.

wisdom, to think about amassing information, creative thinking, and new knowledge if those lack any moral frame of reference?

In the case study "Having a Baby the New-Fashioned Way," it would appear that none of those involved in responding to this complex bioethical dilemma know how to think with higher-level types of thinking, moving beyond convergent thinking (remembering, understanding, applying) to higher-level, divergent thinking (analyzing, evaluating, creating). In moving to higher-level thinking, people gain new insights that make use of original information. They discern truth in ways that are uniquely appropriate to their situation and faithful to truth in Scripture and elsewhere.

Even if there were Scripture passages or insights from other disciplines that shed helpful light on their problems, the simple recall of those passages, understanding their usefulness to the problem, and even being able to apply them to the problem would still be low-level thinking. The complex problem facing Tom and Betty demands the type of process Kilner has modeled, where people ask prior questions (such as, Who are the stakeholders? Is the embryo or the fetus a human being? What constructive way forward will give each person a better life?) and make decisions that will enable all people to have an opportunity to benefit.

It is not evident that any of the main participants have had experience in thinking this way. How different the process might have unfolded for Tom, Betty, and Laura if the church had understood that its educational task, over time, is to train its people to think at higher levels, to be able to take the scriptural teaching and other resources to which a church has access and engage in divergent thinking on the issues.

A SHIFT FROM A TEACHING/TELLING PARADIGM TO A LEARNING PARADIGM

Vanhoozer (chap. 5) raises one of the deceptively simple questions behind this book: How do we teach people to use the Bible to address challenges in bioethics? This question implies that there is more involved than simply knowing the facts or even being able to recall or list the principles involved (convergent thinking). This question speaks of using the Scriptures well, as students and teachers together wrestle with difficult questions. Using Scripture in this process suggests that learners are not merely observers. Rather, the learning process transforms them into participants who take substantial responsibility for their own learning. This process gives them firsthand appreciation of and experience with the application of knowledge to practice. It enables them to think in a divergent manner, resulting in the development of a defensible framework that integrates multiple perspectives (normative, situational, and existential) on the problem at hand.

The church today emphatically needs to embrace a learning paradigm rather than merely a teaching-telling paradigm. If wisdom cannot be told, the role of the educator is no longer simply as a purveyor of information. Though the pastor or teacher may be the expert in the sense of being farther along in the journey, the "sage on the stage" metaphor must give way to the "guide by the side" metaphor. What methods might church educators use to move their people from being recipients of information to being creative thinkers in situations that are new and complex and demanding of creative ideas? One proven educational methodology that offers promise is Problem Based Learning.[30]

PROBLEM BASED LEARNING (PBL)

Problem Based Learning is an educational approach that can help church educators nurture problem-solvers among God's people. PBL develops critical thinking skills in people who are learning to address complex bioethical questions with prudential wisdom from an integrated, cross-disciplinary perspective and within the safety of community.

PBL begins with an authentic problem, need, or challenge as a context in which students learn problem-solving and lifelong learning skills, and in the process acquire knowledge about a particular issue or answers to a complex question. Learners engage an ill-structured problem (i.e., a situation in which initially they are uncertain even about what information they will need to solve the problem). Through a sequence of processes, they ultimately propose solutions that integrate what has been learned. The three case studies at the heart of this book are superb examples of what PBL refers to as ill-structured problems. Each would be an excellent platform from which church educators or pastors could launch a PBL process that would develop in their people critical thinking, problem-solving skills, and lifelong learning skills.

GOALS OF PBL

The genius of a PBL approach to learning is that learners ultimately acquire far more than trustworthy information. They also acquire process skills, problem-solving skills, and other learning skills that can be transferred across various life and work situations (e.g., self-directed learning, independent information mining, collaborative learning, team participation, and reflective thinking).

The following is a simplified presentation of the PBL approach that an educator in the church could use to develop in people the ability to think critically about contemporary bioethical issues. This approach brings to bear on each problem a well-developed scriptural framework and critical information from disciplines that will contribute to making a well-informed decision. In the following discussion, the step-by-step application of the Problem Based Learning method will refer to the case studies central to this book as examples of ill-structured problems that might be used to implement PBL.

---

30. Today, Problem Based Learning is the standard in medical schools around the world; it is also common practice in other fields, such as business, agriculture, law, engineering, social work, and education.

CHARACTERISTICS OF PBL

Problem Based Learning approaches usually include the following characteristics:

- The problem is the *starting point* of learning.
- The problem is usually a *real-world* problem that has no easy or obvious answer. If it is a simulated problem, it is meant to be as authentic as possible.
- The problem calls for *multiple perspectives*. The use of cross-disciplinary knowledge is a key feature in PBL methodology. PBL encourages the solution of the problem by taking into consideration knowledge from various fields, disciplines, and topics.
- The problem challenges students' knowledge, attitudes, and competencies, thus calling for identification of learning needs and *new areas of learning* they will need to explore in order to make a decision.
- *Self-directed learning* is primary, so students assume major responsibility for the acquisition of information and knowledge.
- *Harnessing of a variety of knowledge sources* and the use and evaluation of information resources are essential PBL processes. The facilitator becomes the gatekeeper for these, assuring the quality of resources that learners consult.
- Learning is *collaborative, communicative, and cooperative*. Students work in small groups with a high level of interaction for peer learning, peer teaching, and group presentations, thereby gaining skills they need for real life.
- Development of *inquiry and problem-solving skills* is as important as information acquisition for the solution of the problem. Accordingly, the PBL tutor facilitates by means of questioning and cognitive coaching.
- Closure in the PBL process includes *synthesis and integration* of learning.
- PBL concludes with an *evaluation and review* of the learner's experience and the learning processes.[31]

THE PBL PROCESS — FIVE STAGES

1. Meeting the Problem. Typically learners encounter a real-world scenario as the starting point of learning. The scenario acts as a stimulus to envision a realistic context similar to situations people in the real world will meet. During this initial phase, the facilitator will commit some time to building team dynamics (commitment to team roles and to the group) among small groups that will work together throughout the process of exploring the problem. Other important aspects of this first phase include

31. Oon-Seng Tan, *Problem-Based Learning Innovation: Using Problems to Power Learning in the Twenty-First Century* (Singapore: Thomson Learning, 2003), 31. Among the many excellent resources on Problem Based Learning, Oon-Seng Tan's books are most helpful in that his experience and writing are wider than the North American perspective. The discussion of the PBL process here adopts Tan's five steps. See also Oon-Seng Tan, ed., *Enhancing Thinking through Problem-Based Learning Approaches: International Perspectives* (Singapore: Thomson Learning, 2004).

clarifying the actual process of PBL, brainstorming and articulating probable issues, and seeking consensus on what the problem actually is.

As John Kilner (chap. 4) demonstrates in addressing "Having a Baby the New-Fashioned Way," the temptation is to try to decide immediately whether using the eggs and/or uterus of Betty's sister, Laura, is a good solution. Kilner turns us, instead, to wrestling with less obvious but absolutely primary issues, such as who counts as a stakeholder, whether a fetus has the full moral status that other human stakeholders have, and whether embryos have the full moral status that other human stakeholders have. Thus, in the first step of the PBL process, the articulation of issues and agreement on what the problem statement actually is are important tasks.

2. Analysis of the Problem and Learning Issues. Learners next dive into a self-directed learning phase as they confront the problem together. They share their prior knowledge of the issue and raise questions about the problem by defining it, analyzing it, and generating possible explanations for it. The most important question for identifying learning issues at this stage is, What do we need to know in order to deal with this problem? The facilitator gives guidance, emphasizing that real-life issues require us to look at multidisciplinary knowledge bases. Each of the three sections of this book is an excellent exhibit of the reality that, in addressing ill-structured problems and real-life issues, learners must explore different disciplines and integrate the insights those fields contribute.

Once each group has made a list of learning issues, they discuss where they can find the most trustworthy information (books, journals, experts in their community, etc.) and assign individual research tasks. The notes accompanying each chapter of this book remind us that there are many Christian resources on bioethical issues available. An important task of educators in the church is to teach people to break down complex problems into issues and then assist them in determining what resources they need. Educators may also play a role in helping to connect people with those resources.

Each group divides the task of consulting the resources they think they need in order to address the problem. If the ill-structured problem were the case study "Gaining Every Advantage," the group likely would develop a plan to gather the relevant wisdom to be found in the disciplines of theology (chap. 5), law (chap. 6), intercultural ministry (chap. 7), and neuroethics (chap. 8), among other fields (some of which chap. 8 connects with the case). Netland, Fields, and Sung (chap. 7), for instance, imply that it would be helpful even to understand perspectives that emerge from a religious framework that is not Christian. Therefore, they might suggest that learners need to consult the discipline of cultural sociology.

Determining what constitutes trustworthy resources and where one can find them—whether in the library, in journals, via professionals in the congregation, online, or in the local seminary—are two of the learning processes (life skills) which thinking believers need to master. Ultimately, the task of integration lies with the learner, under the watchful direction of the facilitator.

3. Discovery and Reporting (Exploration of Resources). Learners return to the groups to report discoveries. This is a peer-teaching stage as learners share what they have learned in their individual study. Learners observe and develop group collaboration and communication skills as they question and learn from one another. Such skills are important for functioning in the real world. The PBL facilitator will ensure that the group has not overlooked disciplinary areas that are strategic to understanding the problem, and will confirm the accuracy, reliability, and validity of information obtained by learners.

4. Presentation of the Solution and Reflection. An iterative process follows group members' sharing what they have learned, involving the presentation of possible solutions to the problem. This is both a reflective and an evaluative phase. What one group member suggests could be a solution may need adjustment as other group members share what they have learned in their research. Group members test each other's findings and their implications for the problem at hand. Inevitably, more questions emerge, which may send learners back out to seek further information. The facilitator will assist each group, helping learners to address doubts, recognize gaps in their knowledge, and correct misconceptions or overgeneralizations.

5. Overview, Integration, and Evaluation. Closure in the PBL process happens as participants integrate knowledge from various disciplines and sources, synthesize ideas, and identify possible solutions to the problem. One of the integral parts of the process is for learners and the facilitator to review, evaluate, and reflect on what they have learned, including critiquing the resources they chose (their value, reliability, and usefulness to the process). The facilitator will summarize and integrate major principles and concepts for the group. Group members have the opportunity to evaluate how they, as learners, have functioned as problem-solvers, self-directed learners, and members of a team.

THE HERMENEUTICAL COMMUNITY

The shift from an exclusively teaching-telling paradigm in the church to a learning paradigm will also mean that the role of the learning community takes on new significance. As the contributions of different scholars in this book demonstrate, one cannot expect any individual to have the single, comprehensive, demonstrably right answer to a complex bioethical issue. How important it is to participate in a learning community. Such a community honors each learner as a thinking person, created in the image of God and capable of contributing to a trustworthy framework within which to address complex questions. It is a community where the multiplicity of perspectives enriches the inquiry. The church can and should be such a community, profoundly influencing the way that people in all three of our case studies understand and engage the challenges they face. Accordingly, some further consideration of what this community entails will be helpful here, before looking more carefully at the cases.

Paul Hiebert has advocated a *critical realist position*[32] together with community hermeneutics as a helpful model for equipping God's people in their quest for truth. He wisely observes that the hermeneutic of a community—the way it agrees to go about interpreting the world and its challenges—will guard against the privatization of faith and personal misinterpretation of Scriptures.

In developing his idea of a hermeneutical community, Hiebert commends an approach to learning similar to the PBL process. This manner of investigation helps to decentralize the quest for truth and also prevents its misuse by those desiring to control knowledge for their own ends. Implementation of Problem Based Learning pedagogy in the church requires something like Hiebert's community hermeneutic, a pedagogical approach that acknowledges the frightening complexity of the bioethical questions that the next generations in the church will face and the need for the protection of interpretation in community. This approach suggests an educational method that will enable Christian teachers to nurture problem-solvers among God's people, involving people in the pews in the process, but safeguarding the church body against personal agendas and misinterpretations.

Imagine if a group of believers with increasing experience in an intentional process like that of PBL had already gathered around Dave and Mary ("A Difficult Death") during the agony of dealing with multiple heart-wrenching decisions. Such people could have thoughtfully sought wisdom from appropriate disciplines and assistance from local resources, to be integrated into Dave and Mary's decision-making process. Consider the potential pastoral caregiving that such a hermeneutical community could have provided for Dave and Mary, for Alex as Dave's default primary-care physician, and for others who supported Mary as she persevered. Paramount among the resources that such thinkers would engage would be a biblical understanding of life and death, and its implications for the particular medical challenges of the situation. Imagine what it would mean to all believers like Dave and Mary facing such agonizing end-of-life decisions to be a part of such a hermeneutical community, made up in large measure by people like themselves, people in the pews, who, with feet firmly planted in biblical revelation, seek to work out prudential wisdom among God's people.

Imagine what it would mean to all the Toms and Bettys in churches today ("Having a Baby the New-Fashioned Way"). These are nominal believers who are wrestling with the modern complexities of conception and technologies, both reproductive (e.g.,

---

32. It is helpful to contrast *critical realism* with *naive realism*. Naive realists enjoy 20/20 theological vision; they believe they see things exactly, exhaustively, and without bias. They have no uncertainty, no ambiguity, entertain no mystery. Critical realists, by contrast, affirm objective truth but at the same time recognize that truth is subjectively apprehended. Critical realists realize they know in part and thus acknowledge mystery along with objective truth, and so display a humble need for the views of others. See Paul G. Hiebert, *Missiological Implications of Epistemological Shifts: Affirming Truth in a Modern/Postmodern World* (Harrisburg, Penn.: Trinity Press International, 1999), esp. 37, 69, 70.

in vitro fertilization) and genetic (e.g., preimplantation genetic diagnosis). It would be invaluable to have the wisdom of a hermeneutical community—believing friends under the guidance of a godly pastor or teacher who are committed to developing a trustworthy framework within which to approach the increasingly complex questions of their times. Imagine a community in which, even as the issues become more complex, men and women affirm objective truth but recognize that people apprehend it subjectively. Realizing that they know *in part*, they admit a humble need for the wisdom of others and courageously seek truth in all the data available, from all the revelation of God.

Imagine a local church where young scholars like Roberto, Paul, Akira, and Jill ("Gaining Every Advantage"), whether believers or not, could be involved in hermeneutical communities where emerging and gifted scientists are learning what it means to live within the design of God from a biblically based bioethical point of view (Averbeck, chap. 1). In such communities, biblical principles would form the framework within which bioethical decision-making takes place, people would acknowledge the truth present in other disciplines, and informed decisions would remain anchored in an ever-expanding understanding of the full revelation of God. As in this book, the hermeneutical community might invite wisdom from resident theologians in the congregation or nearby (such as Vanhoozer, chap. 5), wisdom from attorneys who acknowledge the primacy of Scripture (such as Cunningham, chap. 6), and wisdom from disciplines as seemingly disparate as missiology, philosophy, and sociology (such as the insights of Netland, Fields, and Sung in chap. 7), which have something significant to contribute to the church's response to the bioethical challenge at hand.

Such a process would honor Christian thinkers in all professions as precious resources created in the image of God and capable of contributing to a trustworthy framework within which to address tough issues. Such a process would constantly be equipping new leaders to bring a multiplicity of perspectives to bear on the challenges before them. Imagine if students like Paul had the opportunity to observe, within their hermeneutical community, leaders of integrity who live in submission to the Scriptures and understand their application to contemporary culture.

The approach of this book resembles the idea of a hermeneutical community engaged in a Problem Based Learning pursuit. All contributors have begun with a scripted, ill-structured, real-world scenario, from which they have articulated the underlying issues and, in the process, have clarified the issues involved. The authors recognize that they know in part, acknowledging mystery along with a commitment to objective truth. None suggest that the wisdom found in their discipline can fully, and without the assistance of others, respond to the complex bioethical questions in view here. With humility, they affirm the need for the wisdom found in other disciplines. In so doing, they invite into the process of responding to complex bioethical issues people all too easily overlooked: those who might never describe themselves as teachers but who have much to contribute as lifelong learners in the church.

Indeed, the authors affirm that the task of responding as Christians to the complex bioethical issues that will face the coming generation is not the responsibility of a few experts. It is a task for which every member of the body of Christ bears responsibility and for which each has contributions to make. The educational task of the church is to prepare the whole people of God systematically for the burgeoning challenge ahead.

CONCLUSION

CONNECTING THE CHURCH AND BIOETHICS

JOHN F. KILNER

IF you have read the previous chapters and have found some wisdom there for engaging bioethical challenges, then this book has fulfilled one of its purposes. If you find yourself recognizing an even greater need now for such wisdom than you thought you had, then another purpose has been fulfilled. But in some ways, the most important purpose of this book is to motivate and inform your ongoing efforts from this point forward. Will you stay informed about the ever-developing challenges of bioethics? Will you refuse to be satisfied with simplistic answers and biblical proof-texting, endeavoring instead to bring the full message of the gospel to bear on each challenge? Will you take specific steps now to share your bioethical understanding with others? Will you live out this understanding more faithfully in one or more of the areas covered in this book, and help others to do so? Biblical wisdom involves insight that is lived out, not merely thought about.

What this will look like will depend on your personal and vocational situation. The issues of bioethics are practical and profound, touching each person's life in various ways. The desire of Tom and Betty for a healthy baby "like them" is a common human experience, one that is often frustrated by obstacles which new technologies are offering to remove. The desires of Dr. Bright and his four graduate students to gain advantages over others is virtually as old as the human race, but the mental and other enhancements emerging today offering to facilitate such advantages raise the stakes to a new level of promise and peril. The desire of Dave and his family to experience a good death—or at least not a bad one—is essentially universal and fulfillable to some degree, depending on end-of-life plans and decisions one makes.

The people in the case studies of this book are like you and those around you in more ways than you know, but in ways that you will increasingly recognize in the days ahead. Faithfulness to Christ in this biotech century will require awareness, understanding, and intentional action in the face of many bioethical challenges such as these. For you, the next step may be to learn more about the actual impact on human embryos of the contraceptive pills or reproductive technologies you have used or recommended, or the forms of stem cell or genetic research you have condoned by your silence. Or your next step may be a probing self-assessment of your contentment with your human limitations, endeavoring to distinguish between appropriate and inappropriate aspirations to be "like God." Or you may decide to engage in a discussion soon with family members or others close to you—with or without the aid of a written advance directive document[1]—regarding what death entails and what you want to pursue and avoid in the dying process, to the glory of God. Perhaps all of these steps, and more, will be appropriate.

But whatever the next steps are in your personal life, faithfulness to the wisdom that God provides must involve others around you as well. This begins by involving family members, friends, and others in such steps as noted above. For those of you with leadership positions in the church or who are preparing for such opportunities to serve, the church needs to learn from your bioethical insight and commitment to "bioengagement."[2] That means you will need to put to work much of the wisdom that this book's chapters have unearthed.

Bible study is not something "other than" bioethics; it is the very source from which God's people can gain the vision, values, and priorities that shape the understanding and living that bioethics is all about. Preaching is not something "other than" bioethics; it is the very vehicle through which God can speak to the congregation week after week to help people recognize how to live ethically and why it is so important to do so. Pastoral care is not something "other than" bioethics; it is the very demonstration of what commitment to Christ can look like in the midst of the suffering and temptations related to life and health—that is, in the face of bioethical challenges. Similarly, counseling, theology, intercultural ministry, education, and other aspects of church life are not "other than" bioethics; they are the ways that most Christians learn bioethics.

What are the implications of recognizing this? You can help inspire and equip the church to be what the church needs to be in this biotech century. Where bad habits of not mobilizing these aspects of church life to address bioethical challenges have developed over time, you can be a model and a catalyst for change. Demonstrate bioethical awareness and engagement in the illustrations and topics you include in your teaching and preaching. Urge people wrestling with bioethical issues to come to you or your fellow caregivers for pastoral care and counseling. Help others in your congregation to develop information, counseling, and support ministries that focus on bioethical challenges that people are experiencing. People need help not only to wrestle with bioethical issues in their own lives but also in order to provide such help to others around them.

---

1. A simple advance directive form reflecting a biblically sound approach to end-of-life decisions is available from the Christian bioethics center The Center for Bioethics and Human Dignity (*www.cbhd.org*). For a form to facilitate a much more detailed documentation of end-of-life values and priorities, see *http://www.agingwithdignity.org/five-wishes.php*.

2. For strategies of "bioengagement," see Nigel M. de S. Cameron et al., eds., *BioEngagement: Making a Difference through Bioethics Today* (Grand Rapids, Mich.: Eerdmans, 2000).

Moreover, they need equipping if they are to be able to engage such issues effectively in the public arena. Church ministries must help connect people with the insights and resources of medicine, law, and business, among other fields, that public (as well as private) bioengagement requires.

If equipping people for faithful, bioethical living does not characterize your ministry, that may be partly because of inadequate preparation during your theological education. Most seminaries have not done well at constructing curricula that incorporate bioethical education. Some have added elective courses in bioethics to their offerings. Those who have, or will do so in the future, will find much helpful wisdom in the final chapter of this book for that endeavor. However, instituting such a course is a risky first step to take, since it can lead to marginalizing bioethics in two ways. As a merely elective course, bioethics can become branded as a specialty discipline necessary only for those with specialized ministries in health care, public policy, and so on. Moreover, as a stand-alone course, it can foster the model that learning about bioethics best takes place in a class devoted to bioethics. The result is a church in which the occasional adult-education elective on bioethics — reaching a relatively small segment of the congregation — is virtually the only bioethics education that people receive.

This book commends a very different approach to bioethics and the church. Bioethics is an integral part of what Old Testament, counseling, theology, intercultural ministry, New Testament, pastoral care, preaching, and education, among other fields, are all about. Seminary courses in all of these disciplines need to demonstrate what they contribute to a wise understanding and engagement of bioethical challenges. This is not for the sake of bioethics alone; it helps establish the importance of each field for life and ministry.

Theology courses, for example, can demonstrate how one's understanding of who human beings are and what the gospel is makes a profound difference in the treatment of people, from embryos to disabled people to dying patients. Counseling courses can demonstrate how effective counseling can make all the difference for struggles with infertility, temptations to use mind-altering drugs, or care of a demented parent. The list of opportunities is endless. In any course, using case studies is one effective way to connect academic concepts and theories with life situations.

If adding a bioethics course to the curriculum sensitizes the rest of the faculty to the importance of bioethics — if it makes available to them a bioethically informed conversation partner to help them recognize the contributions their fields make to addressing bioethical matters — then that step is a good one. However, seminaries also have an even greater opportunity to use bioethically complex situations, such as the three this book considers, in a way that goes beyond individual courses. Faculties can institute a required end-of-program course, capstone experience, or other venue to help students learn to mobilize all that their separate courses have taught them to help them address such situations. Even better, a seminary could compare students' abilities to understand

and engage such situations in a case analysis they complete at the beginning of their program and then complete again at the end of their program. What a wonderful way to demonstrate to students and churches (and accrediting agencies!) the substantial difference seminary training is making in equipping wise leaders for the church.

Whether you are ministering in a church or seminary, a student preparing to do so, or someone else who wants to be faithful in the face of life's challenges, you need wisdom. But as suggested in the introduction to this book, attempting to attain it on your own is futile. As the wise author of Ecclesiastes long ago testified, "I said, 'I am determined to be wise' — but this was beyond me" (Eccl. 7:23). Rather than this recognition being a reason to despair or give up, it prompts him to do all he can: "I turned my mind to understand, to investigate and to search out wisdom" (v. 25). But he does this because he knows this endeavor itself will please God, not because he is under the illusion that human effort alone can achieve the wisdom the Bible celebrates. He knows well that "to the person who pleases him, God gives wisdom" (Eccl. 2:26).

Since wisdom is more a way of traveling than a particular journey or destination, this book is hardly a compendium of all you need to know in order to "get wisdom." At best it suggests some ways to travel and some ground to cover on your lifelong journey in search of wisdom. But be encouraged. Though the journey may be difficult, it is not impossible—because of Christ. On the cross, he paid the penalty for the self-centeredness and the rejection of God that is our sin, and he rose to new life, giving us access to the power of the Holy Spirit. So it *is* possible to please him, and to find the wisdom that God intends for us, if we identify ourselves wholeheartedly with Christ. His call to people is to "deny themselves and take up their cross and follow" him (Matt. 16:24). In the face of the great challenges of today and tomorrow, including the challenges of bioethics, that is a call not to avoid work but to avidly work, to avail ourselves of the many resources of Christ.

For further reading, see the four annotated bibliographies connected with this book at www.everydaybioethics.org. There is one bibliography for each of the three cases central to this book, highlighting resources relevant to the cluster of issues that the case illustrates. The fourth bibliography includes resources covering the entire range of bioethical challenges.